THE WORLDS OF THE JEAKE FAMILY OF RYE, 1640–1736

Records of Social and Economic History is a British Academy Research Project.

The British Academy, established by Royal Charter in 1902, is the national academy for the humanities and social sciences, promoting, sustaining and representing advanced research. As an academy composed of senior scholars throughout the UK, it gives recognition to academic excellence and achievement, and plays a leadership role in representing the humanities and social sciences nationally and internationally. As a learned society, the British Academy facilitates the research of individuals and groups of scholars.

More information can be found at *www.britishacademy.ac.uk*

RECORDS OF SOCIAL AND ECONOMIC HISTORY
NEW SERIES 56

THE WORLDS OF THE JEAKE FAMILY OF RYE 1640–1736

EDITED BY
ANNE L. MURPHY

Published for THE BRITISH ACADEMY
by OXFORD UNIVERSITY PRESS

Oxford University Press, Great Clarendon Street, Oxford OX2 6DP

First edition published in 2018

British Library Cataloguing in Publication Data
Data available

Library of Congress Cataloging in Publication Data
Data available

Typeset by
New Leaf Design, Scarborough, North Yorkshire
Printed in Great Britain by
T. J. International Ltd, Padstow, Cornwall

ISBN 978–0–19–726636–6

Foreword

Through a modern edition of his Astrological Diary, Samuel Jeake of Rye in Sussex is already known to scholars of the late-seventeenth century. But that knowledge is considerably enlarged and enriched by Anne Murphy's selection from the correspondence of Jeake, his family, and connections. The personal challenges of the life cycle, relationships, well-being, and making a living can all be found in the letters, from a time when written reflections on the self were becoming more frequent—famously in the diaries of Pepys and Evelyn. An important feature of this collection is hearing the voice of Jeake's wife and widow, every bit his partner, and of the melding of family and business matters. Certainly, the wider world was also challenging for the correspondents. Even in small provincial ports like Rye, society was politically and religiously riven, culminating in the 'Glorious' Revolution of 1688–9. Only then were non-conformists like Jeake formally tolerated. But the Revolution led to years of war against France, the greatest European power of the time. That created obvious enough challenges for Jeake's business as a general merchant and financier (in a declining port). It says much about him that in the face of those threats he involved himself in the 'financial revolution' centring on the creation of a national debt and the birth of the Bank of England in 1694—the price of whose stock he watched carefully. This collection well shows the wide geographical spread of connections of Jeake and his family, including with London, south-west England, Ireland, and northern France. Jeakes died in 1699, but as this volume shows his family lived on, until the extinction of his line with the death of his son in Jamaica in 1773.

Julian Hoppit, Chair, Records of Social and Economic History Committee
May 2018

Contents

Acknowledgments

I first encountered Samuel Jeake during studies for my PhD. As the only ordinary investor in the financial revolution of the 1690s who had left a record of his actions and thoughts about those actions, he formed an invaluable case study. When engaging in that desperate struggle to find a job that comes after the PhD, 'the Jeakes' became my exemplar module, the one that everyone puts together because it looks good on a one-page outline and sounds convincing when you sum it up in 5 minutes. It wasn't until I got to teach that module at the University of Exeter's Cornwall Campus that I really came to understand how invaluable a resource are the Jeake archives. Because so much of my knowledge of the Jeakes has come through teaching, my first debt in compiling this volume goes to former students at both the University of Exeter, Cornwall Campus, and the University of Hertfordshire who have studied the 'The World of Samuel and Elizabeth Jeake'. I always feel that when teaching I learn more than my students but hope that those who studied with me enjoyed their excursions into the early modern and their explorations of the extraordinary lives of ordinary people. As with parenting, it is rather bad form to have favourites among students, but I suspect we all do and from those who studied 'the Jeakes', my favourite was the UH class of 2012: Katherine, Annalise, James, William, Hannah, Lattrice, Helen O., Kay, Saarah, Lauren, Nadia, Holly and especially Becca, Vicki, Lewis, Tom and Helen T.

The Jeake papers are kept in the East Sussex Record Office and the Rye Museum. My thanks go to the ESRO for allowing me to photograph the Jeake letters and for dealing with my many requests for information. Linden Thomas, curator of the Rye Museum, kindly allowed me to visit the archive there.

Colleagues and friends have read, commented and advised on sections and chapters including Margrit Schulte Beerbühl, Alan Downie, Jennifer Evans, Anne Laurence, Judy Stephenson, Danae Tankard, Patrick Wallis, and Nuala Zahedieh. Jennifer Basford and Mark Latham transcribed and checked some parts of the volume. Francis Young did the Latin transcriptions and translations and prepared the indexes. Particular thanks must go to the British Academy Records of Social and Economic History Chair, Richard Smith for his patience and to the editorial team, Roger Middleton, Craig Muldrew and especially to Vanessa Harding who read and commented extensively on drafts of the manuscript. All errors that remain are my mine.

Much of the work was completed while I was Head of Subject at the University of Hertfordshire and so I must thank the nicest and (generally) most cooperative colleagues I have ever encountered for making my time as HoS a pleasant one. I was most appreciative of their observation of the 'zombie apocalypse protocol' at times when I have needed to get some work done and especially to Owen Davies and Ciara Meehan for taking over HoS duties in the summer of 2016.

Abbreviations

CSP Dom.	Calendar of State Papers, Domestic, Charles, II, http://www.british-history.ac.uk/search/series/cal-state-papers--domestic--chas2, last accessed 15 August 2015; James II, http://www.british-history.ac.uk/search/series/cal-state-papers--domestic--jas2, last accessed 1 September 2015
DTGC	Nancy Cox and Karin Dannehl, *Dictionary of Traded Goods and Commodities 1550-1820*, http://www.british-history.ac.uk/no-series/traded-goods-dictionary/1550-1820, last accessed 7 July 2016
ESRO	East Sussex Record Office
ESRO, FRE	East Sussex Record Office, Frewen Family Archive
ODNB	Oxford Dictionary of National Biography, http://www.oxforddnb.com/, last accessed 25 August 2016.
OED	Oxford English Dictionary, http://www.oed.com/, last accessed 15 August 2016.
OBPO	Old Bailey Proceedings Online, https://www.oldbaileyonline.org/, last accessed 8 August 2015.
PCC	Prerogative Court of Canterbury Wills
ESRO, RYE	East Sussex Record Office, Rye Corporation Archives
RMA Selmes	Rye Museum Archive, Selmes Manuscripts
TNA PRO	The National Archives, Public Record Office

Introduction

Samuel Jeake the younger (1652–1699) is best known to modern scholars through the edition of his Diary of Actions and Accidents published in 1988 as *An Astrological Diary of the Seventeenth Century*.[1] The diary details events in Samuel's life from his birth until November 1694 and Hunter and Gregory include in their volume a further transliterated shorthand diary for 1699.[2] Aside from its focus on astrological observances, the diary is informative about many aspects of early modern life. It has been employed by scholars in a variety of ways, contributing to analyses of politics, religion and non-conformity, trade and the business community, the financial revolution, health and medicine, fashion and popular culture.[3]

Yet, the *Astrological Diary* has limitations. The Diary of Actions and Accidents from which it was derived was written up by Samuel Jeake from other sources over a five-month period in 1694 and it primarily reflected his desire to 'observe & memorize the Providences therein manifested; & partly to investigate the Measure of Time in Astronomical Directions, and to determine the Astrall Causes, &tc.'[4] It was, in other words, a selection of events made for the purpose of astrological investigations. Hence, as Hunter and Gregory observe, the reader is presented with a fascinating juxtaposition of

[1] M. Hunter and A. Gregory, *An Astrological Diary of the Seventeenth Century: Samuel Jeake of Rye, 1652–1699* (Oxford, 1988). The manuscript diary: Samuel Jeake, *Astrological Experiments Exemplified*, William Andrews Clark Memorial Library, University of California, Los Angeles, MS J43M3/A859.

[2] This document is preserved in the Rye Museum Selmes Family collection and contains entries covering the period between March 28 1699 and October 19 1699. Rye Museum, Selmes MS57.

[3] A select example of scholarly work that has used Jeake's diary includes, Owen Davies, *The Haunted: a social history of ghosts* (Basingstoke, 2007); Mary J. Dobson, *Contours of Death and Disease in Early Modern England* (Cambridge, 2003); Jennifer Evans, *Aphrodisiacs, Fertility and Medicine in Early Modern England* (Woodbridge, 2014); Margaret Hunt, *The Middling Sort: Commerce, Gender and the Family in England, 1680–1780* (Berkeley, 1996); Paul Glennie and Nigel Thrift, *Shaping the Day: a history of timekeeping in England and Wales, 1300–1800* (Oxford, 2011); R. Grassby, *The Business Community of Seventeenth-Century England* (Cambridge, 1995); A. L. Murphy, *The Origins of the English Financial Markets: speculation and investment before the South Sea Bubble* (Cambridge, 2009); Martin Porter, *Windows of the Soul: Physiognomy in European Culture 1470–1780* (Oxford, 2005); Barry Reay, *Popular Cultures in England 1550–1750* (London and New York, 1998); Jane Shaw, *Miracles in Enlightenment England* (New Haven, 2006); Scott Sowerby, *Making Toleration: The Repealers and the Glorious Revolution* (Harvard, 2013); Grant Tapsell, *The Personal Rule of Charles II, 1681–85* (Woodbridge, 2007); A. Wear, *Knowledge and Practice in English Medicine, 1550–1680* (Cambridge, 2000);

[4] Hunter and Gregory, *Astrological Diary*, 83.

personal and business matters with astrological observations but the incidents discussed chiefly are those that suited Samuel's purpose in compiling the diary.[5] Moreover, while Samuel's journals were clearly kept on a daily basis, the Diary of Actions and Accidents was written up with hindsight and some passages were either written or adapted at the time it was compiled.[6] The published *Astrological Diary*, therefore, is perhaps better thought of as a memoir.

The Diary of Actions and Accidents was also introspective, concerned with the writer and not with those who surrounded him. This offers some advantages for modern scholars. The *Astrological Diary*, for example, provides an exceptional account of Samuel's health, both physical and mental. It notes the ailments from which he suffered in almost obsessive detail and records the cures employed. Nonetheless other aspects of Samuel's personal life are neglected and very little detail is presented about his relationships with others. Samuel's wife, Elizabeth Hartshorne (1667–1736) and his mother-in-law, Barbara Hartshorne (?–1707), appeared as bit players on the stage of his life, his children barely received a mention, and a broad network of kin, friends and contacts appeared, sometimes fleetingly, as their business connections allowed. Even his father, also Samuel (1623–1690), was drawn somewhat sketchily.[7] Equally, the *Astrological Diary* covered only Samuel's lifespan, the story of Elizabeth's widowhood and their children's early years has not been told.

Yet there are numerous records held at the East Sussex Record Office and the Rye Museum Archive that would allow scholars to build on the narrative presented in the *Astrological Diary*. These include manuscripts on various subjects prepared by both Samuel Jeake and his father, religious and political pamphlets, collections of medicinal recipes, collections of verse in manuscript and print, sermons, exercise books, account books, legal documents and contracts, horoscopes and over 1500 letters relating to the period between 1580 and 1848 and exchanged between numerous correspondents, including close and distant kin.

This volume employs around 300 of the letters exchanged between various family members, friends and connections of the Jeake family written over the period from 1640 to 1733. Its themes are similar to those covered in the

[5] Samuel's detailed account of his activities during 1687–8, which he titled his 'Astrological Experiments Exemplified' demonstrates that, in some of his journals, he recorded a much fuller version of his life, including such minor things as the packing of wool or negotiations with carriers. Hunter and Gregory, *Astrological Diary*, 22.

[6] Ibid. 25.

[7] Samuel senior's life has, however, been the subject of some scholarly investigation. M. Hunter, G. Mandelbrote, R. Ovenden and N. Smith eds., *A Radical's Books: the library catalogue of Samuel Jeake of Rye, 1623–90* (Woodbridge, 1999); T. W. W. Smart, 'A Biographical Sketch of Samuel Jeake, senr. of Rye', *Sussex Archaeological Collections*, 13 (1861), 57–79.

Astrological Diary. Although astrology does not feature prominently in the letters, they are concerned with everyday life, spiritual matters, religious persecution, trade and the establishment and maintenance of networks of credit and support. This volume also enhances understanding of the Jeakes in a number of important ways. In particular, the 'conversations' provided by the letters create a much more detailed account of the key relationships within the Jeake family, especially those between Samuel junior and his wife, Elizabeth, and between the father, Samuel senior, and his son. Indeed, the most important difference between the *Astrological Diary* and this volume is the number and variety of voices available to the reader. Letters to Samuel Jeake junior from a circle of kin and connections give access to a range of perspectives on everyday life, the practical concerns of worship outside the Church of England, politics and business. Finally, it is particularly significant that, through the letters, it is possible to tell Elizabeth Jeake's story in much greater detail. Series of letters from and to Elizabeth offer an insight into her married life, her day-to-day concerns, her relationships and, most significantly, her contributions to the household economy. Indeed, these exchanges provide a unique understanding of the contribution of a middling-sort woman to the family's business interests.

The letters contained in this volume cover a significant span of time and range of topics. The primary aims of bringing together this collection are to complement and extend the existing scholarship relating to the Jeakes and to provide a sourcebook in the best traditions of the British Academy's Records of Social and Economic History series. Yet, the volume is also offered as more than a collection of correspondence. It has been constructed as a narrative across the seventeenth and eighteenth centuries and through three generations of the Jeake family. With Samuel Jeake junior and his wife Elizabeth at its centre, it also touches on the lives of their parents and their children. The volume begins with a letter written in 1640 about the death of Samuel senior's mother, Anne, and ends with the death of Samuel and Elizabeth's last surviving child, their son Samuel, in Jamaica in 1773. Although the letters in between can by no means create a complete narrative of the family, comprehensive introductions to each chapter, drawing on the *Astrological Diary* and other papers, serve to fill the gaps for the reader. As a starting point the remaining sections in this overview will give an outline of the chapters to follow, draw the reader's attention to the principal letter writers and recipients, discuss the nature of the correspondence contained in the volume and outline the selection of sources.

The Jeakes

The first trace of the Jeake family is a late-sixteenth century record of a William Jeake, who was probably Samuel senior's grandfather. Little is known about William other than the fact that he was a merchant and was probably of Huguenot extraction. It is likely that Jeake was a corruption of the French 'Jaques'.[8] Rye, the small port town in east Sussex where the Jeakes lived, was an obvious destination for Huguenots fleeing persecution because of its proximity to France and its strong traditions of nonconformity. Rye was also attractive for a merchant at the end of the sixteenth century because it had been a prominent port since the medieval period. Although starting to decline at the end of the sixteenth century, it had an active fishing fleet and was one of the centres for export of the products of the Wealden iron industry.[9]

Rye retained some importance as a port because of its position on the south coast, its role as a port of refuge for ships in the channel and as an outlet for various Sussex staple goods, including wool and hops. Nonetheless, it was in decline by the early seventeenth century.[10] Hipkin cites not just the commonly accepted explanation, that of the silting up of the harbour, but also the complex interdependency of trade and fishing in the town. Fishing vessels were regularly deployed in trade during the sixteenth century and boat owners relied upon the exploitation of both economic activities for the protection of profits. A crisis in trade, therefore, significantly weakened the fishing fleet to a point that was beyond recovery by the early seventeenth century.[11] Perhaps as a consequence, William's son, Henry Jeake, took up the occupation of baker. It was a trade which provided him with a secure, and even prosperous, living.[12] Henry married Anne Peerson, the daughter of Reverend John Peerson. They had four children: two daughters, Anne and Elizabeth, who both survived to adulthood, and two sons, Samuel, the diarist's father, and John who died young. Anne Peerson's letters reveal her to have been particularly pious and her son Samuel had equally strong religious beliefs which were to set him against the authorities in Rye.

Rye's charter gave the town the right to govern itself through an assembly of freemen. The freemen elected a mayor who then appointed twelve jurats to assist him. The mayor and jurats governed the port itself and had their own

[8] Smart, 'Biographical Sketch', 57.

[9] Hunter and Gregory, *Astrological Diary*, 62. S. Hipkin, 'The Maritime Economy of Rye, 1560–1640', *Southern History*, 20/21 (1999), 108.

[10] Hunter and Gregory, *Astrological Diary*, p. 62. Anthony Fletcher, *A County Community in Peace and War: Sussex 1600–1660* (London and New York, 1975), 21.

[11] Hipkin, 'Maritime Economy', 136.

[12] Hunter et al., *Radical's Books*, xvii.

court of sessions which was able to try both civil and criminal cases.[13] While a democratic process is implied by these arrangements, Fletcher argues that by the end of the sixteenth century Rye was under the control of a 'tight-knit merchant oligarchy'.[14] The decline of the port and the economic stress that created placed additional strains on local government. Religious discord compounded the problems. Puritanism had been easily established in Rye in the second half of the sixteenth century. It was a town where, as in much of the surrounding area, the established Church was weak, the economy was often vulnerable and families were closely integrated. This, Fletcher argues, encouraged strongly heretical traditions.[15] By the early 1640s the town was riven by political and religious factions and a group, of which Samuel senior was a leading member, had broken away from the Church of England. During the Civil War much of Sussex supported the Parliamentarian cause and there were prominent land battles in the west of the county, notably at Chichester and Arundel. The east of the county saw less fighting but Rye's coastal position made it vulnerable. The town experienced both a threat from the sea and also loss of trade and ships, including, in 1645, five barques taken by Royalist privateers.[16]

Samuel senior did not fight during the war but did rise to political prominence in the town. Having secured his position, he married Frances Hartridge in 1651. She bore him three children but died in 1654 shortly after the birth of her third child. Samuel junior, born in 1652, was the oldest of those children and the only one to survive past infancy. The first chapter of this volume covers the early life of Samuel Jeake senior and includes letters that give an insight into his religious convictions, disputes with the local authorities and responses to the English Civil War. Additionally a selection of letters explores the courtships of Samuel senior and Frances Hartridge. Some of Frances Hartridge's correspondence with her sister and brother-in-law, Mary and Christopher Blackwood, during her short married life is also reproduced.

Far less is known about the family of Elizabeth Hartshorne, Samuel junior's wife. Elizabeth's mother, Barbara, had been twice widowed before she married Richard Hartshorne. Her first husband was John Holman, with whom she had three sons: John, William and Richard. Barbara's second husband was George Harding. She bore him a daughter, Barbara, who died in 1670 at the age of around ten. Richard Hartshorne moved to Rye in 1659

[13] Paul Kleber Monod, *The Murder of Mr Grebell: Madness and Civility in an English Town* (New Haven and London, 2003), 6–7.
[14] Fletcher, *County Community*, 234.
[15] Ibid. 61–2.
[16] Ibid. 270.

to take up the post of schoolmaster. He married Barbara in 1663. They had two children who survived to adulthood, Nathaniel and Elizabeth, and another child, John, who died in infancy. Letters from Richard to Barbara during their tumultuous courtship are also reproduced in chapter one. The letters between Richard and Barbara, like those between Samuel and Frances, offer interesting accounts of the power that women could wield in the course of early modern courtships. While Frances Hartridge and Richard Hartshorne will be met only in chapter one, Samuel senior and Barbara Hartshorne were significant influences in their children's adult lives and on their marriage.

A document listing the names and assessments of those who were asked to pay a 'demobilisation' tax in 1660 can give us an understanding of the nature of Rye's population and economy at the Restoration.[17] The list shows the decline in population during the seventeenth century. In 1565 there had been 530 households recorded in Rye, with 225 of those headed by fishermen.[18] By 1576 there were 407 houses.[19] The 1660 list records 295 dwellings from which Burchall has calculated a population of c. 1,100.[20] Of the occupations mentioned in the list, 117 were associated with the sea trades with the majority of those being seamen and mariners. There were only two 'merchants at sea'.[21] According to Burchall's categorisation, 37 individuals held professional or official positions or were the widows of those persons. There were 8 yeomen, 32 persons engaged in the food and drink industries and 73 involved in trades or crafts.[22] There were 24 labouring households, 79 servants and a small assortment of gardeners and tinkers.[23]

The demobilisation tax assessment shows Samuel Jeake senior to have been comfortable but by no means wealthy compared to some of his neighbours. He was described as a gentleman and assessed on £95 in real estate and £150 in personal estate.[24] He was living in the Middlestreet Ward, a central and relatively affluent area of Rye, home to tradesmen and craftsmen but also a small number of gentlemen, Samuel senior among them.[25] The Restoration, however, was to bring a change of fortunes for Samuel. Charles II's reign was marked by attempts to eliminate dissenting influence in places like Rye whose

[17] ESRO RYE/13/82/82, Precept and rate made for the speedy provision of money for disbanding and paying off the forces in this kingdom, both by land and sea, September 1660.
[18] Michael J. Burchall, 'Inhabitants of Rye, 1660', *Sussex Genealogist and Local Historian*, 4 (1982), 99.
[19] Ibid.
[20] Ibid.
[21] Ibid. 100.
[22] Ibid.
[23] Ibid. 100–101.
[24] Ibid. 105.
[25] Ibid. 98; 101.

independent legislatures made them politically dangerous.[26] The consequences of this were the alteration of municipal charters in some places, a purge of the electorate and the removal of some office holders. Samuel senior was deprived of his rights as a freeman of Rye in October 1662.[27] Equally, despite Charles II's assurances prior to taking the throne that he would grant 'a Liberty to tender Consciences', in fact his reign was marked by religious intolerance backed by a harsh penal code.[28] The Conventicle Act of 1664 and the Five Mile Act of 1665 restricted the activities of dissenting preachers and, as he was one of the principal preachers of the local congregation, these Acts had an impact on Samuel senior.[29]

Nonetheless, it was not until the early 1680s that the Jeakes started to come under significant threat of persecution. The letters in chapter two, which focus on the late 1660s, show no particular concern about the political or religious situation in Rye. The chapter instead introduces Samuel junior as an adolescent, through a series of letters exchanged between father and son. Samuel senior did not marry again after Frances's death and, as his sole carer, developed a close and loving relationship with his son. The letters exchanged during a six-month period in 1668 and 1669 when Samuel junior was in London reveal this close relationship. The father frequently expressed concern for his son's health and welfare and he dispensed spiritual advice. This set of letters also provides details of Samuel junior's continuing education and intellectual life.

Chapter three focuses on the 1670s and details the period in which Samuel junior was attempting to set up in business as a merchant. The late seventeenth century was a key period in the development of English trade and thus the letters provide an invaluable account of the life of someone seeking to enter trade, allowing us to observe the disruption caused by international conflict, the difficulties of controlling cash flow and negotiating credit, and the problems Samuel encountered when attempting to manage the sale of his goods through agents in London who might not always have been acting in his best interests. The letters also reveal difficulties peculiar to Samuel's situation. He did not serve an apprenticeship and thus struggled to make the connections that usually would have come during a period of training. Equally, the letters, and particularly Samuel's attempt to deal in tallow from Ireland in 1678, reveal him to have been rather naïve about both business and business relationships. Above all, while Samuel described himself as a merchant, this chapter demonstrates why trade did not always dominate his business

[26] Hunter and Gregory, *Astrological Diary*, 29.
[27] Ibid.
[28] Tim Harris, *Restoration: Charles II and his kingdoms, 1660–1685* (London, 2006).
[29] Hunter and Gregory, *Astrological Diary*, 29.

activities. Operating out of a small provincial port, Samuel had little opportunity for specialization and frequently had to bear high transaction costs. Trade could not always provide a living for his family.[30] It is not surprising, therefore, that throughout his working life Samuel operated a diversified business model, continuing to earn money through scrivening, money-lending, property and other investments, as well as engaging in domestic and international trade when the occasion arose.

Samuel married Elizabeth Hartshorne in March 1681. He had known her since her childhood and they married when she was just thirteen and he was twenty-eight. The *Astrological Diary* records that Elizabeth was not his first choice but they appear to have had a happy and affectionate marriage. Letters between the couple in chapters four, five and six demonstrate trust, equal contributions to the life and the economy of the household and a desire for each other's companionship which, although perhaps stronger on Elizabeth's side, still seemed to be genuine. The couple were to have six children together, four of whom survived to adulthood. Their first child, Elizabeth, born when her mother was just 15, received injuries during her birth from which she died. The couple's third child, Manasseh, died of a fever at the age of two. A second Elizabeth, known to the family as Betty, Samuel, Barbara and Francis survived into adolescence but only Samuel and Barbara appear to have lived past their late teens or early twenties.

Chapters four and five continue the story of the development of Samuel's various business interests but the early- to mid-1680s were more troubled times. As dissenters, the Jeake family suffered periodic bouts of persecution, the threat of arrest and long periods of exile from Rye. The letters reveal the impact of this oppression on the lives of their family and friends and the extent to which persecution interfered with daily life and business. Elizabeth's brother, Nathaniel, added to the family's trouble. Apprenticed to the radical Whig lawyer, Richard Goodenough, Nathaniel's misbehaviour and poor decision-making led him first into dispute with his master, then into debt and finally involvement in a dangerous political situation. Imprisonment and a capital sentence followed. The letters reveal the family networks that provided support for Nathaniel in London, communicated with his family in Rye when necessary and subsequently attempted to secure his pardon. The letters in these chapters particularly demonstrate the strength and utility of networks of kin and friends.

Chapter six introduces another change in Samuel junior's economic fortunes. The Glorious Revolution of 1688 brought freedom from persecution but the Nine Years' War (1689–1697) prevented Samuel from pursuing

[30] I am grateful to Nuala Zahedieh for instructive discussions about Samuel's business and training in trade.

some of the businesses upon which he had become reliant. Foreign trade was restricted and risky and his business negotiating bills of exchange became unprofitable early in the war. Samuel, therefore, turned to new investment opportunities. The letters in this chapter cover a period not touched on in the *Astrological Diary* and thus they are particularly valuable. They also give a unique and detailed account of the actions and decision-making of an individual who invested in the Bank of England and other forms of public debt right at the start of the financial revolution. Equally importantly, the letters in this chapter offer a window into the world of Elizabeth Jeake. While her husband was in London managing his investments, she remained in Rye, managing both the household and Samuel's businesses.

Samuel Jeake junior died in November 1699 but the surviving correspondence permits an extension of the narrative beyond that point, allowing an exploration of Elizabeth's widowhood and marriage to Joseph Tucker, and her relationships with her adolescent and adult children. Samuel and Elizabeth's four surviving children, Betty, Barbara, Samuel and Francis, all feature in the letters exchanged during the period from 1699 to 1733. Samuel and Elizabeth's children died without legitimate issue so this branch of the Jeake family was extinguished with the death of Samuel III in 1773. An afterword explains his rather chequered legal career and presents his last will and testament. It shows him to have been living a comfortable, if not affluent life, in Jamaica and to have left a significant part of his estate to his black housekeeper, Juno Murphy.

The correspondence and corresponding

The principal recipient of the letters in this volume was Samuel Jeake junior. He also features as a principal letter-writer along with his immediate family, particularly his father and his wife. In some cases Samuel junior preserved copies of the letters he sent, especially during the period when he was establishing himself in trade. These letters have been included in the collection. Likewise Samuel senior preserved copies of his own courtship letters to Frances Hartridge and these have been reproduced. They represent some of the very few occasions when both sides of the conversation are observable by the reader.

Hartshorne voices can be heard particularly in relation to Nathaniel Hartshorne's misadventures. His exchanges with his brother-in-law, sister and mother while in London and then later in prison and on the run provide a fascinating tale of youthful misbehaviour but also an understanding of the management of apprenticeship and the judicial system. Barbara also appeared as a recipient of her daughter Elizabeth's letters during the period of the latter's widowhood, 1699–1703, revealing a different side to the parent and child relationship. Richard Hartshorne, Elizabeth's father, is heard only through his courtship letters to Barbara. The various Jeake children were only occasionally mentioned in the letters, until they became recipients and correspondents during their adolescence and adulthood.

An array of close and distant kin, principally cousins with connections to the Jeake family by blood or by marriage, also sent letters. Connections among the family of Samuel senior's wife, Frances Hartridge, were limited to a cousin, Christopher Blackwood. Blackwood was the son of Frances's sister Mary, who provided Samuel junior with one of his first contacts when he decided to engage in trade. Most prominent among the letter writers with kinship connections to Samuel were members of his father's family. Samuel junior's paternal aunt Elizabeth who had three marriages, the first to Abraham Goph, then to Nathaniel Bonnick and finally to Christopher Dighton, was a regular correspondent but Samuel also had connections with the family of his other aunt, Anne Jeake, who married William Key. Anne died in childbirth in 1665 and William died a year later. Samuel senior then became responsible for five of the Key children, a circumstance which the *Astrological Diary* records 'brought a great deal of trouble'.[31] It also brought lasting connections with the Key cousins especially Elizabeth, Mary and Sarah. Elizabeth married John Mackley, a tallow chandler, who was to become one of Samuel junior's principal London contacts. Mary married an apothecary, John Jaye, who provided a home for the Jeake family and Barbara Hartshorne during their periods of exile from Rye. Sarah married Richard Freebody, with whom contact was regular but less frequent. Connections were also maintained with William Key's daughter, Ann, from a previous marriage. Ann married James Wightman, a watchmaker. Wightman both made watches for the Jeake family and also sourced fashionable goods for Samuel. Both Ann Wightman and Elizabeth Mackley also purchased and sold goods for Samuel and sometimes corresponded with him on behalf of their respective husbands. Appendix 1 provides a set of family trees which explain relationships within the Jeake, Hartshorne, Hartridge and Key families.

Samuel junior established connections with numerous merchants in England and France during the mid- to late-1670s when he was setting up in trade. Yet, because his trading activities waned as political conditions and the threat of religious persecution made business difficult, many of these appear only once or twice in the surviving letters. Samuel's most important and persistent connection outside of his family was, therefore, his relationship with Thomas Miller. Miller was a fellow dissenter who Samuel met in July 1672. As recorded in the *Astrological Diary*, 'occasioned by a casual discourse',

[31] Hunter and Gregory, *Astrological Diary*, 88; 90.

a close friendship, clearly based on much more than business, developed.[32] It was with Miller that Samuel first started to trade actively. When Miller was forced by persecution to leave Rye for London, he became Samuel's principal business connection and correspondent in the capital.

Aside from trading connections, for the most part the Jeakes corresponded with connections in London. Letters were usually exchanged as the need arose or there was something to communicate but there is also some evidence of habits of regularity in letter-writing. Letters exchanged between father and son, husband and wife and daughter and mother while either party was in London for extended periods suggest an expectation that the party left behind would receive a letter once or twice a week. As Whyman notes in her important study of letter-writing, most communication was 'multi-functional' with letters interweaving business and personal lives.[33] Communications about business and requests for, or delivery of, instructions sat easily alongside family matters, spiritual contemplation, an ever-present concern for the health of all correspondents and their connections and the exchange of news, especially on religious or political matters. Very few letters in the collection seem to have been written just for the sake of being in touch.

How and where the correspondents wrote is not often revealed. Writers frequently claimed to be writing 'in haste' but as Daybell suggests, this is likely to have been as much a 'rhetorical or deferential' disclaimer as an expression of the circumstances in which the letter was written'.[34] Correspondents sometimes mentioned writing in the evenings.[35] Elizabeth Jeake wrote one letter at 'past ten a clock'. This was presumably to capture the events of the day, while evening gave solitary space for writing. At other times, though, writing was an almost collaborative affair with other family members and acquaintances seeking to be remembered or to have their greetings passed on. Barbara Hartshorne noted in one letter that 'Cussin Betty came to my chamber to desir me to give you her service'.[36] Remembrances offered in letters or parcels, gifts and other letters sent to be delivered on to someone else indicate the extent to which letters were used to facilitate communication beyond the letter writer and recipient.

The task that letter-writers were engaged in was not necessarily a straight-forward one. Letter-writing was a skill that had to be learned and practised. Comments in the correspondence indicate that this was indeed

[32] Ibid. 125.

[33] Susan E. Whyman, *The Pen and the People: English letter writers 1660–1800* (Oxford, 2009), 113.

[34] James Daybell, *The Material Letter in Early Modern England: manuscript letters and the culture and practices of letter-writing, 1512–1635* (Basingstoke, 2012), 47.

[35] For example, ESRO FRE 5297

[36] ESRO FRE 5360.

expected both of Samuel junior, during his adolescence, and Elizabeth at the start of her marriage.[37] Elizabeth's more mature letters, which are written in a neat hand using mostly standard spelling and grammar, can provide a significant contrast to others in the collection. Both Ann Wightman and Elizabeth Mackley, for example, used idiosyncratic spelling and grammar, perhaps betraying a lack of education.

Daybell also points to the practical requirements for letter-writing. Letter writers had to gather the accoutrements needed for writing, notably paper, which was expensive, suitable quills and penknives for shaping those quills, ink, sand for blotting the wet ink and wax and seals for sealing letters.[38] The size and quality of paper used by the Jeake correspondents varies greatly but in general it was of good quality and watermarked. Purchase of paper would have undoubtedly been a regular occurrence in the Jeake household and could involve communication with London to arrange the purchase.

Letters were sent by post, by carrier or in the hands of friends and acquaintances travelling to the letter's destination. Where it was possible the Jeakes sent letters by carrier or with friends and acquaintances. This was sometimes for safety and sometimes to avoid charges.[39] There was a particular emphasis on the safety of the goods being carried in the letters where those goods were valuable. Samuel junior notes having received his wife's stays, presumably as a template for having more made in London, but with 'Mr Tournays bond enclosed in them'.[40] While the safe passage of letters and goods clearly was a concern, there appear to have been relatively few cases of problems in the transmission of letters. Communicating with the Continent was somewhat more complex but the delays, infrequently mentioned, were seen to be due to the inattentiveness of the carrier rather than delays in transportation.[41]

The letters offer a constant reminder that members of the Jeake family spent a significant amount of time in London, especially during the persecutions of the early 1680s. Thus they also acted as part of a network of letter carrying and communication with the capital. The family's modes of travel varied. Sometimes travellers walked part of the way; journeys were also made on horseback, in a coach, and via coastal waterways. Often journeys combined a variety of modes of transport. In one letter Samuel junior described hiring horses to get the party to Maidstone, going by river to Rochester, walking from there to Gravesend and then taking another boat to London.[42]

[37] ESRO FRE 4827 and FRE 5141.
[38] Daybell, *Material Letter*, 30.
[39] ESRO FRE 5197.
[40] ESRO FRE 5331.
[41] ESRO FRE 4943.
[42] ESRO FRE 5206.

While in London, the letters reveal that correspondents were not only conducting their own business but also acting for immediate family members and a variety of acquaintances who would give instruction for information to be sought and goods to be sourced and bought.[43]

The postal service was resorted to when nobody was available to carry a letter. The postal service, although relatively reliable, had developed primarily to meet the intelligence needs of the State. These were intensified at the Restoration when Charles II's Secretaries of State worked with the Postmaster General to intercept, read and make copies of letters deemed useful in intelligence gathering.[44] As dissenters regarded as politically active, there is no question that the Jeake family letters sent through the Post Office were subject to such treatment. Samuel junior mentioned to his wife the possibility of his letters being opened 'you know where' in 1699, long after the family's direct political problems had ended.[45] Nonetheless the postal service was a relatively efficient way of communicating especially with contacts in London. The costs of postage for a single sheet letter were 2d. for a journey of up to 80 miles, 4d. for up to 140 miles and 6d. for longer journeys. Postage could be paid at the start or the end of the journey.[46] Nonetheless, the efficacy of not paying post at the start of a letter's journey was mentioned by Samuel senior in 1668. He noted that he did not pay in Rye because the letters 'should come the better to your [Samuel junior's] hands'.[47] Again, however, there are relatively few mentions of letters going astray.

The selection of sources

Sources relating to the Jeake and associated families are preserved in numerous official and private records, including parish records, State Papers, the Bank of England archive, the Old Bailey Proceedings and books, personal papers, accounts and correspondence preserved in the Frewen family archive at the East Sussex Record Office (ESRO) and in the Selmes manuscripts in Rye Museum Archive. The means by which the collections survived have been reconstructed by Michael Hunter *et al.* The papers were initially preserved by Elizabeth Jeake and passed to her daughter from her second marriage to Joseph Tucker. Philadelphia Tucker (1707–1795) married Dr Thomas Frewen and, as far as it is possible to ascertain, she was the only one of Elizabeth's

[43] See particularly chapters 2 and 7.
[44] Whyman, *Pen and the People*, 49.
[45] ESRO FRE 5326.
[46] Whyman, *Pen and the People*, 50.
[47] ESRO FRE 4817.

eight children to have legitimate children of her own. It is possible that throughout this time the papers remained at the Hartshorne/Jeake family home in what is now Mermaid Street in Rye. That house was still in the possession of Philadelphia's daughter, also Philadelphia, in 1837.[48] In 1858, and following the younger Philadelphia's death in 1841, one of her relatives, Mrs Moreton Frewen, appears to have made some of the papers and manuscripts available to the antiquary T. W. W. Smart, and that loan subsequently became a gift. That collection survives in the Rye Museum as the Selmes collection. Much of the remainder of the collection was retained in the hands of the Frewen family and is now deposited in the East Sussex Record Office.[49] Although it appears that the majority of the archive was kept in these two collections, along with other items, including most of Samuel Jeake senior's books, the Diary of Actions and Accidents, from which the *Astrological Diary* is derived, was sold. The Diary was thought for many years to be lost until it was uncovered at the William Andrews Clark Memorial Library at the University of California, Los Angeles. The Library had apparently purchased it from an English bookseller in 1959 but it is not clear how it came into the bookseller's possession.[50]

Although the entire Frewen archive is significant, its huge extent makes it impossible to reproduce in full. The primary focus of this volume, therefore, is just under 300 letters between the immediate Jeake family and their close and distant kin, friends and business connections. The selection has been made primarily from the collection in the East Sussex Record Office and includes letters from the following series:

FRE 4223 Volume of correspondence of John Peerson, Ann Jeake (née Peerson) and Samuel Jeake the elder: 1589–1675;
FRE 4814–5249 Letters to Samuel Jeake the younger: 1664–1686;
FRE 5263–5300 Letters to Samuel Jeake the younger's mother-in-law, Barbara Hartshorne: 1654–1689;
FRE 5301–5333 Letters from Samuel Jeake the younger to his wife Elizabeth: 1696-1699;
FRE 5334–5336 Letters to Elizabeth Jeake: 1693;
FRE 5337–5358 Letters from Elizabeth Jeake, widow to her mother Barbara Hartshorne: 1701;
FRE 5359–5420 Miscellaneous correspondence: 1661–1748.

[48] The Jeake house is still standing on Mermaid Street in Rye, as is the storehouse that Samuel junior built during the 1690s and the meeting house completed by Elizabeth Jeake, after Samuel's death.
[49] Hunter et al., *Radical's Books*, lx–lxiv.
[50] Hunter and Gregory, *Astrological Diary*, 1.

Significant collections of letters and papers relating to Samuel Jeake senior (FRE 4224–4813) and correspondence with the Reverend John Allin[51] and Philip Frith[52] have not been included in this collection. For the interested reader the ESRO online catalogue provides detailed descriptions of these letters and the remainder of the Frewen family collection.

For the most part the letters are now stored as a chronological collection, loose, flattened and grouped according to principal recipient. The majority of the letters are in good order, although there is some damage especially to the series FRE 5301–33, 'letters from Samuel to Elizabeth Jeake covering the period from 1696–1699'. One notable exception to the mode of preservation is a letter-book complied by Samuel Jeake senior, possibly during the 1670s. This was not a letter-book in the formal sense of a book into which was copied both incoming and outgoing correspondence.[53] The volume covers the period from the early seventeenth century to 1675 and includes letters to and from Samuel senior's maternal grandfather, John Peerson, his mother Anne Peerson, letters addressed to Samuel Jeake senior and copies of letters that he sent. The original letters are stitched together and copies appear to have been written into the volume at the time it was compiled but there is no indication of where these were copied from and, of course, it is impossible to tell whether or not they were copied accurately from the originals. The purpose of the volume is unclear but given the majority of the letters relate to matters of religion, it might be argued that they trace a spiritual journey. This is certainly the view taken by Hunter *et al.* and Daybell also argues that such letter books might be seen as a form of life writing.[54] Samuel senior's letter-book has been used extensively in Fletcher's study of godly communities in Sussex.[55] In this volume, however, it is used as a means of representing the man and experiences relevant to our understanding of Samuel junior's upbringing and formative experiences.

The Selmes collection at the Rye Museum is somewhat less accessible than the records in the ESRO and much more eclectic. The collection includes various of the manuscripts written by Samuel senior and junior, some of Samuel junior's accounts and collections of horoscopes and numerous papers relating to Elizabeth's children from her two marriages. There are relatively

[51] Allin was a former vicar of Rye and a close friend of Samuel Jeake senior. He was ejected from his post in 1662 and, thereafter, took up medical practice in London. Hunter et al, *Radical's Books*, xxii. Allin's letters to Samuel senior and Philip Frith were used extensively in Walter George Bell, *The Great Plague in London* (London, 1924), particularly 255–265.

[52] Philip Frith was a resident of Rye and, although may have started out as a lawyer, he developed a career as a surgeon-apothecary. Hunter et al., *Radical's Books*, xxii. .

[53] For a discussion of early modern letter-books see Daybell, *Material Letter*, 177–190.

[54] Hunter et al., *Radical's Books*, xiii; Daybell, *Material Letter*, 188.

[55] Fletcher, *County Community*.

few letters in the collection and thus volume includes only a very few of the Selmes papers, notably letters from Francis Jeake, Samuel and Elizabeth's youngest son, written to his mother and step-father, Joseph Tucker.

Editorial conventions

The abundance of correspondence in the Frewen family archive has meant that most of the collections of correspondence in the following chapters have been sampled. Letters containing content that is repetitive or not central to the narrative have not been included in this volume. This is particularly the case with letters relating to trade and Samuel junior's activities in discounting bills of exchange during the period from 1678 to 1686. The latter are often perfunctory, simply giving details of successful negotiation of the bill. In other cases discrete runs of letters relating to particular topics or events have been included. Thus, all letters relating to the escapades of Samuel's brother-in-law, Nathaniel Hartshorne, are reproduced, and a series of thirty-three letters sent from Samuel, in London, to Elizabeth, in Rye, between 1697 and 1699 are included in their entirety. The letters in the collection have been organised chronologically, as far as it is possible to ascertain. Sub-headings have been included in each chapter as a means of organising the material but the letters within each section are sometimes an eclectic mix with not all being central to the overall theme of the section.

Throughout the chapters, the following conventions apply:

Most letters in the collection were sent using the 'tuck and seal' method and postal directions are, therefore, preserved on the reverse of the letters. Where these directions occur they have been reproduced at the end of each letter.

The letters preserved in the ESRO have been catalogued in what was presumed to be chronological order. In the course of transcription it has become clear that some letters have been catalogued out of sequence. In such cases the editor's assumption of chronological order has been imposed.

Some of the letters are faded or damaged in places and in some cases text has been obscured by the placement of seals. In cases where single or several words have proved unrecoverable this is indicated by [word/s lost]. Where a longer section is obscure this is indicated by the inclusion of the words [section damaged] in the text. In cases where a fair guess can be made at the missing sections, this is indicated in the text by the inclusion of the phrase in square brackets.

With regard to erasures and crossings out in letters, where the original text is clear, this has been reproduced with a line through to indicate that the text was struck through. Where the original text is not recoverable this has been indicated in the text thus: [words struck out].

Where possible definitions of archaic or dialect words used in the correspondence have been given in footnotes.

Where possible printed books referred to in the correspondence have been identified in footnotes using either Hunter, M., Mandelbrote, G., Ovenden R. and Smith, N., eds., *A Radical's Books: the library catalogue of Samuel Jeake of Rye, 1623–90* (Woodbridge, 1999) or *Early English Books Online*: http://eebo.chadwyck.com/home

As with many early modern letter writers, Samuel, Elizabeth and their correspondents tended to write lengthy texts with little or no use of punctuation or paragraph breaks. This style of writing has been preserved as far as possible, but some punctuation has been added for clarification and ease of access for the reader.

Spelling and capitalisation used by the letter writers has been followed consistently. In some cases, where clarification has been deemed necessary, modernised spelling has been added as a footnote.

Where it has proved impossible to distinguish between upper and lower case forms of certain letters, the choice is editorial.

As Hunter and Gregory note with regard to the *Astrological Diary*, abbreviations were used, for the most part, as a purely functional device relating to both expedition and space.[56] All mechanical abbreviations have therefore been expanded with the exception of abbreviations of proper nouns.

Ampersands have been retained but dipthongs have been spelt out.

For clarity, the £ sign, rather than l. has been used where money is mentioned.

[56] Hunter and Gregory, *Astrological Diary*, 78.

1

Conflicts and courtships, 1640–*c.*1662

Preserved among the Jeake family papers are letters relating to the courtships of Samuel's and Elizabeth's parents: Samuel Jeake senior and Frances Hartridge, and Richard Hartshorne and Barbara Harding. Since Samuel's father and Elizabeth's mother played significant roles in their children's adult lives, this first chapter explores elements of their courtships and marriages and, through other letters written by and to Samuel senior, explores his early life and beliefs, and involvement in the religious and political conflicts of the 1640s and 1650s.

The life of the elder Samuel has been the subject of some scholarly attention, especially with regard to his intellectual pursuits and activities as a radical preacher from the 1640s.[1] Much detail about his life can be drawn from a letter book compiled by Samuel and containing not just papers relating to his courtship but also correspondence to and from his mother, Anne (neé Peerson), letters from the Civil War period and numerous exchanges detailing religious disputes and dispensing spiritual guidance.[2] Deserving of a volume to itself, the letter book cannot be reproduced in full here but a small sample of the letters is included to give insight into the milieu into which Samuel Jeake junior was born.

The elder Samuel grew up in a deeply religious household. Letters to his mother show her to have been pious, of the 'hotter sort' of Protestant, although in need of regular encouragement in her faith. One of her chief correspondents and spiritual adviser, John Wilmshurst, wrote to reassure her that her 'thirsting after grace and heavenly things [was] an evident signe that you have true grace in you, provided this thirsting be constant and continuing'.[3] This chapter opens with a letter from Samuel senior to one of Anne's friends describing his mother's final acts of piety. Anne achieved a 'good death', 'sweetly yield[ing] up her soule into her Fathers hands' (FRE 4223, fo. 60). The letter serves not only to illustrate the relationship between mother and son but also to provide an example of a common godly trope. Such descriptions of deathbed scenes were regarded as inspirational by the godly, bringing both strength to the writer and spiritual instruction to the recipient.[4] It was a letter that Samuel wrote when he was sixteen.

Clearly precocious in his intellectual and religious development, also around this time Samuel became involved in religious disputes within Rye. Rye was a divided town. From the Reformation, Sussex had been strongly and stridently godly, with the more radical worshippers harbouring tendencies towards separatism.[5] John Wilmshurst had warned Anne Jeake to keep apart from the ungodly in Rye, informing her that she would find the town 'given to much prophaneness…swearinge, curseing,

[1] Fletcher, *County Community*; Hunter *et al.*, G. *Radical's Books*; Smart, 'Biographical Sketch'.
[2] ESRO, FRE 4223.
[3] Quoted in Fletcher, *County Community*, 64.
[4] Fletcher, *County Community*, 68.
[5] Ibid. 62; 117.

whoredome, skolding, and many such sinnes'.[6] Although in 1640 Samuel Jeake still worshipped within the Church of England, religious divides were deepening, in part, as Fletcher argues, because the then minister, John Harrison, did not have the strength of personality to unite the differing views of Protestantism.[7] An exchange of letters between Samuel and another parishioner, John Coulton, illustrates the febrile atmosphere in the town (FRE 4223, fos. 61–4).

The origins of the disagreement seemingly lay in decisions made by John Harrison to ask the congregation to pray for a woman dangerously ill after having given birth to an illegitimate child, and to preside over the burial of a Catholic woman using the words 'dear sister' in the service. Samuel objected strongly to both actions and clearly was willing to say so publicly, rather than privately, to Harrison. He criticised not only the minister but also Coulton. Coulton supported Harrison but in Samuel's eyes was no better. He had also left his wife to come to live in Rye. This Samuel found scandalous and said so. Yet he regarded Coulton as a powerful influence and a powerful preacher, much more so than John Harrison. The quarrel between the two men was not long lasting. Their mutual disagreements with Harrison's practices united them, especially his decision in 1642 to baptise the children of 'visible unbelievers'.[8] Disagreements of this nature and a tendency towards separate gatherings of worshippers did not always lead to a break with the parish church but in this case they did.[9] Samuel, Coulton and others had, by 1642, broken away from the Church of England and thus Samuel became one of the leaders of a newly independent congregation.[10]

Religious factionalism was to persist in Rye throughout the seventeenth century but the Civil War would bring greater prominence for Samuel. He did not fight, but his views at the time were firmly with the Parliamentarian cause and are exemplified in a letter written to General Fairfax at the end of the war (FRE 4223, fos. 102–3). In the letter, which was signed by Samuel and others in the town, he called for retribution against the king and his advisers and any who criticised the army. With regard to government he called for the purging of corruption and better communications so that the army could contribute more effectively to the hoped-for programmes of reform.[11] As the writing of the letter suggests, by this time Samuel was playing a leading role not just in the religious affairs of the town but also in local politics. He had also embarked upon a legal career although how his education fitted him for this role is unclear.[12] From 1651 he was appointed town clerk, a role which apparently he performed with diligence and efficiency until 1662 when the Restoration deprived him of his office. He served as the town's registrar for births, deaths and marriages from 1653 to 1656.[13]

It was perhaps the greater economic and political stability of the post-Civil War period that prompted Samuel to seek a wife. His courtship of Frances Hartridge began in 1650. She was twenty and he was twenty-seven. The couple appear to have met when Samuel visited the Blackwood family at Marden in Kent. Christopher

[6] Quoted in Smart, 'Biographical Sketch', 58.
[7] Fletcher, *County Community*, 117.
[8] ESRO, FRE 4223, fos. 64–9. Letter not reproduced in this collection.
[9] John Spurr, *English Puritanism 1603–1689* (Basingstoke, 1998), 198–9.
[10] Fletcher, *County Community*, 117–19.
[11] See also Fletcher, *County Community*, 292–3.
[12] Michael Hunter, 'Jeake, Samuel (1623–1690)', *ODNB*.
[13] Ibid.

Blackwood, Frances's brother-in-law, had been the vicar of Rye during the 1630s and acquaintance between Samuel and Blackwood had been made then. Blackwood had married Frances's sister Mary after the death of his first wife in 1646.[14] Mary and Frances's parents appear to have died by this time and Frances was living with her sister and brother-in-law.

Although the letters suggest that Frances had given some encouragement to Samuel while they were together (FRE 4223, fos. 106–7), his declarations of love in writing were rejected. One of Blackwood's letters suggests that Frances's objection to the match lay merely in the matter of her jointure (FRE 4223, fo. 107), yet she was much more determined in her refusal. She informed Samuel that 'a soveraigne influence upon my will bends it the cleane contrary way from you' (FRE 4223, fo. 104). Frances's determination would seem to suggest there was something more to the refusal than just a disagreement about a jointure. Financial arrangements were after all open to negotiation. Perhaps Frances feared that Samuel would be an oppressive husband. His letters demonstrate him to have been highly opinionated and, in his own analysis of his nativity, he admitted to a propensity to be somewhat bookish, 'a little solitary, taciturne & laborious'.[15] Certainly like many other godly women Frances valued, and was concerned to preserve, her individual religious freedom.[16] In a highly unusual 'contract' drawn up by Frances prior to her marriage (FRE 4223, fo. 111) two of the five clauses related to freedom of worship and conscience, giving these issues equal weight with Frances's financial concerns.

Although his advances were rebuffed, Samuel was persistent and ardent in his affections (FRE 4223, fos. 106–7). Yet, it was not Samuel's persistence but rather the intercession of Christopher Blackwood that brought the couple to an agreement. It was Blackwood who offered encouragement to Samuel's suit and perhaps persuaded Frances to accept (FRE 4223, fo. 107, fo. 111). The interference of friends and family in a match was typical of an early modern society in which couples were generally free to make their own choices but at the same time subject to the approval of those closest to them.[17] The courtship of Samuel and Frances, therefore, seems to illustrate the 'subtle system' described by Diana O'Hara, in which love was only part of a set of economic, social and familial considerations.[18]

Once committed, Frances offered affection to her future husband but was still careful to extract what she thought was owing to her. As noted above, a contract was drawn up by Frances to protect her religious freedoms, to assert her economic rights and ensure that she could maintain links with her family. In addition, Frances reminded Samuel of the love tokens due to her. In one letter she asked for gloves and 'a ring with a diamond in it' (FRE 4223, fo. 118). These tokens were typical of those exchanged in early modern courtships and, while of dubious value in legal cases, there were considered to be of importance as modes of sealing a contract.[19]

[14] Richard L. Greaves, 'Blackwood, Christopher (1607/8–1670)', *ODNB.*

[15] Quoted in Hunter *et al.*, *Radical's Books*, xix.

[16] Diane Willen, 'Godly Women in Early Modern England: Puritanism and Gender', *Journal of Ecclesiastical History*, 43 (1992), 566.

[17] Alan Macfarlane, *Marriage and Love in England: Modes of reproduction 1300–1840* (Oxford, 1986), 301.

[18] Diana O'Hara, *Courtship and Constraint: Rethinking the making of marriage in Tudor England* (Manchester, 2000), 5.

[19] O'Hara, *Courtship and Constraint*, 62–4; Macfarlane, *Marriage and Love*, 300–1.

Although Frances's contract suggests she expected to retain some independence within her marriage, her brother-in-law urged her to conform to accepted gender roles. He told Frances to 'Endeavour to please him that shall be your husband and dwell with him with an amiable meekenes & contendedness of minde' (FRE 4223, fo. 114). Frances's own views on her relationship with Samuel do not emerge from the letters she wrote during her marriage but she did express longing for the company of her sister and brother-in-law (FRE 4223, fo. 122; fo. 124). She also was clearly distressed by the factionalism within Rye, noting in one letter 'We looke for peace and behold truble, for righteousness and behold oppression…' (FRE 4223, fo. 120). She was not, however, to experience that trouble and oppression for long. After her marriage she bore three children in quick succession: Samuel, born 4 July 1652; Thomas, born 29 June 1653 and died in July 1656; and Frances, born and died on 3 December 1654. Having contracted smallpox in the later stages of her final pregnancy, Frances died on 9 December 1654, six days after her infant daughter.

Elizabeth's mother, Barbara, had been twice widowed before she married Richard Hartshorne, the local school-master. She bore three sons to her first husband, John Holman: John, William and Richard. Barbara's second husband was George Harding. The only child of that marriage was a daughter, named Barbara, who died in 1670 at the age of around nine or ten. Richard Hartshorne and Barbara were married in 1662 and had three children, Elizabeth, Nathaniel, who we shall meet again in chapters four and five, and John, who died in infancy.

As an affluent widow and a woman who had proved herself fertile, Barbara was a good catch.[20] That she was also attractive is demonstrated by an extant letter from another suitor, Richard Langdon. Writing after the death of her first husband, Langdon described Barbara as incomparable in beauty and virtues and claimed that on meeting her he thought 'that havens choosest jewell was there Locked up in Erthes Richest Cabbinet' (FRE 5264). Richard Hartshorne was a relative newcomer to Rye, having moved there in 1659 from Leigh in Staffordshire to take up the post of master of the grammar school. The testimonials that accompanied him described him as 'able, industrious, & successfull in the education of the Youth committed to his charge: as also of a temperate & unblameable conversation'.[21] However, at the age of around 40 and with only a school master's salary, Richard was somewhat less marriageable than Barbara.[22]

As a couple in their middle age with, apparently, no living parents to interfere in their match, it might have been expected that Barbara and Richard's courtship would have proceeded smoothly. There was, however, a serious disagreement between them which was the cause of the letters reproduced in this collection. Although we only have Richard's side of the story, it is clear that a dispute had arisen over a love token, a watch, given by Barbara to Richard and intended to be a secret between themselves. The gift, however, had become known to at least some in Rye despite Richard's strong denial that he had ever wound it or looked at it in company (FRE 5268).

[20] Barbara left significant sums in her will, see chapter 7. She was also able to provide Elizabeth with a substantial dowry, Hunter and Gregory, *Astrological Diary*, 150.

[21] ESRO, RYE 47/162/11, General Files, Mayoralty of Thomas Greenfield; uncalendared, 1659–60.

[22] J. L. Chester, compiler, and G. J. Armytage, ed., *Allegations for marriage licences issued by the Dean and Chapter of Westminster, 1558 to 1699: also, for those issued by the Vicar-General of the Archbishop of Canterbury, 1660 to 1679* (London, 1886), 73.

A close relationship between the two prior to the disagreement is indicated not only by the exchange of a token but also by Richard's intimate knowledge of Barbara's previous relationships. In his letters he made several mentions of her second husband, Mr Harding, and demonstrated an awareness that Barbara had already married twice against her will (FRE 5270). The intimacy of the relationship in also indicated by the promise of 'letters full of kisses' and Richard's desire to 'injoy thee one night instead of every nights dreames on thee' (FRE 5269). The question of whether this indicates an already physical relationship is problematic but it was certainly not unusual for engaged couples to become physically intimate.[23] Another clue to Barbara and Richard's relationship is his claimed affection for her young daughter, Bab. Barbara had left Rye during their quarrel and Bab was being cared for by a local woman. Richard visited her on at least one occasion so that he 'might kisse mine owne' (FRE 5270). No other indications about Richard's connection with Bab are given in the letters making this tantalising phrase impossible to interpret but the fact that Richard felt able to visit the child must indicate an already close relationship.

Richard's letters are equally interesting because they expose the nature of his, not unjustified, doubts about the relationship. Fletcher argues that men were expected to take an assertive role in early modern courtships but, even without the quarrel, there was a serious impediment to Richard's dominance of the relationship.[24] Notably, he claimed that he was 'not borne to a great inheritance' and could offer only 'love and poverty' (FRE 5269). Richard obviously feared that Barbara saw him as a poor economic prospect as he questioned whether 'A better fortune make a lesser love far more worthy in thy eyes' (FRE 5269). Barbara's anger over the exposure of the watch subjected Richard to additional doubts. He doubted her love, accused her of picking a quarrel about the watch on purpose to end the relationship and expressed jealousy about the prospect that Barbara might have other suitors (FRE 5268 and 5270).

Although Richard was eloquent in his pleadings on his own behalf he also employed what we might now describe as emotional blackmail to convince Barbara to return home in his use of little Bab's crying for her 'moda, moda, moda [mother, mother, mother]' (FRE 5269). Moreover, he threatened both the judgment of god and society against Barbara's behaviour. He reminded her: 'my Love there will be atime of searching, all the secrets of our hearts, no covers nor pretences can cloake us from the all seeing eye of God'. Equally, he asked her 'consider how many have been ruined by breaking their engaged faith' (FRE 5269). Unfortunately, the surviving letters do not tell us which of Richard's arguments persuaded Barbara to accept his suit but the couple did marry. There is also no record of whether Barbara's third and final marriage was a happy one. Although Barbara will appear regularly in the chapters to follow, Richard has left few traces in the records.

[23] R. Adair, *Courtship, Illegitimacy and Marriage in Early Modern England* (Manchester, 1996), 129–33.

[24] Anthony Fletcher, 'Manhood, the Male Body, Courtship and the Household in Early Modern England', *History*, 84 (1999), 431.

A 'good death'

[1] *Samuel Jeake senior to Mrs Wenborn, 24 March 1639/40. Copy letter with heading.* ESRO FRE 4223 fo. 60

My Letter to Mrs Wenborn of Mayfield who before was the wife of Mr John Wilmshurst[25]

Godly friend
You may thinke me too bold in presuming to present these confused lines unto your view, which will but trouble you to read but more trouble to me to write in regard of the old friendship & acquaintance betweene you & my mother having now this opportunity could not but acquaint you with that which I wish rather you had beene an eye witness of, even the death of my dearest friend under God. It is now .22. weekes ago she finished her course, she sickened first like an Ague, upon the 29th of October being Tuesday, on the wednesday she went out to Goodman Millers to repetition, the thursday the fit tooke her againe & held her as before, & on the friday she went out to a buriall which was the last time she was forth. On the Saterday she was tooke againe & so it held her all night & the next day being Sabbath she was very sicke, yet in the Afternoone she rose, but still continuing sicke, on the Monday as she lay, she read the .102. Psalme,[26] for the Lord seemed to hide himselfe from her, but he did not forsake her over long, in that night hee revealed himselfe to her in a sweet manner, so that her bruised bones leapt for joy, in the morning she revealed to us what a sweet night she had enjoyed, & how the Lord had let out him selfe to her from these words of the .36. Psalme 5.6.7.8.9. verses[27] and that now she had found by experience what we have yet but by promise, that heaviness may endure for a night but joy cometh in the morning. Continuing sicke we sought to the Physician, this weeke like a Saint, her words ministered grace to the hearers, & she was perswaded she should dye on the Sabbath & that having done a weekes work she should enter into his rest yet God otherwise prevented & that Satan might take his last farewell of troubling her tooke occasion hereby to molest her but at length the Lord

[25] Letter refers to the death of Samuel Senior's mother, Anne Jeake neé Peerson.

[26] Psalm 102 is 'A prayer for the afflicted, when he is overwhelmed, and poureth out his complaint before the Lord'.

[27] Psalms 36: 5–9, 'Thy mercy, O Lord, is in the heavens; and thy faithfulness reaches unto the clouds. Thy righteousness is like the great mountains; thy judgments are a great deep: O Lord thou preservest man and beast. How excellent is thy loving kindness, O God! Therefore the children of men put their trust under the shadow of thy wings. They shall be abundantly satisfied with the fatness of thy house: and thou shalt make them drink of the river of thy pleasures. For with thee is the fountain of life: in thy light shall we see light'.

revealed himselfe to her more fully then before, so that about the middle of the weeke she told us she was as full of joy as her heart could hold. The Lord had now afflicted her with a sore mouth, which much troubled her to speake, about the latter end of the weeke we had good hope of her recovery, but God ordered it better for her gaine though for our losse, on the saterday night & Sabbath following she could take downe nothing but beere & suger with a feather & on the monday & tuesday she waxing worse & worse, we had little hope of life left in her, on the Wednesday being the .20th. day of November about .4. a clocke in the afternoone she sweetly yielded up her soule into her Fathers hands, catching up her hands together uttered these words Come Lord but what more could not be heard. Thus as you had acquaintance of her in her life, you are acquainted with a true relation of her death, that you may rejoyce with her & weepe with me, & that God to whom alone belong the issues of life & death helpe us to glorifie him in either of both conditions. So praieth

Your poore friend lately robbed of his chiefest jewell
Samuel Jeake

Rie March 24th
1639/40

Religious conflicts in Rye

[2] *Exchange of letters between Samuel Jeake senior and John Coulton with explanatory heading. Original letter from Coulton dated 20 May 1641. Copy letter from Samuel senior, undated.* ESRO FRE 4223 fos. 61–4

1640. When Mr John Harrison was minister at Rye, one M. M. had a bastard & in her lying in being dangerously ill was praied for in the publique congregation, also old Mrs Anne Threele as I minde or another professed papist was buried & in the doing of either my tender yeares[28] & apprehensions tooke offense being then under the ministry of the Church of England as so called this occasioned me to say something of my dislike and the same misreported to John Coulton he sent me the following Letter May 20th 1641 to which I returned him this Answer.

Dearely beloved
Unto you I write (with this apelation Beloved) Grace, mercy, and peace be unto you; from God our father and from our Lord Jesus Christ. The motive induceing my pen to scrible these few lines unto you is notoriouse and very urgent to any honest hart at the first riseing of this storme, I had well hoped

[28] Samuel would have been seventeen in 1640.

a strong gale of patience would have blowen it over, and those whisperings thatt are now soe curant amongst you would have beene killed in the shell butt my patience can hold noe longer, and soe you have compelled me if any thing be nott to your compelatary motion thanke your selves and excuse him thatt dare nott now butt acuse you, least guilt of selfe violente should ly upon my selfe: neither have you stayed heare butt soe great Caracters have you written them in, thatt he that runs may read it: and I thatt had thought to have prest my pen for silent service must now stepp forth in a [word illegible] defence to releave my selfe againest your calumniations which now foloweth, I shall sume them up, they are the fo[llowing]

That I hold and mentione dangerouse erours, before ignorante people to deceive them, butt if it weare before my match I would be delte with well inough: (and they are these) as that Mr Harrison did well in praying for the woman falen into the scandalous sine of fornication, when shee sent her bill to the congregation also that I mentione thatt it was well done in him to use the word (deare sister) at the buriall of the Romane Catholique that I have medled with one of the cheefest of the Towne which I had best lett aloane, least it be worse for me then I am aware of.

That it is become a wonder unto you thatt I am sufered to be in the Towne and nott rather to live with my wife as a man of knowledge.

That you wonder thatt mother Renard will sufer me to use her house soe much and will nott reprove me for these things you have amongst you transferred that eternall ministeriall dignitie, atending your owne pastour: (and that unto me undiservedly) in these words (thatt I was more able in in gifts then Mr Harison wish my that he could pray as well as I can doe which I utterly disclaime, thus I have summed by the Cheefe [word illegible] me laine in a succinct way to give you some short answer.

For the first obiection I scorne to deceive the simple or to delude the ignorant by overpowering them with knowledg butt bring me before whome you please what ever I have said, I shall nott feare to justifie whatt I said; soe long as I have one drop of blood in my vaines: therefore you utter a dareing falacy againe indesence of Mr Harison praying for the woman I spoke whatt I thought on it, and now doe positively afirme it before whome you please, and to whome you will, that he did well in it and had comitted a great sinne if he had nott prayed for her, therefore I produce these scriptures read them your selfe. It is both commanded and practised as a duty in the word of God as a rule for us to walke by, it is commanded in Math: 5: 44,[29] Jer: 29: 7[30] soe

[29] Matthew 5: 44, 'But I say unto you. Love your enemies, bless them that curse you, do good to them that hate you, and pray for them which despitefully use you, and persecute you'.
[30] Jeremiah 29: 7, 'And seek the peace of the city whither I have cause you to be carried away captives, and pray unto the Lord for it: for in the peace thereof shall ye have peace'.

it is practised by the people of God also 1 Sam: 12: 19[31] very pertinent to the purpose as will appeare if you examine these texts with a curious eie soe to this purpose is that of Steven, Acts 7: 60[32] these are [word illegible] for the [word illegible] of such a cleare truth as this is soe thatt I hope you will nott deny this seing it carieth maiesty from heaven with it, and I suppose I need nott be ashamed to mentaine the truth, nott onely before weake Christians, but also the strongest that are.

Also for his using the word (deare Sister) it was nott unlawfull as I conceive, for first she was a deare sister by creation, we had all one father by creation soe she was a sister, again she was a sister by profession, she professed Jesus Christ, and also she was a sister by Baptisme, sow (as I can prove) she was baptised into the church and as yet never cutt of by noe censure of the church therefore deare sister also she was deare in regard of the sufficiency of the meritt of Christs death that was ofered for the elect, and that unto salutation; for the wicked that soe he might judge them, as psalme 2: 8 verse aske of me and I shall give the the [*sic*] heathen for thy Inheritance and the out most parts of the earth and thou shalt bruse them with a rod of Iron soe much for that obiection.[33]

The secondeth foloweth I answer for my medleing with great ones, I feare not to give an account when ever I am Called unto it I that know I may nott curse the king in my chamber, I that know the apostle recons it by far a grand imposture to speake evell of dignities, it weare grosse impietie in me to fall thus grosely, and if you lett me butt have the conceite of an hypocrite in your head, you may well know it is nott the way to gaine creditt to my selfe, butt indeed I have alwayes beene soe wary of speaking evell of honest dignities that I dare nott entertaine the least irreverent thought and whatt sover our evell envieing Christians doe report, whose glory and practise it is to run prateing from house to house to heare and tell (as I by experience know some) yet what danger soever may come to me I pas nott, because if I doe suffer I canott sufer as a delinquent and lett me speake to you Samuell I hope you will nott believe it, but yet soe far am I from feareing whatt I have said or done that in stead of crying petavi, I rather say facere pesimus[34] but I hope I shall nott have cause to feare any such tryall I have done with this also.

[31] I Samuel 12: 19, 'And all the people said unto Samuel. Pray for thy servants unto the Lord thy God, that we die not: for we have added unto all our sins this evil, to ask us a king'.

[32] Acts 7: 60, 'And he kneeled down, and cried with a loud voice. Lord, lay not this sin to their charge. And when he had said this, he fell asleep'.

[33] Psalms 2: 8–9, 'Ask of me and I shall give thee the heathen for thine inheritance and the uttermost parts of the earth for thy possession. Thou shalt break them with a rod of iron: thou shalt dash them in pieces like a potter's vessel'.

[34] Do thy worst.

To the third particular I answer it is nott convenient for me to write the reason of my being absent from my wife neither would my sheete containe it yett as you are a Christian and as you are an unquestionable believer in my opinion, I hold my selfe bound to signifie to you thatt it is nott oute of any dislike each of other, we live apart: butt onely for some reasons which if you be curious to know when you and I meet I shall lay them downe to your satisfaction, I hope; and tell me Samuell what hurte have I done in your Towne sure I first know it speake plaine I have prayed for the peace and prosperity of it, whether they have beene answered or noe that must be (for the most of them both to you and me) counsell or at least a secrett not to be [word illegible] I have spent my time if it fell to my lot to doe good not onely to my selfe but others I have undergone many hot thunderbolts amongst you, troubles doe surround me dayly from abroad, and what out with day by contestings and a man of temptations which with sorow I am faine now to boast of unto you own of myne infirmities, and why you would have one sent out of the Towne I know nott I am sory thatt the saints are weary of me for wicked men it is noe nuse to heare there rebylenys both of you and me, and liveing and the dead butt you to be weary of me toucheth me verie much butt noe marvell sometimes I am a burthen to my selfe, and yet if you know any course or way to have me out spare nott however this I canott butt take as an affliction sent of God to weed out some hurt, oh that I may make a hapie use of it soe much for that.

For the 4th thing I have nott much to say to it, it is rather bent upon her (whoe as I have heard since I began this letter) hath beene the [word lost] of this storme, god grant I may make a hapie use of it soe I leave that and her too worse then I though to have done.

The last is something worse then the rest, for your comparsisons betweene Mr Harison and my selfe, that I was more able then he for discourse and prayer, I doe nott aprove of it butt doe protest in the presence of God I desire nott for to be accounted neither Doe I believe it to be true in part or in whole, whatt shall I say, I utterly disclaime it I say noe more onely dearely beloved had you seene these faults in me this ~~had~~ was not the way to reclame me, in whispering behind my backe noe Samuell these rather stur up wrath and envy, and evell surmises, butt our saviour layes downe another way 6 Gall 1[35] Math 18th 15[36] which course if you take what [word illegible] my time, when you se me fall, lett me nott be [word illegible] then lett the righteous smite me thatt shall be good for me, soe shall nott my head be broken I shall make prayers

[35] Galatians 6: 1, Brethren, if a man be overtaken in a fault, ye which are spiritual, restore such an one in the spirit of meekness: considering thyself, lest thou also be tempted.

[36] Matthew 18: 15, Moreover if thy brother shall trespass against thee, go and tell him his fault between thee and him alone: if he shall hear thee, thou hast gained thy brother.

for you, both now, and ever, while time lasts to me, or I to it and you eternised in the heavens.

Soe praieth your unworthy friend
John Coulton

Rey May 20th 1641
What ever from my pen doeth fall
Oh lord take thou the glory of all

Goodman Coulton
I salute you, I perceive I am growne odious in your sight and become very obnoxious to you, by reason of some false accusations & calumnious aspersions cast on me by some that are seeming friends onely. I have now received your Letter, wherein you charge me with divers & severall false positions, at which I marvaile but I pray expect not such a circumspect answer as if I had learned the [words struck out] art to comprehend much matter in a few lines, or as if I had a helper to instruct & teach me, yet thinke not that it shall altogether die in silence when as for what I spoke I know how to answere if I goe awry teach me & I will learne, raise me to understand where in I have erred.

First you impute to me, that I should report you hold and maintaine dangerous errors before ignorant people &tc. to notifie to you the words that I then said in every particular as neere as I can remember (speaking the truth in Christ before whose dreadfull tribunall I must give accompt as of all my words & workes, so of this also whether they be good or evill) were these, that some of your Reasons to uphold praying for the Fornicator, & the words, Deare Sister, at the buriall of the Papist were very weake.

And now to insist a little larger on it, you would go about to prove it, you bring me scripture indeed, which as I conceive are nothing correspondent to the purpose, you quote me the precept of Christ & example of Steven, which instances onely praying for our enemies. I conceive there to be two sorts of enemies to be praied for & that after a double manner, the enemies of the Church of God in generall and our owne enemies in particular. For the first sort we are to pray either for their conversion (because we know not whether they belong to God or no) or confusion (as David imprecates in some of his Psalmes against such enemies) & this may be done in the publicke congregation. For our owne particular enemies, we may pray for them generally in the publicke congregation but not particularly, for if any have wronged abused or reviled us, so as it tends to the dishonour of God & scandall of his Gospell, though we are to forgive them in our heart & earnestly pray for their pardon & to qualifie our heat of malice with some affection of love: Yet not to testifie our forgiveness outwardly by praying for them publiquely till such time as they seeke reconciliation & submit themselves lest we confirme the verity of the former & insure the like upon our selves in future times.

Now for your place in Jeremy 29.7.[37] where the prophet exhorts the people of the Jewes, to pray for the peace and prosperity of the city whether they were led captive producing this reason for in the peace of that, they shall have peace. Those words as I perceive are no proofe of the point in hand, when the prophets drift is to teach & divert the people how to undergoe their captivity with the more ease by praying that the city might be at peace freed from trouble & warre & perplexity, for they being there resident, if any such combustions be must be sure to share in them, therefore seeke the prosperity of the city & pray to the Lord for it, that so they might with the more patience & lesse grief waite upon God, for the time of their deliverance, not for any affection that the Prophet beareth to the Tyrant or to the City (which may seeme if you take the words too literally) noe for not onely the Israelites but all the world yea & the very insensible creatures should rejoyce when these Tyrants should be destroyed as we may read Isaiah .14. 4. 5. 6. 7. 8. & so forward.[38]

And for that in Samuel, unlesse you will prove the Israelites to be such as she is, is very impertinent, but if it were soe (which is a gross falsity to thinke,) yet its to no purpose for first its a question whether he praied for them in private or in publique, but if he did pray for them in publique, yet they first confess their sinnes & humble them selves openly before him, but you may tell me, so did she in regard she sent to be praied for, but it is apparent to the contrary whatever she seemingly pretends, witness her vile words spoken to one that professt Godlyness, about that time, which though she now deny yet can be justified on oath to the contrary, so that it is cleare she had no love nor liking to the waies of God, neither to humiliation nor prayer but onely to have her sickness removed (which many an honest woman endures more in the common disease of child bearing) it's true we must judge charitably, but charity judges not absolutely not peremptorily & though it hope well of all things: yet it is not a toole to conclude all things. Again the prophet convicts them of & laies open unto them the hainousness of their sinne & reproves them sharpely & severely for it, & that before he prayes for or at the least manifests his prayer to them which may be plainly seene by viewing the context, which if she had beene (as the manner of some other reformed churches are) I could have held well with. But for to be praied for in the publique congregation before she had testified her humiliation & repentance

[37] As fn. 30.

[38] Isaiah 14: 4–8, 'That thou shalt take up this proverb against the king of Babylon, and say, How hath the oppressor ceased! The golden city ceased! The Lord hath broken the staff of the wicked, and the sceptre of the rulers. He who smote the people in wrath with a continual stroke, he that ruled the nations in anger, is persecuted, and none hindreth. The whole earth is at rest, and is quiet: they break forth into singing'.

& before she had beene soundly reproved, I cannot thinke to be lawfull since her fault was so scandalous, lest it were a countenancing of her in it. For the Apostle saith plaine .1.Tim. 5. 20.[39] them that sinne rebuke openly that the rest may feare, thus much for that.

Now for your Reasons to prove the words Deare Sister at the buriall of the Papist to be lawfull, I thinke them little lesse than cavills, it's true, we had all one father by creation, & we are all by nature the children of wrath, but now nature is changed by grace in the godly & old things are passed away, & we are now no more strangers & foreiners but citizens with the saints & houshold of God, and now what fellowship hath righteousness with unrighteousness what communion hath light with darkness? What concord hath Christ with Belial? and what part hath a believer with an Infidell? I leave to the learned to judge.

And for her profession, I pray how did she professe Jesus Christ, was it not after a wrong manner? are not all the tenents of the papisticall religion for the most part egregious & pernicious errors, derogatory to the honour & dignity of Christ, and that in a high degree, I presume your selfe can witness, nay she was an Infidell being a papist, for they deny the faith of us Christians & cleave to the covenant of workes which is now abrogated, and no man is able to performe neither is any man justified by it. Gal. 3. 11.[40] And as I said before what communion or fellowship hath a believer with them? And especially in such a neere bond of relation as to be a Sister or Brother to them by profession. I thinke it little lesse then to partake of their sinnes, wherein we lye lyable to partake of her plagues.

And for Baptisme, when she was baptized she knew not what she did, but others were surely for her, which when she came to age, was bound to performe, but refused (violating her covenant she there made & judged her selfe unworthy of eternall life, following dumbe Idolls as she was led) and joyned unto a false church: that the Apostles words might be verified they went out from us for they were not of us, if they had beene of us, they would no doubt have continued with us still. So that Antichristians & Christs followers have no relation nor affinity to or with one another.

But you may object, it may be said to them as well as to carnall men living in this Church. I deny it, for they submitting themselves to the ordinances of God (though perhaps church papists) are under the compass of a true visible church (as farre as I yet see) when as the Papists are of a false church &c. so much for that.

[39] I Timothy 5: 20, 'Them that sin rebuke before all, that others also may fear'.

[40] Galatians 3: 11, 'But that no man is justified by the law in the sight of God, it is evident: for, the just shall live by faith'.

Secondly you blame me for saying you meddled with great ones which you had best let alone &c. I protest unto you, I never said it. The words that I said (as neere as I can remember without either addition or detraction) were these: you had discanted on some randome, concerning praying for Maudline, which if you have done, you know, whether they be great one or little ones, if you have not then you may repute me a lying Christian (as well as envying Christ) but I know on what grounds I spake it.

For your third it is partly true & partly false. I then spake in the words of the Apostle that you ought to live with your wife as a man of knowledge, which I thinke you cannot take distast at since it was the words of the Holy Ghost, & for your propounding to me the reasons of your living asunder, I desire it not. Thinke not (I pray) that I harbour curiosity so much in me, as to be a meddler in other folkes matters, lest I come under the Apostles reproofe, onely I thinke it occasion of scandall for a professor & his wife to live at variance. For the other part I disclaime it utterly & therefore cannot nor will not Answer for that which I never said nor thought.

For the fourth also is partly true & partly false, for the first I said it if I were to live in the house as Goody Kennard is I should not endure, but to reprove you plainly, which was all to my knowledge that I said, wherein I meant plainly & simply as I wish any one would do to me when they see amisse in me. But for the other that she should not suffer you to use her house, it is others slanders and not my words.

For your last I have nothing to do with it, neither did I know any word to that effect was spoke till I questioned about it & neither were as you have set them downe, but I wonder why you should burden me with it, seeing you know I spoke it not except by your denying the negative, you would have others prove the affirmative, which I know none meanes to doe.

This I hope will give you satisfaction for that I spake, without any further contention, & whereas you reprove me for whispering behind your backe I may justly retort it on your selfe; for I spake it to one of your sociable companions, but you noised it abroad before divers as I had notice, before you knew the truth. Thus craving pardon for my boldness intreating you to make a favourable construction of all my Errors. I commit you to your safest conduct of the surest conductor and so remaine

Sometime your loved Sometime
your loathed
Sa: Jeake

The English Civil War

[3] *Samuel Jeake senior to his friends in the army, undated. Copy letter with heading.* ESRO FRE 4223 fos. 69–70

My letter as a last farewell sent to my friends in the Army Jn° Coulton, Joseph Relfe, Thomas Caven & others.

Dearest and most entirely beloved friends
My best love salutes you. My tenderest Affections are toward you, whom I love as my owne soule, whose happines is my rejoycing, whose griefe is my Dollour, whose victories shall be my crowne, whose societies I judge my selfe unworthy to enjoy, because the Lord hath deprived me of it: & that I feare in anger. I am right glad to heare from you. Your letters did not a little refresh my dropping spirits. Oh how I long to see you! much more to abide with you; that so we have beene comely in our lives, in our deaths we might not have beene divided. & now what adds downe weight to my sorrowe? but that I feare I shall never see your faces more. But the will of the Lord must be done. I know mine iniquities are of such a distracting power that they do not onely sequester my friends but labour to separate my God from me. I have little to write to you, but a last farewell. I can do nothing for you but that which I daily do (to wit) often ply heaven with prayers for your good whose conditions all joyntly & every one severally according to my weake abillity both are & shall be commended to God continually by me. What shall I say? I desire your safe returne againe if the will of the Lord be so. I desire victory for you, against your & the Lords enemies. I desire you may (as I heare you are) be couragious, having so good a cause call & captaine. I desire you may keepe your selves from spiritual pollutions: Babes keepe yourselves from Idolls Amen.[41] And what you are deprived of in respect of publick Administrations, I desire the Lord by the immediate workings & conveyance of his spirit to make good to you. When you go forward, or shall set upon any attempt what is my desire? but that the Lord would rise up before you & scatter your enemies: and when you rest, that the Lord would returne to the many thousands of Israel. In a word I desire your happiness, & in some respect I could even wish my selfe miserable to attaine my desire. I cannot make an end or give over the multiplication of my soules wishes for your soules & bodies good. I am full of matter, & the spirit within me constraines me to go on; let your love pardon my excesse, it may be the last time that ever you may heare from me, I know not, but might my speech be long as my heart is large, or could it possibly be soe: when should I surcease, these my hartiest benedictions, these

[41] 1 John 5: 21.

my kindest valedictions? Yet I must conquer my selfe & spite of my longing heart to wish longer. Desiring onely this one thing that what good I am not able to intreat God for you, the Lord of his goodness may please freely & fully to give downe upon you all for ever, that so it may come to passe that in all respects & estates what soever wherein you are or may be considered you may in every of them be truly blessed that as men you may be faithfull, as souldiers couragious as Christians gracious, & as Saints glorious, more than these I cannot pray for & I do & will pray that you may never enjoy less from the hands of the living God, who giveth abundantly and upbraideth no man, who sincerely seeketh his face for any present or future favour. And so deare Christians and Brethren, my faithfull & affectionate heart bids you all farewell, you are all beloved of me, & I must now leave you to the love of God, whose power guard you from all evill, grace guide you unto all good, peace rule in your hearts & mercy compasse you about in all estates. As my loving friends I leave you to him that is the helper of the friendlesse. As warriours I leave you to the Lord of Hosts who is the mighty God of battell, as Christians I leave you to Jesus Christ both your Lord and mine. He abide with you, his grace abound in you, his Holy Spirit be your comforter on Earth, your conductor to heaven. And now the God of peace that brought againe from the Dead the Lord Jesus Christ , that great Shephard of the sheepe through the blood of the everlasting covenant make you perfect in every good worke to do his will working in you that which is well pleasing in his sight through Jesus Christ, to whom be glory for ever and ever

Soe prayeth yours whilst his owne
Samuel Jeake

[4] *Samuel Jeake senior and others to General Fairfax, undated. Copy letter with heading.* ESRO FRE 4223 fos. 102–3

Copy of the Letter sent by my selfe & some others to the Lord General Fairfax

Right Honourable
It were lost labour to enumerate to you (who have beene a deepe sufferer under) the plurality of Evills that have attended this seven yeares warre. Your faithfull fellow feeling with the poore oppressed Kingdome, hath hitherto beene manifested in your appearing as a Saviour unto it & your unwearied undertaking for publique good both in former and later actings. You have waded through the Kingdome in blood & carrying your life on the point of your sword have (by the strength of God in you) woone that you weare, & in valour beene victor.

Yet it is not unknowne to you that the Kingdome yet groanes (for liberty as waiting for the manifestacon of the Sonnes of God) for shall a Nation be borne at once? or in one day delivered from the monstrous Mola's or conceptions its wombe hath inclosed & hatched these many ages? our miseries were breeding many generations agoe, we must turne over yeares & reignes ere we read their Original, yea runne & rowle beyond the Norman Conquest, & there finde some seeds of our divisions sowne, some men's wills made laws, some publique persons act to privat ends, & judgment inverted into gall & wormwood, this we know what it meanes by wofull experience our diseases are not of yesterday, they are more desperate than will admit of a tedious cure, & what more bitter! our physicians have beene of no value, our remedies have beene our diseases, he that helped & they that were helpen have both fallen & perished together.

But though our freedome be too intricate for man to recuperate yet are we not left either hopeless or helpless, our great Jehovah being engaged to effect it, & for that purpose impower such Actors as majesty from heaven dwells upon, amongst the which your honour challenges the foremost place, the anointing upon you being evidenced by the power with & in you, under whom though but the other day (in the Enemies account) wee were fallen & as dry bones, yet now are Risen & stand upright the tempestuous & thunder threatening cloudes that darkened our Horizon being dispersed through the power of the most High over shaddowing you. Oh loose not the things you have wrought, let there not be a prize in the hand & no heart to improve it, lest we complaine at last the harvest is past, the summer is ended & we are not saved.

And though our present grievances have beene more lively represented by others & our petitions begged before for us: yet in the manifold experiences we already have of your unparalel'd endeavours for generall good & our continual confidence of your perseverance therein, reminding your present engagements: we earnestly crave that amongst your midst & multiplicity of your weighty agitations, these our few petitionary proposals may have admission into your serious thoughts, which out of our faithfull affection [word struck out] to your honour & tender care of the weale of the Republique we as humbly & earnestly remonstrating both declare and desire.

First that as we do fully adhere to the late Remonstrance & are resolved to venture lives & fortunes in defence of the Army in the just prosecution of it: so doe we desire that no delayes (as conceiving them altogether unsafe) may be admitted therein.

2ly considering that want of care & vigilancy (as well as fidelity) in Comittees & others betrusted with publique affaires hath beene the seminary of many evils to this Kingdome: we intreat that care may be taken to refine them, & that such as shall in any waies be obstructers of justice ether by opposing it, or not improving their intrusted power to that purpose may be excluded & also that the like sedulity may be used in removing the Committee of Accompts & appointing others others in their places they being such whose endeavours are more to ensnare than to advance the publique good.

3ly The Kingdomes groaning under the burden of freequarter & (yet) unreasonable taxes, occasioned by the unfaithfull dealing of those entrusted with the publique treasure: requires (as we humbly conceive) some exquisite search: & those being found that have any way abused the state by such fraudulent practises, as to designe the publique treasure to their private advantage deserve to be severly dealt withall.

4ly minding the nakedness of those marine parts & the great dangers we lie exposed to, if any new commotions (which God forbid) should break forth. We earnestly sue that some carefull provision may be made for the sea coast, & especially neere this place the better to strengthen the hands of the Kingdomes friends, & to prevent (at present) unthought of mischiefs.

5ly Being grieved to heare the slanderous aspersions the Army is & hath beene loaded with, notwithstanding its desert to the contrary: we heartily desire, that all such as shall be knowne to asperse them or to act or speake against their proceedings in reference to the execution of justice & righteousness may be brought to condigne punishment.

6ly The principall Actors in and Abbettors of our miserable differences by reason of prominence in some alliance in others with other such wiseblinding bribes have regained strength to rally againe & againe when we had well hoped were irrecoverable: wherefore we humbly intreat your honour that some commissioners may be appointed to find out the Actors & fomenters of the late warre & bringing in of the Scots & being found to secure them or otherwise, without superficial dealing in matters of this concernment. yet a speciall care to be had of the non oppressing their families.

7ly Because of the distance of this & many other Garrisons from the Head quarters, & the necessity of intelligence from thence to animate the souldiery & wel affected residing therein, to joyne with and in defense of the just proceedings of the Army: we therefore humbly beseech that there may be an impartiall communication of the Actions of the Army to the respective Garrisons that shall remonstrate with them by such actors as each Garrison shall to that purpose appoint & yet all such of the countrey as either have or shall shew themselves worthy to be confided in may be put in to a posture of defence.

The courtship and marriage of Samuel Jeake, senior and Frances Hartridge

[5] *Samuel Jeake senior to Frances Hartridge, 1 July 1650. Copy letter.*
ESRO FRE 4223 fo. 104

Most deare & entirely beloved friend
My heart cannot but emanate unto thee, after whom such a tendency of my whole selfe is effluxed; as I can no longer enjoy my selfe but in thee for truly I have not beheld in all the world one so able to reciprocate my longings & retaliate that love which will never expire but with life. & may I speake, & yet but modestly in my owne behalf. I can in speaking truth, say, I am not my owne to be thine.

Deare Heart, pardon my boldnes & consider that I neither can nor dare eclipse the truth of thy well deservings with complementing vanities or Nugations: but in reality professe I must needs deviate from truth if I should speake lesse then venerably of the unworthiest carriage I ever beheld in thee; so as to me I thinke subordinate to the most High, my joy, solace, comfort, and foelicitous welbeing are concentiring in thee. Much more I long thou shouldst experiment, but at present because of the porters speedy returne I cannot enlarge. With my prayers for your health & presentation of my unfained loves, intending my presence shall shortly excuse my rusticke lines, I shall humbly kisse your hand.

Madame
Yours as his owne and more
Samuel Jeake

Rye July 1
1650

These To Mrs Frances Hartridge with care, private

[6] *Frances Hartridge to Samuel Jeake senior, 16 July 1650. Original letter.*
ESRO FRE 4223 fo. 104

Sir,
I perceived by your conferencs when you were last with us that you intended us a further visit if as a freind without any further reference you will be welcome to us all but if you intend to pursue your former sute I must hearin that you may not fall into a laborious losse of time professe my selfe by this finall negative a totall dissenter. Christian plainenesse ought to proceed from me who professe my selfe to be a Christian to declare reasons of my totall

deniall might be tedious to you and perhaps a ground of further trouble your desires possiblye putting you upon an endevor of counterballancing reasons ~~wich~~ which to you might perhaps seame probable but to me impossible and therfore I forbeare to perticularize. [word struck out] Take it in [word illegible] the most high who hath a soveraigne influence upon my will bends it the cleane contrary way from you not in relation of freind ship for I wish you the choysest shee upon the earth and the plentivel of all happines heare and hearafter but in the relation of wife being resolved in my selfe not as yet to marrye this I thought good to signifye to you that you might not loose opportunities [*sic*] else where nor create future affliction to your selfe by an affection of any long standing. Pardon my freenes in speaking my heart seing in matters of this natuer wee cannot bee too plaine, I need not write any thing to stay your spirit from sinking at the disposall of these affaires, the soveraigne will and providence of god is a resting point for belevers besides would you turne the tables and looke upon the unworthines and unhansomnes of the object perhaps better lost then found this might further compose your spirit with which compare those many who exceed me far in portion proportion virtue and discent of one which you are capable but in so plaine a case I need not adde reasons in the addition wherof my lines perhaps might swell and perhaps overflow the banks of reason which if they should might chalenge excuse from my sex and yeares so desiring the god of peace to quiet your heart at all times and perticularly in this my totall and finall deniall I take leave and rest Sir

Your well wishing
Freind & servant
Frances Hartredge
the 16 of July 1650

[7] *Samuel Jeake senior to Frances Hartridge, 1 August 1650. Copy letter.*
ESRO FRE 4223 fos. 106–7

Dearest friend
I cannot but contemplate the Metamorphosis of thy aspect towards me and as ponderously ballance the cause: the which (ah my hart) am I neither sophicall enough to know, nor physicall enough to cure; but must rest super magnum Medicum[42] although that I may use the poets words Omnia in pejus ruerê et retro pede lapsa referri.[43] I wish my selfe under a capacity of deserving

[42] Upon the great Physician.
[43] A misquotation of Virgil, Georgics 1:199–200, *sic omnia fatis in peius ruere et retro sublapsa referri*: 'Thus all things, by the fates, rush to the worse and, having slipped, are carried backwards'.

your love; but the way thither is to me uncouth, & soe intricate câ causâ. For I waver in a sea of uncertainty, believing thy selfe can fancie me (or else I should desist,) and not knowing what inferior reasons can counterpoise; but so faine a bloome might have as fertill a harvest. Yet may I not see thee upon any other accoumpt then as a common friend, as the letter didascalizeth, on paine of the forfeiture of my welcome the which though I cannot ceremonize yet I confesse hath exceeded my deserts. If I answer to one objection, [word struck out] another succeeds, and a third dethrones a second & which is more, each reply ingerminates more scruples in thee: yet what should I not endeavour so I might be ascertained of thy love? But to fight still in the aire, amounts to nothing but vapours of victory. And if to satisfy thee I should administer to the deceased & contract for the payment of some long past debts, purchasing to my selfe trouble enough besides an undoubted resurrection of jealousies (if of no more) that I as conscious to my selfe of former fraude (cuius contrarium verum est[44]) should now administer which I have till now refused: being assured it will nothing else but expose me & through me the Gospell to the vituperie of the world and resurge matters now more than five yeares obliterate and buried, alwaies minding that it cannot adde to my foelicity, nor enfranchise me, either in point of conscience or the law with any cleerer right or title unto what I enjoy than what I already have & enjoy it with: and yet then not to be certaine of acceptation with thee neither, & so to loose the end of my engagement, would but render me ridiculous, if not Bipedum Stultissimus.[45]

My friend I confesse with thee, the will of God is a resting point for believers, & therefore I cannot say much though my heart be enlarged, yet had need to desire submission to his will & herein implore your helpe. Yet I know not how upon so slender a testimony as one letter to receive such a selfe denying dissent. But if still the prevalency of that soveraigne influence (as you dogmatize) hath resolvedly bent your will to an everlasting blast of my hopes, as a token you have blotted out all thoughts of love toward me, take your pen & rase out my lines & returne them to me in that mourning garbe, the which after I have embalmed with a few brinish drops, I shall crave strength of the most High to bowe to his will, but shall never cease to wish well to you, because I am

Mrs
Your true & affectionate friend & servant
S. J.

Rye 1 August
1650

These To Mrs Frances Hartridge in Marden private

[44] Contrary to the truth
[45] The most foolish of bipeds.

[8] *Samuel Jeake senior to Frances Hartridge, 23 August 1650. Copy letter.*
ESRO FRE 4223 fo. 107

Sweet friend,
My Letters as my love to you have beene most unfortunate, since I have failed though I have looked for a requitall of both. Ah unhappy me! not worthy the answer of a few lines, your receipt I question not because of the former faithfulness of the Messenger. I may not see thee, I cannot heare from thee. Ah! what a deluge of doubt I drive in, & yet more I know no ende. Nullis amor est medicabilis herbis.[46] How faire could I further engage for thy sake (if it might be accepted) I here neither say nor can. But I beseech you in all tenderness of bowells, even as I at your request have forborne to visit you, you will at mine be pleased to honour me with a perspective of your mind, the which I daily expect & now begge at your hands, or returne my papers with a blacke face that I may solemnize their dislike & mine in mournfull eulogies the which though I professe I know not how I shall beare nor scarce can write without excruciate ____ yet I am but clay & in the hands of the potter, who will do what he pleases, to whom I shall supplicate for your welfare continually, longing [words struck out] to heare therof, intreating your excuse on my confused lines because they come frome a confused minde & that in

Mrs
Your true friend & servant
Sa: Jeake

Rye August 23
1650

To Mrs Frances Hartridge these private trust

[9] *Christopher Blackwood to Samuel Jeake senior, 3 September 1650. Original letter.*
ESRO FRE 4223 fo. 107

Lo[ving] Sir,
Yours I received both first and second together with rules about the rule of three for all which with other your [word illegible] I returne you many thankes my sister[47] remaines as she was in a negative posture whose inclosed letter I have hearein sent, the great shirke as to me seameth and truly the only shirk is feare of and doubt about a good tithe about the things to be possessed from you which though to many others might seame a thing of nought yet to her

[46] Love is not to be cured by medicinal herbs, Ovid.
[47] Frances Hartridge.

its of that moment that shee cannot goe forward for were there but £200 of just tithe shee is of such nimble minde that I doe imagen shee would content her selfe so far is shee from looking after great things, these things I speake as my own apprehensions I am sorye that you should finde so troublesome business herein but as our comforts so our troubles are appointed by god. The cause why you had no sooner an Answer was my forgetfulness for my sister went to London (where she tarried about a fortnight) & left [word struck out] this letter to be sent to you I ~~might~~ met with a sure messenger from Rye three weeks agoe or thereabouts & forgot to give it to him & since we had not an opportunity till this day. My wife desires to be remembered to you. No more at present save that I am

Your assured frend
Ch: Blackwood

Marden
~~Aug~~ September 3
1650

[10] *Frances Hartridge to Samuel Jeake senior, 14 August 1650. Original letter, assumed enclosure with Christopher Blackwood's letter of 3 September.*
ESRO FRE 4223 fo. 108

Sir,
I had well thought that I had in my former paper as well as by a living voyce set the impassable bounds of a nonplus ultra to your sute by rendering myself totally and finallye negative thereunto as my lines upon perusall will further demonstrate but seing you further try me whether time or sum new emergent occation or reason have wrought any change in me from what I was I must declare ingeniously that I am hearin to use queene elizabeths [word struck out] motto semper eadem[48] that is as absolute in my deniall as formerly I was. I must by this silent messenger returne you many thanks for your loving opinion and affections towards me towards me which I shall in a way of freindship though not of mariage endeavor to requite pardon mee if I speake plaine language for it is in reference to you that I may not put you ~~uon~~ upon ~~any~~ a laborious losse of time & cost for me to put you to any hard taske of restitution or any thing else and heareby give away my liberty were but folly and madnes in me and so much the more in a matter wherein your conscience is so fully satisfied and the effects of the busines so uncertaine and troublesome truly I shall forbeare hearein and all together counsell you in patience and silence to rest in the pleasuer of that god who worketh all things after the

[48] Always the same.

counsell ~~will~~ of his owne will who [words struck out] knoweth what you have need of and I hope will wherto my wishes are provide you a helpmeet. I have returned your lines rased as a token that I have blootted all thoughts of love to you in relation to wedlocke though not in relation to freindship if the certificate wherof shall create any sorrowes in you it will be your wisdome to take the advantage of them and turn them into godly sorrow I count it some part of my unhappines that I should occation sorrow to any much lesse to a freind yea such a freind that hath had so large affections as you have I doubt not in truth profest. Sir I have no more at present save that I am your

assured freind & servant
Frances Hartredge

August the 14: 1650:

[11] *Copy of a contract between Samuel Jeake senior and Frances Hartridge, with heading in Samuel's hand.* ESRO FRE 4223 fo. 111

Afterwards having some discourse with Mr Blackwood & receiving some incouragement I went againe and after a right understanding of things she consented upon the proposalls following, readily granted by me, and we were happily married July 17th 1651.

Propositions which I[49] judge reasonable, which being granted I know not of any other thing I shall desire

1.	I desire libertie of conscience & that I may have all conveniencies for a journey to the church whereof I am a Member fower times in the yeare.	This was performed as oft as shee desired after marriage.
2.	For the goods which were your fathers, because I am not established in conscience about the title of them & so consequently not of the use of them, though you your selfe be; I desire that so much of it as will be worse for using may be changed with what convenience may be and some other which will be of a right propertie in my conscience purchased, which I may use in the roome thereof.	Some goods were sold & others the property altered & she better satisfied therein

[49] Frances Hartridge.

3. That forasmuch as I know not the manner of your worship nor whether there will be any thing that will offend my conscience therein: I desire that if there should be such worship as my heart cannot close withall nor my bodily presence allow of without sin, that it may be no alienation of conjugall affection if I should absent herein.

   She never tooke offence that I ever learned, nor at any time when in Towne or case to go forth did absent her selfe.

4. That whereas my Brother Mr Blackwood told me that he had proposed no other condition about temporal estate save the joynture of the house unto me: yet this thing I shall adde that in case we have no issue and if you should dye first I desire it may be given to me & my heires for ever.

   The joynture was accordingly made but I being the survivor & she leaving issue is voide

5. That you will be pleased for as much as I see my sister Blackwood over burthened with young children to let me keepe Mary Blackwood her daughter till we have children of our owne.

   Mary Blackwood was brought down & kept here till my wife desired to send her home.

Which things being by you subscribed I trust I shall show my selfe a loyall loving & dutifull wife.

[12] *Frances Hartridge to Samuel Jeake senior, 28 May 1651. Original letter.*
ESRO FRE 4223 fo. 112

My deare,
having this opportunity I could not but salute you with this paper not ~~d~~ doubting of you had providence offered you the first opportunity as it hath done mee, I can but give you [word struck out] only hearin a testimoniall of the confirmation of that fidelitye and love wherein I am ingaged to you be assured that true affection is lodged in my hart to you wards which nothing I hope save death ~~sall~~ shall remove, I shall not bee much in declaring that which if by you I am confident unsuspected freinds in there absence are wont to speake their hearts by letters I hope you forget not to implore the most high touching our intended busines my broken praiers shall not bee wanting one thing I shall propose as a quere whether it bee expede for you to lay any thing out in building seing in a short time god may offer you a more convenient house upon easie tearmes and then you may let out your owne but this I onely propose: God evermore blesses you and direct all your waies in reference to his owne glory and your everlasting ~~good~~ peace is the praier of

your most affectionate
freind and servant
F H

May 28 1651

My Brother went to London on ~~ty~~ tuesday
My Sister and the familie are well

[13] *Samuel Jeake senior to Frances Hartridge, 30 May 1651. Copy letter.*
ESRO FRE 4223 fo. 113

Deare Heart
I kindly thanke thee for thy loveing letter my tyme is soe short; that I cannot write what I would, but I trust to speake with thee shortly: yet it will be middle of next weeke before I can come for I had thoughts to have beene with thee on munday next but I have employments with the mayor. Prethee excuse my brevity & present my kind respects to Mrs Blackwood & thus with my prayers for you I remaine

your ever lo: consort
Samuell Jeake

May 30th 1651

[14] *Christopher Blackwood to Frances Hartridge, 30 May 1651. Original letter.*
ESRO FRE 4223 fo. 114

Deare Sister
I have sent your joynture ready for sealing if you proceed on in finishing your marriage before I come backe which I would counsell now to doe (especially if it be his desire) then let Mr Jeake seale the joynture first to my unkle John Hartridge for you and then let him seale the bond but if you see the bond be offensive to him you wave it for it is of no great moment where wee deale with honest persons of which I judge him to be one. Though I bee put in as a feoffee for you with my unkle yet if I could not come so soone as I desire & your occation will require yet will it be sufficient without me if made over to my unkle my praiers shall not bee wanting for your good success in your business. I have sent Goodye Darbye her virginall strings they cost a shilling. If you should marrye before I come backe yet would I not have you to goe to Rye till my returne if the Lord shall please to bring me backe but if he should not bring me backe the journey being long and my bodily strength weake yet I hope wee shall meete and bee for ever with the lord. Remember my warning take heed of hardness of heart in time of prosperitie [words struck out] endeavour to please him that shall be your husband and dwell with him with an amiable meekenes & contendedness of minde and doe not greeve his spirit

with the least forwardness affections may be easilye lost but hardly recovered be courteous to all & loving to ~~sts in~~ saints in speciall remember mine when I am dead for ther fathers sake who loved you dearlye and would have showen more tokens of it had not outward straits stood in the way follow your latine still at spare times when you are married. I thinke to bee onely three lords dayes whither I goe and then (if the lord will) to make my returne for Kent ~~but~~ man purposes but god determines the extreame pressures that have lyon on me this yeare or two have some thing interrupted my communion with my god but now I find him returning towards me in my ancient way of acquaintance for I desire you to give thanks keepe close with god take heed the desires of your knowledge of the latine tongue doe not take of your heart from tend pietye in your heart and life is ther anything like to Jesus Christ and commune with him. The lord perfect that which I trust so hath begun in you that you may be presented spotless at the coming of X with exceeding joy my dearest sister farwell

Your assured loving Br[other] till death
Ch: Blackwood

May 30
1651

I am sorye that I could not tarye at home till your business was whollye effected but sadly had in probability lost this present opportunity which providence seames to offer & ~~the~~ your business could in a manner effected.

When I come backe from my journey I thinke to pay Mary Streater what you owe her but I dar not before for feare monye should fall short & I in a strange place remember my kind love and respects to Mr Jeake.

[15] *Christopher Blackwood to Frances Hartridge, 11 June 1651. Original letter.*
ESRO FRE 4223 fo. 115

Deare & loving sister
The last time I did not write to you because I was in a hurrye of business now having a little leasure I would have you see a glymse of that true affection I beare to you. What god will do with mee I cannot tell I am as clay in the hand of the potter when he hath tryed me I shall come forth as gold. I long for the time of our meeting together remember my kind love & respects to your freind Mr Jeake I am heartily sory your business should be delaied by my meanes. I have no more but onely to exhort you to stand fast in your faith & to cleave unto god who will never faile you nor forsake you if you cleave to him remember ther are eternall joyes with X far beyond all the married joyes

of this world in the enjoyment of our god let us a little encourage ourselves, hoping for a fuller [word struck out] enjoyment hereafter. Deare sister take heed you bee not wicked with the pompe & glory of this world keepe your acquaintance with X renew it every day for my affaires my wives letter can tell you how it is. Remember mee in your praiers. Let your heart be drawen up often to prize X in adverse times if ever you be cast upon them ther you will finde lasting consolation. It is he that is able to supply your want of father Brother freind. Strive to live to god make him your end make him your joy beware of declining in affection to the lord seing so it ever [word illegible] if the world come upon you let ther be largeness of heart to doe good that fruits may abound in the day of your account remembering that a fruitfull life never wants [word illegible] of assurance. My dearest sister farwell the lord grant us a joyfull meeting. I rest your affectionate Brother till death.

Ch: Blackwood

From Collonel Duckenfields in Duckenfield thirtye miles wide of Chester this 11th day of June Ann 1651.

[16] *Christopher Blackwood to Frances Hartridge, 17 June 1651. Original letter.*
ESRO FRE 4223 fo. 116

Deare Sister
I wrote to you June 14th I hope you received it. This is to informe that god willing about the 8th or 9th of July I purpose god assisting to bee in Marden against which time let all your business bee readye and if you please you may write to Mr Jeake to bee for about the tenth of Julye. Remember my cordiall respects to him. I shall desire your happines in your proceedings I suppose as much as any freind you have in the world. Dicere qua puduit scribere jussit amor.[50] One of my greatest southerne sorrowes is that wee must part but this comforts me that it is for your good and that I trust once more I shall behold you in this world if not oftner how much more I shall behold you at the right hand of the judge in reference whereto goe onto follow your god who never failes his make him your joy in whom is lasting comfort let your meditation be much with him make him your joy make him your treasure pray for mee. I expect to be saluted with a letter from you at London my dearest sister farwell I shall pay Mary Streater at my returne if god will. Present my true love to Mr Jeake. May god keepe you all in whose eternall armes I leave you hoping ther to finde you in Christ fraterally yours

C. Blackwood

Chester June 17

[50] What I was ashamed to say, love has commanded me to write, Ovid.

[17] *Christopher Blackwood to Frances Hartridge, 21 June 1651. Original letter.*
ESRO FRE 4223 fo. 117

Deare Sister
I cannot passe by you unsaluted. I wrote in my former which I suppose you have received that about the 10th or 11th of July I hope your business will bee finished. If the Lord bring mee home sowbeit because things are casuall in so long a journey doe not appoint it till I come home & then wee will send a messenger over to him. Pray for mee that the lord may bring us once more together which is my exceeding desire. Encourage your selfe in god in all hard times grow out of love with the world stay your selfe on that all sufficiency who hath not failed you in a time of need neither will it faile mee. Remember X & all things goe together feare nothing but him. Love god soveraignelye. Pray fervently & looke for answers to your praiers be affraid of delayes & tremble at declinings cleath often towards X & let things bee on such good tearmes betwixt X & you that you may long for his appearance. I have noe more to offer save the affections of him who loves you with an unfained dearenes & rest yours C. B.
June 21 1651

Remember my kind & hearty respects to Mr Jeak

[18] *Frances Hartridge to Samuel Jeake senior, 9 July 1651. Original letter.*
ESRO FRE 4223 fo. 118

Deare love
that no weeke might passe with out sume visit personall or signall as preparatorye to that immediate mutuall fruition wherto the providence of our god I trust hath designed us I have put pen to paper and so much more in that absent freinds are wont to keepe affections alive this way. I shall not forget to informe you of my Br Blackwood his safe returne on July the 5 Saturday who with the rest of the family are in health hee desires [word struck out] to have his respects presented I intend to send a trunk of cloathes and other things by Champ or Johnson I have all things ready for our business be assured of the tender affections of her that loves you till time and death sever. Things are appointed towards the nuptials according to your appointed time on thursday July 17 hast calles me away I shall not word any further which is but superfluous where affections are not questioned ~~in~~ so desireing your prayers for a good succes upon the ~~inten~~ intended busines I rest

yours till
death F H

July the 9 1651
I desire you to buy me a ring with a diamond in it and bring it with you and be not unmindfull of the gloves I spake to you of.

[19] *Christopher Blackwood to Frances Jeake (neé Hartridge), 9 August 1652.*[51]
Original letter. ESRO FRE 4223 fos. 119–120

Deare sister
I received my Brothers letter and perceive you had beene downe out of your chamber & were somthing recovered from your sickness, I desire to blesse god for his goodness to you & desire that you may make a sanctified use of ~~his~~ the chastisement of the lord learne to see that those visitations to the elect are as cups out of the hand of a father who are chastened of the lord that you may not be condemned with the world. Let it be your wisedom to profit by the lords hand on you who delivered you from a double danger that you may hearby double your prayses to our god, in your prayses remember that god had respect to your strength, and that he was your present refuge in your trouble. Let the use of this triall bee to make you humble before the lord & meeke towards them [words struck out] with whom you doe converse & to search for the sin which hath caused the lord to break in upon you. Remember to pay the resolutions you made to god in the time of your trouble. Strive to be cheerfull the righteous are oft called to rejoyce in god as well as tomorrow for corruption; too much melancholye doth not credit our profession we are called to serve the lord with gladness. Strive for contentedness of spirit. It will not onely make your condition easie but the condition of others in your familye you are as a citye set on a hill labour to hold forth a holy life, least it [be] said what doe you more than others. Regard not any ornament so much as that of a meek spirit which beautifyes in the sight of god. Let your heart breath after ordinances in the want of them. ~~I des~~ We desire to see you and my brother as soone as god shall make you fit for travell.

All our family are through mercy in health but many about us verye sicke. I desire you to excuse my suddaine departure when I was last at Rye which was for diverse causes necessitated, but future opportunity god willing may occation a longer tariance. My wife received her things by Rich. Johnson remember my kind love to Goody Shoesmith & the rest of my friends also my wives [word illegible] present my love & duty to my mother & tell her that I

[51] The marriage took place on 17 July 1651.

expect her to come over shortly unto us. So with both our loves to you & my Brother very kindly remembred I take leave & I rest

Your assured loving Br
Ch: Blackwood

Marden
August 9
1652

[20] *Frances Jeake (neé Hartridge) to Christopher and Mary Hartridge, undated. Original letter.* ESRO FRE 4223 fo. 120

deare and well beloved brother and sister
after my deare love to you both and my littell cousins remembered I greete you in the lord Jesus the captaine of our salvation who throu [word struck out] the bloud of the everlasting covenant hath made ~~and~~ us perfect and compleat in himselfe to his [word struck out] apearing. I having an oppertunitie cannot but let you heare that we are all in health throwh the mercy of our good god hoping the same of you and yours the last I wrot to you was about the later end of June which was scent by brother Covenye I suppose you have receved it. It hath pleased the lord since your departure to give me a safe deliverance of another son[52] which my husband acquainted you of in his last letter they are both very thriving childrin[53] throwgh gods mercy I desire we may be thankfull I have littell good news to acquaint you with. We looke for peace and behold truble, for righteousness and behold opression, our eyes evne faile with looking but I trust the lord will support his people in times of truble: your frinds her are for the most part in health [words struck out] but it hath pleased god to release out of this life our Brother Jacson which is a greate lost to the saints I was at his funerall and went from thence to Marden he died above ten weeks agoe we have not heard from you but once sinc you went but I [words struck out] hope ~~I~~ you will not neglect to scend when oppertunitie shall serve I shall be very glad to heare of your well being thought I cannot inioy you heare yet this is my comfort that if I cannot behold you [words struck out] in this world I shall behold you at the right hand of the judge in refernce wherto let us goe onto folow our god who will never faile us in a time of neede. O let us labor to have our harts low in time of prosperitie and to live on god in time of adversitie for it is but a litell while and he that shall come will come and not tary and then what will these things profit I beseech you remember me at the throne of grace that I may walke close with

[52] Thomas, born 29 June 1653.
[53] Samuel junior and Thomas.

god in this crooked and perverse generation among whome I live. My dearest Br and sister farewell my good god keepe you all in whose eternall armes I leave you and rest

your assured
loving sister
Frances Jeake

Rye

[21] *Frances Jeake (neé Hartridge) to Mary Hartridge, 24 March 1653. Original letter.* ESRO FRE 4223 fos. 122; 124

deare sister
my tender love to you with my deare brother and ~~my~~ cousins ~~and the rest yours~~ remembered I have receved dated the 24 of October and am ioyful to heare of your health this is the 4 letter as I thinke I have wrot to you sence your departure and I have had 3 of yours these few lines are to let you know that we are all in health bessed [*sic*] be god hoping the same of you and youres I ~~have~~ understand you licke well of your habitation and ther is hope of your returning which if there were I sould be glad if it were for your good otherwise I am content with the will of god it is the lord let him doe what seemeth him good therefore deare sister seing the lord hath bestowed so many mercys on you first and above all things consider that as every good and perfect gift pertaining to soule and body is given ~~fom~~ from above and commeth from the father of light even so to whomsoever the lord dealeth any of his benefit of them he doth ~~chifely~~ chiefly require a thankful heart for the same which my desire is may not be wanting in any of us that profess his name but I feare there is much backwards even in the best of us and for my owne part I may speeke by experienc I inioy many mercys from the lord but walke so unworthy under them that I may iustly feare the lord will turne the same into my greate disprofit and discomfort at the last: I am glad to hear of the increase of the gosple amongst you and of your walking sweetely to gather ~~my ear~~ earnest desire is that that grace of love may exceedingly abound ~~which~~ toward onanother though difrent in sum points love is that which doth most beautifie a Christian [word illegible] Christ saith by this shall all men know that ye are my disciples if ye love one another but this is much wanting amongst the saints and in stead therof division which brings much dishoner to the truth and causeth many to stumble at the ways of god [words struck out] for which we have cause to morne. I have ~~not any good~~ littell to acquaint you with only hear are sum changs since you went I acquainted you in my last of the death of Brother Jackson Go Coveny I heare is dead at Bristo I supose you have heard of it and Mr Gorge Mapliessden of Marden hath buried his wife and

his son in law Mr Busbedg and his eldest son Mr Edward and for the rest of your acquaintance there were well not long sence Mr William Davis intended to have came for Ierland this march but god hath prevented him by death his Buried this day. Good Crouch of this town is also dead [words struck out]. Mrs Hollman is well and desires kindly to be remembered to you and my brother and to the children ~~and many more I supose~~. Goody Shosmith desres to be remembered to you both and many more I supose would if they had knowne of this present writing thus I comend you to god desiring him to blesse you with all spirituall blessings in heavenly things and allso with the deale of heaven and fatnesse of the earth that in all things you may be made rich in Christ to the praise of his name is the praier of of [*sic*]

your affectionat
sister Frances
Jeake

March the 24 1653

Wooing Barbara Holman

[22] *Richard Langdon to Barbara Holman, 20 September 1659. Original letter.* ESRO FRE 5264

Most Excelent Lady
The excesse and incomparablenesse of your Beautey withe your Transendance And never paralleled vertues causes all your beholders too Admier and Mee by a devine providence too fixing my Affextions upon you Like a pole in the senter which is impossible too Remoove without the Destroying of the whole boddy pardon Mee Maddam if I disclose what Extreame faureyes my Affections hath Led mee too and caused in mee for when I first behelde that stately fabrick natuers choosest Architecture I then concluded that havens Choosest Jewell was there Locked up in Erthes Richest Cabbinet. And when nature Maide you shee playde the Alchimist and Extracted all the Spirits of the Elements Leste a Dressy Body should clogg soe Devine a soule Thousands of More Could I Let you understand but for Intruding too much on your patience. But Really by you Maddam Am I Involved in as sea of Missery and am Like too drowne in Love without houlden by you. And wounded I am too the very harte soo that it is Incurable without your selfe Maddam too be prostrated so At the throne of your Mercy. It would Make the veryest Addamentall Harte in the world to Relent and if any dropes was left too distill them from the Limbeck of their Eyes. Considder seriously I beseech you Maddam of things of this natuer and transfix your Eyes too Hero and Leander and you shall finde Love Caused them too Mudder themselves Besides in thousands

Examples you shall finde it no sleight thing. If you considder how it hath Maide princes becom slaves too their Affections. Pardon I beseech you how ever love will Apology for mee for being soo much over burdensum too your patience with Excese of time I would a wayted upon you too day but my orrations call me too Capt. Turkers but as soone as I Returne god willing I shall Make bould too pay a vissit too you and shall bee at your servis while I have Breath to Certyfy you Maddam that I am your thrise humble

Faithfull and
Captived vassell
Rich Langdon

September the 20th
Anno Domini
1659

These to the Most worthy and his hihly honred [friend] Mrs Barbara Holman, present with care

[23] *Richard Hartshorne to Barbara Harding (previously Holman), 11 May 1662. Original letter.* ESRO FRE 5268

May 11th 62
Madam,
(For the motion's Retrograde but not on my part) I am astonished to admiration (though not utterly stript of hope) to read your satyricall lines tis an easy thing I confes to find a staffe to beat a dog, but tis no victory to conquer the disarm'd nor badge of honour to trample on the Captive but tell me my Dear, are all crimes capitall? all sins mortall? all transgressions piacular: or is there no veniall errour under the Sun? I appeale to the barre of judgement, let not passion sway the Scepter nor Will bias your Reason: had I exposed your watch by tongue or hand to publique view (which so let me prosper in your favour & the other world) had I thereby now more than formerly merited a finall exclusion a for-ever excommunication out of your favours? easily this crime augmented by a magnifying glasse to the highest aggravation were but veniall, though I doe professe I know not how it should happen for I neither looked upon it nor wound it up, but when alone, unless some[one] saw me invisibly or pict my pocket when asleepe, but if it were granted which I cannot acknowledge unless I bely my selfe, as you in effect are pleased to say I doe though I can bear that very well from your pen innocently, notwithstanding I say is there no absolution for such a mistake or no intercession for such an errour? Is all compassion banish? is every sparke of respect extinct. Be intreated to be a little more tender-hearted for indeed

you are in this unlike your selfe. You say my Deare shortest errours are best, and must this be rankt among the most hainous? Alas! Will nothing les satisfy. Could I improve the greatest favour, as much as you the least mistake I should hope to sinke all my fears, split all my doubts and arrive with safety at the desired Haven. But wo is me! If I have a fair gale one day, I am in danger of shipwrecke the next, so unfortunate is my bitter-sweet voyage. But would you not have me think you picke a quarrell on purpose to make a breach of our society, why doe then upbraid me with my fair but you please to stile them false promises and unregarded now for all kindness. My Deare though but for a — extinguisht before the time? Put a Period to this high Career, reflect a little upon your last favour: how doth my heart ake to compare those 2 together! Doe not banish me by a new [word illegible] before the appoynted time, if it must be then be not so tart to your poor supplicant, nor suffer this passion to grow inveterate. Can you delight in cruelty & take pleasure in afflicting your unfeigned but distressed friend & servant doe not make the worst of every thing, nor conclude of betraying worst part if any were betwixt us, because your watch hath sounded so loud. I would with all me soule I had never desired to keepe it. I beseech you pardon the penitent, & Remember the good old rule doe as you would be done unto, and sound a Retreat to this first charge, yea renew again my Deare Love the League already made, & grant me the sight of your face again with comfort that I may inioy some part of my late & sweet felicity, if you please to honour me with a line or 2 before I see you I hope 'twill a little revive my drooping heart unfeignedly God knows devoted to you, and wishing your welfare every way equall with my owne yea & shall pray for your prosperity though you procure my sorrow of heart. The God of all flesh deale with me according to the integrity of my heart towards you and make up this breach betwixt your selfe and, him that loves you as himselfe, though now accounted unworthy your favour, yet cannot crafe to be indeed what his pen can subscribe to wit

My Deare Love
Your faithfull friend & servant
and intire Lover (though know
unworthy of your favour),
Richard Hartshorne.

What intelligence so ever you had that told you I had your watch, is nothing, no nothing at all but imagination to pump you, for there's neither a man nor woman upon earth that hath either seen it or heard so much from my mouth save your selfe. I wish with all my heart that you doe not or have not ere this comes to hand, comfort and then tis well enough. As God shall save my soule which is of far greater worth than a watch this is true.

[24] *Richard Hartshorne to Barbara Harding (previously Holman), undated. Original letter.* ESRO FRE 5269

Ah my dear (but unkind) Heart
Hath not all my love merited a line from thee to be satisfied of thy welfare? I have not forgotten since I was promised letters full of kisses, and that often. Prithee my Deare if my love deserue any thing, let me know where thou art, how thou dost, and when I may comfort my languishing and sorrowful heart with hopes to see thee thou never wentest away from me so, but wouldest tell me some time of returne. For my part I take God to witness I am very restles, discontented and cannot tell by what means to injoy any thing of my selfe without thee. I know not and that grieves mee whether this will come to thy hand, if it doenot what shall I doe, oh that I might injoy thee one night instead of every nights dreames on thee. I confes I live a most wretched comfortless solitary and indeed heartles life. Oh that my heart should have such a fresh spring of love, so lasting, and so coming after its deare Jewell & not decay! Truly it makes me astonished and amazed at my selfe. I could (but that experience too sadly convincedth me) have believed it impossible love could after so many sharp incourters, so many grand repulses, remaine unconquered imperfection of it first springing. But God knows I know not any thing thou canst doe to me, or against me, can subdue it. It hath been used too barbarously and heathenishly, yet it is not offended, & that addeth to my misery. My love me thinks tis too unnaturall to render contempt for love, slighting for a deare affection. Thou know it how boundless my love hath been, how unfeigned I need not here rehearse, and how durable the weariness of my many & great repulses too much to testify. Is there noe reward for vertue? Is there no jewell transparent but gold? Ah my Dear Heart consider how many have been ruined by breaking their engaged faith & promise there is a time for every thing and certainly if thou wast afraid of God's Judgements in poor Mr Harding's case I know not how it can be otherwise, may I believe tis much worse in mine: for I suppose he might in proces of time have married another, I must not. Thou wouldst be accounted iust in thy dealing, I pray God give thee a heart to be so to me but yet I believe never poor lover had more iniury and harder dealing than I have. Good my Dear Heart think upon me, and consider what I suffer for thy sake, poise the burden that lies on my heart but in thy thoughts, make but my case thine a little & weigh it in equity and doe not let all my life be spent in sorrows, and all comforts taken from me att all my Daies. I would I could but send thee one of my present bitter groanes or that thou mightest but for the twinkling of an eye feel my aking heart, surely thy closed nature could not but relent and a little dissolve from its frozen hardnes. The God of Heaven mollify thy hard hart and make it more naturall and not so stony to me. I know thou expectest mercy at Gods

hands (which I pray God grant in the hour at death & day of Judgement) but how canst though looke for any & exercise so much cruelty and falseness. Indeed if there were not another world it would not at all matter what our actions were, but my Love there will be atime of searching all the secrets of our hearts, no covers nor pretences can cloake us from the all seeing eye of God. Didst thou ever read or canst thou believe faithless & merciles shall find mercy without repentance or amendment? Thous hast separated mee from the society of men & from thy presence I must be excluded. What heart is able to beare and endure these, this hard measure and not complain? Or who can undergo so great a punishment. Where poor Mr Harding had one trouble I must have 20. The God of heaven some way put an end to my wretchedness or my life or some way helpe me. I am not able to sustaine this cruelty. Poor I that want nothing can be laid to my charge, but that I am not borne to a great inheritance, that only abound in love and poverty, the last [word lost] the former filthy and of noe beauty. A better fortune [may] make a lesser love far more worthy in thy eyes, have a better lustere though never to good a relish. I waited a Saturday [to see] poor little Bab but when I consider her parting from mee [words lost] it even makes me curse the day of my birth & the hour when it was said a son is borne. She cald moda, moda, moda[54] [words lost] shall not do away! Truly I am not satisfied at her [word lost] though I found the old woman having her on her knee, but the house is old & the roofe is much unthatcht and open to the cold & raine. Good dear heart therefore take some care of thy deare babe she yet complains of her poor belly, but is merryish & something chearfull [words illegible] a teach as well as she can speake, & I beseech & conjured thee to returne home again thy business being dispatcht that was undertaken and make noe quivocations with my poor heart, nor delaies to take care of thy dear Image. I would to god either time or sorrow would cut the thred of my dismall dayes, or consummate the ioys & desires of my too much abjured though yet valient heart. No more now.

From that hand whose guide
is clouded with tears to thinke
of thy cruelty, yet must ever be
thine till he be not Richard Hartshorne.

For my much honoured and very good friend Mrs Barbara Harding, these in London

[54] Mother, mother, mother.

[25] *Richard Hartshorne to Barbara Harding (previously Holman), undated. Original letter.* ESRO FRE 5270

My Hard Deare Heart
I have received thy deare & bitter lines, would to God they were not so deare to mee, then should I not meake and worthless, naked and unarmed be continually necessitated to assault an invincible Castle fortified with stone walls, harder than Adament stronger than marble through which there is noe gate, no entrance, so high, no accesse, nay and which is far worse, might be betrayed with gold, cannot be won with virtue. Wilt thou never assuage this scorching flame? Hast thou only added fewell to make a sacrifice? If it were ligated what more comfortable? continually fed, what more cruell? Oh that I had any thing but bitterness, teares, & a broken heart to send thee: I would I had the treasures of the Indians to make access for my Petition or the fortune of ten thousand [words illegible] than I for my succes. But thou hast only loved mee to make me miserable, a by-word and a spectacle which my misery too sadly proves, wert thou not mine by the comfort of thy fond dear Heart (how often given I shall not say) I would ingeniously acknowledge my importunity presumption and more then [word illegible] but what is freer then gifts? or what can be more mine owne then what is freely given? Nay and if thou avert not that inestimable Pearle farre above the worth of this faire world. I should not account thee worth my seeking. but alas my dull pen cannot describe thy Deare value that my forlorne and dying heart hath put upon thee. If I had only Complements to devise my fancy might be undervalued by its invention but I have nothing but faithlessnes & broken promises to breake my broken heart. Oh that it might be broken at once for all, that I might once put an end to my grevious & just complaint! Could I have found any meanes to quench this burning flame, I would not send to thee who wilt rather suffer my to dye for thirst then give a drop of water to coole my scorched heart. If thou enduredst such a captivity so cruel a prison, so bad companions, and with all soe continually inbittered with most exquisite Torment thou wouldst thinke it were more then barbarous, more cruel then heathenish, more savage then bestiall. but I, poor I, have lost my Reason, the guide of my life, my liberty, the inioyment of my selfe, my hopes, the comfort of my beeing, what have then I left but a life not worth the name. I am sure death is a thousand times more acceptable to mee then anything I enioy.

If others covet thee, thou art pleased to say thou wilt not forget what is betwixt thy selfe & me, alas, if thou deny them, am I any better than they? And have not they as much as I nay more they are at liberty, so am not I, they may make a new choice, so cannot I, they may have many, I must not have one, mine owne. Surely thy thoughts are very bad of mee and thy love very small to mee to say I may make a new choyce when thou knowest I am bound under an eternall course to marry none but thy deare selfe. It is not a wife, nor a woman that I so much dote upon a tis none but thee who to me art the quintessence of all thy sexe, who though thou art so cruell wouldst give my soule to Hell, God I hope will have more mercy for it. But why (if it be lawfull to expostulate) didst thou urge me to engage my selfe by tongue, who was thy own in heart long before and told thee I rather desired to doe it my [word illegible] as thou knowest to this day, and now thus to sleight all my love, to eat up all thy promises in effect, and pretend to give me my liberty againe prithe tell me, can a man hanged dead have his life restored? but be it soe, twas thy will. I satisfied it and it had satisfied mee had it been the same as I have been, had it been true as I have been to the swearing away of my life, my misery will never redound to thy honour, nor the breach of thy promises make thee happy. For I beseech thee consider thy dealing with me, than knowest none hath above one heart (but thy selfe) how long thou hast had 2 thou art not ignorant, doe but tell me then with what I shall love another woman? Besides have I had so good success that if I were at liberty I could hope to be more fortunate. God blesse me till then and not longer. But alas my Dear Heart tis nothing for thee to bid one leaden to run that cannot go. I am sure thou wast pleased in thy deare arms to call me husband, before I durst dare to honour my selfe with the name of wife. But I perceive thy [word illegible] is apart of thy selfe subject to forget what it loves not, & very to continue in the contrary. I visit thy Dear Bab last Saturday that I might kisse mine owne. Why dost thou tell me thou canst not satisfy my Love God hath made thee willing, there wants nothing but performance. Thou toldst me thou marriedst twice against thy will why not a third time to thy poor friend? See if thou canst perswade thy hard heart a little to relent and with mee I beg of as for my life a faster hand since (my heart) thou thinkst I deserve thee for my love before the God of Heaven conscious of my love & thy promises I beg, beg & beseech thee let me be once rewarded with that treasure which I am devoted to serve and honour to the breathing out of my last gasps, which if this may not be I pray the God of Heaven put an end to my long lingering sorrowes & give thee peace and forgive thy hard dealing to

Thy Poor distressed but ever
Loyall servant
Richard Hartshorne

These for my dear but unkind Mrs Barbara Harding

2

Adolescence and starting out, 1668–1669

The younger Samuel Jeake was born on 4 July 1652, at '1/4 of an hour past 6 a Clock in the morning', according to the record made by his father. Samuel senior continued noting the milestones of his son's early life. He was weaned at around seven months and started to teethe at nine months. At a year old he began to walk and was talking at the age of fifteen months.[1] The loss of his mother and both siblings in very early childhood meant that Samuel junior's life thereafter was dominated by his relationship with his father. Samuel senior did not marry again after Frances's death, and the close and loving relationship that father and son enjoyed until the death of the former in 1690 is demonstrated not only throughout the *Astrological Diary* but also in many letters in this collection.

Samuel Jeake's diary, which as noted above was more of a memoir than a journal, is the principal source of information about his childhood and early adolescence. There are no surviving runs of letters relating to Samuel junior until 1668. Prior to that, he spent most of his time in Rye and in the care of his father who was his primary spiritual and intellectual influence. Aside from a very short period of time when he attended a school run by the wife of a local craftsman, Samuel junior was educated at home. Tutoring had provided a source of income for Samuel senior and thus he was well-equipped to teach his son.[2] Samuel junior's education was broad. He read widely, recorded learning Greek, Hebrew, shorthand, 'Rhetorick', arithmetic and compiling a 'Manuscript for my own use called Epitome Grammaticae Latinae'.[3] He also taught himself to draw and became 'indifferently skilled in the Theory or Rules of Poetry', although his 'fancy never ran much to practise'.[4] He recorded his first forays into astrology, noting that he began to learn on 25 June 1667, at about noon.[5]

The *Astrological Diary* also records Samuel junior's spiritual development. Regular domestic devotion would have been typical in a godly household and his father's strong beliefs must have shaped Samuel's early religious experiences.[6] Yet, his own reading matter included numerous godly books and a number of Puritan biographies chronicling individual spiritual progress.[7] As Hunter and Gregory argue, Samuel junior's first purpose in keeping a diary might have been to track and assess his own spiritual development.[8] Nonetheless, this active piety did not persist in the diary and,

[1] Hunter and Gregory, *Astrological Diary*, 85–6. Hunter and Gregory argue that these early milestones might have been recorded by Jeake senior for astrological purposes.
[2] Ibid. 40.
[3] Ibid. 87–8.
[4] Ibid. 91.
[5] Ibid. 92.
[6] Fletcher, *County Community*, 69; Hunter and Gregory, *Astrological Diary*, 6.
[7] Hunter and Gregory, *Astrological Diary*, 7.
[8] Ibid. 7.

unlike his father's letters, it was not a dominant theme in the younger Samuel's surviving correspondence.

Samuel junior's first extended period away from his father's influence came at the age of sixteen when he visited London for a period of nearly six months. He had travelled before but only for short visits. As noted in the *Astrological Diary*, he made visits in Sussex and Kent and to London where he went to Deptford, to see the ruins made by the fire of 1666, to Greenwich, Westminster Abbey and the Tower of London.[9] The purpose of the visit to London from October 1668 was 'to tarry there some time for diversion'. He stayed with his father's sister, Elizabeth, and her second husband Nicholas Bonnick in Salisbury Lane near Redriffe Wall in Rotherhithe. He did not return to Rye until the following March.[10] The *Astrological Diary* is generally silent on this time, recording only an incident where he came close to having a cart run over his foot.[11] But Samuel senior wrote to his son regularly while he was away. These letters are brought together in this chapter.

This period of time away from his father must have been a significant rite of passage for Samuel junior: a time when, although in the care of his aunt and uncle, he could assert some measure of independence. Many of his contemporaries would, by the age of sixteen, have been leaving home to enter an apprenticeship or some other form of service. As such Samuel may have regarded himself, and have been regarded, as having sufficient judgement and discretion to make his own decisions.[12] The following letters do indeed demonstrate that he was both trusted and trustworthy. Nonetheless, Samuel senior's solicitude for his son is apparent in every exchange. The letters contain warnings to take care when out and about in London (FRE 4816), spiritual guidance (FRE 4823) and regular references to his son's health. The journey home to Rye also generated concern with Samuel senior being reluctant that his son should over-exert himself, travel alone, or travel on foot (FRE 4838). Samuel junior's correspondence from that period does not survive in large numbers. This does not necessarily mean that the younger man was a poor correspondent although there are some hints that the father wanted reassurance about his son's welfare and to hear more about how his son was using his time in London (FRE 4820, 4826, 4832). There are also some signs of resistance to his father's concerns, with correspondence indicating that the younger man had been arguing that his physical strength had increased and that he was able to make the journey back to Rye on foot (FRE 4833).

As the correspondence surviving from the time Samuel junior was in London is rather one-sided, the diversions he enjoyed while away are not detailed in the letters. It is probable that like many other young men in his position he found London an intimidating but exciting place.[13] It was, however also a place to learn new skills and hone existing ones. Plans to learn French were mentioned (FRE 4828, FRE 4832), along with the purchase of 'graving tooles' (FRE 4822). The fact that the few surviving letters written by Samuel junior in 1668 and 1669 were written in Latin appears to be a further indication that both father and son regarded this period as one in which the younger man's education was continuing. The teaching of letter-writing was often

[9] Ibid. 98–9.
[10] Ibid. 100–2.
[11] Ibid. 101.
[12] Ilana Krausman Ben-Amos, *Adolescence & Youth in Early Modern England* (New Haven and London, 1994), 30.
[13] Ibid. 99.

Latin-based, deriving examples to copy and emulate from writers like Cicero and Horace. Aside from conveying their message in an exemplary format, the letter also might incorporate a lesson in rhetoric, grammar and composition.[14]

Aside from educational activities, Samuel junior's time in London was occupied by errands for acquaintances in Rye. In particular, as London was the centre of the early modern book trade, Samuel senior and friends in Rye took advantage of having a London contact to acquire information and negotiate purchases.[15] This was no small endeavour for the younger man. Book browsing and buying expeditions would have taken him a long way from Rotherhithe, at least on to London Bridge and probably across the river to the primary book market around St Paul's Churchyard.[16] Nor was the acquisition of books straightforward. Hunter *et al.* detail Samuel senior's acquisition strategies in the Introduction to their edition of Jeake's Library Catalogue.[17] Samuel senior was careful with his purchases, well aware of the merits or otherwise of various editions and committed to sourcing books as cheaply as possible.[18] He clearly expected his son to do likewise (FRE 4819, 4825, 4827, 4833).

The letters demonstrate Samuel junior's acquisition of another set of skills. While he was in London, he was active in undertaking business for his father. Samuel senior had understandably found himself side-lined after the Restoration. He lost his job as town clerk and was deprived of his voting rights.[19] While he continued to be influential as one of the leaders of the nonconformists in Rye, his work focused more on his legal business and investments and, throughout the letters below, we see evidence of that work. Samuel junior was asked to negotiate bills and manage debt collection (for example FRE 4819, 4820, 4821) and to gather and dispense business intelligence, especially in the case of Samuel senior's dispute with the 'dishonest' Mr Bennetland (FRE 4829, 4840). In addition, he managed his own finances and negotiated with his aunt and uncle about the costs of his keep. His business errands for his father again took Samuel junior away from the immediate environs of his uncle's house. Even the seemingly simple business of collecting letters required him to go across London Bridge to Bishopsgate Street.[20] There is, however, every indication that the younger Samuel negotiated the space and the business with relative ease.

As we shall see in the following chapters, Samuel junior was eventually to earn his living as a merchant but, unusually, he did not serve an apprenticeship. It is possible that he was initially intending to follow in his father's footsteps and enter the legal profession. Equally, an apprenticeship in trade was an expensive commitment, successful merchants could demand upwards of £500 and perhaps as much as £1,000 to take on an apprentice, with no guarantee that a successful career would follow.[21] Hunter and Gregory argue that Samuel junior's early forays into trade were guided by

[14] James Daybell, *The Material Letter in Early Modern England: manuscript letters and the culture and practice of letter-writing, 1512–1635* (Basingstoke, 2012), 55–7.

[15] James Raven, *The Business of Books: booksellers and the English book trade, 1450–1850* (New Haven and London, 2007), 135.

[16] Ibid. 84;114.

[17] Hunter *et al.*, *Radical's Books.*

[18] Ibid. xxix; xxxiii.

[19] Ibid. xx.

[20] Hunter and Gregory, *Astrological Diary*, 101.

[21] Perry Gauci, *The Politics of Trade: The overseas merchant in state and society, 1660–1720* (Oxford, 2001), 71.

his friend Thomas Miller.[22] This series of letters, however, offers a corrective to that view and suggest that Samuel junior's introduction into the London business world, and the key skills required by a merchant, was guided by his father.

Samuel junior in London, October 1668 to March 1669

[26] *Samuel Jeake senior to Samuel Jeake junior, 17 October 1668. Original letter.* ESRO FRE 4816

Lo: sonne
[Top portion of the letter damaged: transcription begins at line 5]
...expect you render me an Accompt that is what you lay out for clothes, & pay to any by my Order, you should have paid all the expenses of your journey because Thomas went with you for company, when you send my watch buy a penny boxe fit to put him in & so seale the boxe & let Thomas either bring it in his pocket or else put it up in the Trowzes in the boxe you carried up. Here inclosed is one of your cuffes forgot to be put up. Remember me to your uncle, Aunt, cosin Anne, Samuel, & to Thomas. Had you a Horse there I could afford you should go to Maidstone with your cosin but you have none & besides if you go then you must come back alone which I do not like you should. Mr Wightman wrot to me to let you go to Maidstone but I have answered him that you being gone to London the day I had his letter I could not see how with conveniency you could, tell Thomas his mother remembers her love to him & she saieth Mrs Grebell desires him to buy her two pound of Ginger bread & she also desires him to buy her some, she remembers to you, your Aunt and cosin, pray have a care of your selfe and take heed of being out late alone or going crosse the Thames in foule weather, much desiring your wellbeing in this world & in that which is to come I remaine

Your ever lo: father
Sa: Jeake

Rye Oct 17th 1668

To his lo: sonne Samuel Jeake at Br Bonnick's House in Salisbury Lane neere Redriffe Wall these.

[22] Hunter and Gregory, *Astrological Diary*, 61.

[27] *Samuel Jeake senior to Samuel Jeake junior, 24 October 1668. Original letter.* ESRO FRE 4817

Lo: sonne
Yours by Thomas who is well come home this night with my watch & your Accompt I have received. I am well satisfied with what you laid out. The other monies keepe in your hands till I or you have occasion for it, what you have occasion to lay out for necessaries or other wise to good uses I shall not be against I intend to writ more largely to you some time next weeke. The charge of the letters set downe to my Accompt for I do not pay here because they should come the better to your hands. My love to you & prayers for you, your uncle, Aunt & cosin Sam. That is all from

your very lo: father
Sa: Jeake.

Rye October 24th 1668.

Thomas Shoosmith & his mother remember to you.[23]

To his lo: sonne Samuel Jeake at Br: Bonnick's house in Salisbury Lane neere Redriffe Wall, these.

[28] *Samuel Jeake senior to Samuel Jeake junior, 26 October 1668. Original letter.* ESRO FRE 4818

Sonne
My love to you, your unckle & Aunt. Thomas Shoosmith remembers to you & them & desires you to deliver these inclosed to the man he had his hoe of. I am in hast but your cosins remember to you.
Rye Oct 26th Your lo: father
1668 Sa: Jeake

To his lo: sonne Samuel Jeake at Br: Bonnick's house in Salisbury Lane neere Redriffe Wall.

[23] There were two families called Shoosmiths in Rye at the time of the 1660 Demobilisation Tax, both headed by widows. It is assumed that Jeake refers to Mary Shoosmith, the widow of a tailor, Nicholas Shoosmith, who lived in Middlestreet Ward near the Jeakes. There is no mention of her son in this record, indicating that he was under the age of 16 at the time the tax was collected. Mary was assessed at the basic rate suggesting she had no taxable real or personal estate. Burchall, 'Inhabitants of Rye', 105, 107.

[29] *Samuel Jeake senior to Samuel Jeake junior, 6 November 1668. Original letter.* ESRO FRE 4819

My deare child
Yesternight I received yours by Mr Cadman & thereby perceive you had my former lines which I did feare were miscarried as I wrot you in the letter I sent yesterday to the posthouse before I had yours. This night by post I have your other letter, I am sorry to heare your Aunt continues ill. I hope this may find her somewhat better I hope she is not dangerous. Thos: Gram: Ling Hebrae before the fire in London cost betweene .3s. & 4s. Mr Hartshorne[24] gave full 4s for his as he told me if you have a desire to one you may buy one. The Relation of Dr Dees actions with spirits[25] I have seene and by what I have elswhere met with of the Dr it is as much like him as an Apple, an Oyster. If Mr Gingey will buy the part of the vessel hee late sailed in or any other of his friends & pay you thirty pounds sterl[ing] as you write I am content to sell and shall signe & seale a bill of sale for an Eight part of her & so pray acquaint him but I expect ready money downe at the sale. Remember me to him his wife & her mother & other friends that you see at any time aske after me as if named deliver the inclosed to Mr Boys when you have sealed it. Present my love to your uncle, Aunt & cosin with my hearty desires & prayers for all their & your welfare expecting to heare how you enjoy your health in body & minde I remaine

Your truly lo: father
Sa: Jeake.

Rye Nov 6th 1668

Postscript.
As soone as you have received this letter if in the day time go to Mr Bourbes and shew him the bill & if he accept it & pay not the Tenne pounds presently let him underwrite I accept this Bill and subscribe his name & advise me the first post if he accept or pay the money. When you have the money I would have you pay the Tenne pounds to Mr William Sleed at the Red Lion in Southwarke an ironmonger and take an acquittance of him thus

[24] Richard Hartshorne, schoolmaster father of Elizabeth, Samuel junior's future wife.
[25] Probably *A true & faithful relation of what passed for many yeers between Dr. John Dee ... and some spirits* (London, printed by D. Maxwell for T. Garthwait, 1659).

Copy

Received Nov: 1668 of Mr Jeake of Rye by the hands of his sonne Samuel Jeake the sume of Tenne pounds sterling for the use of & by the order of Mr Henry Wightman of Maidstone	£ 10:	s 00:	d 00

I say received as aforesaid

Send me the Acquittance put in the day when you pay it.

To his lo: sonne Samuel Jeake at Br: Bonnick's house in Salisbury Lane neere Redriffe Wall, these.

[30] *Samuel Jeake junior to Samuel Jeake senior, 10 November 1668. Original letter.* ESRO FRE 4820

Londini. 10. Nov[em]bris 1668.
Pater Charissime
Circa Decimam horam ante-meridianam huius diei allatæ sunt mihi Epistolae duæ à te Nov. 5. &. 6. datæ. quæ quidem gratisimè advenerint. Timui enim antea Litteras aut meas aut tuas p[er]iisse viâ. Adsint (divina Clementiâ) valetudine favor, ac tibi eandem Misericordiam cordialiter opto. si autem unqu[a]m æger fuero admittam tibi citissimè verbum, Precor ut occasione causā[.] Absit à me ut negligerem asperemve amorem tuum, Non unqu[a]m Cogitationes tales in Animum intraverant, nec (Dei Auspicio) intrabunt. Ne verbum quidem de peste audivi post adcessum Thomæ Shoosmith. Billam mortalitatis vidi quâ nulli de Peste moriuntur. Etsi non multum fidei adhibeatur billa Thomâ Shoosmith præsente audivi à D. Martin. 2. Obijsse hodie interrogavi ab Avunculo; ille non iuravit puerum mortuum esse in hac P[ar]ochia cum Tho[ma] Shoosmith me comitatus est; Post illud nil audivi. Amita expectat Mariam Key, illa nunc convalescit. Salutat te et Avunculus. Consobrinus valet. Emui Buxtoni [words lost]. Thesaurum Volsij Rhetoricam de magnitudine Amosij medulla paginus 559. & Joh[annis] Bulweri Pathomyatomia.[26] 8o parvo, paginus 240. & 6.s 6.d. Profectus sum D. Gingæum & alloquitur uxorem ejus. quæ dixit si transmittam Billam vendit[i] o[n]is hos 30to representatus & p[ar]te Navis. Tradidi Epistolam D[omi]no Boys. responsum tibi mittet; Recepi 10.l à M. Boucker, Vidi M. W. Stedd

[26] John Bulwer, *Pathomyotamia, or, A dissection of the significative muscles of the affections of the minde* (London: Printed by W.W. for Humphrey Moseley, 1649); Hunter *et al. A Radical's Books*, 28–9.

cujus edicto solvi 10.l servo suo, cujus acceptilator[e]m Epistola indidi, Vidi M[agistr]um Allin.[27] Salutæ Amicos T. Shoosmith cum Matre &c.

Preces impetro tuas tam p[ro] Anima qu[am] Corpore; De Incolumitate tua audiendi cupidus maneo, scribebam Raptissime

Filius tuus obedientis[simu]s:
Sa[muel] Jeake jun[io]r

Translation:
London, 10 November 1668
Dearest father,
Two letters of yours to me, dated 5 and 6 November, were brought to me today at around 10 o'clock in the morning. These, indeed, thankfully arrived. For I feared that either my or your previous letters had perished on the way. May favour be present with health, and I cordially desire for you the same mercy. But if I shall ever have been ill, I will most speedily send you word, [and] I pray that in this case, may it be far from me to neglect or scorn your love. Such thoughts had never entered into my mind, nor (by God's grace) will they enter. I have heard no word of the plague since the arrival of Thomas Shoosmith. I have seen a bill of mortality in which none died of the plague. Although the bill does not engender much faith, I heard from D. Martin (with Thomas Shoosmith present) that two had died. Today I asked uncle; he did not swear that a boy died in this parish when Thomas Shoosmith was accompanying me. After this I have heard nothing. Aunt is waiting for Mary Key, who has now recovered. Uncle also greets you. My cousin is well. I bought Buxton's *Treasury of Volsius' Rhetoric concerning the size of the kernel of Amosius*, 559 pages, and John Bulwer's *Pathomyatomia*, a small octavo, 240 pages, and 6s. 6d. I set out for D. Gingey and spoke to his wife. She said that if I send a bill of sale, this would be payment for a thirtieth part of a ship. I handed over the letter to Mr Boys. He will send you a reply. I have received £10 from Mr Boucker; I have seen M. W. Stedd at whose instruction I have released £10 to his servant, [and] introduced the receiver of his letter. I saw Mr Allin. Friendly greetings to T. Shoosmith, with [his] mother etc.

I ask your prayers as well for my soul as for my body; I remain desirous of hearing of your safety; I have written very hurriedly.
Your most obedient son
Samuel Jeake junior

[27] John Allin, former vicar of Rye.

[31] *Samuel Jeake senior to Samuel Jeake junior, 12 November 1668. Original letter.* ESRO FRE 4821

Loving sonne
My love to you, your uncle Aunt, cosin & other friends & am glad to heare of your health. Yours of the 10th instant received with the Receit you sent for the .£10. you received of Mr Bourbes & paid Mr Sledd for your cosin Wightman. I have here inclosed sent a Bill of Sale to Mr Gingey and when you deliver it & have the .£30. you may pay the same .£30. to Mr Sledd also and take such an Acquittance as you did before and send me. Mr Boys hath writ me that he will pay me .£20. of the .£100. he owes me. So when you see him you may tell him that I desire he would pay it to you & when you have it I will direct you how to dispose of it. You may give Mr Boys a receit thus:

	£	s	d
Received Nov. .th 1668 of Mr Joseph Boys by the order & for the use of my Father Twenty pounds sterling in part of the Hundred pounds due from that said Mr Boys to my Father. I say received as aforesaid	20:	00:	00

The last Monday was put aboard Mr White bound for London a bundle of Mary Keys clothes to be brought to your uncles, and a basket of Apples which the widdow Winterburne sent you, have acare of the basket & if Mr White come hither send the basket againe by him if not by the next boate of Rye that comes home. Thomas White said he would bring them to you. I did put aboard the Barque 4 Trunks to be sent to Maidstone to your cosins but they you need not speake of for he is to put them aboard a Maidstone Hoye[28] but if there should be none there pray your Aunt to get some place to get them in neere the waterside till some Hoye comes up when your cosin Wightman shall appoint to take them in. I am in hast but abide

Rye Nov 12th 1668 — Your truly lo: Father Sa: Jeake

The old woman & her son[29] with other your friends remember to you

To his lo: sonne Samuel Jeake at Br: Bonnick's house in Salisbury Lane neere Redriffe Wall, these.

[28] A hoy was a 'small vessel, usually rigged as a sloop, and employed in carrying passengers and goods, particularly in short distances on the sea-coast', *OED*.
[29] Probably Thomas Shoosmith and his mother.

[32] *Samuel Jeake senior to Samuel Jeake junior, 26 November 1668. Original letter.* ESRO FRE 4822

My Child
Yours of the 21th & 24th instant I have received & am glad you have received the £30 & paid it as I ordered. I wish that part of Mr Bennetland's vessel were as well sold when you heare he is come home write me word, & if you heare of any that would buy such a part I have but a 1/16 of that send me word & do your endeavour to put it off. I have not yet seene R Frebody since he was with you. What Graving tooles you have a minde to you may buy but you were best buy them with handles for you cannot well use them without when you receive the .£20. of Mr Boys pray Tenne pounds thereof to Mr Sledd for your Cosin Wightman & take an Acquittance as far as the former summes paid & send me if I could tell how to get your cosin Mary up or had knowne of your Cosin Wightmans coming to London she should have gone up with him. But I do intend ere long to get her up one way or other remember me to your Aunt uncle cosin & other friends. I am in hast but abide

Your lo: father
Sa: Jeake

Rye Nov 26th
1668

Mr Marshall Mr Miller & Mrs Mr Boys Mr Frith,[30] Mrs & Frank Sarke, Edw. Newton, Tho. Carew & [word illegible] Tho. Shoosmith & his mother remember to you.

To his lo: sonne Samuel Jeake at Br: Bonnick's house in Salisbury Lane neere Redriffe Wall.

[33] *Samuel Jeake senior to Samuel Jeake junior, 10 December 1668. Original letter.* ESRO FRE 4823

Lov: sonne,
Yours I received last post with the Acquittance for the .£10. paid Mr Ellis & seeing Mr Bennetland is come home I doe intend to writ to him when I heare what answere hee gives you if you can speake to him, but it is to little end to speake to his wife. If you can get some candied cowslips or conserve of them you may buy some and eate in a morning before breakfast they are good for your head. I suppose you have heard that Henry Man is lost coming from

[30] Philip Frith, primary correspondent of John Allin and Samuel senior.

Diepe on the 24th of October last but how none of them in the vessel lived to tell, nor where can yet be discovered. Your calls you wrot me in your former from heaven are to be harkened to & so farre from grounds of discouragment that they provoke to runn the faster, God hath not yet done calling. Behold now is the acceptable time, & this the day of salvation, to day therefore heare his voice, get a true sight of sinne & a hatred of it & holy purposes & earnest prayers against it & although an answer come not presently yet every delay is not a deniall God will come & tarry not. Looke into the freeness of grace in the Gospell tendered to unworthy soules, thiefe sinners &c. who have no money or prize in their hands to buy or purchase & if you can do no more yet hope, and wait for God hath promised to be gracious to the soule that waiteth for him he knows our strength & remembers that we are but dust & he will not contend for ever, we are not choise of mercy because we believe are holy &c but because we should believe & be holy being chosen thereunto. In all with Gods free grace and Christs free laying downe his life even when we were enemies do sufficiently demonstrate our inability & insufficiencie to procure merit purchase worke out or deserve our owne salvation & if so why should you or any other that is sensible of sinne & brought into a longing after & loving of Jesus Christ thinke your selves excluded. Where hath God excluded any that are become willing to be divorced from their sinnes and married to their saviour? That God hath touched your heart is good, that he will heal it as well as wound it I doubt not, & if he hide his face some time he will after two daies revive & you shall live in his sight. Remember me to your uncle Aunt &c. Farewell in hast

Rye Dec 10th
1668

Your lo: Father
Sa: Jeake

To his lo: sonne Samuel Jeake at Br: Bonnick's house in Salisbury Lane neere Redriffe Wall, these.

[34] *Samuel Jeake senior to Samuel Jeake junior, 17 December 1668. Original letter.* ESRO FRE 4824

Lov: sonne

Yours of the 15th instant I received & am glad to heare of your health your Aunt & Relacions with you. I did write to you by Jn° Hounsell which I suppose by this may come to your hands. Mr White by reason of the foule weather is not yet arrived at Rye but I hope well in the Downes. If any of Lillies

Almonacks[31] do come out buy a couple & one of Gadburyes[32] & send by the carrier. George Marsoone desired me to write to you to enquire among the stationers for a little book called the Kings high way treating of the cure of seven diseases in Horses commonly counted incurable[33] & if it be of small price to buy it & send it, if of high price send the price downe before you buy it. Mr Hartshorne desires you to enquire for Behmens Mysterium Magnum[34] & his three principles & the lowest price & send word accordingly. Also Mr Shinner desires you to enquire the price of your uncle Blackwood's[35] book which I have being an exposition of the first ten chapters of Matthew be carefull of your selfe in taking cold this wet weather. I have this weeke given order by Letter to cosin Wightman to carry Mary Key up to you which I would have done before if I could have sent to him but had no opportunity of writing. Remember me to your uncle Aunt cosin & friends. I am in hast but abide

Rye Dec: 17th Your truly lo: father
1668 Sa: Jeake

Severall remember to you besides the old woman & her sonne.

To his lov: sonne Samuel Jeake at Br: Bonnick's house in Salisbury Lane neere Redriffe Wall, these.

[31] William Lilly, Astrologer (1602–81). Patrick Curry, 'Lilly, William (1602–1681)', *ODNB.* The Jeake library contained Lilly's Almanacks for the years from 1645–64 and 1681, along with other works by the author. Hunter *et al., Radical's Books*, 310–11; 142–3.

[32] John Gadbury, Astrologer (1627–1704). Patrick Curry, 'Gadbury, John (1627–1704)', *ODNB.* The Jeake library likewise contained a series of Gadbury's Almanacks, along with numerous other works by the author. Hunter *et al., Radical's Books*, 308–9; 102–3.

[33] Probably either Gervase Markham, *How to chuse, ride, trayne, and dyet, both hunting-horses and running horses vvith all the secrets thereto belonging discovered* (London, printed by E. Allde for Ed. White, 1606) STC 17350 or the abridged version: Gervase Markham, *The complete farriar, or The kings high-way to horsemanship* (London, printed by I. Dawson for R. Young, 1639) STC 17341.

[34] Jakob Böhme [Jacob Behman] *Mysterium magnum, or An exposition of the first book of Moses called Genesis* (London, printed by M. Simmons for H. Blunden, 1654).

[35] Christopher Blackwood published a variety of works on spiritual matters. Richard L. Greaves, 'Blackwood, Christopher (1607/8–1670)', *ODNB.* The Jeake library contained several of Blackwood's publications. Hunter *et al. Radical's Books*, 24–5.

[35] *Samuel Jeake senior to Samuel Jeake junior, 24 December 1668. Original letter.* ESRO FRE 4825

Lov: sonne,
My love to you, your uncle Aunt & cosin, I have received yours of the 22nd instant, and it seems John Hounsell did not go so soone as I expected by reason the weather was so bad, but when he comes up he will give you the Letter. I do not remember that I wrot to you for Erastus, The nullity of church censures[36] yet if it be not too great of price you may buy it. You writ not any thing whether you have spoken to Mr Bennetland so I have forborne writing till I heare from you. Thomas Shoosmith remembers to you also his mother & she intends next weeke to send you a Goose for a token & she would have you call for it on Thursday morning (this day sennight) at Mr Joseph Boys to whom commend me. Mr White came not in this harbor till this day. I have not yet seene him, with my prayers for you I rest

Rye Dec. 24th 1668 — Your lo: father Sa: Jeake

If any news worth communicating at any time you may write.

To his lov: sonne Samuel Jeake at Br: Bonnick's house in Salisbury Lane neere Redriffe Wall, these.

[36] *Samuel Jeake senior to Samuel Jeake junior, 30 December 1668. Original letter.* ESRO FRE 4826

Lo: sonne
Yours of the 29th I have just now received & having opportunity by Mr White I have wrot these to let you know I am indifferent in health & am glad to heare of yours. I have put aboard Wm Oake who is bound for London a little fardell of your cosin Mary's clothes & a bagg of nutts that George Marsoone hath sent you who remembers to you when he comes up you may call aboard of him & take them. Pray tell your Aunt that I have received the coat and the old woman hath offered it to sell & cannot be bid above seven shillings for it great fault is found that the moths have beene in it & it is threadbare before, now your order being not to sell it under .9s. it must be sent backe againe unless she will take 7s which I desire to know by the first opportunity. The 2 Bibles you write of if you thinke good you may buy. Yet if they be both alike

[36] Thomas Erastus, *The Nullity of Church-censures: Or A Dispute* (London, printed for G.L., 1659); Hunter *et al.*, *Radical's Books*, 80–1.

one will serve. I would faine you should write me a line or two how you like your being in London & if you have any disrellishment in your Quarters. I pray remember me to your uncle Aunt cosin & other friends. I wish well to you all write me when Mr Martin comes home. I wish you could heare of one that would buy the part of Mr Bennetlands vessell I must be content to come off at loss with his dishonesty. Mr Boys the old woman & her sonne & others remember to you, I am

Rye Dec 30th
1668

Your very lo: father
Sa: Jeake

To his lov: sonne Samuel Jeake at Br: Bonnick's house in Salisbury Lane neere Redriffe Wall, these.

[37] *Samuel Jeake senior to Samuel Jeake junior, 14 January 1668/9. Original letter.* ESRO FRE 4827

Lov: sonne
My love to you, your uncle Aunt & Cosins, I have received yours of the 12th instant, I hope your Cosin Mary is well after her Journey. I have shewed Mr Hartshorne what you wrot who desires you to buy the two Bookes for .32s. seeing you cannot have them under & keepe them till some Barque of our Towne comes downe to Rye & put them aboard to bring to me in your Buying them see they be perfect. I shall willingly joyne with Mr Martin in what he doeth concerning Mr Bennetlands vessell & thinke it will be little end to write to him seeing he refuseth to give Mr Martin an accompt. I have received of Mr White the Prot: Almanack[37] & Erastus.[38] The Booke called Secrets revealed[39] if of any biggness may be worth .18d. you may buy & send it when you have opportunity if Mr Frith should not like it, it is no great matter. Marke Chiswell I understand cannot yet deliver because of the [word illegible] You may let me know what money you have yet in your hands, your writing & Latine in some things want excuse, I hope you enjoy your health, you writ me not whether the noise in your head continue I am in hast but wish you well & abide.

Rye Jan 14th
1668/9

Your truly lo: father
Sa: Jeake

[37] Copies of the Protestant Almanack from 1668 and 1669 were noted in the Jeake Library catalogue. Hunter *et al.*, *Radical's Books*, 310–11.
[38] Possibly *The Nullity of Church Censures* noted above.
[39] Possibly *Secrets reveal'd, or an open entrance to the shut-place of the king*, authorship unclear but noted in Hunter *et al.*, *Radical's Books*, 280–1.

Tho Crouch[40] the old woman & her sonne with others remember to you.

To his lo: sonne Samuel Jeake at Br: Bonnick's house in Salisbury Lane neere Redriffe Wall, these.

[38] *Samuel Jeake senior to Samuel Jeake junior, 21 January 1668/9. Original letter.* ESRO FRE 4828

My Child
Yours last post I received & am glad to heare of your health. I have wrot to Marke Chiswell to go along with you to Mr Salter & receive for me £3 for which you may give an Acquittance thus

	£	s	d
Received Nov. .th 1668 of Mr Joseph Boys by the order &			
Received January ..th 1668 of Mr George Salter Three	03:	00:	00
pounds for one yeares interest of fifty pounds due in August			
last from the said Mr Salter & Mr Edw: Nunne I say			
received for the use of my Father Mr Sa: Jeake of Rye			

And putting in the date when you receive it subscribe it. I understand Marke Chiswell comes home so you may now put aboard the Mortar & Mr Hartshornes bookes but direct them to ~~you~~ me. I am willing to allow your uncle fifty shillings for your quarters board if that do not give content lay them downe more for you shall be no charge to them. I cannot heare that France is yet cleare of the pest but I had rather you would get a Frenchman that [is in] London to teach you for there be them that teach the French tongue there, and then if you should be ill I can be with you. But I am in hast at present & with my love to you & all friends with you remaine
Rye Jan 21th Your lo: father
1668/9 Sa: Jeake

To his lo: sonne Samuel Jeake at Br: Bonnick's house in Salisbury Lane neere Redriffe Wall, these.

[40] There were at least two individuals named Thomas Crouch living in Rye according to the 1660 Demobilisation Tax record. One was Thomas Crouch, leader of the Court party in Rye, who went on 'in an insolent and Violent manner' to usurp the mayoralty of the town in 1681. The Thomas Crouch referred to here is more likely to have been apprentice to the barber-surgeon Edward Gee. Burchall, 'Inhabitants of Rye', 102–8; Hunter and Gregory, *Astrological Diary*, 31, 57.

[39] *Samuel Jeake senior to Samuel Jeake junior, 28 January 1668/9. Original letter.* ESRO FRE 4829

Lov: sonne,
Yours last post I received as also one from Mr Martin concerning Mr Bennetland & when you see Mr Martin thanke him & let him know I shall joyne with him at any time to put out such a dishonest man as Mr Bennetland is if Marke Chiswell be not come away if he be by any vessel of Towne that comes home send me a dozen of parchment, if you know not where to buy it Mr Boys will direct you or buy it for you. Wm Harnet desired me to write to you to buy him a boxe of Lockyers pills[41] a whole boxe will cost 4s & they be to be had at the Three Boares Heads over against the meale market in Southwarke you need have no booke of directions how to use them for he hath a booke already this little boxe if Mr Boys send any thing to his Father or Br Curtis he may put it up in it, if not when you have any opportunity you may send it by Boat or otherwise. Although I have declared that you would have nothing sent you yet I understand Mrs Curtis will send you something next weeke & seeing she will I have ordered a Capon sent me to be put up with it so on Thursday morning next weeke call to Mr Boys for it & tell your Aunt I have sent her the Capon. You have not deducted out of the money in your hands your owne .16s. 6d. which I did formerly order you & you may do & more if you have occasion. I suppose Wm Oake is now come to London aboard of whom are your nutts & a bundle of Mary's clothes as I wrot you formerly. Pray desire your Aunt keepe an Accompt particularly of what she layes out for Mary for her clothes & such things as she wants & tell Mary that I charge her to be a good girle. I suppose your cosin Wightman brought up such clothes of Mary's as were at Maidston. The little Booke of Tho Savage[42] I have seene. Have a care of your health. With my love to you, your Aunt & cosins I remaine

Rye January 28th 1668/9 — Your very lo: father Sa: Jeake

To his lo: sonne Samuel Jeake at Br: Bonnick's house in Salisbury Lane neere Redriffe Wall, these.

[41] Lionel Lockyer (c.1600–72), famous for his 'miracle' remedies. A. S. Hargreaves, 'Lionel Lockyer (1600–72) & his Pillulae Radiis Solis Extractae', *Pharm Hist (London)*, 29 (1999), 55–63.

[42] This does not appear in the Jeake Library catalogue. Hunter *et al.*, *Radical's Books*.

[40] *Samuel Jeake junior to Samuel Jeake senior, 9 February 1668/9. Original letter.* ESRO FRE 4830

Londini 9o Februarij. 1668/9
Pater Charissime
Post debitas salutat[i]o[n]es tibi ac omnib[us] Amicis n[ost]ris; his lineis quas tibi hoc temporis exaratæ sunt intelligas nos recepisse Caponem à te Amitæ, & Meleagridum à M[agist]ro Curtis mihi missos pro Capone gratias tibi Reddit Amita téque salutat; pro Meleagride[m] gratias meo nomine quæso ut M[agrist]ro Curtis reddas, quem ut salutas oro & hanc Epistolam inclusam, quam tibi aptam mitto obsignatam illi tradas; Amita mea orat te scribere, an misisti nobis tunicam illam, quam demisit illa Riæ, an non, Si autem misisti p[er] quem. Vidi M[agistrum] White & ab illo accepi pignus tuum Amoris gratiasq[ue] tibi hoc.

Recepi p[er] manus Marci Chiswell à M[agrist]ro Salter. 3. Saluta T. Shoosmith cum matre &c, Non mihi plus negotij, sed non recepi Epistolam à te ha[n]c septimana[m]. Vale salutis tuæ cupidus
Filius tuus obedientis[simu]s:
Sa[muel] Jeake jun[io]r

Translation:
London, 9 February 1668/9
Dearest father,
After the due greetings to you and all our friends, know by these lines which are scribbled down for you in this time that we have received the capon from you to Aunt, and the guineafowl sent to me by Mr Curtis. Aunt thanks you for the capon and greets you; I ask that you return my thanks for the guineafowl in my name to Mr Curtis, whom I also ask you to greet, and to hand over this enclosed letter, which I send attached and signed by me. Aunt asks me to write to you whether you have sent us her gown, which she left behind at Rye, or not, and by whom you have sent it. I have seen Mr White and received from him a pledge of your love; thank you for this. I have received by the hand of Mark Chiswell from Mr Salter £3. Greet T. Shoosmith with [his] mother, etc. I have no more business, but I have not received a letter from you this week. Farewell, desirous of your health,
Your most obedient son
Samuel Jeake junior

[41] *Samuel Jeake senior to Samuel Jeake junior, 11 February 1668/9. Original letter.* ESRO FRE 4831

Lov: Sonne
I had last night yours of the 9th instant but perceive thereby you had not my last for therein I wrot that you could acquaint your Aunt that I had sold her coat for 9 s which was the most I could get & did order you to pay her the money. Marke Chiswell is not yet come home by reason of contrary winds. I did write to you to desire your Aunt to buy Mary a coate & such other things as she wanted & keepe an accompt thereof. I wonder Cosin Wightman hath not brought up such clothes as she had at Maidstone for I thinke she had some with her there. You do not write me that she goes to schoole I would not have her idle. Remember me to your uncle Aunt & cosins & so in hast remaineth

Rye Febr 11th
1668/9

Your lo: father
Sa: Jeake

To his lo: sonne Samuel Jeake at Br: Bonnick's house in Salisbury Lane neere Redriffe Wall, these.

[42] *Samuel Jeake senior to Samuel Jeake junior, 18 February 1668/9. Original letter.* ESRO FRE 4832

My deare child
I have yours of the 16th instant & am very willing you shall take a purge this spring but yet the weather is too cold. I hope you are well though you do not write anything thereof. I desire you to go to Mr Allin & receive of him .£3. according to the receit herein inclosed which I doubt not but he will pay because he hath wrot to Mr Frith to know to whom he shall pay it. & by the post to be here on Wednesday next advise me because I suppose the day after the party will come to me for the money which I shall pay if I heare you have received it. Marke Chiswell is now upon coming in & my next I intend shall give you a accompt of what I have from him. The French schoole at the Spittle will be too farre off. I wish there were one nearer you. I am in hast at present but not forgetting my love to you, Mr Allin, your uncle Aunt & cosins, I remaine

Rye Febr 18th
1668/9

Your lo: father
Sa: Jeake

To his lo: sonne Samuel Jeake at Br: Bonnick's house in Salisbury Lane neere Redriffe Wall, these.

[43] *Samuel Jeake senior to Samuel Jeake junior, 4 March 1668/9. Original letter.* ESRO FRE 4833

Lov: sonne
I forgot in my last in my last to bid you get your watch mended. I am glad by yours of the 2nd instant to heare your increase in naturall strength if you thinke you can walke on foote. Tho: Crouch & Tho: Shoosmith will come up when the footwaies are a little better & then you may come down with them. Mr Frith hath given me the inclosed note which showes the title of Wrayes booke that I wrot about before & he also desires you buy the Improvements of Walker[43] if you can meet with it but if it should bee very deare you were best to write word of the price first. Mr Hartshorne desire you to enquire of the price of Pagnino his Hebrew Lexicon[44] but whether so called or not I well know not but I thinke it is for I have seene it, it is in folio, & gives the Latine of the Hebrew words. I am in hast, wish you well and am
Rye Mar 4th Your lo: father
1668/9 Sa: Jeake
Remember me to all friends, yours here remember to you.

To his lo: sonne Samuel Jeake at Br: Bonnicks house in Salisbury Lane neere Redriffe Wall, these.

[44] *Samuel Jeake junior to Samuel Jeake senior, 6 March 1668/9. Original letter.* ESRO FRE 4834

Londini. 6o Martij. 1668.
Pater Charissime
Tuæ Mar[tis] 4. Datæ hodie allatæ mihi sunt. At opinor meip[s]um potentem à Londino Riam ambulam & consortium propositum (viz T. Crouch & T. Shoosmith) libenter Amplector. Emi 2 Libros pro Mr Frith viz. Walkers Improvem[en]ts[45] C[hapter] 18. & Drages Experim[en]ts[46] C[hapter] 3d,

[43] Probably William Walker, *Some improvements to the art of teaching especially in the first grounding of a young scholar in grammar learning* (London, printed by S. Griffin, 1669); Hunter *et al.*, *Radical's Books*, 250–1.
[44] Probably Santes Pagnino [also known as Pagninus or Pagnini], *Thesaurus linguae sanctae*. See reference in FRE 4834. This is not recorded in the Jeake Library catalogue. Hunter *et al.*, *Radical's Books*.
[45] See fn. 43.
[46] William Drage, *Physical experiments being a plain description of the causes, signes, and cures of most diseases incident to the body of man* (London, Printed for Simon Miller, 1669); Hunter *et al.*, *Radical's Books*, 74–5.

demittam Riæ p[ro] M[agistro] White. Pretium Thesauri Santis Pagnini[47] est circa 30^{s}. Pretium Epitomes ejus circa 2s. Audio q[uo]d Guil[elmus] Coventry Miles in Turri Londiniensi incarceratur quonia[m] monomachiam cum Duce Buckinghamiensi (ut memini) inire voluit. Prætoris Londiniensis Guil[elmus] Turneri Ensis à Legis-positis Templi interioris ibidem vi defenditur. Saluta Amicos no[m]i[n]atim D[ominus] Boys, D[ominus] Miller, D[ominus] Frith, T. Shoosmith T. Crouch, [word struck out] Salutant te Amita M. Key &c Vale, & vive n[ost]ri memor.
Filius tuus obedientijs [sic]:
Sa[muel] Jeake jun[io]r

Translation:
London, 6 March 1668
Dearest father,
Yours dated 4 March were brought to me today. But I think I would rather walk from London to Rye. And I gladly embrace the proposed partnership (that is to say, T. Crouch and T. Shoosmith). I have bought two books for Mr Frith, that is to say Walker's *Improvements*, Chapter 18 and Drage's *Experiments*, Chapter 3. The price of the *Thesaurus* of Santus Pagninus is around 30 shillings. The price of his *Epitome* is around 2 shillings. I hear that Sir William Coventry has been imprisoned in the Tower because he sought a duel with the Duke of Buckingham, as I recall. The sword of the Lord Mayor of London William Turner was defended there/in that matter by force by the lawyers of the Inner Temple.[48] Greet our friends by name: Mr Boys, Mr Miller, Mr Frith, T. Shoosmith, T. Crouch. Aunt and M. Key greet you, etc. Farewell, and live mindful of us.
Your most obedient son
Samuel Jeake junior

[47] See fn. 44.
[48] Jeake's statement is unclear. For Coventry's arrest, 3 March 1668/9, and release, 20 March, see *CSPDom:* 'Charles II: March 1669', in *Calendar of State Papers Domestic: Charles II, 1668–9*, ed. Mary Anne Everett Green (London, 1894), pp. 219–58. *British History Online* http://www.british-history.ac.uk/cal-state-papers/domestic/chas2/1668-9/pp219-258 [accessed 28 July 2017].

[45] *Samuel Jeake senior to Samuel Jeake junior, 13 March 1668/9. Original letter.* ESRO FRE 4835

Lov: Sonne
Through mercy I am in health & hope you are the same. I have not heard of you since Lordsday last, & I have beene busie this weeke & little time to write, nor any great businesse to write to you, only to let you know that I thinke if the weather hold good, T. C. & T. S.[49] will come up to London the weeke after this next that comes in & then if you thinke you can hold out you may come downe with them, but I shall write to you God willing betweene this & that, Mr White is not yet come in, remember me to your uncle Aunt & Cosins wishing you all health & prosperity inwardly & outwardly I remaine

Rye March 13th 1668/9 — Your lo: father Sa: Jeake

To his lo: sonne Sam: Jeake at Br: Bonnick's house in Salisbury Lane neere Redriffe Wall, these.

[46] *Samuel Jeake senior to Samuel Jeake junior, 16 March 1668/9. Original letter.* ESRO FRE 4836

My deare child
I have this day received from Mr White the piece of Chyrology, scripture Almanack & Manuscript but have not yet purused any of them. I reckon at the end of this weeke your friends T C & T S[50] will be with you and so you may get all ready to come away the next weeke with them. Pay your uncle for the time you have beene there since the last quarter you paid & take an acquittance of him, or your Aunt & take the Accompt with you of what you have laid out for Mary Key & bring with you & when you have brought any thing that you want if you have more money spare than will bring you downe you may pay your uncle what overplus you have towards that accompt of Mary. If more than the accompt comes to cleare that accompt & leave the residue in your uncles hands towards the accrewing Arrears. My love to them all, the Lord be with you & blesse you is the hearty prayer of

Rye March 16th 1668/9 — Your lo: father Sa: Jeake

To his lo: sonne Samuel Jeake at Br: Bonnickes house in Salisbury Lane neere Redriffe Wall, these.

[49] Thomas Crouch and Thomas Shoosmith.
[50] Thomas Crouch and Thomas Shoosmith.

[47] *Samuel Jeake junior to Samuel Jeake senior, 18 March 1668/9. Original letter.* ESRO FRE 4837

Londini 18o Martis 1668/9
Pater Charissime
Per manus D[omi]ni Miller (hesternâ luce) tuas Mar[tis] 13. datas ad me scriptas recepi, gaudeóq[ue] de valetudine tuâ audisse, Cum T. S. & T. C. advenerint paratus fuero (Divinâ Clementiâ) domum cum illis redire. Mittas (si placeat) verbum quomodo demittam vestim[en]ta & mea Riæ. Tibi p[ro] M[agistro] White misi Bulweri Chirologiam (or Naturall Language of ye hand)[51] ac Kalendarium cui Titulus The Scripture Kalendar revived. denique Manuscriptum vocatum Considerat[i]ons about ye condit[i]on of Christ's visible Church on Earth; Misi antea tibi transmittere p[ro] Avunculo Galerum Gallicum oro si possis [word lost] transmittas, vel (si conveniens judicetur) ut T. S. Galerum tale recens super Capite Londini adferat, hic autem Avunculo vendat et domum Galero meo veteri redeat: sed vx[or]æ prudentae com[m] itto. salutant te nostrates. Saluta Amicos nominatim. Plura non addo
Vale
Filius tuus obedientis[simu]s:
Sa[muel] Jeake jun[io]r

Translation:
London, 18 March 1668/9
Dearest father,
I received yours written to me, dated 13 March, by the hand of Mr Miller at dawn yesterday, and I rejoice to hear of your recovery. When T. S. [Thomas Shoesmith] and T. C. [Thomas Crouch] arrive I shall be ready (by God's mercy) to return home with them. Send me, if you please, a word concerning how I shall send my clothes to Rye. I have sent you for Mr White, Bulwer's Chirologia (or Natural Language of the Hand) and the calendar entitled The Scripture Calendar Reviv'd, and finally the manuscript called Considerations upon the Condition of Christ's Visible Church on Earth; I sent you before, to send over to uncle, a French hat. I pray you, if you are able, do not send it, or that (if it should be judged convenient) T. S. may wear such a clean hat on his head in London, let this one be sold to uncle and let him return home with my

[51] John Bulwer, *Chirologia: or, The natural language of the hand. Composed of the speaking motions, and discoursing gestures thereof* (London, printed by T. H., 1648); Hunter *et al.*, *Radical's Books*, 30–1.

old hat; but I commit it to your prudent wife. Our folks greet you. Greet our friends by name. I add no more. Farewell.
Your most obedient son
Samuel Jeake junior

[48] *Samuel Jeake senior to Samuel Jeake junior, 20 March 1668/9. Original letter.* ESRO FRE 4838

My sonne
I had yours last post as to the things you have to send downe you may send by the carrier for I thinke there's no Boats of our Towne at London but it is best by the carrier. A Hat for your uncle Tho: Shoosmith will bring up as you write I did minde it before but here hath none or very few come over a great while, onely Tho: Shoosmith saith he will let your uncle have his. If you had my last letter you will remember to bring with you what Accompt your Aunt hath for Mary & leave what money you spare with her. I have wrot to your Cosin at Maidstone to give you Accompt of what is due to him there, which bring with you, if you find your selfe weary coming thither, you may hire a horse there. Pray have a care of going beyond your strength or drinking when you are hot, except it be hot liquors. Present my love to your uncle, Aunt & Cosins & when you come away you may give your Cosin Sam: a shilling & the little maide that was with your Aunt if she be there still six pence or if another be there the like. I commit you to the blessed protection of the Almighty & remaine
Rye Mar 20 Your lo: father
1668/9 Sa: Jeake

I would not have you come downe to Gravesend in the night.

To his lo: sonne Samuel Jeake at Br: Bonnicks house in Salisbury Lane neere Redriffe Wall, these.

3

Samuel, the Merchant, 1672–1680

On 4 July 1671, his nineteenth birthday, Samuel Jeake junior took account of himself. He listed his accomplishments, having acquainted himself with Latin, Greek and Hebrew but also 'Rhetorick, Logick, Poetry, Natural Philosophy, Artihmetick, Geometry, Cosmography, Astronomy, Astrology, Geography, Theology, Physick, Dialling, Navigation, Calligraphy, Stenography, Drawing, Heraldry and History'. He noted his physical description. He was short, 5 ft 4 5/8 inches, small in stature, pale and lean. His complexion was 'melancholy', 'Eyes Grey, Nose large, Teeth bad & distorted'. His hair was of 'a sad brown', curly but thinning by his early twenties. His eyesight had been affected by smallpox, which had also made his voice grow hoarse.[1] He gave no description of his state of mind at this time as it was 'inconvenient for me to relate, and liable to certain exposure: it being not possible for me in this particular to saile between Scylla and Charybdis'.[2] This points towards the depression that Samuel suffered throughout his life and which appears to have been particularly pronounced during his teenage years and twenties. Indeed, he noted in his diary in 1667 'an excessive Melancholy, which continued with Violence till July 1670...But its' continuance was full 7 years; Nay not quite gone in 10 years time'.[3]

At this time Samuel had still not entered a formal occupation. There are no surviving runs of letters between 1668 and 1672 but the *Astrological Diary* shows that he was continuing with his education and various diversions, including keeping a weather diary for Rye.[4] He did suffer long bouts of ill health, most particularly very severe attacks of what he describes as ague, probably malaria, which was prevalent in low-lying coastal areas around Rye.[5] He also travelled to London in May and June of 1672 with the intention of finding a medicine for his eyes.[6] In the midst of the Third Anglo-Dutch War (1672–4), this was a rather dangerous time to be in London and the letters mention fear of the possibility of impressment, as well as giving news from the Battle of Solebay (FRE 4841, 4842). While Samuel was once again doing some business for his father during his time in London, it was not until he turned twenty-one that he began to give his attention towards building his own career as a merchant.

Post-Restoration England was experiencing a 'revolution in trade'.[7] Supported by Charles II's navigation policies, growing domestic wealth and demand, and nascent colonisation, there was a significant growth in all aspects of foreign trade. Merchants were increasing in number, growing rich and trade was becoming a more acceptable occupation. Although not universally approved, the very visible growth of trade

[1] Hunter and Gregory, *Astrological Diary*, 117–18.
[2] Ibid. 118.
[3] Ibid. 98.
[4] Ibid. 107
[5] Ibid. 107–16, 51.
[6] Ibid. 120–1.
[7] R. Davis, 'English foreign trade, 1660–1700', *Economic History Review*, 7 (1954–5), 162.

underpinned its importance to the country.[8] By the end of the seventeenth century it could be argued that although in former times 'Trading…rendered a Gentleman ignoble [now] an ignoble Person makes himself by Merchandizing as good as a Gentleman'.[9]

As noted in the previous chapter, Samuel did not serve an apprenticeship. Hunter and Gregory confirm this as unusual and suggest that his first steps into the business of becoming a merchant were overseen by Thomas Miller and facilitated by the commercial links of the Jeake and Hartridge families.[10] The importance of having 'ready made connections' in trade should not be underestimated.[11] We have, however, already seen the adolescent Samuel in London and undertaking business dealings for his father suggesting that his entrance into trade was facilitated in a number of ways. The *Astrological Diary* and the letters in this chapter offer us several possible starting points for Samuel junior's more formal working life. On 11 December 1673 he recorded in his diary that he 'Resolved to set apart the Tenth part of my Annual Income & Profits arising by Trade for the Relief of the Poor & other Charitable uses'. His initial resolve was to commence the following year in January but he then backdated the commencement to the previous April 'that it might comprehend the first of my profits'.[12] Neither the *Astrological Diary* nor the surviving letters record this first profit but Hunter and Gregory argue that it was money made from scrivening, an occupation for which Samuel had received training from his father and to which he was to turn on and off throughout his adult life as a way of supplementing his income.[13] Samuel recorded his 'first entrance into trade' as being a venture in August 1674 to purchase linen from St Malo in partnership with his friend Thomas Miller. But it is clear that he had been building to this point for some months. In April 1674 Samuel and Miller had taken a trip together to Dieppe. Amongst other distractions, some of which Samuel had cause to regret because he engaged in sight-seeing 'instead of keeping holy the Sabbath day', they also visited the Exchange and bought a small amount of bone lace in partnership.[14] This was not his only small venture in the summer of 1674. One of the letters below shows that in July Samuel had purchased a barrel of meal from James Le Griell in Dieppe and had also enquired about glass pendants and bees wax (FRE 4847). He had also made contact with his cousin Christopher Blackwood, the son of his mother's sister, in mid-1674 to enquire about the prospects for trade. Blackwood was based in Dublin. He responded acknowledging Samuel junior's intention to engage in trade and detailing the state of trade in Dublin. Blackwood assured him 'that if in any respect it Lyes in my power to serve you hither in these parts or Else where it shall not be wanting' (FRE 4846).

The importing of French linens and lockrams was the most dominant and most lucrative of Samuel's early ventures. In this business he operated in partnership with Thomas Miller, imported from St Malo and Morlaix and sold in a quite wide area around Sussex. Other commodities, including herrings, and goods from France,

[8] R. Grassby, *The Business Community of Seventeenth-Century England* (Cambridge, 1995), 52

[9] [Guy Miège] *The New State of England* (London, 1699) quoted in N. Glaisyer, *The Culture of Commerce in England, 1660–1720* (Woodbridge, 2006), 17.

[10] Hunter and Gregory, *Astrological Diary*, 61.

[11] Gauci, *Emporium of the World*, 123.

[12] Hunter and Gregory, *Astrological Diary*, 126.

[13] Ibid. 60.

[14] Ibid. 126–7.

notably gloves, fans, lace, paper, wine and brandy, were traded from time to time with mixed success. Samuel's links with France, however, were brought to a halt in March 1678 when Parliament prohibited the trade. He did continue to trade with France illegally from time to time but came to regard the connection as 'too full of Snares & Temptations to be exercised with a good Conscience'.[15] The letters below chiefly relate to the period from 1678 when Samuel was casting around for sources of income and trying to establish new contacts. During the period prior to 1680 when trade with France was restored, he traded in wool, in tallow from Dublin, in timber with Thomas Markwick, a close friend and fellow nonconformist, and in purchasing French boats captured as prizes with Lewis Gillart, a supporter of the court faction in Rye and, therefore, on the opposite side of the political divide from the Jeakes. Gillart was to become one of Samuel junior's primary tormentors during the 1680s when the persecution of dissenters increased.[16]

Samuel also diversified through money-lending activities. He lent on bottomry, an arrangement that allowed the master of a ship to borrow using the ship itself as collateral. Samuel also began to negotiate bills of exchange. The bill of exchange was the standard means of making payments between merchants based in different countries. Enforcement of this payment system was through the law merchant, underpinned by sound institutions in most cities which supported trade.[17] Inland bills of exchange were used by persons trading within the same country and were becoming increasingly common by the mid-seventeenth century.[18] Bills were used because they were a secure form of lending. They were drawn up using a proper legal form, often by a lawyer or scrivener, and always in front of witnesses. They were accepted in court as evidence of a debt and, as a consequence, were usually paid 'without hesitation of any kind whatsoever'.[19] Bills were also assignable to a third party, which meant that the person to whom money was owed could 'sell' the debt on. When Samuel moved into the business of negotiating bills of exchange, therefore, he was acting as a third party taking on debts at a discounted rate and, so long as the debt was paid when due, eventually making a small profit.

The funding for Samuel's initial ventures came from various sources. At the end of 1674 had Samuel computed his stock at £305, including £70 employed in trade and £140 held in land.[20] That land, and the timber grown on it, was sold in 1676. It had been left to him by his mother and he had received it when he was twenty-one. Although a lengthy and problematic negotiation, the sale of the timber and land yielded him nearly £150 (FRE 4851, 4852 and 4855). Samuel's capital was further enhanced by gifts and loans from his father. At the start of 1675, Samuel senior made his son three gifts of money totalling just over £110.[21] In this, Samuel was like many other early modern young men who relied on their parents to fund their first steps into

[15] Ibid. 147.

[16] Ibid. 146; 30; 165; 170–1.

[17] C. Muldrew, *The Economy of Obligation: The Culture of Credit and Social Relations in Early Modern England* (Basingstoke, 1998), 115; Jeremy Edwards and Sheilagh Ogilvie, 'What lessons for economic development can we draw from the Champagne fairs?', *Explorations in Economic History*, 49 (2012), 131–48.

[18] Muldrew, *Economy of Obligation*, 111.

[19] Daniel Defoe quoted in Muldrew, *Economy of Obligation*, 192.

[20] RMA, Selmes, Stock Accounts, RYEYT, N39.39.1

[21] Hunter and Gregory, *Astrological Diary*, 128–9.

business.[22] Over the period from 1674 to 1680 Samuel's annual profits were relatively modest. He made £31 15s in the year from January 1674 to January 1675. Profits did not exceed £30 in the following two years. In 1677/8 he made close to £50 in profit and in the following two years £71 10s and £59 12s respectively. By January 1680 his stock stood at £685, with nearly £370 in cash, gold, annuities and on account with John Mackley; £92 was held in trade goods, including lockrams, and £210 had been lent on bonds.[23]

The level of diversification adopted by Samuel junior was not unusual. Some trades, of course, were restricted by monopolies such as that held by the East India Company. Nonetheless, many merchants, like William Cotesworth, would have 'dealt in any thing I cd gaine by'.[24] Equally a provincial merchant like Samuel would have found that there was simply not enough foreign trade coming into local ports to sustain an entire business.[25] Acting in partnership with others also spread costs and risk and allowed Samuel to make the best of the capital he had acquired.

Rye was still a relatively active port during the late seventeenth century and some of Samuel's trade came through either Rye or nearby Hastings and was sold in the local area. Nonetheless, he needed to establish a broader network of contacts both in the areas with which he traded and most especially in London. London was key because, since he did not own ships, he always had to contract space for his goods on someone else's vessels, many of which came to London, which was England's chief port. London was also the place where Samuel was most likely to sell some of the fancier goods he purchased. The letters below reveal much about the establishment of the relationships that facilitated his business. Most, but not all, of his contacts were fellow nonconformists and close or distant relations. This should not surprise. Many merchants made kin or co-religionists their primary contacts, if the opportunity arose.[26] Ties of kinship helped to establish trust and provided another imperative for acting well although, as Zahedieh points out, kin did not always live up to expectations.[27] One important relationship for Samuel junior was that with John Mackley, a tallow chandler and the husband of his first cousin Elizabeth (née Key, the daughter of Anne Jeake and William Key). Mackley was to be Samuel's principal correspondent in London until the mid-1680s when Thomas Miller moved to the capital to avoid persecution in Rye. Also interesting in this collection are business connections with Elizabeth Mackley and Ann Wightman, Samuel's cousins and, at times, his regular correspondents.[28] Both of these women, although married, were clearly working when the occasion called for it and were Samuel's principal contacts when it came to trying to procure items and sell some of the fancy goods, such as the gloves, that he had imported from France. Samuel was right to rely on women whose husbands' livelihood depending on selling. James Wightman was a watchmaker and John Mackley was a tallow chandler. There is plentiful evidence of married women working on the

[22] Grassby, *Business Community*, 84.

[23] RMA Selmes, Stock Accounts RYEYT, N39.39.1–5; Profit Accounts N39.41.1–6.

[24] Quoted in Grassby, *Business Community*, 54

[25] Grassby, *Business Community*, 63.

[26] P. Gauci, *Emporium of the World: The merchants of London 1660–1800* (London, 2007), 97.

[27] N. Zahedieh, *The Capital and the Colonies: London and the Atlantic Economy 1660–1700* (Cambridge, 2010), 106–7

[28] Ann Wightman was a cousin by marriage. She was the daughter of William Key by his first marriage. William later married Samuel junior's aunt, Anne Jeake.

retail side of their husbands' business.[29] Moreover, women would have been responsible for household provisioning and thus familiar with London's wider retail environment.[30]

Had Samuel served a formal apprenticeship as a merchant part of his training might have included a spell abroad to establish vital contacts.[31] He had no such advantage, but we get in this series of letters a rare insight into the little-understood process of establishing and cultivating contacts.[32] This was not always an easy task. The *Astrological Diary* shows Samuel to have visited London in 1679 in an attempt to establish correspondents there, 'but the times favoured not my indeavours'.[33] Matching supply with need in these relationships seems to have been one stumbling block, as a letter Samuel junior drafted to a Major Childs in London showed. Having made enquiries for Childs as to whether it was possible sell Madeira wine in Rye, Samuel was forced to conclude that he found 'no great probability, they being neither used nor indeed well knowne here' (FRE 4886). Another problem was delays in communications. Richard Pickersgill wrote to Samuel to 'verey muche wonder wheare [his letter] hathe Lain soe longe…for I none had any lettres soe longe on the way from Rye before this' (FRE 4943). Nonetheless, Samuel did make connections, principally in France. Indeed we can observe a fairly systematic covering of the north and north-west coast of France with contacts at Calais, Dieppe, Caen and Nantes. He also made contacts in the south-west of England at Exeter and Padstow.

Notable in these exchanges establishing new contacts were the methods used to demonstrate reputation. For businessmen like Samuel who participated in, and depended often upon, complicated credit networks, the ability to prove oneself trustworthy and determine the trustworthiness of others was of paramount importance.[34] Thus he relied on personal recommendations. As he informed John Jewell, he had contacted 'Mr Wm Jennens of Plimo[uth] [to request] him to recommend me to a good correspondent in your parts, in answer to which he was readily pleased to direct me to your selfe' (FRE 4885). In making initial contacts it was also important to advertise one's reputation and one's connections.[35] John Cooke of Exeter told Samuel junior 'you come recommended by my good friend Mr Thomas Morris of London but as by your style you manifest an ingenious disposition' (FRE 4881).

Although solid and trustworthy contacts offered some protection against the dangers inherent in early modern trade, Samuel's chosen business was fraught with risk. The following chapters will show that his profits were affected by the persecution of dissenters and the onset of war with France. Even during times of greater economic and political stability, merchants were at the mercy of the weather which acted to determine the availability of goods, speed of transportation and the condition of cargoes. Markets were volatile and subject to the vagaries of fashion.[36] Samuel, for example, lost money on jessamy gloves. Ann Wightman, who had tried to sell his goods at the Royal Exchange but found no interest there, told him, 'They would Aben

[29] Amanda Flather, *Gender and Space in Early Modern England* (Woodbridge, 2007), 91.
[30] Sara Mendelson and Patricia Crawford, *Women in Early Modern England, 1550–1720* (Oxford, 1998), 307.
[31] Gauci, *Politics of Trade*, 72.
[32] Pat Hudson, 'Correspondence and Commitment: British traders' letters in the long eighteenth century', *Cultural and Social History*, 11 (2014), 527–53.
[33] Hunter and Gregory, *Astrological Diary*, 146.
[34] Muldrew, *Economy of Obligation*, 148.
[35] Zahedieh, *Capital and the Colonies*, 95.
[36] Grassby, *Business Community*, 91.

glad to have had them if they had ben fashonable they tell me they were in fashon last yeare they shewd me sume that wher now in fashon and they much defer from youers' (FRE 4941). Ann promised to try to sell the goods at the 'street shops' but a following letter showed she was having little luck and had received complaints that they had 'lost there sent' (FRE 4945).

Samuel was generally risk-averse and often cautious especially when approaching new ventures.[37] The purchase in 1678 of 4 tons of tallow demonstrated the usefulness of that caution. The transaction was organised by Daniel Hays in Dublin, managed by John Mackley in London and purchased in a partnership with Thomas Miller and Richard Freebody of Rye and John Mackley (FRE 4868). This new venture was prompted by the prohibition of trade with France mentioned above and it was the first time that Samuel had worked with John Mackley.[38] The younger Christopher Blackwood had been Samuel's first point of contact in this venture and, with admirable prescience, he had warned of the risks and the uncertainty of the market (FRE 4864). Nonetheless, Samuel and company were determined to try with this 'small parcel…preparatory to a greater quantity after Michaelmas' (FRE 4868). Blackwood found it difficult to source the tallow and arrange freight and advised delay but, possibly at John Mackley's insistence, Samuel wrote to an alternative correspondent, Daniel Hays, and sourced the tallow from him (FRE 4869–4871).[39] The letters give us an account of the incidental costs of the trade as incurred by John Mackley who was managing the London end of the transaction (FRE 4876) but also reveal the suspicions that might result from working in a partnership and trusting a distant correspondent to act on one's behalf. Mackley had clearly sold what he could and then had 'done Like a kind partner in ofring to take the rest of the parcel att the prise'. The price, however, was the market price and implied a loss to the rest of the partners. Mackley was a tallow chandler and thus could both afford to take on stock and was able to sell at retail, rather than wholesale prices. Although Samuel did not keep a copy of his letter to Mackley there was a clear implication that Mackley was taking advantage of his partners. On Mackley's part he laid blame on the high quantity of tallow already in London and on Daniel Hays for purchasing poor quality goods at too high rates (FRE 4877).

As Grassby asserts, perhaps the most serious risk an early modern businessman faced was from the misdealings, misfortunes and possible bankruptcies of third parties.[40] This was an issue with which Samuel was confronted over and over again and with which his own conscience wrestled. He recorded feeling guilt about a transaction with Edward Cross of Exeter where he had made around £12 by being less than honest when selling Cross some hops. Cross had died before Samuel could make restitution and this prompted him to consider other occasions where he might have 'wronged any person' in business. He made restitution of around £20 to various unnamed persons.[41] The letters below are distinctive because they offer an insight into the process of learning how to deal with a debt that had gone unpaid. In this case John Mackley, Samuel's inexperienced contact in London, had made the wrong choices about how to proceed.

[37] Hunter and Gregory, *Astrological Diary*, 59

[38] Ibid. 138.

[39] There are no extant letters to or from Hays. The details are recorded in Hunter and Gregory, *Astrological Diary*, 139.

[40] Grassby, *Business Community*, 93.

[41] Hunter and Gregory, *Astrological Diary*, 219.

He was apparently well-intentioned but acting on limited experience and received wisdom about the 'Custome of Marchant' (FRE 4919). Thus, we see Samuel turning to a more experienced merchant, Thomas Morris, for advice about how to protest a bill (FRE 4917). The matter was resolved but not without a considerable commitment in time, effort and persistence (FRE 4940). It was not to be the last time in Samuel's career that he faced such difficulties and, unfortunately as we shall see, not all turned out so favourably.

Visits to London, 1672–1673

[49] *Samuel Jeake junior to Samuel Jeake senior, 4 June 1672. Original letter.*
ESRO FRE 4841

London June 4th 1672
Dear Father
I have spoken with Mr Wm Langley who tells me he hath received of Mr Nun £10 06s due on the bond but could not get him to pay any interest & so thought it good rather to take this whilst he might have it. The money he could not pay me (he said) when I spake to him which was May 30th because he had not so much in the house, but hath promised I shall without faile have it next Thursday morning. I could not get him to deduct any thing for his charge. Yours of May 28th I received May 31st and the same day presented the bill, was ordered to come for the money this day morning. I went but Mr Norton hath put me off till the afternoon & then he promised I shall have it. I could not get above £3 10s for the Rings & 5s for the spoon. The money I have received for the Rings, & hope to have of Mr Langley, with what I brought up will serve to pay off my Aunts accompt of £15 17s 10 ½d & to serve my owne occasions & something over. I had wrote you how the price of Turky work cushions & carpets was but that my Aunt mistook & enquired for chairs & goeth not out again till to morrow. I heard yesterday by Mr Byndlos that he saw a Letter for me at the Posthouse but I cannot light upon it nor hear of it since nor what is become of it & therefore cannot understand whether you have ordered me any other business or no, for mine is now finished so as to come away upon a days warning. As for news I cannot write you so certain as I judge you have already, for reports are to this day infinitely various, howbeit tis certain that the hospitalls are very full of wounded men.[42] Here is not yet any danger of pressing if there be I shall be very carefull of my selfe nevertheless I would not care how soon I were at home. If there be any

[42] A reference to the Third Anglo-Dutch War, 1672–74 and possibly the result of the Battle of Solebay, 28 May 1672.

presse I will not lye at my Aunt's:[43] If you please to speak to the Carrier to bring me up a horse next week that I may have him next Thursday come sevennight in the morning. I shall God willing be at Tunbridg the same night, I am not willing to stay any longer. I intend to lodge there at Petly's at the signe of the Bull. Tis hoped there will be no pressing yet for severall of the Seamen are dismissed for the present (till the ships be fitted) & walk the streets daily. My Aunt remembers her love to you, she is well with my Cousins & selfe thanks be to God. I have no more but my humble duty to your selfe, love to friends & Earnest desires of your welfare

Your obedient son
Sa: Jeake

To his honoured Father Mr Samuel Jeake in Rye in Sussex

[50] *Samuel Jeake junior to Samuel Jeake senior, 6 June 1672. Original letter.*
ESRO FRE 4842

London, June 6th 1672
Dear Father
Yours of 1st instant came not to my hands till yesterday; when I had received (after 3 times attendance) £7 of Mr Norton in payment of the bill, & therefore shall not now need any of Jn° Swaine. The Guineys I did put away for 21s 6d. we have Enquired the price of Turky work cushions were asked 5s for a good large one without the back the carpets being different according to their bigness. As for news of the Fight I have none of the best intelligence the best accompt I can give concerning the English is that many Commanders are killed, the Henry 'tis said had not one officer left alive. The E[arl] of Sandwich most say is lost, his ship the Royal James is agreed on all hands to be burnt.[44] Capt Digby, son to the E[arl] of Bristol slain & Sir Freshevile Hollis,[45] the Ld Maidstone, & sevral of the Gentry the French they say never came up. The number of men slain some estimate at 6000 of which almost 1000 in the Royal James. Here have not been any publick demonstrations of joy shown since the

[43] Probably referring to his aunt Elizabeth Bonnick. Her husband, Nathaniel, had died in October 1670. She would marry Christopher Dighton, a glazier, in March 1673. Smart, 'Biographical Sketch', 79.

[44] Samuel was referring to the indecisive Battle of Solebay off Southwold, 28 May 1672, when the Royal James was attacked by a fire ship. The Earl was indeed lost, his body was washed ashore after the battle and he was buried in Henry VIII's chapel in Westminster Abbey. J. D. Davies, 'Montagu, Edward, first earl of Sandwich (1625–1672)', *ODNB*.

[45] Sir Frescheville Holles, commander of the Cambridge, also killed at the Battle of Solebay. J. D. Davies, 'Holles, Sir Frescheville (1642–1672)', *ODNB*.

fight. Of the Dutch I have no certain news. My Aunt hath not heard any thing of her sonne, but the ship he is in is said to come to Queenborough; I wrote to you the 4th instant which I hope you have received but lest it should not come to your hand pray sir fail not to speak for an horse of the Carrier which I may have this day sennight, & ride to Tunbridge the same day. I have to day received the other £5 due on the bill of Mr Norton, who presents his service to you. But Mr Langley hath disappointed me, I intend to call upon him ere long. We are thanks be to God in health. My Aunt remembers to you, with my humble duty to your selfe, love to Thomas, his mother &c and desires of your welfare is all at present from

Your obed[ien]t son
Sa: Jeake, junior

To his honoured Father Mr Samuel Jeake in Rye in Sussex

[51] *Samuel Jeake junior to Samuel Jeake senior, 11 June 1672. Original letter.*
ESRO FRE 4843

London June 11th 1672
Dear Father
Yours of the 6th instant received & am glad to hear you had mine of the 4th since which I wrote you [word lost] the 6th in answer to yours of the 1st which I hope is come safe to your hands. Mr Langley hath not yet paid me the money I went thither last Thursday, he was not within, his wife said they had not so much money then as would pay if off but her husband should bring it me, yet I question whether I shall have it ere I come away. My Aunt & cosin Sarah remember to you, Cannot hear any news of Cosin Sam: he went in the Constant Warwick which tis said is come up to the Buoy of the Nore, I intend (God willing) to be at Tunbridge on Thursday night. Not else but my humble duty presented to your selfe as being

Your obed[ien]t son
Sa: Jeake

Tis said the French have taken Arnhoym and Nimmegen.

To his honoured Father Mr Samuel Jeake in Rye in Sussex

[52] *Samuel Jeake senior to Samuel Jeake junior, 17 July 1673. Original letter.*
ESRO FRE 4844

Son,
These are only to let you know I got well to London on Wednesday but when I shall be at home I cannot well say having some other business then I knew off ere I came & have some thoughts of going to Maidstone if things concurre in order thereto remember me to Mr Boys & tell him his son presents him his duty & is well with his family. His horse will be sold you may tell him & if he can by any conveniency send me a horse next weeke to Maidstone to be there on Thursday then I would come thence God willing on Friday if he cannot [word struck out] send me one to be there accordingly then do you write me to be here by next post on Monday & speake to Slowman on Monday to send me up a Horse to be here next Thursday. Tell Mr Miller I thinke I shall bring home his Rings againe I am offered so little for them remember me to him & other friends in general as if named. I have no newes to write you save the story of the press in the countrey was more then I have found here unlesse for seaman but is less now than formerly ere the fleet was fallen downe I enquired of Marke Chiswell & he went home the day I came out of Rye, and I heare hath got his two men released & you may tell Mrs Cadman she may expect him home the first faire winde. I am in hast but remaine

Southwarke — Your truly lo: father
July 17th — Sa: Jeake
1673

To his lo: sonne Samuel Jeake in Rye Sussex

Samuel's first ventures into trade, 1674

[53] *Christopher Blackwood to Samuel Jeake junior, 18 April 1674. Original letter.*
ESRO FRE 4845

Dublin Aprill the 18th 1674
Lo: Cozin:
I have yours per sea of the 6th Instant which was right truely welcome to mee: I ame heartily Glad to heere of my uncles and your welfare; though truely I must needs acknowledge my Greate neglect in not paying the tribute of those Great Kindnesses & favours I am indebted for to your father & selfe in my thankfull acknowledgements in some lynes unto you; but it was not for want

of any Reall & Cordiall respects but onely Loth to putt you to an Extraordinary Charge haveing onely my hearty wishes to recomend unto you: & the desier of understanding your welfare.
Since my being with you it hath please God by his providence wonderfully to blesse mee & direct mee: in my Imployment of ~~Mer~~ Merchandizeing which I tooke in hand and doe now follow: I am still a single man: & yett in noe provible way as to my owne Intentions of Changeing my Condition: Though I doe keepe house & my mother is with mee: & in Good helth who desiers her hearty recommendations to my unkle & your selfe. I understand your Intentions as to Asume Merchandize for your Imployment: the Lord direct you in that which is best, & if you be any ways Intending to Enter Into a maryed Estate [word struck out] my hearty well wishes Attend you; & as to your Imployment you Intend: Assure your selfe that if in any respect it Lyes in my power to serve you: either in these partes or Else where: it ~~should~~ shall not be wanting to the utmost: & shall bee acknowledged but as a parte retaliation of those obligations: wherein I stand Ingaged [to] my unkle & your selfe: & I am suer: [words lost] these partes I am at present as capa[ble] [words lost] to pleasure you [word illegible] any things you should in joyne mee: as [word lost] one is: I am sorry to heere of the scarcity of Corne with you: thanks be to God who affords us heere both plenty & liberty to the full. My brother Timothy wife & children are well & desiers to be kindly recomended to my unkle & your self with my Reall Service to my unkle & hearty respects to your selfe: I haveing beene to prolix sh[all] not ad but that I am

Your assured truely lo:
Chr: Black[wood]

Excuse the necessary charge of postage for I knew noe other wayes of conveyance

For Mr Samuell Jeake Junior at Rye in Sussex, these.
Rye forward per post to Lond 6d.

[54] *Christopher Blackwood to Samuel Jeake junior, 27 June 1674. Original letter.*

ESRO FRE 4846

Dublin June the 27th 1674
Lo: Cousin,
I have yours of the 4th Instant And doe thankfully acknowledge your kinde remembrance of mee therein, as also your Cordiall respects therein expressed: I shall onely retturne mine in my harty recommendations to your selfe: &

Good father my unkle ~~for~~ without further complement for want of further Ability to manifest it though as to your Appology therein made: certainley is unessesary: where there is nothing obligeing from mee [word illegible]. I am heartily Glad to heere of [word struck out] my unkles & your welfare: and doe observe your Entrance & Intentions In trade: and as to what you write for my advise in, I must needs expresse the Begerlynesse of the trade of this country ~~as~~ in a few words: As to all Goods imported: and more essentially at this dead tyme in trade noe Goods imported heere will sell for mony, but at very long tyme: and then mony very hard to bee Gott: All Goods of the product of this country Exportable: must bee Bought with reddy mony, if to be had. As wooll, tallo, sable hids, tannd leather, & Butter: As for Hopps they are heere now very Low worth But £4 per hundred[46] & a meere Drugge at that to: & noe mony suddenly to be raised uppon them: they are subject to rises & falls heere according as with you in England: I would not advise you to send any not noe Lining's neither: nor Can I advise the comodity import that I thinke will turne to accountt any wayes to your satisfaction: reddy Cash is the onely comodity heere to buy up the Comodities of this Country, the prises of which I have underwritten: And now wee make £ 5 per Cent heere Ex[change] of our mony, provided it Lyes in London to Draw uppon it there: Sometimes the Ex[change] is at 7 & 8 & £10 per cent to according as it happens: My mother & Brother are well with his family & desiers their hearty recommendations to my unkle & your selfe with my hearty service to my unkle & respects to your selfe wishing you all health & happiness: I am

Your truely lo: Cousin & s[ervant]
Chr: Blackwood

Wooll is heere pretty low at variable prises according to the severall sortes. Tallos at £30 & £31 per Tunne the charge heere is aboute 40s per Tunne. Tanned Leather uppers at 6d, soles at 7d. Sable hids smale at 16 s p hundred with the Dutys of Both sable & tanned hids will be about 5d per hide. Butter if good at £28 per Tunne, the charge heere 20s per Tunne. The Ex[change] of mony for London at £5 per Cent.

For Mr Samuell Jeake Jun merchant at Rye in Sussex, these.
Rye forward per p[o]st to Lond 6d.

[46] 20 hundred[weight] = one ton.

[55] *James le Griell to Samuel Jeake junior, 12 July 1674. Original letter.*
ESRO FRE 4847

Mr Sa: Jeake Deepe[47] This 12th July 1674

Sir I have received yours of the 17th of passe what I have done for you when you was heere is nott worthy of eny tanks [*sic*]. According to your order I doe sent you by this baeror Robert Berthemew his vessell one baerrell of mealle accordinge to the nott here under which doest amont to the summe of £19 10s French which you shall plaese to pay to my good frind Mr Thomas Miller and agreed with him for the exchange as concerning glass pendants such commoditie arre nott of my trade and such businesse arre both att Paris from whense thatt Comme: In what ells I can serve you you must allwaisse command mee and shall ever ~~Remag~~ Remayne

Your most humble servant
James le Griell

One small barrell of mealle for the accoumpt of Master Jeake
Weighinge 225 lb tarre[48] for the barrel 21 lb

Is net 204 lb att £7 10s	£ 15 : 6
For the barrel and hoope worke	£ 1 : 10
For all duties	£ 2 : 10
and for portage	£ 4
	£ 19 : 10

When you shall send mee some bees wax, shall selle it the most I can att your most and best advantege.

Sir you shall have for agreeable my kind respect unto you I doe kindly salute you and rest your att command John Le Griell

To Master Samuell Jeake Junior in Rye
By en[closed] R. B whom G. S

[47] Dieppe.
[48] *OED*, tare, n. 2. The weight of the wrapping or packaging of goods which is deducted from the gross in order to ascertain the net weight.

[56] *Elizabeth Dighton*[49] *to Samuel Jeake junior, 8 September 1674. Original letter.* ESRO FRE 4848

Loveing Cosin after my kind love to thee this is to let thee know that I am not altogether unmindfull of thee cosin I have some perswadans that thy deare father might like hannah desir a son: and the Lord hath given him a son which he hath indued with wisdom and understanding in a great mesur above many and so he did the son of hannah for wee read that he did ministred before the Lord when he was a childe and thy deare father hathe known the holy scriptures from a childe: and thou hast been brought up with him and by him: as his dayly [word illegible]: and therefore it will be aspected that thou shoudlest be as a fruitful bough even a fruitful bough by a well: whose branches may well out run all thy fellow cosins: and I hop thou will labor after the same faith to dwel in thee that dwelt first in thy grandmother and after ward in thy father: and by what I have heard in thy mother also: as to the well that I [word illegible] thou hast been by is in on some the water of life that Christ hath given to thy deare father which hath been in him a well of water which hath its springing from a pressious Jesus: this is a samle [*sic*] token of my true love to thee and I pray cosin to give Mary this lettel letter and if she cannot read it then read to her: and Sarah hears also: and pray tel them what is missin in them it may be thy deare fathers eye may not always over them: so with cosins that thou mast know more of the Lord I take leave of thee and remain thy truly loveing

Aunt Elizabeth Dighton

Sept the 8 1674

[57] *James le Griell to Samuel Jeake junior, 29 September 1674. Original letter.* ESRO FRE 4849

Mr Sam: Jeake Jun Deepe[50] This 19th/9 September 1674

Sir I have received yours of the 21st passe by the which you give mee advis you had well received the barrell of maell I did sent you by R. Bartholomew and that you had paye to Mr Miller the £19 10s for which I have discharge you of them. I gave you many tanks for the paere of glowfs you have sent mee for my sonne I keese your hand and shall Remayne

Your most humble Servant
James le Griell

To Mr Samuell Jeake Jun in Rye

[49] See above, fn. 43.
[50] Dieppe.

[58] *Mary Freebody to Samuel Jeake junior, 14 October 1674. Original letter.*
ESRO FRE 4850

Sir
Cosin Jeak I am sory that tis my unhapines to be troblesam two my frends as I must be for I must beg the favor of you not two fail coming two Cranbrook the day and time apoynted two testifie my cosin your fathars hand and your own for my cosin made the mortgage and hee and you ar the only witnes as two it tis my childrens possions and a busines of great consarn it must not be omited because of the date of the comision and had bin soonar had not other disapoyntments fallen in of which I shall give farther acount when we meet at Cranbrook whear god wiling we shall be two make satisfaction for your troble and pains not douting but you will grant my reques with my husbands and my sarvis two you and our cosin sir I am your obliged frend

Mary Freebody

Benanden this
14 of October 1674

Pray fail not on sattarday by 8 or 9 a clock at the farthest

To Mr Samuell Jeake Jun at his house in Rie this with care and speed

Raising capital, 1676

[59] *George Castell to Samuel Jeake junior, 26 June 1676. Original letter.*
ESRO FRE 4851

Sir
I and my freinds was showed your land by John Inge: I wish I had known that you would a sold it halfe a yeare agoe: if the timber were standing I would give as much more for the land, as now I will doe. Sir my friends judgments are that you enjured your selfe by takeing downe soe much fine young Timber, which is a great wrong to you or they that shall have it (you might a taken 30 or 40 trees very well) for the growth of the Timber would be the choose of the landlord gaine in that place and if you had been a towner (considering the timber the fences take (you would not a cut [word struck out] now exsept you had proseeded to destroy the wood: your whooler timber: fine boosh tillowes[51] are cut for ages, it is true there is some fine tillowe left for other ages, but harly a nofe to suplie the farme for this, and I here that [Wayhouse] intends to cut

[51] *OED*, tiller or tallow a. to produce side shoots from the root or base of the stem.

the wood that is standing, and to leave the land, for hee hieres, a way to your land, and the man knowes that loses his way: at [word illegible]: and if great care be not taken, in the carrying out all this timber and wood and faggotts (the coppice are very thin of wood all Ready) by breaking and [word illegible] of [word illegible] will be much damnified, and the land is fit for little Else but wood. I did looke on John Inge house and land and the [word illegible] but now find the marle not good, with a elienge[52] plane: and hard to get a good Tenant not soo is it fit but for a Trade man or laborer if I bought your land lend to it I understood neere what hee gave for it, and I asked him where hee would expect of soo much money, and hee told mee no: hee could have more: but truly there are noe [word illegible] times to bye, a man doth not know whom hee has a bargain hee did cale at mee foure but I was not at whom: Our wood masters are doubtfull that within this 7 yeares that the price of wood will be much lease and [words illegible] lowe, but god be thanked for a plentie. Sir pardon my [word illegible] having considered the thinnesse of the coppice, and the great spoyle that will be made in them: and most of the land fitt for little but wood, and the plaine land that is no good [word illegible] neere; and great store of fences to be made and maintained with posts and [word illegible] and little timber left to doe it with, and I feare a tenant to seeke and there must be a batment of Rent, but however because I live neere, I will give you for your land fower score pounds provided you make mee a good title, and I will pay you money at lamasse day the first of August at Mr Hoppers in Tunbridge and if you will take my money pray send your writing and instructions to Mr George Hopper to be made againest that time. And I pray send mee an answer with out fayle on fryday next, by the post, to be left for mee with Mr Carter [word illegible] of Tunbridge because I shall cale for the money in, that shall pay you, this with my respects and my wife presented to you. I take my leave and remaine sir

Your sav[t] George Castell

Somerhill 26th June 1676

For Mr Jeakes the younger liveing neere the kingshead in Rye these delivered with speede and care

[52] Possibly elenge, *OED* adj. 2. Remote, lonely, dreary or miserable.

[60] *Samuel Jeake junior to George Castell, 29 June 1676. Assumed draft letter.*
ESRO FRE 4852

Mr George Castell Rye June 29th 1676

Sir
I have yours of the 26th Instant wherein ~~you offer me but 80 which is so~~ I perceive you under valued my land below what ~~without your advance we are not like to deale over the lesse~~ others that know the land have already found it to be worth but seeing you have taken the pains to view the Land & ~~that you desire a speedy Answer~~ write to me there about, I shall be out in the countrey next week, and will call on you at Somerhill on this day sennight being the 6th of July about noon where shall treat with you about it. I shall bring the writings with me which I do the rather because if we should deale I should be unwilling to send them lest they might be lost. Pray let me find you at home. Not else but my serice to your selfe & wife I remaine

Sir Your Lo: friend & servant
Sa: Jeake jun

To Mr George Castell at Somerhill in Kent. Leave this with Mr Carter the post at Tunbridge to be delivered as abovest

[61] *Elizabeth Dighton to Samuel Jeake junior, 16 July 1676. Original letter.*
ESRO FRE 4853

Loveing cosin
This to let you know that we have received your token and letter and we do find therby: that it is sent to my daughter: securely it is very welcome: and we do take it as a very great kindness from you and cosin Mary both: and give you both thankes for it: I hop you will never want it againe: it is wonderfull mercy that even wee were brought forth in a land of plenty both for soule and body: O that wee may walke worthy of such mercy and not foolishly requite the lord as I may say I have so oft done: the lord be with you and guid you in the narrow way which leadeth to life and when you have enter through the strait gate you will have a full reward for al your good works: then is not a alme forgoten if it be but a cup of could watter: I hop my Brother is well I should be glad to see a letter from him. Wish my husband and my kind love to him and son and daughter servis: and all our kind love to you and Cosin Mary. I remain your ever

Lo: aunt Eliz Dighton

July the 16

Thankes be to the lord wee are all pretty well at present Mr kennedy son was buried 10 weeks agoe he have lost his mother wife and son he is now sengel agane if Mrs Miller can doe him a kindness to [see] him to a good wife for he doth deserve on: and I know not but it may comfort him now in his grife. My love to him.

Cosin I doe [word illegible] you would does me that kindness as to by me 6 paer of [word illegible] when the new saltfish come to use and what mony you lay out for me send word how I shall pay it so I would not have of the [word illegible] sort but indeed on lettel one: and let them be put up safe:

This for her very loveing cosin Mr Samuel Jeake in Rye

[62] *John Wagon*[53] *to Samuel Jeake junior and senior, 29 September 1676. Original letter.* ESRO FRE 4855

Loving Bro & Cosin Pembery September 29th 1676
Yours of the 2nd & 3rd of August I received wherby I understand that you have sould the Land unto Mr Castell & that you desire me to pay the Mich[aelmas] rent to him which will not be conveniant for me to doe because I have suffered much damage by the workmen & carryers in rutting open severall hedges & leaveing opent the Barrs & other fences soe that I had a piece of oats quite spilt & a piece of wheat very much dampnified & alsoe in the pasture I hope you doe not desin that I should bear the loss of it & if I can requir nothing of Mr Castell & therfor aply my selfe to you who I hope will allow me what in equity I shall deserve & I desire noe more now. Pray let me know your Answer by the next soe with my kind Love & respects to you both I rest

Your Loving Brother & Uncle
John Wagon

These for Mr Samuel Jeake at Rie

[53] John Wagon was brother-in-law to Samuel Jeake senior. Wagon was married to Frances Jeake's sister Elizabeth, see Appendix B.

[63] *Thomas Miller to Samuel Jeake junior, 7 November 1676. Original letter.* ESRO FRE 4856

Rye the 7th Nov: 1676
Mr Sa: Jeake
Sir I am sorry our master Holmes hath lost his oppertunity, these are to advise you nothing was wanting in me, but munday morning was his time which can not now be recovered, these are to desire you to se if you can get a boate at Hasting that will carry them on bord, if Rob: Moore should com with his vessel into the road and at what price per barrell for I feare we must do so at last for I feare Holmes fech she. Praye do what you can to get on, these are also to advise you that I have just now agreed with Mr Lewis Gillart Junior for what quantity of Red Herrings we shall want at 22s per barrel all full & very good ware, so that if you have not bought any more herrings I would advise you not to bye any more then to make up just 120 barrells of full repacked, and the shotton[54] only to full packe them for London market & we will fill up the vessel with red heare Mr Gillart hath about 30 barrells if we can take them all in we may have them. I have acquainted your Father with it who doth very well approve of it, if this com to you before you com out of Towne faile not to se to get a boat or at least to know if a boate can be had if we should so do & at what price per barrell & if it be late before you com home you shall be shure of comming over the ferry for I will speake to Joseph the ferryman to waite for your coming tho late. My respects to you & to my Cousans, I rest

Sir Yours to Comand
Tho: Miller

To Mr Samuel Jeake Merchant At Mr Naldreds house in Hasting, Sussex

Family matters, 1677–1678

[64] *Elizabeth Dighton to Samuel Jeake junior, via Richard Freebody, 20 July 1677. Original letter.* ESRO FRE 4858

My deare and loveing Cosin
This to let you know that I did deliver the token to her to whom you sent it and she doe give you many thanks for it: She wish you may have it made up to you again: so I hop you will have it made good to you: and much more for that: either in this life or in that which is to come: for God is not forgetfull of

[54] Shotten. *OED*, 3a. a herring that has spawned.

your labor of love which you have [showed] to any of his poore ones: I was a dream last night that Mrs Weekes had me to her house and me thought when I came there was to spits of meat at the fire: I was thinking this morning whether ther might be weding then or no. I pray you when you see her and Mrs Mary to remember me kindly to them both and give them my thankes for ther love to me and to my frend: when wee were at ther house: he remembers to you all and write to that he thinke to come home shortly: So with my husband and my love to your father and selfe and Cosin Mary: and son and daughter service to ther unkel and love to ther cosins

I am in hast but remain your
very loveing aunt Eliz: dighton

July the 20
1677

For Mr Richard Freebody in Rye in Susex pare give this letter to my Coz Samuel

[65] *J. Relfe to Samuel Jeake junior, 15 August 1677. Original letter.*
ESRO FRE 4859

Sir
Yours of the 13th instant I received, but not until this present day being Wednesday after 5 of the clocke in the Afternoone. By yours I understand that your Fathers fitt proved worse that day I left you then wee expected that it would be, as alsoe you let me know what happened to him unto the time that you wrott your Letter. Sir I hope that the many stooles that you mention were criticall & soe a benigne action of nature in casting out what was inimicatiall to it; for in all Evacuations there is some expense of vitall spiritts with the offending matter, even in evacuating of purulent & corrupted humours from an Imposthume in the externall parts of the body as Mr Gee can tell you. And that I apprehend is the cause of his much increasing weaknesse & faintnesse. Many alterations may happen since you wrott your Letter, therefore I know not what to advise you to better, then to continue the use of strengthening & cordiall meanes. I doe long to heare further how it pleaseth the Lord to deale with him. I have not else at present who am

Cranbrooke Aug
15th At 7 at night 1677

Yours to serve you to my
power J Relfe

Sir pray remember me to your Father, my Cosin Boys, Mr Miller, Mr Gee, & all other Friends with you, & if you have any new Intelligence for France or elsewhere, to give me 2 or 3 lines of it.

To Mr Samuel Jeake Jun in Rye these

[66] *Samuel Jeake senior to Samuel Jeake junior, 23 February 1678. Original letter.* ESRO FRE 4862

Loving son
These are only to acquaint you that through mercy I got well to London this Afternoone about 4 a clocke our Company riding but softly & Mr Crouch desires you would let his family know that he got well up also. I can write you no news yet for the war[55] the talke is as various here as in the countrey & wayers. I heare at the Coffee houses some for warr & some for peace, Cosins here are in different but Cosin Mackley's little one is dead, & Cosin Jane hath got a cold. My horse carried me very well & I am not very weary. Remember me to Cosin Freebody and his wife & Cosin Mary & all my friends that aske after my welfare not else but my kind love to you & hearty desire of a blessing on you all in hast I subscribe
London Febr 23th
1677/8

Your lo: father
Sa: Jeake

To his lo sonne Samuel Jeake in Rye Sussex these

Trading in Tallow, 1678

[67] *Christopher Blackwood to Samuel Jeake junior, 23 April 1678. Original letter.* ESRO FRE 4864

Dublin Aprill the 23rd 1678

Deare Cousin
I have yours of the 11th Instant And am rejoyced to heere of my unckle & your welfare I observe the Contents is for Information of the trade of this place In Genererall And for mee at this juncture to Give you a phuller account of trade heere or rates of Goods would bee. Wholy on uncertainties for this Longer suspicion of A warr with France putts A Delema on all Trade here, till wee see what the results will bear In Generall I would not Advise you to

[55] Possibly a reference to the Franco-Dutch war, 1672–8.

Concerne your selfe in Any Goods whatsoever to Importe them heere for the trade of this countery is to sell all Imported Goods at Longe trust and badd pay of. And all Goods of the product of this countery wee are force to buy with our reddy money, nay, & Advance beforehand. Therefore if you Concerne your selfe heere, it must bee in hides tan'd Leather Tallow Butter Beefe Salted Mutton & Wooll. Now in the paying for said Goods, you may Either remitt your mony By Bills you may take up at London on this place, or by ordering your correspondent heere to drawe for the same on London and In soe Doeing you Advance In profitt by the Ex[change] from £5 to £10 per Cent. In retturneing your mony over hither, and that is according as the Current of the Ex[change] happens heere and In London. Now the times of the yeere for beeing concerned in said Goods are for Leather all the yeere round dewty heere 6s per hide besides some small contingent charges. Rawe hides from Michaelmas to Candlemas, dewty 6s per hide. Beef & mutton from Michaelmas to Candlemas, dewty 12s per Barrell, tallow to be had all the yeere but the plentyfullest tyme is from Michaelmas to Candlemas, dewty 18s per hund. Butter the best tyme is from Midsummer to Michaelmas the dewty 6s per hund. As for wooll it will not Lye in your way to deal there in Comitions heere for Exportations are at £2 ½ per Cent, there are some contingent charges in the exportation of said Goods as at all places and for the freights, its Divers according to the places you Designe for And applenty of shipping are to bee had for mee to Give you the rate of Goods as they now are signe-fyes not for if wee have A war all Goods with us will imediatly fall: if noe war then all goods will immediatly Advance againe. Now if there bee A war your Hazard will bee very Greate in trade especially from heere to London very Dangerous. In time of peace, freight for London is commonly from 32 to 36s per Tunnes. I suppose you may have much A Designe on Tallow the rates whereof are very uncertaine, according as marketts are Abroad, soe it Advances or falls heere and I have knowne it to varey heere soe much as from £22 to £36 per Tunne. Coz Assure your selfe In any things you may freely Command mee and assoone as wee have some settlement concerning this war you shall heere from mee fully, as to phuller rates of Goods as also advise as to plausible Designes soe farr as I Apprehend and in the Interime, if you Ex[change] A Letter now and then desireing Information, as to any phuller Designe you have thoughts of, or any phuller comodities you shall have my full Answer thereto. I have been Married this 12 months past & have one Daughter. With tenders of my Humble service to my Good unckle & hearty respects to your selfe I am

Your moste Affectionate Lo Cousin
& Humble Servant
Chri: Blackwood

If you Designe any trade heere, I shall also Direct you in ordering your mony to best advantage in the Ex[change] which often proves as much advantage, as the profit by the Goods. There is now Advantage in the Ex[change] of mony from £8 to £9 per cent.

For Mr Samuel Jeake Jun Mercht in Rye in Sussex

[68] *Samuel Jeake junior to Christopher Blackwood, 9 May 1678. Copy of letter made by Samuel Jeake.* ESRO FRE 4866

Rye May 9th 1678
Lo: Cousin
Mr Miller & myselfe, are intended to send to Dublin in Ireland for a small parcell of Tallow to be brought to London & disposed off there. If you think meet to venture you shall have a part with us. I suppose Cos: Freebody will also be interested in it; we shall send now only for a Triall that if it please God it prove of any advantage we may gain some experience & prepare for a greater Quantity the next winter it being the best time to buy in Irel: between Michaelmass & Candlemas. And therefore we now shall not exceed a Tonne apiece at most if so much what we order. If you write your mind you shall have equal with any of the partners. I desire your answer next post for the Exchange now being between 8 & 9 per Cent profit to remitt moneys into Ireland we think to give order assoon as your answer comes to hand. Pray with all advise mee how Irish Tallow bears prices in Lon[don]. ~~We cannot promise ourselves~~ If you have any intentions of joyning in with us I shall in my next God willing acquaint you of our proceedings about it & so from time to time [words struck out]. We are all through mercy in health & hope the like of you & that littler Cousin Tho: is upon recovery. With respects I remaine

[69] *John Mackley to Samuel Jeake junior, 11 May 1678. Original letter.* ESRO FRE 4867

Southwark May the 11th 78

Lo Cousin
Yours I received and tharby understand you be minded to send to Dublin in Irland for a small parcell of talow which I am Free and willing to bare a part with you and the others whom you have menshoned in such a parcell as you write of that tharin we may see how our Corospondant doth Deale with ous in sending that which is good and then as we like to Rosgoe for a bigger parcell one thing I would disier of you to give order it may be put up in prity

bige Caske for if thay be small Caske we shall Luse by them in tear[56] for I thinke the Custom howse Doth alowe but £12 per hundred tear hear so the bigger the Caske be the beter, I am to waye of a parcell of Irish talow which Came from bristowe one Tusday next which Coste me 37s a hundred. I doe not knowe of any that hath bein Bought Cheaper. I hear it is worth but 32s a hundred att Bristowe it is my mind and som others that I have discoursed that if we have a war it will be Cheaper for we have always knowen it to be so, but if no war I think it will be Rather dearer. We are all through marcy in health excep my sonn who hath the small pox & was blind with them 3 dayes but thanks be to God he is pretty well and Doth Come Dowen in the kiching & we have much adoe to kepe him out of the shope my sarvis to my uncle & Kind love to youre selfe & other Relaitions. I Rest & Remaine

Youre Loving Cousin
John Mackley

A too hundred Cask thay alow 24 lb & I have known such Caske way 36 lb. If the Caske be beg or lettel that is the tear the Custom howse alowes if they be 4:5:6 or 7 hundred or thar aboute it will be best.

To his Loving Cousin Mr Samuel Jeake Junior in Rye Sussex

[70] *Samuel Jeake junior to Christopher Blackwood, 14 May 1678. Assumed draft letter.* ESRO FRE 4868

Rye May 14th 1678

Respected Cousin
By yours of the 23rd past I have to satisfaction your full answer to my former since which I have communicated my intentions to those that will be interested with me with such goods as I shall send for from Ireland to London whose names you have at foot: and having last post received advise from London that Excha[nge] continues good for Ireland, with an accompt of the present price of Irish tallow in London being at £37 per Ton. We have concluded that though it be not the best time of yeare to buy in Ireland yet to try now with a small parcell that if it please God to give success with it may be preparatory to a greater quantity after Michaelmas. And therefore I do hereby order you to buy for my selfe & Company 4 Tonnes of good Tallow at the best rates the present market with you will affoord. In your Choice whereof do as for your selfe that it may be good white & well tryned into the Cask & such as is fitt for London market & be pleased when bought to ship the same in the first good English vessel bound for

[56] See fn 48, above.

London marked MCo & consigned to Mr Jno Mackley Tallow chandler in Tooleys Street neer London bridge in Southwark, London. Pray ~~but it~~ let it be in great Cask or 5. 6. & 7. hundr with the Cask which saves us something at the Customehouse in the tare. And for the cost please to draw on me & Company at the usuall time of payment payable in the house of the said Jo: Mackley London for which you may take the best Excha[nge] that presents to my advantage. I should have remitted but that it would have been impossible to have fitted the money exactly & this being only for a Tryal we know not how our Resolutions will be to continue the trade. I hope the profit of Excha[nge] may not be much less to us for being drawn on. Moneys were remitted from London last week to Dublin at 10 per % profit. Pray put the order hereby given you in Execution with all convenient speed & without hesitation. I have fully considered of the suspences and demurr on Trade you write of & fear not that hazard you mention. Let not uncertain Rumors delay your following my order, I think the Excha[nge] can never be better for me [words struck out] My partners are Mr Tho: Miller & Mr Rich Freebody of Rye & the said Mr John Mackley to which last consign the goods as above & send the bill of Lading but the invoice enclose in yours to me. My Father & selfe are through mercy in health & presenting your selfe with our respects & congratulations of your mutual happiness. Expecting your answer per first I remaine

Sir Your most affectionate Cousin
& most faithful humble servant
Sa: Jeake jun

[71] *Christopher Blackwood to Samuel Jeake junior, 25 May 1678. Original letter.* ESRO FRE 4869

Dublin May the 25th 1678

Deare Cousin
I have yours of 14th Instant & observe your orders to buy 4 tunns of tallo, to send to London. I should redily observe your orders but at this tyme of yeere, its seldome freight is to bee had for London, and at present none at all is to bee had heere being one vessell heere, but shee was fully loaded before your orders came, for though at tyme of yeare vizt after Michaelmas when goods are to bee had then plenty of freight is to bee had for London; But till then I Doubt I shall get noe freight for your 4 tunns of tallo unlesse I should freight a whole vessell off, which is beyond your orders & also such a Quantity of tallo could not nowe bee perused therefore I shall wave buying any untill I meet with opertunity of freight which when it happens I shall fullfill your orders in Buying 4 tunns of tallo for you, consigneing it as Directed & Drawe

on you for the mony. The Exch[ange] is heere at £8 pcent, it's comonly £3 per cent more Advance remitt from London then to Drawe heere, besides if I Drawe money, it must bee on Mr John Mackley in London Directly, whoe must accept & pay the sight is as common for to have bills presented at Rye though paid in London would occasion losse in the Exch[ange]. Tallo is nowe heere at £32: 10 per Tunn, it haveing kept up its price heere, this yeare beyond Expectation, soe that I feare, there will bee losse by it considereing the charges that you will not Gett soe much as the Advance of [the] Exch[ange] by it, therefore I shall wave y[our] orders untill I can meete with freight & then I shall fullfill them, unlesse, in the interime, I receive your orders to the conterary with humble service, to my good unckle and your selfe, I am

Your moste Affec^{t} Lo Cousin
Chr: Blackwood

For Mr Samuel Jeake Junior merchant in Rye in Sussex

[72] *Samuel Jeake junior to Christopher Blackwood, 22 June 1678. Assumed draft letter.* ESRO FRE 4870

Dear Cousin

Rye June 22nd 1678

In Answer to yours of the 25th past. If none [words struck out] Tallow in regard you had not have presented since & you have not bought [words struck out], before this comes to your hand. Then I desire you not to buy any for I will not venture to give such a price ~~at this time of year seeing it will come to late to London~~ now unless you had ~~there had an~~ [words struck out] met with a freight [words illegible] my former Letter. So if you have not bought before you receive this, I desire you to forbear, & do hereby make void any former order. I expect not an Answer at present but after Michaelmas when you find some good may be done, advise me without faile in time & I shall give you a new order. If you had bought you might have drawn on Mr Jo: Mackley directly giving him advise thereof though the way I proposed is usuall from France; And unless I lived in London my selfe I chuse to be drawn on rather then run the hazard of remitting. I have no more but respects to your selfe & good wife. I remaine

Dear Cousin your assured Lo: Cousin
& humble servant
Sa: Jeake jun

[73] *John Mackley to Samuel Jeake junior, 6 July 1678. Original letter.*
ESRO FRE 4871

Southwark July the 6th 1678

Lo Cousin
Youer I Received and tharby understand you are minded to lay by ouer Intenshon of Ireland while Michaelmas, I doe understand that then we shall lose the advantages that we nowe can make in the Returning of ouer money for it now goes att 10 per cent and att that tim marchant are Glad to Return att Even hand, if you & the Rest are willing as I am I would have you Give order by the nex post to them for to draw a bill for such a sum of money to by such a parcell of goods as you ordered be for and that it may be Redy to be shipped by the first that present, so then we shall have the advantadge of the Returns of money, and the advantedge of the bying ouer goods, Irish talow is worth £39 a tun, so as they write it would be best for me to Except and pay, I thinke it would for it will be a grate troble to send them to you, if you doe anything in it advise them to send me a letter that I may know thar hand, it being all but my sarvis to my uncle, we being all throw marcy in health, with my kind love to youer selfe & other Relations I Rest

Your Lo: Cousin
John Mackley

To his Lo: Cousin Mr Sam Jeake Jun in Rye Sussex

[74] *Elizabeth Dighton to Samuel Jeake junior, 17 August 1678. Original letter.*
ESRO FRE 4872

Loveing Cosin
I haveing had long knowledge of the poverty of a sober family and this yeare it hath pleased the Lord to lay sickness on them first on: on of the children: and after on the mother and then after on the father: and now the man is pretty well: the woman is downe agane and weaker than before and I feare much is come on them for want of food and with drinkeing water: and haveing mett with desapointments in the world by which they were low and under many temptation and in det: but now the distress is so great that I was thinking unles the Lord did open some way for them no lese I know not what they would doe: he tol me last weeke that he had sold some thinges: and in his wife first sickness he caryed the best of her things with wearing clothes to pane: and he pay us for the mony: and if they not be redeeme be that since the peance is up he shall lose them I did tel him I would doe some thing about that. But that will be littel to their present want: as I was comeing from him

you came on my mind: and the kindness which you had shew to Copland upon which I had thought to write to you to see if you would show kindness to this distressed case: I being sad in thoughts about it that saying which the man said to Christ: if thou cant doe any thing come and help: me thinks by this word given in to me to write to you the Lord show you the case more fully than I can write it since this I have met wish of and are about writeing of this wanton to you but this last night in my sleep and in my last dream I dreamed that you did put the mony in my hand for a poor body: and me thoughts a littel after Mr Miller come to me and put mony in my hand for the poor also: and then I awake and thought on my [dream] and on the case: and my starkness in writeing that which was so full intended: then I commended god had now quicken to write by a dream so I thought I would not delaye on day more. I could produce many words to promot this good worke but I thinke need not to you: it is but a littel while that the Lord will need to borrow money of us: a word to the wise I am in hast and must write less then I intended: so with my kind love to your deare father and selfe and cosins all freinds I remaine your very loveing aunt

Eliz: Dighton

Aug the 17th 1678

If you can get any mony of any body els I think it may be apeace of good serves to the Lord. Lately I have beg so oft of my aquaintance here for some poor that I cannot tel how to aske them agane.

Copland give you many thanks for the last and all the rest of your love to hear she said she hop god will make it good to you againe

I have sold but on [word illegible] of the bodes for 6 sillings which cost 6 sillings 6 pence and have had but half the money as yet. I know not when I shall sell the other they be so so hig price. I receaved 8 sillings 6 pences from Martha Grebell I hop she will be willing to tarry for her mony tel thay be sold.

[In Samuel Jeake's hand:] ordered Cos: Mackley to pay 10 s Aug. 20th 1678.

This for my very loveing Cosin Mr Samuel Jeake the younger in Rye

[75] *John Mackley to Samuel Jeake junior, 29 August 1678. Original letter.*
ESRO FRE 4874

Lo Cousin
According to youer disier I have Inquieried & have not any nues of the aRiviell of the Shipe as yet but being bisiey this day could not Inquire but doe Intende to make Inquiery tomorrowe of Mr Claude Hays, and when I hear of the aRivell to send you word. I have Received youer 2 letters and allso a bill of Laden whearing I understand what fraight to pay & shall take care to and gite a friend that shall direcke me in the entry of them, as to ouer markets they are fall Conceveable & therefore disier a Lien from you by the next post what I shall doe in it, as to sell ore to lay by for I canot make above 36s or 37s per cent at most & if it had bein heer aboute 3 weeks agoe I could have mad 39s per cent, so acording as you order I shall doe my best in selling it, my thinkes thay bought att a very hie prise more than I heare hath being given thare. My sarvis with my wives to my Uncle with kind love to youer selfe being Glad to heare you are in hope of amendment. I wrest

Youer Lo Cousin
John Mackley

August the 29th 1678

To his Lo: Cousin In Samuel Jeake Junior in Rye Sussex

[76] *John Mackley to Samuel Jeake junior, 12 September 1678. Original letter.*
ESRO FRE 4875

Lo: Cousin
Youers of the 7th Instant I Received and also my Uncles and acordingly have payed the bill Mr Miller Drawe one me for £7 19s and Intrest. Thanks be to god ouer talow is arrived the vesell doth lie att Dise Key.[57] I have this day intred the talow and I think it will be Landed tomorrow. I have some that doe Intend to see it tomorrow so when I have sould I shall give you a further acount pray Remember my sarvis to my uncle and aquante him that I have sould the [word illegible] att 11 ½s & thar was £47 so I had for them 45s. Mrs Gant hath not as yet Coled for the 20s my Uncle ordered me to pay her, my Aunt had 10s of me. We are all blessed be god in health but sorey to hear you

[57] Dice Key, London.

have gotton an ague & Couteney[58] so weake it being all but disiering the Lord to give you stranth & Restore you againe to helth. I wrest

Your Lo Cousin
John Mackley

Southwark Sept. the 12th 1678

Pray Remember my Kind love to all ouer Relaitions & to Mr Miller. Hear is the bill for my Uncle.

To his Lo: Cousin Mr Samuell Jeake Jun in Rye Sussex

[77] *John Mackley to Samuel Jeake junior, 18 September 1678. Original letter.*
ESRO FRE 4876

Southwark September the 18th 78

Lo Cousin
My kind love with my wives to you, with ouer sarvis to my Uncle hoping youer helth as blessed be god we are att present theas are to Lett you Knowe that I have sould the fore Grate Caske of talow att 36s per cent thay take them att Irish wt & tare only I alowe 2s one a Caske super tare & the other 13 I have taken home to my selfe & will take them att that prise only I thinke you must alowe 3s one them for by the Kings coine I fall shorte in every Caske in wt. I would have sould more but I could not be bid above 35s 6d for the Rest. Ouer markets are solowe I do hear thar is a parsell sould sences for 35s a hundred, how ever I ame free to take them to my selfe. I shall Received the money for thowes fore a Monday & as for my money it shall be Redy in a fortnight so you may Caste up what it Comes to by youer Invoyes & Charge me Dr: I Rest

Youer lo Cousin
John Mackley

[58] Continue.

An account by the Kings Coine of the wt			An account of what mony I have laid out	
No. 1 =	4 = 3 = 00			£ s d
2 =	4 = 3 = 10	May the 9	paid for a letter	00 = 00 = 02
3 =	4 = 2 = 12	25	paid for a letter	00 = 00 = 02
4 =	8 = 3 = 00	July the 16	paid for a letter	00 = 00 = 04
5 =	8 = 0 = 22	16	paid to Mr Mounke	25 = 00 = 00
6 =	4 = 1 = 8	August 20	paid for a letter	00 = 00 = 02
7 =	2 = 0 = 16	27	paid for a letter	00 = 00 = 04
8 =	4 = 2 = 0	Sept 7	paid to Mr Tillotson	07 = 19 = 00
9 =	4 = 2 = 10	7	paid for a letter	00 = 00 = 04
10 =	4 = 1 = 0	11	paid for Custom of 4 tun	03 = 03 = 04
11 =	5 = 2 = 0	11	paid for writing a bill	00 = 00 = 06
12 =	8 = 2 = 0	11	paid for bill mony	00 = 02 = 06
13 =	6 = 0 = 16	12	paid to the Landwater[59] for Bill Mo:	00 = 02 = 00
14 =	4 = 3 = 3	12	give to those that wayed	00 = 00 = 06
15 =	2 = 1 = 15	12	paid to the Cuper for huping & heading som	00 = 01 = 06
16 =	3 = 0 = 10	12	paid too shilling a tun landing and warfidge	00 = 08 = 00
17 =	8 = 0 = 8		Spent	00 = 00 = 06
Grose	89 = 1 = 18	Septem the 18	paid for fraite & primidas & caridge	06 = 12 = 02
				43 = 11 = 04
				32 = 19 = 00
				10 = 12 = 04

GE	82 = 0 = 27	to alow	8 s one the 4 Caske
Tar	1 = 19	ditto	39 one the 13 Caske
Nett	81 = 3 = 08 att 36 per Cent	47	

36
486
243
291/6
145:16
1:7
2:7
147 = 5 = 7

All Limons hath be in a Grate fier that hath burnt above 20 howses. It broke oute one Wensday morning. Pray give my uncle Mrs Gants Res[pects]

To his Lo: Cousin Mr Samuell Jeake Jun in Rye in Sussex

[59] *OED* land-waiter or landing waiter n. a customs officer whose duty it is to superintend the landing of goods and examine them.

[78] *John Mackley to Samuel Jeake junior, 24 September 1678. Original letter.*
ESRO FRE 4877

Southwark Sept. the 24 1678

Lo Cousin

Youers of the 18 Instant Received and for Anser I will asuer you I have done Like a kind partner in ofring to take the Reste of the parcell att the prise I sould tho to my one Lose when I Can by Nuecastell talow att the same prise which is better talow, thou the Irish talow I would have sould more then I did Could I have Reched the prise. I ofred it to Sevrell that I ame aquanted with & we doe by together ofingtimes & thay would not give me more than 35s 6d & thought it would be a Grate kindness in them to take it so you write if I cane aforde it to give the 42s which you will be Lusers by it, truly I canot give any More for it is above the market what I ofer, yesterday I Received the Money for the fore Gr[e]at Caske of talow & one of them proves so Corse that he did say had he sein it he would not have Given above 32 s per cent it was so bad thay was all aborde the shipe when I sould them so thay take them by the numbers not seing what they Bought. Some of this that I have att home is very corse, as to ouer markets I doe not thinke thay cane be dearer for hear is a Grate dell of talow in London & more Irish talow Exported in Every day. I have Broken open 5 of the Caske & I have 8 hole that I have not Luked one so if you be wiling to venter the market those shall stand att ouer howse & if thar shall be any Rise this winter I shall doe my best to sell them as Dear as I can for you. I Cane doe no more than what I have ofred so I wrest disiring youer Anser by the next post.

Youer lo Cousin
John Mackley

I wonder ouer Correspondent shuld by so dear for ouse.

The charge for bring in howse of the 13 Cask
Cost me

	£ s d
For 2 Cartes	0 – 7 – 0
For loding	0 – 2 – 6
	0 = 9 = 6

Pray Remember ouer servis to my uncle & kind love to all ouer Relaitions.

To his Lo: Cousin Mr Samuell Jeake Jun in Rye Sussex

Making new contacts, 1679

[79] *John Cooke to Samuel Jeake junior, 26 March 1679. Original letter.*
ESRO FRE 4881

Exon 26th March 1679

Mr Sam Jeake Junior
Sir I am favoured with yours of 19th Current & with great readiness & satisfaction shall I embrace the honour of your correspondence & service here wherein you judge mee capable not only as you come recommended by my good friend Mr Thomas Morris of London but as by your style you manifest an ingenious disposition & as I have occasion of service in your partes, I shall address my selfe to you desiring att the season you would advise mee [your price] of hopps &c. as also whither for the present there are any ships about 25 the Marchant tonnage to be disposed off & whither you conceive a penny worth[60] may bee obtained wherein you will oblidge mee ever to approve my selfe

Yours att Com[man]d
Jn° Cooke 1678

To Mr Sam Jeake Jun Merchant in Rye pd 3d

[80] *Samuel Jeake junior to John Cooke, 3 April 1679. Assumed draft letter.*
ESRO FRE 4883

Mr John Cooke Rye Apr .3. 1679.
Sir as the obligation you have put upon me by your kind entertainment of my last devotes me to your service. To the character which though superior to my deserts you are pleased to honor me with by yours of the 26 past fills me with desire of opportunity to manifest at least in the sincerity of my service a supply of any failure in its merit. I shall not omitt God permitting to advise you the price of hops for the next season & in due time, being extremely satisfied in the Reflection of your favour so far as to intimate your making use of me in any concerns hereabouts, requesting the continuance of your good affections that I may be interested in the execution of such commissions as you shall find occasion to give in these parts & that your curtesy may likewise diffuse it selfe in procuring me those of your good acquaintance that may be subject to your influence. I have made Enquiry about such a ship as you mention, but find not one of that burden or neer it to be disposed off ~~nor indeed~~

[60] *OED*, n. 3a. a bargain or good return.

~~any that I can urge a [word lost] as times now are~~ that I can either commend for penny worth or [word illegible]. I deferr'd my writing ~~last post~~ on purpose last post to learn if any ~~had a mind to sell~~ that were worth your purchase would bee sold but I see myself not so happy to accomplish your desires herein. However if hereafter I meet with one, I shall not forget to advise you. In the interim I crave leave to subscribe

Sir Your most humb: & obliged servt
S. J. j

* ~~Here is one of~~ If you had occasion of one about 70 ton of ~~stowage~~ cask ~~w of dead wt or near~~ here is a very ~~a new~~ & good pinke[61] & well fitted & almost new ~~you had occasion~~ belonging to this towne one Rob: Nicholl mt which I saw one of the owners tells me will be sold & somewhat under £400 he saith have been bid £400 for her. I do believe were the times any think favourable she were a penyworth, but as they now are I know not what to say, though I believe her well worth what she will be sold for. If [you] have employment for one so bigg I believe she would do very well which you may consider of & if it will fit you [section damaged] or on the Receit of your answer I shall be ready to treat ~~with the owners~~ [words illegible] what service I can in treating with the owners.

[81] *Samuel Jeake junior to John Jewell, 15 April 1679. Assumed draft letter.*
ESRO FRE 4885

Copy to Padstow

Mr John Jewell Rye Apr .15. 1679.
Sir having not long since occasion to write to Mr Wm Jennens of Plimo[uth] I was requesting him to recommend me to a good correspondent in your parts, in answer to which he was readily pleased to direct me to your selfe. Whence I assume the liberty to give you the trouble of a Line or two to advise me the price of wheat now with you, & whether if I should find it worth while (on your information of the present price) [words struck out] to give order for a parcell. There be plenty & not like to be inhanced in the rates. I desire also an account of the correspondence of your measure & a different estimate of the price as you buy it of the country or when it is milled and the soyle & drake taken out. Red wheat is that which usually is sold with us if very good I praye therefore chiefly intimate the price of that & such as is good & new. [words struck out] And whether you will buy by Commission at 2 per % or keep

[61] *OED*, n. a. a small sailing vessel.

stores your selfe, which if you do at what rate you [wi]ll sell the best red wheat milled & free from soyle. If I find probability of a sale here I do intend when I heare from you or within some short time after (if the prizes you write me will beare it) to order a parcell to be bought the quantity I cannot yet resolve though twill not at most exceed 250 quarters Winchester[62] maybe but 200 perhaps not above 120 only would know ~~whether~~ if could have the greater quantity bought without a rise of the price or whether must have been shipped already & consequently be like to advance & also ~~whether~~ your harbour be good & fit for great vessells as well as small. As to the Cost if I should do anything I can order you where to draw in London & remitt money there which you may have in your hands before I send a vessell for I shall not send money by sea. I wait the honour of your answer per first which as it shall be thankfully accepted so if your owne affaires or friends should at any time be concerned in these parts I shall be ambitious to repay it with equal gratitude and never forget the obligation you will hereby put upon

Sir Yours att Command
S J junior

My name is Samuel.

[82] *Samuel Jeake junior to Major Childs, 19 April 1679. Assumed draft letter.*
ESRO FRE 4886

Copy to Major Childs in Gracechurch Street London Rye Apr. 19 1679
Since sir I had the happiness of seeing you in London I have been enquiring whether I could dispose of any madera wines at this place but find no great probability, they being neither used nor indeed well knowne here. Yet I met with one that told me he might buy if had a tast & did like it, so if you think meet to send * ~~a small bottle (less than a pint will doe)~~ by the Hawkhurst Carrier *(next Thursday) lodging at the Greyhound in Southwark a small bottle (less than a pint will do) of the very best, pure & ~~unsophisticate~~ unmixed I will try whether the tast will please him. If it doe & can fasten a pipe or haste upon him I shall order you by what vessell to send it & for what I buy shall ~~expect you~~ pay ready money expecting usage according [words struck out]. But if find it prove not acceptable to the country shall then desist & not trouble you with impertinences. Not else but that I am

Sir Your servt to Command
Sa: J j.

[62] *OED*, n. 1a. dry and liquid measures the standards of which were originally deposited at Winchester.

[83] *William Delamare to Samuel Jeake junior, 28 April 1679. Original letter.*
ESRO FRE 4887

To Mr Samuel Jeake junior Caen 28 April 1679
Sir I received but yesterday your Letter of the 29/19th of March: and the day before I received sum from London of the 20/10 of this month. So that if your said letter had required a speedy answer, the long staing of it by the way, might have caused a prejudice to your affaires, which accident I do intimate that you might prevent it hereafter. Being you are pleased to desire my corre-spond in this Town, I am very willing to accept any occasion to render you my service in whatsoever shall concerne you in these parts, and to that effect you may commande mee when you please but, as the affaires stand as yet between France & England, there is, I thinke, no hopes of sending any goods from hence to you, till the deffence of it be taken off in England, and I know not what could bee brought from your Town to Caen. So expecting then your further desire, and instruct about it, I shall in the meane time assure you of my service, and willingness to continue our correspondence togather, for which, I see, I am beholding to Mr Savary. I do send you this answer by the maister of a Vessel that is [going] from Caen to London, seeing there is no hast for it; and do direct my Letters to the said Mr Savary. If you any other friend in London to whom I may addresse my Letters to you hereafter, you shall bee pleased to let me know it by your first, and so remaine

Sir Yours at Command
Wm Delamare

For Mr Samuel Jeake merchant in Rie

[84] *Richard Pickersgill to Samuel Jeake junior, 2 May 1679. Original letter.*
ESRO FRE 4943[63]

Samuel Jeake
Sir,
Yesterday came to my handes your acceptable Lettre of 19/29 Marche, I doe verey muche wonder wheare whear it hathe Lain soe longe beinge come by way of diepe soe must be fault by him you delivert it to, for I none had aney lettres soe longe on the way from Rye Before this. I am muche oblidged to you for your kind ofer what Lyes in my power for your servis heare you may fre[ly] comand me, at all tymes as for Messrs Proctor & Sidgwicke & Morlaix as also Mr Godfrey in London there is noe neede to write them, nor nobody else

[63] Catalogued out of sequence, letter was catalogued as if sent in 1680.

about our Consarnes but if you please to informe your selfe of Mr Cadman or Capt. Hall I am verey well knowne by bothe.
Now Sir, as for what you desire which is fans & Jessemy gloves[64] with other things of the Like natur you know these Comodityes are desending in England yet since you are please to expleake your selfe soe muche I shall doe the same to you for the things you desire. Am Soure Noebody can fournish you better, nor cheaper I have drive the trade somme tyme and have a frind at Paris who I imploy that byes att the first hand and the best soe, if you desire, to make a tryall must send me a not of what you desire. Right Jessemy gloves will cost £12 the dozene, fannes according as they are in good not noe prise can be lemited if you can give me any incouragement, I will take somme in trust with you in case you desire it but you must send me a memoir what you desire which I shall be exact to observe soe at present shall not fourder [further] inlarge but remaine

Sir your most humble servant
Richard Pickersgill

Pray when have your ordres lett me know what way moust convay the goods.

To Mr Samuel Jeake Junior Marchant in Rye
By the Recomandation of your most humble servant D Lesport in Deepe the 2th of May 1679

[85] *James le Griell to Samuel Jeake junior, 4 May 1679. Original letter.*
ESRO FRE 4889

Mr Samuell Jeake Deepe this 4th May 1679
Sir your letter of the 19/29 March with divers letters in itt I have received butt this last voiage of this [baeror] John Jacob I do suppose that your said letter was wraitt long beefore your said letters I have sent them by the post according to their direction you do desire to have a friend or a good anist man and correspondence att Paris. If you plaece to make yusse of my friend Master Charles Derosnel marchant in St Denis Street. I am suere that hee will serve

[64] Jessamy is now known as jasmine. The Dictionary of Traded Goods is not clear whether jessamy gloves were so-called because they were coloured yellow or because they were perfumed with jessamy. In either case they were luxury goods. *DTGC*, 'Jessamy – Jinny screw'.

you well and anistly what shall laye in my power to serve you you shall plaece to command mee and shall Remayne

Your humble servant
James le Griell

To Master Samuell Jeake in Rye

[86] *Bernard Coudert to Samuel Jeake junior, 6 May 1679. Original letter.*
ESRO FRE 4890

Samuel Jeake Junior Nants, May 6th 1679
Sir I am Honoured with yours of the 19th March wherein I Doe obsarve By the Recommendation of Mr Claude Hays of London you are pleased to apply your selfe unto mee for your correspondant. In answer I doe acknowlidge my selfe oblidged unto Mr Hays for his kindness to Procure me your acquaintance when occasion shall present on the parts to sarve you may be assured of my Readyness with all the care & punctualitie that can be expected. In doeing my best Endeavour for Promotteing your Intrest as my owne. Our Brandys are this day sould att 45 lb 10s [words illegible] whitte from 80 to 85 lb the tyn, Best High country claretts from 88 to 100 lb the ton, [words lost] 95 lb Nante wines from 36 to 45 lb, Black Borneef Salt 20 lb. The charge croisie & Pouliquer 18 lb. the [word illegible]. If you order me to Loade any Goods for your account may bee pleased to remitte mee the Provision Bills upon Paris. If nott [word lost] order somes eminent freinds in London to accept my bills for your account. I [do] nott know what manifactures you have in your Parts that I may advise you as for Lead is att 30 [word illegible] the 100/00 Suffolk Butter 24lb the gall. I doe kindely value you & as for my commission I tacke 2 ½ per %

Sir Yours att Command
Bernard Coudert

I have forgotten to tell you that your letter dated of the 19th March I did receave it onely this day By addresse of Mr L'homme of Paris have a care of him for his Business were nott curr[en]t a whille ago. This for your Government.

To Mr Samuel Jeake Junior Merchand in Rye via London

[87] *Michel Savary to Samuel Jeake junior, 19 May 1679. Original letter.*
ESRO FRE 4895

London 19th May 1679

Mr Jeake
Sir
I have yours before mee of the 12th Instant per answer I have spoken with sume acquaintance, touching those things you writte of, I perseive will doe well to send them up, on such apart as you thinke good to Mr Mackley that the same may bee seen, for without no one will treate to any purpose, & farther tis high time to expose the fans Especially to salle, for if they bee not sold in a month will indanger to keepe them till next yeare & in that time, the fashons may differ which is your [word illegible] & if soe will indanger to loose by them this being the advise I can give you will accordingly [word illegible] as shall seeme good, if you send [word illegible] things, & you judge me cappable to serve in it, may freely Command him who is

Your humble Servant
Mich: Savary Jun

Pray bee pleased to present my humble Service unto your good father.

For Mr Samuel Jeake Merchant in Rye Sussex

[88] *James & John Hays to Samuel Jeake junior, 26 May 1679. Original letter.*
ESRO FRE 4897

M. Samuel Jeake Junior Calais the 26th May 1679
Sir
Wee have yours of the 6/16th Instant by which perceave that you beeing about desiring an acquainttance here, of our brother Cl: Hays of London[65] he hath directed you to us, In answer wee kindley returne you thancks of all civiletyes In case of any Concerns of ours in your parts, you may alsoe as any occasion offers to Dispose of us, whoe shall be glad to receave your Command in any tyme as beeing

Sir Your very humble servants
James & John Hays

Monsieur Samuel Jeake Le Jeune

[65] Claude Hays, a London business contact of Samuel junior's mentioned in FRE 4894, which is not included in this collection.

[89] *Samuel Jeake junior to Peter Swymmer, 29 May 1679. Draft letter, not sent.* ESRO FRE 4898

Mr Peter Swymmer Not sent Rye May 29 1679
Sir
Yours of the 13th Instant came to hand but yesterday, whereby perceive it difficult to buy any great quantity of wheat with you & the time of year is so far come on that we shall not have liberty if it could be bought to send a vessell from hence to fetch it. We see but one way to doe any good which in short is if you see any likelihood of buying a lesser quantity as of 200 or 150 or if not above 120 quarters Winchester, & can be certain to fit ~~freight~~ a vessell to what you buy it & freight her from Padstow to Rye with it for 2s the Winch[ester] quarter or thereabouts; If you judge it to be effected and could for a beginning buy 50 quarters or more of good wheat at 12 or 13 your bushel of 21 gallons as you write the price it was then its possible you might pick up enough in smaller parcells to freight a small vessell provided you can have one in your Port. And we should be content to advance to 14 your bushel if the cargo might be made up at different prizes not exceeding that. If you have any prospect of accomplishment it will be requisite to be very diligent & speedy & yet to do it without clamour, if you could make a beginning & buy some indiff[erent] parcells of the principal farms we hope the rest might comply & not advance much. We cannot allow more time for the buying & shipping it then a month after the receipt of this Letter. So if you can effect it as above you must not lose any time but fall to buying immediately with what privacy you can, And for moneys draw on Mr Walter Monkeat at the Goate in Lothbury London. Your bills shall be well paid, And if you fraight a vessell must agree with the master to stay 14 days at Rye & if you can get him under 2 s per quarter Winch[ester] but for a small matter we must not stand. We desire your answer per first & if you proceed then every post or two as the business goes forward. But if you see that neither such a quantity can be bought nor a vessell hired at Padstow then pray desist altogether & only favour us with a Line of answer.

[90] *Bernard Coudert to Samuel Jeake junior, 15 July 1679. Original letter.* ESRO FRE 4903

Mr Samuel Jeake Junior Nants Jully 15th 1679
Sir
I am Honoured with yours of the 19th Ultimo which I have this day Receaved By convoyance of Mr Richard Pickersgill of Rouen, I am sorrie to hear the Parliament hath noe Inclination of Reversing the Prohibition of French

Goods in your Parts, which Did Prevent you to Give your orders for Buying any Goods for your account, But when it Please God to send us againe an open Trade you may macke a Tryall of us & then may Be assured of my Readynesse to sarve you with the Best of my Endeavours for answering your Desires. If I had some occasions in your Parts I would Presume to accepte of your Proffers & though I have non In your Place I am noe lesse engaged unto your civillities for which I Doe Retturne you my Humble Thanskes. I kindely salute you & Remayne

Sir Yours att Command
Bernard Coudert

Brandy att 40lb the 29/8

To Mr Samuel Jeake Junior Merchant in Rye by via London

Negotiating Debts, 1679–1680

[91] *John Mackley to Samuel Jeake junior, 16 August 1679. Original letter.*
ESRO FRE 4907

Southwark August the 16th 1679

Lo Cousin
Youer of the 12th Instant Received with a bill which I have bein att the Exchange to gite it accepted but the marchant is oute of towen & will not be att home tell Monday so it is not as yet accepted & I was this Day att the Excise Office & spake to Mr Laurences & he Direcked me to another man which Informes me that Mr Johnson will goes Dowen in Sussex next weake & if I would pay the money hear he would give me a offices bill to be payed att sight by Mr Johnson. He telles me it is better to have affices bill then to have it Drowen by Mr Laurence. I thought it good furst to aquainte you of it before I payed the Money for I advisied which one & thay sayed thay would not Doe so So I thinke it may be the better way for you to Repay to Mr Johnson when he is in the Country to Gite him to pay you so much money & so to Drawe youer Bill one me & then you will be suer, but if you be satisfied other wayes send word & I shall proceed as you shall order. I have payed youer bill of 6:13 to Mr Robert Hayle I was with Mr Byndlos man & he hath not heared from Mr Gillart so he informed me latter it being all but mine with my wives kind love to you & sarvis to my uncle with love to other Relaitions we being got well at home but my sonn hath gote an ague and is very Bad. I wreste

Youers Lo Cousin
To Command
John Mackley

Marke Chiswell hath so layed his bissness that we canot come to spake with him thoues whear we have thought he hath layon hath Denye it & som that Doth knowe whar he is will not tell ous for thay say the Reison is thay understand thar is a Difference between ous he is afraid we will wrest him his wife has promised that he should come to ous but I beleve we shall not like of him.

To His Lo Cousin Mr Samuel Jeake Jun in Rye Sussex

[92] *Elizabeth Mackley to Samuel Jeake junior, 12 September 1679. Original letter.* ESRO FRE 4911

Lo: Cousin
these fue lines are of lett you understand that my husband hath bouth your stif and he did goe to Apotercarey Halle and the Gentell man did say that if he had not come in thy Gentell nam he would not have it for the prise and he had 25s for the haulf onces and sefapneces [sic] for the boll my husband hath som busens fell out more then we looked for soe that he could not give you an Acount for he is very hard at work. My humbell serves to my uncel with my due Respetes to your slef [*sic*] and my husband allsoe. I thenk the Lord my childeren be indefrent prer disire my uncle to Remember me in his pries my Lo: to sone I Ramin your lone [*sic*] Cozen and Sernt to com[mand]

Elizabeth Mackley

Sept the 12 1679

We will send it by Sloman this wake. This night my Coz Gofe is a bead of A grill se.

To her Respected Cos Mr Samuell Jacke Junior marchent in Rye in Susex with care

[93] *Elizabeth Mackley to Samuel Jeake junior, 14 September 1679. Original letter.* ESRO FRE 4912

Lo: Coz:
I am very sory that I should be soe unwordey as to send you A Letter Aboute your stufe and to forgeet it but I hope your Good nataer will pardon my unwordess but if it be possebol to get any body that will bring it safe to your hands I shall be very dilleinet [in] the sending of it by the furst ouptry I can get. Pare coz plesed to pardon me In this ~~unham~~ unhamson crime I much

Relie upon your good nuter and subcribe myself to be your Lo: Cozen and most humbull sernt to command

Elizabeth Mackley

Sept the 14 1679

My serves to my uncle & husband

To her Respted Lo: Cos Mr Samuell Jeacke Junior marchant in Rye in Susex

[94] *John Mackley to Samuel Jeake junior, 20 September 1679. Original letter.* ESRO FRE 4913

Southwark Sept. the 20th 79

Lo Cousin

Theas are to acquaint you that I have sente you Dowen the valantin salte of vipers[66] in a littell box. I ame sorey my wife shuld be so forgitfull as not to send it the weak before the acaision was she was coled to my Cousin Goffe & I was upe all the night at work so I hope you will not take it a mis frome ous I have maide Inquiery concerning the selling those things you write aboute & thay are not willing to by it being so late in the year, but I understand that he gives 22s & 24s & 26s a Dozen if thay bee good but hee is not willing to by them. I have payed the to bills one to Mr Briant & the other to Mr Carbine it being all but my kind love to youer good selfe with sarvis to my uncle & love to other Relaitions I wrest

Youers to Command
John Mackley

If I had not menshoned Esqe byol name, I had not bought the meadson which

I thinke is very Dear. I could not gite anything abated of	25s 0d
& I was forced to by a Bottell which cost	0 6
For a box	0 1
	25 7

I thanke you for writing for me to your Cosin I sent it by the post that night

[66] The flesh and skin of the viper, or adder, was used in a variety of preparations and was thought to have great restorative powers. Nancy Cox and Karin Dannehl, 'Viol – Vizard mask', in *Dictionary of Traded Goods and Commodities 1550–1820* (Wolverhampton, 2007), *British History Online* http://www.british-history.ac.uk/no-series/traded-goods-dictionary/1550-1820/viol-vizard-mask [accessed 7 July 2016].

Talow is now [worth] £42 a tun I hear, a [words lost] would not fech above [word lost] a hund[red].

To Mr Samuel Jeake Marchant in Rye Sussex

[95] *John Mackley to Samuel Jeake junior, 30 September 1679. Original letter.*
ESRO FRE 4916

Lo: Cousin
In Anser to yours of the 27th Instant I have this Day bein at Mr Hayes who I understand will now accept the bill which before he would not it was his man that Denied me & to Day he tells me that thay have Received order from Lointhier, who befor had ordered them not to accept any more bills till further order frome him so you may please to send it up & I will gite it accept & will send that & this I nowe have Dowen together tomorowe morning. I shall goe & Received this bill of £38 I have Discorsed Mr Savery & he telles me one the not accepting a bill I must proteste it presently & then you have the Law one him to make you satisfaction who In Doss it to you & so it goes frome one to aother tell it comes to him that was the Drawer to make good but he tells me if a marchant tells me I have nowe advise pray kept it a poste or to one would Gratifie so far as to Doe it but in so Doing you run a hazard for maybe the marchant may Brake & then you cannot protest it so as to make him make it good as you had it frome 2ly I may proteste it in youer name or my one which you thinke fite, thurdly you may come one after the proteste is maid & make him alowe all Charges, as for a bill that is accept if thay Refues to pay the money it must be protested before sun sete It being all but my kind love to y[our] selfe & sarvis to my uncle. I wrest

Your lo Cousin
John Mackley

Sept. the 30th 79

To Mr Samuel Jeake Junior Marchant in Rye Sussex

[96] *Thomas Morris to Samuel Jeake junior, 30 September 1679. Original letter.* ESRO FRE 4917

London the 30th Septem 1679

Sir & Worthy Friend

In answere to yours of the 27th Instant, I am heartily sorry you are like to have any trouble, ~~but~~ if the man be but good that you delivered your mony to, you will have the ~~the~~ loss, But your friend here ought to have had the Bill protested for non acceptance, before he has return'd it to you; As the case now stands, you must send up the bill immediately, & gett it protested if the man refuses still to accept it, if you please to send it to me or direct [words struck out] your Cozin Mackley to come to me with it, I will gett it protested for you, it must be without delay, and then that protest for non acceptance being sent to you, you must goe with it to the man that endorsed the Bill to you, and demand either your mony or security from him which if he be honest & will stand, he cannot refuse you, for no merchant howe ever refuses it upon the sight of any Protest, except he goes a one side ~~and who~~ But if he should refuse to give you Security I suppose you may either make an attachment or bring your action against him, But when the bill comes to be due, then if it be not paid, you must have another Protest made for non payment (& that protest must be made in due time, on the last day, or also it will be insignificant) and then you may certainly maintaine an action against him, & tis but letting your first action fall, when you commence a new one against him. But if he be a substantiall man & no danger of his breaking or Running away, I think it [words struck out] might be as well to bring your action against him for non Payment of the Bill, & not before or to make an attachment, then if you can as well have opportunity then to doe it. In this I think you will find a particular answere to all your Queries, and it is the best advise I can at present give you, & if I can doe you any further service therein, you may freely command me who am

Your assured loveing friend & servant
Thomas Morris

My Cordiall Respects to your Father.

To Mr Samuel Jeake Junior Merchant in Rye

[97] *John Mackley to Samuel Jeake junior, 4 October 1679. Original letter.*
ESRO FRE 4919

Lo: Cousin
Youers of the 2nd Instant this day Came to my hand with the bill I formerly sente you which I have goten accept & sente you with the other bill I had of yours. I had Received youer bill of £38 and as I write you confering a bill bieing protested be fore sun set it must be one the 3rd day which marchants alowe as a Custome & if one shuld Doe it one the Day it is presisly Due thay would Reck[on] one Redickles & plead the Custome of Marchant which is the 3 dayes alowants. I have not as yet coled on Mr Tho: Morris to Returne him youer thanks but Doe intende it when I have a opertunety, I did think to my selfe that the bill I sente you would come to me againe to be protested hear but that it fell out outherways for I could Remember Mr Godfrey sarved one that I was against which so but I thought beter to send it you againe, Rather then to medell tell you ordered me it being all but mine with my wives [kind] love to youer good selfe & sarvis to my uncle & Lo: to all other Relations. I wrest

Your Lo Cousin to Command
John Mackley

Southwark October 4th 79

I shall att any time Indeavour if I mete with a disipointement to advise my selfe the best I cane to searve you.

To Mr Sam Jeake Junior Marchant in Rye Sussex

[98] *D. Lesport to Samuel Jeake junior, 22 December? 1679. Original letter.*
ESRO FRE 4925

Deepe the 22th [Dec?]1679

Sir
The hon[our] of yours was given from Robert Moore with & inclosed for Mr Pickersgill which I send to his wiffe to send them forward for London where hee is at present. I am glad that the goods I sent you came safe to your hands. As to the Backwardnesse of them is none of my fault Being I shipped them two days after Receipt of said Mr Pickersgill.
As for the provision that you dosire to pay [mee it] is not worth whille. Assuring you that when you shall order mee any other Bussinesse I shall use

you favourally that you shall acknowledge for the effects. Desiring to Rest all my life

Your humble serv
D Lesport

As for the £2 2 by Mr Pickersgill passing by this place for England made mee passe them to his accompt soe I Received nothing of Robert Moore.

To Mr Sa: Jeake Junior Marchant in Rye

[99] *Richard Pickersgill to Samuel Jeake junior, 22 January 1679/80. Original letter.* ESRO FRE 4927

Mr Samuel Jeake London the 22nd January 1679
Sir I have not for some tyme wrot you beinge when came for England did desine to come by way of Rye but, after to oblidge some frindes I went by way of Callais & dover but this day haveing receiving one from my wife at Rouen she advisethe me that had receiving yours & that you had not had the Invoyce of the small parsell goods sent you soe heare inclosed you have the coppie a wantinge unto £214 which is w 71 1/3 Att 55d par Crowne, as the Charges then went make £16: 6: 11d which I desire you would be pleased to rem[it] heare & make said bill payable at sight unto Mr Benj[a] Smartt under whose covert you may please to write me in answer to the present, soe humbly saluting you I Remaine

Your most humble Servant
Richard Pickersgill

Pray adres for me at Mr Benj[a] Smart Marchand in London

To Mr Samuel Jeake Junior Marchant in Rye

[100] *Elizabeth Dighton to Samuel Jeake junior, 12 March 1679/80. Original letter.* ESRO FRE 4938

Cozen Samuell
I have sent a bundle & a letter by the Caryer & gave him 2d to drinck to put it up dry that it may com to no whet & directions is in the letter what must be done with the bundle & when it is sould let not the carrier pray exact upon you, but take out the money out of it to pay for the Carage. With many

thancks for all your kindness & if you have anything for me to doe hear I shall Recompense your love. I

Remaine your truly loving Aunt till death
Eliz Dighton

Southwark
March 12 1679

My kind love to my Cozen Mary Key. I pray her to Remember my love to Martha Gribble & tell her I have been faine to loose 3s in her Bodies: if this thing bee sould pray give her 5s of the money if she will have mee be at the loss, for no more will com to her, I have not took the money for them yet, last summer I was offered twelve shillings for them & was lought to loose soe much on them: & while I sent to her to know of her they had bought, & have gon about, till I have been weary to sell them, & could never com to the price again:

For Mr Samuell Jeake Junior at his Fathers house in Rye Sussex

[101] *John Mackley to Samuel Jeake junior, 13 March 1679/80. Original letter.*
ESRO FRE 4939

Southwark March the 13th 1679/80

Lo Cousin
I thought good to write you word what I have done Conserning the bill of £40 payable by Mr Smith. I have beine att his house 3 times this Day to have Received the money but he had Lefte no order for the payment of it & I understand by his sarvants that he is gon in the country so thay still ordered me to come frome time to time tell it was 4 a Clocke which time I thought was as Long as as mite be Deferred for I could have but a slite Anser & thar one I advised with Mr Savary & Mr Morris who wished me to convey it to a Notorey [that] I missed the money att 4 a Clocke so acording as thay ordered me I have left it att a Notterey to be protested so I ame to cole for it one Monday. Tis like thay will take the protest of & pay the money. The man promesed me to take caer in it, tis thar usiall way after a bill is left with them to send thar man to make a Demand of the Money which if thay Refuses to pay thay protested for it I shall give you an accomt by next poste what is Done in it. I have carried it to a suer man by Mr Savary advise. I shall be very Carefull in youer other bill when Due to Received it or take the Care that no Damages shall happen by neglect from me it being all frome youer Lo: Cousin

John Mackley

I sente you all the billes by Mr Miller.

To his Lo: Cousin Mr Sam Jeake Junior Marchant in Rye Sussex

[102] *John Mackley to Samuel Jeake junior, 16 March 1679/80. Original letter.*
ESRO FRE 4940

Southwark March the 16th 1679/80
Lo Cousin
My Laste to you was the 13th Instant wharing I give you an accomt howe I had proceded in the bill of £40 of Mr Smith & sences Did goe to the Noterey & had the bill which cost me 1s: 6d so he tould me Mr Smith would pay it so I wente & Did Received the money & had my charges againe he was unwilling to pay the 1s: 6d it Coste me but I would not luse it for I Knowe it to be his Due to pay it for I give tendants a note if thay had bene minded to pay it. Pray present my sarvis to my uncle & love to my sister Mary with Love to youer good selfe I wrest in hast

Youer Loving Cousin
John Mackley

To Mr Samuel Jeake Junior Marchant in Rye Sussex

[103] *Ann Wightman to Samuel Jeake junior, 19 March 1679/80. Original letter.*
ESRO FRE 4941

Loveing Coson
Youer I received with the things and I did send to sume of my Acquaintance to se them as sone has they came to my hands they would Aben glad to have had them if they had ben fashonable they tell me they were in fashon last yeare they shewd me sume that wher now in fashon and they much defer from youers therof they will not goe of at the Change.[67] I doe Intend to see at the street shops and [then] I will doe my best endeavour to put them of and then you shall heare further from me. This with our loves to sister Mary and sarves to my uncle and youre selfe [word illegible]
Your loveing Coson

Ann Wightman

London March 19 1679/80

[67] Probably the Royal Exchange but could also be New Exchange, both known for selling haberdashery wares and gloves.

[104] *John Mackley to Samuel Jeake junior, 27 March 1680. Original letter.*
ESRO FRE 4944

Southwarke March the 27th 1680

Lo Cousin
Youers of the 16th Instant I have Received & tharby understand you have Received the bills which I sente by Mr Miller. I gave you an acount in my laste that I had Received the bill of £40 & sences I was att Mr Jorrays 3 times & spake with him my selfe & he kepe me of tell 5 a clock & then would have given me a bill one a goldsmith, but I prevented his Dlayes Refused to write my bill at his house tell I knowe the gouldsmith would accept his so we went & when we came thar he Refused but after some Discourse between them he Gave ouse a bill one a other so when we came thar they would not pay it so I Returned thar againe, but att Laste he payed me the money it was paste 8 a clocke before I had Received it & gote home with it. Lo Cousin I see you are willing to let me have £30 for a year. I shall note faile you to Let you have it againe in that time & thinke my selfe very much behoulding to you for it. I have payed to Mr Gibbing £16 & to Mr Burkes £20 by youer order. I have not as yet seine my Aunt to tell her what you write. I shall take youer advise to Lay oute as lettell as I cane. It being all att present but my kind love to youer good selfe & service to my uncle with love to sister. I wreste,

Youer Lo: Cousin
John Mackley

I shall be at the sine of the sune the very next Dore att Mr Jn° Peake.

To Mr Samuel Jeake Junior Marchant in Rye Sussex

[105] *Ann Wightman to Samuel Jeake junior, 11 April 1680. Original letter.*
ESRO FRE 4945

Loveing Coson
These are after our love to you and sarving to my uncle to lett you understand that I have safe received the box you send as allsoe youre letter; I have endevored all that I can to put of the things but are profeard very little above halfe what they cost you and is but here and there one that will buy any of them att all for them ther is one as ofered me for five of them just soe much as you say they cost you an I am loft to take it tell I now your mind in it if you will take it pray send me word next post. If they were mine owne I could not doe more to get them of and to get gaine for them if you paid soe much for them you whas not well used as for those things wee received this day I have showed

them to one first ~~could he agreed~~ and he would give me but twenty shillings a dosen he says they have lost there sent but I will trye more and hope I shall put them of. This desireing to here from you what I shall doe in it as soone as you can possible. The meane time I [word illegible] as much as I can be done this being all att present from youer cosen

Ann Wightman

Apr [11th] 1680

To Mr Samuel Jeak Junior in Rye Sussex

[106] *Christopher Blackwood to Samuel Jeake junior, 3 April 1679/80. Original letter.* ESRO FRE 4946

Dublin Aprill the 3rd 1680

Deare Cozin
I had your of 3rd Febb some tyme since And I have nowe at last mett with Mrs Joane Booth the Executrix to Mr Mackley. Shee will shee tells mee see to pay those £5 Legacies I am ordered to receive assoone as shee cann but that as shee is a Legatee her selfe shee thinks it reason to pay her owne Legacy firste I Doe believe I shall gett said £5 Legacies in some tyme which when Received I shall remit the mony persuant to your order it being not worth while to Lay out soe smale a sume in talo. Mrs Booth Desires to knowe where and who arre the 10 children of Wm Mackley's Brother & Sister to whome are left £5 a peece by the will and also Desires to knowe in what condition they are because if they bee any way nessesitous I thinke shee will the rather discharge their legacies first Conserning the which when you write againe signify a Lyne. I doe thinke the woman means very honestly. Deare Cos I am Heartily glad to heere of your welfare, as also that my good unckle is liveing and in helth to whome presente my Reall Dewes And a Lyne from you nowe and then is very acceptable to mee as wee are the onely children liveing of two sisters Soe I desire to manifeste my selfe in all the bonds of Friendshipp and kindness and should be rejoyct in any things to serve you which with mine and my wives true love presented to your selfe, wishing you all prosperity in this world and true happiness hereafter, I rest

Your affect lo Cozen
Chr Blackwood

For Mr Sam Jeake Junior Merchant in Rye in Sussex Rye, these in all 8d

[107] *Ann Wightman to Samuel Jeake junior, 20 April 1680. Original letter.*
ESRO FRE 4948

Loveing Cosen,
Mine and my husbans kind loves remember to you with our sarves to my unkle this to let you know that I have put of the the [*sic*] things but with a great dealle of lose and could not put them of better that very night received your last I sould that passele wich I wrott to you abouth for Aleven shillings and for all the other things I have lost greatly and soe you will find I wrot you word that I whas bed twenty shillings A dosen I only showed the lite coller wich was laid uppermost and I did thinke they where all one coller tell I came to sea them then they would give for them but twell shillings a dosen and I lost my chapman at last I met with one wich bed for all of both sorths. I had five pounds, three shillings and twenty I considered of it and I did thinke I had better take him then let him goe for I had bid up and could not mette with one that would give me soe as he did Soe of the things I have maid five pounds, fourteen shillings. If it had bene my owne I could not a sould them for more the mony my husband hath tell you please to order him where he shall paid it soe not ous at present but remaine your Loveing cosen to sarve

Ann Wightman

London April 20 1680

To Mr Samuel Jeak Junior in Rye Sussex

[108] *John Mackley to Samuel Jeake junior, 30 October 1680. Original letter.*
ESRO FRE 4976

October the 30th 1680

Lo Cousin
Youers of 26 Instant Received with a bill for forty pounds one Mr Olnius to be accept & when Due shall Goe & Received it I have spake to Mr Hayes who tells me that he sent the to billes by Thursday past he semes to be disgusted that you send youer bills to him he has so much bisness of his one that he canot mind other on less thar was a protest in it for he said he had nothing for provision nor posteds or porters of letters. He tould me he had Rather you shuld send them to me then trubell him so if you pleas Rather than he shuld be disgusted att youer sending to him I am freely willing to Due you any sarvis that lie in my power to Due you. I ame sory to hear my uncle hath bein ill but Glad to hear he is prety well againe pray present mine with my wives

sarvis to him with kind love to youer good selfe hopin youer health as blessed be good we are att present I wrest

Youer Lo Cousin
To Command
John Mackley

My Brother Freebody is att ouer howse & disiers to be Remembered to you he mete with som Brokers that maid bould to take moste of his Clothes & money from him he Disiers to be Remembered to Mr Miller.

To Mr Sam Jeake Junior Marchant in Rye, Sussex

[109] *Michel Savary to Samuel Jeake junior, 23 December 1680. Original letter.*
ESRO FRE 4984

Mr Samuel Jeake Junior London the 23th December 1680
Sir
About 4 years since Robert Bartholomew useing betweene London & France I Brought in my Brother Mr Mathieu Hebert for 1/8 part of his ketch, expecting would have followed imply as hee promised to doe & therby might have been a comfort to them both. But since has Ever done his pleasure & gone weather has Lusted without Ever giving any accompte, which is a greate disheartening to that End he having noe acquaintance with you I take the liberty to trouble you in it & to desire you would bee pleased to speake with him & to know his designes therein being uneasie to bring [word illegible] one, & take his money which was £25 afterwards to deale soe unworthylie especially with a man who has been Ready att all times to service him to his power Being therefore wearied with the same I farther intreate you to Indeavour if possible to sell the same 1/8 part provided £20 & with all pray tell him when ever hee comes here, hee will not lett him goes untell hee has both given him an account & disposed of his part, poss[ibl]e hee may doe it himselfe when you propose the same to prevent greate trouble unto him I am sorry to trouble you but crave excuse, being for a meane friend & in the like occasion pray freely command him who is wishing you all happinesse in this new yeare comeing, my service to your good father & unto your selfe being

Your humble servant
Michel Savary

For Mr Samuel Jeake Marchant in Rye Sussex

4

Marriage, Trouble and Strife, 1681–1684

Samuel Jeake junior began to consider marriage in 1676, when he was around twenty-four and, as we have seen, had begun to establish himself in business. He was not initially lucky in love. His first attempt at making a match was instigated by his aunt, Elizabeth Dighton (previously Bonnick).[1] Elizabeth recommended Mary Weeks. Samuel junior had a long-standing friendship with Mary's brother, John, and had visited the Weeks' home several times while Samuel senior had undertaken legal work for the family.[2] However, Elizabeth had misjudged and Mary's parents found Samuel junior unsuitable.[3] An attempt in 1677, brokered by an unnamed cousin and a Mr Jenkins of Hothfield, Kent, to woo Ann File was equally unsuccessful. The Files were an affluent family from Wye in Kent and Samuel visited in June 1677. Subsequent to this visit Ann File refused to consider the suit.[4] Samuel accepted this decision but was more persistent in his pursuit of Mary Weeks. When her mother died in 1679 he approached her again, only giving up when, at a final meeting on 21 January 1680, he found 'no inclination in her'. With the benefit of hindsight, Samuel recorded, in shorthand, in his diary 'Nor were I at all concerned about it, and have since seen it a most happy circumstance that prevented it'.[5]

In June 1680 Samuel junior resolved to offer marriage to Elizabeth Hartshorne. He was twenty-seven and she was, at that point, just twelve years and eight months. He claimed an affection for her from childhood but the *Astrological Diary* records no expressions of the romantic love that had characterised the courtships of their parents.[6] It may be that Elizabeth had much to recommend her. The nineteenth-century antiquarian William Holloway claimed to have seen a portrait of her and furthermore described her as 'eminent for beauty, virtue, wit, and the talents of conversation'.[7] It is, nonetheless, more likely that her substantial dowry was a prime motivation. Although the financial negotiations with Barbara Hartshorne were long

[1] Hunter and Gregory, *Astrological Diary*, 129. See above, chapter 3.

[2] Hunter and Gregory, *Astrological Diary*, 117; 123; 124.

[3] Ibid. 36; 138.

[4] Ibid. 134–6.

[5] Ibid. 149.

[6] Ibid. 151.

[7] W. Holloway, *The History and Antiquities of the Ancient Town and Port of Rye in the County of Sussex* (London, 1847), 573. Two portraits identified as members of the Jeake family were, until recently, in the possession of Frewen College, Northiam. They were sold at auction in 2003. Michael Hunter identifies these portraits as being of two of Samuel and Elizabeth's children: Barbara and Francis and notes there was a third portrait of Elizabeth. Michael Hunter, 'Jeake, Samuel (1652–1699)', *ODNB.* Consultation with the College revealed there was no third portrait. Further investigation by Danae Tankard suggests that the portraits were painted by John Closterman (1660–1711) and thus could not have been of Francis and Barbara Jeake, who would have still been children in Closterman's lifetime. I am grateful to Danae Tankard for sharing this information.

and complex, on his marriage Samuel received around £1,000 in money, property and household goods.[8] The advantages of the match for Barbara were also clear. Her husband, Richard Hartshorne, had died in early 1680 and her son, Nathaniel, was already proving difficult to manage.[9] It seems likely that she sought to establish a positive male influence in the household.

Elizabeth's own initial views on the marriage were not recorded. Later letters in this chapter and the following two will show Samuel and Elizabeth to have had a happy and affectionate marriage. However, modern writers have suggested that early modern women often would have experienced the first phase of marriage as a 'violent discontinuity', a transition which gave their husband sexual access to their bodies and the right to inflict physical chastisement.[10] Many women also experienced a sense of displacement as they moved from their family homes into that of their husband. This was not the case for Elizabeth, but she did experience domestic disruption, as Barbara had offered her house as part of the dowry and both Samuels, son and father, moved into the Hartshorne home in April 1680 after the formal betrothal, and prior to the wedding. Soon afterwards Samuel junior suffered a recurrence of the depression that he had experienced since adolescence which created 'great displeasure and difference between me & my intended Mother in Law & Wife'.[11] Although the rift was mended before the end of that year, with that experience in mind Elizabeth may have approached her marriage with some trepidation.

Elizabeth was an unusually young bride. The majority of early modern women married in their early to mid-twenties and, even among the nobility and gentry, by the end of the seventeenth century, child marriages were decreasing.[12] Equally unusual was the fact that the Jeake marriage was consummated almost immediately.[13] Although the legal age of consent was 12, girls were not usually perceived to be sexually mature until they had reached the menarche, which, at this time, was likely to have been around the age of fourteen or fifteen, although it could, of course, have been earlier or later in individual cases.[14] The question of whether or not Elizabeth had begun to menstruate at the time of her marriage is impossible to answer. She was just thirteen years and three months. Barbara would, of course, have known whether or not Elizabeth had begun to menstruate and might have advised against consummation of the marriage if she had not. Medical advice was certainly clear that there was a risk of damage to the girl's reproductive health through intercourse prior to sexual maturity.[15] Our main clue to Elizabeth's reproductive health is the history of her first pregnancy. While most early modern women bore their first child within ten months of their marriage, Elizabeth was a year into her marriage before she fell pregnant with a child she carried to term.[16] Admittedly, there might have been miscarriages during that year and these might not have been spotted or understood in a girl so young but there are no mentions of miscarriages during that period in the *Astrological Diary*. The birth of

[8] Hunter and Gregory, *Astrological Diary*, 150–5.
[9] Holloway, *History and Antiquities*, 574.
[10] Mendelson and Crawford, *Women*, 129.
[11] Hunter and Gregory, *Astrological Diary*, 153.
[12] Mendelson and Crawford, *Women*, 125, 128.
[13] Hunter and Gregory, *Astrological Diary*, 154.
[14] Sara Read, *Menstruation and the Female Body in Early Modern England* (Basingstoke, 2013), 42–5.
[15] Ibid. 44.
[16] Mendelson and Crawford, *Women*, 149.

that first child was difficult and, as her father-in-law wrote, was attended with 'so much paine' (FRE 5141). The child lived only a few days having been 'hurt in the Birth in the right Temple'. Elizabeth was, however, pregnant again six months later with a pregnancy she successfully carried to term and resulted in a thriving infant, Elizabeth (known throughout the correspondence as Betty), born in March 1684.[17] Elizabeth went on to have another six children, four more with Samuel and two with her second husband, Joseph Tucker. Out of her eight children, six survived to adulthood.

For Samuel, marriage might have transformed his view of himself and marked the completion of his transition to manhood. It certainly would have made him master of his own household and elevated his position in society.[18] His consciousness of a new role is illustrated in the series of letters that begin this chapter. Those letters from James Wightman,[19] a cousin by marriage and a watchmaker, show Samuel purchasing a new watch and suit of clothes with an obvious regard for the the concerns of fashion. The watch was as much for display as for time-keeping and Wightman offered advice on fashionable cuts and colours for the suit (FRE 4992; 5047). The bill for Samuel's new clothes exceeded £20 (FRE 5011) but this may have been seen as a good investment. Gauci indicates the importance to merchants of 'cutting a figure of substance and probity'.[20] Danae Tankard argues that Samuel would have cut a fine figure in Rye with his clothes 'marking him out as a young man on the rise'.[21]

Yet the 1680s brought not only the transition of marriage but also a difficult period of persecution against dissenters. Thus, although the letters in this chapter show Samuel junior engaged in money lending (FRE 4996; 5014), negotiating bills of exchange (FRE 5015; 5017) and pursuing legal business in his father's absence from Rye (FRE 5083), the principal concerns of the remaining letters were not business but politics and persecution.

The Restoration had brought a series of Acts to curtail freedom of worship for dissenters. A new Act of Uniformity, passed in 1662, deprived clergy who failed to accept the Book of Common Prayer and episcopal ordination, and rejected the Solemn League and Covenant and the right of political resistance.[22] Legislation in 1664 and 1665 further curtailed the activities of dissenting clergy and targeted the laity, restricting worship outside the Church of England.[23] These restrictions were pushed not by the new king, who was inclined towards toleration, but by the Anglican gentry who after the experience of the Interregnum resented and feared Puritanism. The restrictions were implemented unevenly. Much depended on the attitudes of local officials and the prevailing national political situation.

Persecution increased during the late 1670s and early 1680s as a result of a series of political crises surrounding the succession. Since Charles II had no legitimate children, his heir was his Catholic brother, James, Duke of York. The scene was set by Titus Oates's revelations about a Popish Plot to assassinate Charles II and destroy

[17] Hunter and Gregory, *Astrological Diary*, 162; 168.

[18] A. Shepard, *Meanings of Manhood in Early Modern England* (Oxford, 2003), 73–4.

[19] James Wightman was the husband of Anne Key, daughter of William Key by his first wife, Jane. William Key later married Anne Jeake.

[20] Gauci, *Emporium of the World*, 99.

[21] D. Tankard, 'They tell me they were in fashion last year': Samuel and Elizabeth Jeake and clothing fashions in late seventeenth-century London and Rye', *Costume*, 50 (2016), 20–41. I am grateful to Danae Tankard for allowing me sight of this article prior to publication.

[22] G. S. De Krey, *London and the Restoration 1659–1683* (Cambridge, 2005), 72.

[23] The Conventicle Act, 1664 and Five Mile Act, 1665.

Protestantism in Britain. The Plot was, as is well known, an utter fabrication but the political consequences of Oates's mendacity were far-reaching. James was implicated in the Plot when Oates accused his former secretary, Edward Coleman, of treason. Sufficient evidence was found against Coleman to warrant a charge of high treason and his later execution. Fearing a Catholic succession and seizing the chance presented by the fallout from the Plot, the Country party in Parliament, led by the Earl of Shaftesbury, sought to pass an Act which would exclude James from the throne. The crisis rumbled on for close to two years with the exclusionists' aims hampered by Charles's successive dissolutions of Parliament. By early 1681, however, it was clear that Charles had defeated the opposition.

Thereafter, persecution of dissenting Protestants increased. Meetings were broken up, sometimes violently, and thousands of dissenters were fined, arrested, prosecuted and sometimes imprisoned.[24] It was the elder Samuel, as one of the leaders of the dissenting congregation in Rye, who suffered most under this regime. He had already been deprived of his voting rights during the 1660s and then was excommunicated from the Church of England in 1676. In early 1681 his situation was made more precarious by political squabbles in Rye. Local politics had been characterised by 'great heats & animosities' throughout the Exclusion Crisis.[25] The election of the mayor in August 1681 caused further disagreement when the loyalist candidate, Thomas Crouch, was accused of usurping the position of the Country party's Thomas Tournay. The disagreement culminated in a petition to the king. Charles II summoned both parties to appear before him, found for Crouch and outlawed Samuel senior's conventicle.[26] In 1682 Samuel senior was forced to leave Rye in order to avoid arrest. He remained in London for the next five years.[27] Samuel junior was not politically active nor one of the leaders of Rye's dissenting congregation but nonetheless the *Astrological Diary* details the tumultuous local political and religious situation, the persecution that he also suffered and the economic consequences of periods when heightened persecution forced him to absent himself from Rye.[28] The letters in this chapter complement this story by revealing the persecution of friends, acquaintances and kin (for example, FRE 5030; 5055; 5086; 5095; 5097).

Equally, they offer the chance to explore further the relationship between father and son and the impact of the absence of the older man. He was clearly missed, and missed his son in return. His letters continued to dispense both practical and spiritual advice. As he was ageing and sometimes sickly, there was a fear that he would die without the chance to say goodbye to his son. Thus Samuel senior wrote in February 1683 'If in my absence I shall find my life in jeopardy I shall be willing you have timely notice that I may set mine eyes upon you before I dye & you may put your hands upon mine when dying' (FRE 5090).

This period was further complicated for the family by the misadventures of Elizabeth's brother, Nathaniel. In March 1681 Samuel junior recorded that 'my Mother in law sent her son Brother Nath: Hartshorn [to London]; because of a report of Infamy that she heard of him a day or two before'.[29] The infamy was unfortunately

[24] J. Coffey, *Persecution and Toleration in Protestant England, 1558–1689* (Harlow, 2000), 168–70.
[25] Hunter and Gregory, *Astrological Diary*, 155.
[26] Ibid. 30–1.
[27] Ibid. 33.
[28] Ibid. 156–74.
[29] Ibid. 156.

never specified. Nathaniel was seventeen when he was sent to London and he was apprenticed to a lawyer. This might have seemed a good choice as the legal professional offered significant social and economic opportunities to an early modern gentleman.[30] Nathaniel's apprenticeship, however, removed him from the frying pan to cast him into the fire. His master Richard Goodenough was a lawyer admitted to the Inner Temple in 1671 and to the Middle Temple in 1679. He was also a Whig, member of the Green Ribbon Club, and spy for the Duke of Buckingham. He was involved in the Exclusion Crisis, and in the Rye House plot to assassinate Charles II in 1683 and the Monmouth Rebellion of 1685. While Goodenough's more serious radicalism emerged after Nathaniel's apprenticeship was agreed, his reputation was already well-known. He had been involved in pro-Dutch intrigue during the 1670s and acquired a reputation as a 'pestilent attorney'.[31] The apprenticeship was arranged by a prominent Rye resident, John Tudman, who perhaps should have been aware of this reputation. Apprenticeships were usually handled with great care and due consideration to the character of the master as well as the apprentice.[32]

It seems unlikely that Goodenough did much to keep Nathaniel's rebellious tendencies in check. Moreover, the temptations of London were great. Urban areas offered plenty of opportunity for youthful misbehaviour: disruptiveness, excessive drinking and illicit sexual activity.[33] Nathaniel obviously wasted little effort in resisting those temptations. As early as August 1681, Goodenough was complaining of his poor attitude and accusing him of ribaldry, impudence, mischief-making and lying (FRE 5290). Nathaniel, in his turn, was complaining that his mistress was 'not so good as she should be', and was telling lies about him, and that he was not being well fed (FRE 5020; 5290). In October 1681 Goodenough asked Samuel junior to remove Nathaniel from his service (FRE 5025). How this was resolved is not recorded but Nathaniel was not removed at this time.

In March 1682 Nathaniel was back in Rye claiming Goodenough had given him permission to go to see his mother, while the lawyer wrote to tell Samuel junior that Nathaniel had been dismissed for 'severall notorious faults' (FRE 5045; 5046). The disagreement was smoothed over and Nathaniel was placed once again with his master in May 1682.[34] In August Nathaniel wrote to Samuel junior to say that he had discovered the root of the problem. His 'fellow Clerke was the occasion of my Masters parting with me now he hath gott our 2 maids with child as it is reported and another maid' (FRE 5065). Given that Goodenough had already complained of Nathaniel's dishonesty and lewdness, it might be unwise to trust his version of events. Nor, if he had been engaging in sexual activity, would Nathaniel have been untypical of a young man living in London in a household large enough for more than one apprentice and several maids and thus offering space and opportunity for promiscuity.[35] Nonetheless,

[30] P. Wallis and C. Webb, 'The education and training of gentry sons in early modern England', *Social History*, 36 (2011), 46.

[31] G. S. De Krey, 'Goodenough, Richard (*fl.* 1671–1687)', *ODNB.*

[32] Ben-Amos, *Adolesence and Youth*, 109.

[33] Shepard, *Meanings of Manhood*, 94–7.

[34] Hunter and Gregory, *Astrological Diary*, 159. Family and friends would often intervene to smooth over differences between masters and their apprentices. P. Wallis, 'Labor, Law and Training in Early Modern London: Apprenticeship and the City's Institutions', *Journal of British Studies*, 51 (2012), 795.

[35] P. Griffiths, *Youth and Authority: formative experiences in England 1560–1640* (Oxford, 1996), 236; 281–2.

Nathaniel's tone in his letter to Samuel junior was reassuring. He wrote 'the whole family are very sivill to me. I have behaved my self so as to gaine theire good opinion' (FRE 5065). By November of that year Nathaniel had been indicted and imprisoned for debt.

Nathaniel's indebtedness may not have been surprising to his family. There were early signs of profligacy. In one letter home during 1681 he wrote 'my Mother told me when I were at Rye she would willingly allow me money in my pocket, provided I were not extravagant. I have now a care of it when I have it I find it is no so easily gotten as spent' (FRE 5020). Aside from the abundant opportunities for drinking, dining out and other activities afforded by London, Nathaniel also succumbed to the delights of conspicuous consumption.[36] His tailor's bill shows him to have been purchasing fine textiles and running an account that was certainly beyond the means of an apprentice (FRE 5294). The letters also reveal him to have tried to lie his way out of his problem. Nonetheless, his family rallied round. A number of Samuel junior's London connections were drawn into the resolution of this affair, including his cousins by marriage, John Mackley, James Wightman, John Jaye and Samuel senior (FRE 5071–73; 5076). Nathaniel was bailed out, his debts paid off and he was sent back down to Rye (FRE 5081).

In the meantime Nathaniel's master, Richard Goodenough, already heavily involved in London politics as under-sheriff for London and Middlesex during the early 1680s, was becoming more deeply embroiled in opposition to Charles II. He had been imprisoned for his efforts to frustrate the prosecution of the Popish Plot informant, Edward Fitzharris, and continued to be involved in legal efforts to incapacitate Tory control in London. Goodenough was also one of the principals of the Rye House plot, an abortive attempt to assassinate Charles II.[37] What Nathaniel knew of all this activity is not clear but by the early summer of 1683, and probably with an eye to the main chance, he was back in London and had turned informer against his former master.

Nathaniel then joined forces with Samuel Starkey, the servant of Aaron Smith, a dissenting lawyer, a member of the Green Ribbon Club and possibly involved in the Rye House plot.[38] The pair were then employed by the secretary of state, the Earl of Sutherland, to search the houses of those involved in the Rye House plot and attempt to locate Goodenough and others who were on the run. Nathaniel and Starkey pursued their task with some vigour and soon were exceeding the limits of the warrants issued to them. By early August the tables had turned and warrants had been issued for the arrest of Starkey and Nathaniel for theft of a horse, of money and jewels from the house of Sir Roger Hill and for searching the house of Lord Paget without appropriate cause.[39] Sunderland, when consulted, disowned them as 'rogues' and regretted giving them money and being kinder to them 'than they deserved by what I have heard since'.[40] The Earl of Bridgewater similarly commenting on Starkey's behaviour noted: 'I am afraid he has not well demeaned himself in what he was employed in, but sought

[36] Griffiths, *Youth and Authority*, 213–21. Griffiths points to significant use of prostitutes by London apprentices.

[37] De Krey, 'Goodenough', *ODNB*. De Krey, *London and the Restoration*, 362.

[38] Paul Hopkins, 'Smith, Aaron (*d.* 1701)', *ODNB.*

[39] 'Charles II: August 1–10, 1683' in *CSP Dom.*, 238–77.

[40] Ibid.

his own private profit more than the advantage of the service'.[41] Starkey's defence was that Hill had given them money as a bribe so that they 'should not ill represent his resistance nor take away a book of the *Growth of Popery* sent him by Andrew Johnson and some other papers'.[42] This was to no avail. Both Starkey and Nathaniel were arrested and imprisoned in the Gatehouse at Westminster.

The *Astrological Diary* records Nathaniel's misadventures in only the briefest of detail, noting that Samuel junior rode with Barbara Hartshorne to London when they received news of the arrest. The letters below offer a much more detailed insight into Nathaniel's behaviour and the family's efforts to protect him and to secure his pardon. These include several from Nathaniel which explain the indictments against him and his fears about the punishments that awaited him (FRE 5291). Whilst in turns pleading with, cajoling and threatening his mother, at one point telling her that 'all this treates jelousy in me to thinke you never designed to save my life and now in a manner convince me that you had rather I should be hanged than not' (FRE 5292), Nathaniel was also pursuing other means to extricate himself from prison. He turned on Samuel Starkey, writing to tell Sir Roger Hill that 'Mr. Starkey…has often offered to swear treason against you…and has often importuned me to swear the same, but I refused'. He wrote also to the Earl of Clare saying 'I have been tempted by another prisoner here to swear treason against you and some other persons of quality…I beg you to come and see me here, where I am ready to give you a true account of this villainous design. Your lady knows me and has lain at my mother's house in Rye'.[43] Then in October 1683 Nathaniel attempted a daring escape. He was at large for several days during that time writing to his mother, under an assumed name, to tell her that he was 'dayly sought after and alwaies driven out from place to place' and had whilst hiding out in York Buildings been forced by a 'search of 2 or 300 men … naked as we were out on the Topp of the house', shot at and only rescued by the kindness of strangers. He begged his mother to send money so that he could not only escape to France but also live comfortably since 'without money friend acquaintance or Creditt I must be forced to steale and there I should be starved in Gaole and hanged at last' (FRE 5292).

Nathaniel was retaken and, with Starkey, was subsequently tried at the Old Bailey for assault and trespass against Lord Paget. They were found guilty and fined £100.[44] They were subsequently tried at the Lent 1684 assizes at Aylesbury for the theft against Sir Richard Hill and sentenced to death. The story, however, did not end there. We will meet Nathaniel again in the next chapter.

[41] 'Charles II: August 11–20, 1683', in *CSP Dom.*, 277–311.

[42] 'Charles II: August 21–31, 1683' in *CSP Dom.*, 311–46.

[43] 'Charles II: September 21–30, 1683' in *CSP Dom.*, 410–44.

[44] *Old Bailey Proceedings Online* (www.oldbaileyonline.org, version 6.0, 17 April 2011), December 1683, trial of Nathaniel Hartshorn and Samuel Starkey (t16831212-28).

The well-dressed man about town, 1681

[110] *James Wightman to Samuel Jeake junior, 12 February 1681. Original letter.* ESRO FRE 4992

London 12th Feb: 1680/1

Loving Cousin
Yours I received this day and understand you would have a fashionable watch, that which I would advise you to is a pendulum watch as wee call them, which is with a spring under the balanc which regulats the worke soe that it goes better then one with a balance onely as for the studed caces they are still in fashon onely some allteration in the order of them the price of such a watch will be £7: but if you fix upon such a one as Mr Smiths it was a shillin or two under five pounds and ten shilling, pray be pleased to send which you pleas to have and I shall take extraordinary care in making it, this with our respects to your selfe and second with our sarvis to my uncle I rest

Your loving Cosin
James Wightman

To Mr Samuel Jeake Junior in Rye Sussex

[111] *James Wightman to Samuel Jeake junior, 19 February 1681. Original letter.* ESRO FRE 4993

London Feb 19th 1680/1

Loving Cousin
Yours I received and acording to youer desire have sent the bonds and the Ring by Moone the carrier and hope they will come safe to hand, the Ring was three peny wait seven grains, the watch I shall be very carefull in the doing of it and shall be as speedy as I can this with our sarvis to youer selfe and your Lady and allsoe to my uncle I remaine

Your loving Cosin
James Wightman

To Mr Samuel Jeake Junior in Rye Sussex

[112] *Mark Chiswell to Samuel Jeake junior, 15 March 1680/1. Original letter.*
ESRO FRE 4996

Sir
My kind Respects to you and youer Father Sir I doe understand that you doe lett out money by the voage to Newcastell for twelve pence in the pound I am short of money my fraight will not [stock] me to Newcastell I shall want about Fivtenn pounds If you please to lett me have it here I shall pay it you at the Return of my voage with the intrest implyment is verey dead here I cannot get affraight that will produce aney proffitt they proffer me but thirtey five shillings alast to goe to Stockholm and back to London for France I cannot find affraight. Sir I doe desier youer anser by the post this is all that I have at present to troboll you. I Remain youer loving Frend to command

Mark Chiswell

London the 15 day
of March 1680

Pray derect youer letter to my Brother Mackley house.

This for Mr Samuell Jeak Junior Living in Rye in Sussex

[113] *John Mackley to Samuel Jeake junior, 24 March 1680/1. Original letter.*
ESRO FRE 4998

March the 24th 1680/1

Lo Cousin
Youers of the 17th & 19 Instant I Received & this Day have bein att Mr Peter Bar & Received those 2 bills of one hundred pounds a peas & I have payed to Mrs Eliz: Chadwick a bill of 16:16 as by youer order & I have hear inclosed & sente the Rest the bound is not yet sealed by Marke Chiswell for he hath the ofer of a vidge to Ireland & he shall not knowne the Resulte tell to morrow when sealed by him I shall take care & sende it to you it being all but min with my wives sarvis to youer selfe & wife & good uncle & to youer mother. I wrest

Youer Lo Cousin
John Mackley

My aunte Dighton Remembers her kind love to youer selfe & wife & to my uncle & mother. Lo Cousin I understand by youer bro: Mr Miller hath sume moskets to sell if so I Disier you to by me one if thay be not to Dear & send by the Carrier.

To Mr Sa Jeake Jun Marchant in Rye Sussex

[114] *John Mackley to Samuel Jeake junior, 26 March 1681. Original letter.*
ESRO FRE 4999

March the 26th 1681

Lo Cousin
I write you laste poste war in I aquanted you that I had Received the too bills you sente me the acaison of writing now to you is to Disier you to write me a letter to youer Cousin in Irland about that small Leagcy that was leafte me I having a opertunity to send by my Brother Chiswell he hath taken a vidge to Dublin: in Ireland so if you please to menshon in youer letter if he hath Received it to pay it to my Bro: Chiswell & Disier he would Indeavour to gite it when he is thar, my Bro: hath hyered his wife to lode corne hear & to lode back againe & he hath bargned to have £60 for the vidge he will not make use of youer money. [With] my sarvis to my uncle & to youer good selfe & wife I wrest

Youer Lo Cousin
John Mackley

I ame Deter somethin about this bisness for posted of letter Disier you to write me next post for he will I beleve be gon att the later end of the weak.

To Mr Sa Jeake Junior Marchant in Rye Sussex

[115] *James Wightman to Samuel Jeake junior, 19 April 1681. Original letter.*
ESRO FRE 5002

London April 19th 1681

Loving Cousin
After our kind loves to you and my Cosin these are to acquaint you that I sent the gloves and braslets and allsoe the ring in a peec of paper put between the Gloves and hope they came safe to your hands they being sent by the Carier last weeke there was allsoe a booke sent att the same time for my uncle pray present my sarvis to him and tell him the booke cost twenty shilling I hope it such a one that he writ for, if it be not pray desire him to send it up and I shall readily chang it; the most I could make of the thing he sent was 18 s – 6 d I intend to send your watch by the Carier Moone this week by whome you may expect it; I would intreat you to doe me the favour to receive about eleven pound of my Bro: Holt for me and returne it to me when you can conveniently this being all att present From your loving cosin

James Wightman

My sister Wightman is well and my cosin they being in London.

For Mr Samuel Jeake Junior in Rye Sussex

[116] *James Wightman to Samuel Jeake junior, undated. Original letter.*
ESRO FRE 5003

Lo: Cosin
I have hear sent you a very good watch one the upper plate where the Endles screw use to be there is a screw to turne which comands the spring under the Balanc which will make it goe faster or slower as you please as you turne it you will find a little brass peer slide two and from which poynts to the fugars that ar graven .1:2:3:4: to increase the fugars make it goe faster and decrease slower the lowest price will be £6 15s which is 5s cheaper than I have sould the worst that I have made of this sorte this with our kind loves and sarvis to you and your wife and all friends I remaine your loving

Cosin James Wightman

Pray lett me have a line or two whether it comes safe to your hands.

[117] *Ann Wightman to Samuel Jeake junior, 30 April 1681. Original letter.*
ESRO FRE 5005

Loveing Coson
Youre noe received by Mrs Miller and this day one by the post with the Abill in it Acording to your desire I did goe with intent to bye the clouth but when I came I could not gett one under to shillings and to pence and to shillings the ell that ples me and that whas very good but I intend to se further next weke and sene it truly I did bed to shillings for that they assks to shilling one to pence but they would not let me have it soe for I bye for you as I woude for my selfe if you be free [words struck out] to goe soe hie pray sen[d] me word next post and what [word illegible] me with. Send it all together next weke soe mine and husbands sarvis to my unkle and kind respects to you and wife in hast I wrest your loveing coson to sarve

Ann Wightman

April the 30 1681

[118] *Elizabeth Dighton to Samuel Jeake junior, 16 May 1681[?] Original letter.*
ESRO FRE 5007

Loveing Cosin
I pray you would excuse my unthankfullness that have not write sence wee received our gloves: It hath not been for want of acceptance in mee but for want of time I wish you true happiness in your match I have sent my cousin your wife 6 pounds of sugar by Mr Benby: though a small token I pray accept my love in it: I shall be glad to see a letter from you when you receved it: my mind is not compose to write much so at present but shall wish your welfare so with all our love and thanks to you and cosin your wife I take leave of you and remain your

Truely loveing aunt
Eliz: Dighton

May the 16

Through the descomposer of my mind I have write badly but I hop you will read it. I pray remember me to your mother.

This for my cousin Mr Samuel Jeake

[119] *James Wightman to Samuel Jeake junior, 17 May 1681. Original letter.*
ESRO FRE 5009

London May 17 1681

Loving Cosin
Yours I Received with the Bill and have allsoe Received the mony and your other letter about the watch for Mr Waylett I supose he means to have a spring watch by the price which shall be made with all speed, but it will not be as soon as he might have a chain watch for those I have ready made, which will cost him butt £4 12 s in a plain leather case and will be more convenient for him, because not subject to Breake; pray cosin let me have a line or two from you of his minde, as for your shute and other things that you writ for I intend to send god willing the next weeke the Taylor being not able to finish them before Whitson tide this with mine and my wifes love and sarvis to you and my cosen and all friends in hast I rest

Your loving cosin
James Wightman

Pray when you send be pleased to lett me know how Mr Miller doth and present my sarvis to him.

To Mr Samuel Jeak Junior in Rye Sussex

[120] *James Wightman to Samuel Jeake junior, undated. Original letter.*
ESRO FRE 5047[45]

Loving Cousin
I received yours this day and have been with my Taylor about your shute but find him unwilling to make it except he may have a measure sent up or else one of your coatse for he siath it will not be well made without one of them if you send a measure he desires that they that take it may write one it which is the breasst and which the wast and the rest; he tells me that wast coats are in fashon and they weare them very long but flowerd silk is little worne but goold and silver striped is much worne, and if you lace it before it must allsoe be laced round the skirt and and the slitts allsoe as for the lining he sais it will not be sutable to the rest if you line it with Persian tafety, but it should be a richer silke frost button is still in weare and Goold or Goold and silver, upon sad colour cloath which is much worne, as allsoe dark greys are much in weare, the button that is in fashon is a prity high button with ridges but they doe not weare very well as I am informed but looke hansom on a shute; I think a hatt of the price you write of will be two meane for you; I think a beaver would doe well and for £3 you may have good one, but you may does as you please and lett me know your mind about these things and I shall sarve you to the utmost of my abilitty. This with our harty respects to your selfe and cosin and sarvis to father and mother is all att present from your loving cosin

James Wightman

If you send your coat it may doe well and if I could know your mind I would indeavour to have it done the next weeke; if you send a measure. I believe it will not be much charge to send it in a letter.

To Mr Samuel Jeak Jun in Rye Sussex

[121] *James Wightman to Samuel Jeake junior, 28 May 1681. Original letter.*
ESRO FRE 5011

London May the 28th: 1681

Loving Cosin
After mine and my wifes Respects to you and my cosen with my sarvis to my uncle and your mother unknown these are to lett you understand that I have

[45] This letter has been placed here, rather than in the order indicated by the ESRO catalogue as it makes reference to the purchase of Samuel junior's suit.

sent those things you sent for viz your shute hatt and band, for I am tould a Ribon the same of the shoulder knot is quite out of weare and this very fashonable there is allsoe sent 19 ells of doulass[46] and pomeander braslets[47] and a paire of stokens you will find in the box a peece of silk and what cloath that was left allsoe two or three o[ld] buttons in the pocket as I am tould I hope all things will fit and please you allsoe I having done my best Indeavor pray lett me have a line or two that I may know whether the shute fitts for I have a great desire to heare you will find under written an account of all which will be all att present from your loving cosin

James Wightman

A wedding ring the paire about 13 or 14 s for which I desire you to looke in my letter having lost the paper I set it downe one, as alsoe for the first bonds which was in the same paper

[48]3 pwts 7 gr – 13s: 2d. Fashion 2s: 6d – 15s: 8d. Bonds 1s: 6d	00-17-02
a Joynt Ring	00-10-00
a pendelum wattch	06-15-00
two Pomander Brasletts	00-02-00
two paire of white gloves	00-04-00
2 yards and quarter of cloath att 15s 06d per yard	01-14-09
5 yards of silk with goold and silver att 12 s per yard	03-00-00
19 ells of doulass att 01s – 09d	01-13-03
a white hatt	00-15-06
a band to the hatt	00-05-06
a pair stokens	00-04-00
a quire of bonds	00-01-06
for 8 doz Buttons att 3s- 6d per doz	01-08-00
for 4 doz and half of brest buttons	00-07-06
for 4 yards and quarter of tafetty	00-07-00
for a shoulderknot	00-14-00
for goold and silver stichin	00-09-00
for making a coate, hose and wastcoate	00-14-00
for Colard Calecoe	00-02-06
for whit Calecoe to your wast Coate	00-01-06
for silke and 4 yds of galome[49]	00-02-06
for Calecoe to your hoase pockets and reviting	00-05-00
for Stayes and fine drawing	00-02-06
A box and postedge	1s 6d

[46] Dowlass was a coarse linen cloth. *DTGC*, 'Doublet – Dozens'.

[47] A pomander was a mix of aromatic substances usually fashioned into a ball and contained in a small bag. They were made to be carried in the hand or pocket or, as is seems in this case, suspended from a chain to be worn around the neck or waist. *DTGC*, 'Pocket – Pompon'.

[48] This line inserted in Samuel junior's hand.

[49] *OED*, galloom or galloon a. A kind of narrow, close-woven ribbon or braid, of gold, silver, or silk thread, used for trimming articles of apparel; a trimming of this material.

[50]Summe Tot	£21 – 7s – 8d
Letters	0 – 0 – 8
	21: 8 – 4

To Mr Samuel Jeak Junior in Rye Sussex

[122] *James Wightman to Samuel Jeake junior, 9 June 1681. Original letter.*
ESRO FRE 5014

London June 9th 1681

Loving Cosin
Yours I receved as allsoe the bill and the mony up one it I am very glad to hear that your shute fits reasonable well, if ther be anything worth the sending up to alltter pray send it and it shall be done; the taylors bill came to £5– 3s – 6d and I could get him to abate but one shilin; which I have in my hands of yours; the occatione of my writing now is to desire you to lend me fifty pounds for six months att the end of which you shall have it againe with Interest it will doe me a great kindness att this time for I have a bout a hundred and fifty pounds worth of watches and clocks bespoke for turkey and have none by me of the sort they would have of, therefore must make with all speed they being to goe in the next shiping, which will be a bout 6 weeks henc as they tell me, and it is the shortnes of the time puts me to this straight for our workmen never tryst but rather have ther mony before hand; therfor I shall not be able well to compas my bisnes without asistance. I could have mony heare but not without paying extortione; which I am not willing to doe; therfore if you have soe much to spare and are willing to let me have it for the time above mentioned pray lett me have a line or two of it and I shall be willing to give you any security you shall desire; this with our respects and sarvis to you all I remaine
Your loving Cosin
James Wightman

This morning hapned a great fire in the maze in Southwark[51] and burnt down about 25 or 30 houses. This day Fitzharis was tryed att the Kings b[enc]h bar and was bought in guilty of high treasons.[52] He supeanied severall witness one his be halfe but the particulars of his tryall I know not having not had time to

[50] Calculations of total inserted in Jeake junior's hand.
[51] The walks and gardens belonging to the inn called the Abbot of Battle, on the north side of Tooley Street were known as the Maze. 'The borough of Southwark: Manors', in *A History of the County of Surrey: Volume 4*, ed. H. E. Malden (London, 1912), pp. 141–51. *British History Online* http://www.british-history.ac.uk/vch/surrey/vol4/pp141-151 [accessed 24 July 2016].
[52] Edward Fitzharris, implicated in the Popish Plot, executed in July 1681. Alan Marshall, 'Fitzharris, Edward (*d.* 1681)', *ODNB*.

inquire, but I supose Mr Miller hath sent a more particular account to his brother for he tould me he would write. Yesterday Plunket the titular primat of Ireland was tryde and found guilty of high treason.[53]

[123] *John Mackley to Samuel Jeake junior, 9 June 1681. Original letter.*
ESRO FRE 5015

Jun the 9th 1681

Respected Cousin
I had thought not to have written you tell Saterday but we haveing bein frighted with a fier which hath burnte a boute 30 housis thought good to give you an account it was att the uper end of the Maies as you goe to Mr Winson Milleing howes tis thought it came by trichery I have Received the bill of £5 of Mr John Burke & have payed to Br: Whightman £21: 8: 4 & to Mr Bateman the bill of £8 & when these other bills are Due shall Received them & pay according to youer order this Day. [Words lost] to youer mothers order my wife being near [h]er time of travell I Disier youer prayers with my uncle for her that the Lord would be pleased to give her a safe delivery. It being all but my sarvis to your good selfe & wife & uncle & to youer mother. I wrest youer Lo: Cousin

John Mackley

The bill of Mr Hayes I this Day luking one it find it to be Dated 15th/5 which makes the 5 & 3 Days of the alowance makes the 8 Day. I Canot tell but I may be mistaken you write tis not Due tell the 16 of June if it be sooner I have sliped the time.

To Mr Sa Jeake Junior Marchant in Rye Sussex

[124] *James Wightman to Samuel Jeake junior, 18 June 1681. Original letter.*
ESRO FRE 5017

London June 18: 1681

Loving Cosin
Yours I received with a bill for £45 and did allsoe receve the mony one the bill you did in your letter desire a bond for the mony, [word lost] which I did signe and seale in the presents of my bro: and sister Mackley and a neighbour of

[53] Oliver Plunkett, titular primate of Ireland, implicated in the Popish Plot and executed in July 1681. John Hanly, 'Plunket, Oliver [St Oliver Plunket] (1625–1681)', *ODNB*.

his, and did deliver it to your use, and take it kindly that you give me Credit for 6 months; att which time god willing it shall be punctually paid, I have sent the bond downe by the Carrier and the watch for Mr Waylet the price is £4 5s, I hope it will pleas him, it being a very strong and good one as he desired and his name one the case allsoe. This with mine and my wifes respects to you and my cosin, with our sarvis to my uncle is all att present from

Your loving cosin
James Wightman

I would desire you if Mr Waylet pays you, to pay your selfe what charg you have been att for letters and allsoe the shilen that I have of yours.

It is not the fashon to wear the coat loosse in the body therefore it will be convenient to alter it and as for it being short wasted it is much easier to mend then if it had been to long in the wast.

To Mr Samuel Jeake Junior in Rye Sussex

Nathaniel in London, 1681–1682

[125] *John Mackley to Samuel Jeake junior, 21 June 1681. Original letter.*
ESRO FRE 5018

Jun the 21st: 1681

Lo Cousin

After my kind love to youer good selfe & wife with my sarvis to my uncle theas are to acquainte you that my wife was taken ill one Saterday night about 12 a clock and was brought to bead of a sonn just be fore the clock struck 2 which I Disier youers with my uncle prayers of thankes to the Lord that he hath bein pleased to give her a safe delivery shee is nowe not very well which we judge is by Reason of her Milke, Mr Laines Disiered me to write to you aboute your kinswoman lying sicke of the small pox which sences he spake to me we understand shee is this Day Dead I have payed Mr Goodenough the £100 & to my Bro: Wightman the £45 all which you ordered it being all att present frome

youer lo Cousin
John Mackley

We did not knowe that youer kinswoman was sicke tell yesterday. He tould me the Doctor had given her over.

To Mr Sa Jeake Junior Marchant in Rye

[126] *Nathaniel Hartshorne to Samuel Jeake junior, 28 June 1681. Original letter.* ESRO FRE 5020

Deare Brother

Yours of the 20th wherein my mother saith she is not willing that I should make any such composition with my Mrs whither her truly am I willing forby some of my Friends I am advised to the contrary it tendeth wholy to my ruine, I confess my selfe in error in not returning thankes but yet now I would not have my Mother thinke that now I suppose my selfe provided for that I disrespect her or any one else for I write without dissimulation that I do as faithfully love and respect you all as ever I did and I hope that no one thinketh any other by me neither will I give any occasion. I thanke you heartily for your good advise I were something in hast when I wrote my last or else I had expressed my selfe forever bound in duty to my Deare Mother for this which she hath now done for me, I feare I shall never be capable to retaliate, I am still I must say with as good a Mrs as I desire but she is not so good as she should be But I told my Master how I were used and he hath in some measure regulated that concerning my Victuales, I have borrowed six shillings to purchase me another hatt and I had four shillings left and added to it but will not buy me so good an hatt as I would have, I didn't write for money for any extravigant expenses but merely necessary, I want a paire of sleves to save my Cloths For my old Cloths are quite done. And my Mother told me when I were at Rye she would willingly allow me money in my pocket, provided I were not extravagant, I have now a care of it when I have it I find it is no so easily gotten as spent I am now very sensible Mistris is a woman that doth me a greate deale of injury in exporting of false things to my Mr But I have made somethings appeare false a little publiquely which hat put a stopp to her infamous proceedings. Pray remember my Duty to Mother and intreat her not to be discomfited for I hope we shall all one day meet together, I should be glad and returne you hearty thankes if I could have once a weeke a lettre of good advise from and Uncle so with my Sincere respects To my Uncle, selfe and wife I Rest

Your Sure Loving Brother
Nath: Hartshorne

London June the 28th
1681

For Mr Samuel Jeake Junior in Rye Sussex

[127] *Richard Goodenough to Barbara Hartshorne, 2 August 1681. Original letter.* ESRO FRE 5290

London 2° Aug 1681
Madam,
I received yours in its proper time and should have long before now have returned you an Answere had not some accidentall affaire prevented it, I wondered to heare of your sons complaints that he wants Victualls; The reason I suppose is for that he having had whole Joynts of meat sometimes set before him & being left to help himselfe, he hast so indulged it that what remained was not fit to be set before any man, for which he hath been often reproved by me & my wife. As for beaff also he hath allowed him Bread & Beere which is more than was allowed me when I was a Clerk, He hath constantly hot meat for dinner & bread & butter or cheese for supper which is as much as I allow my own children, & the course I have always observed in house-keeping, which was never so traduced (as I know of till now) till this done by your son, His Ribaldry I complain off is down right bawdry, no man I beleeve can think me so [word lost] or ridiculous to accuse him for such things for asking for Victualls only, besides he was generally doing mischiefe (whereof I have severall instances) to the goods in & about my house. And though catched in the Act yet did as impudently deny all as he doe to you his ribaldry, for your sake I am willing to trye him a little longer hopeing his Amendment, which if he doth not we shall not continue long togather, And as for the Termes if he should persist in his impudence & by Acting & writeing lyes endeavour to expose me, that shall be settled by indifferent persons. But if he wants Victualls (as I understand he hast writ to you he does) I suppose you'll be ready to remove him, which you may so soon as you please with all my heart, And in that case alsoe the same Method shall if you think fit be used to adjust what shall be returned, I am very sincere in what I now write, & should be loath to say more (though I could inlarge very much in this matter) seeing my credit must be brought in competition with your sons (according as he boasts himselfe) [words struck out] In your not believing anything against him, notwithstanding which I am Madam
your humble servant
Richard Goodenough.

[128] *Richard Goodenough to Samuel Jeake junior, 1 October 1681. Original letter.*
ESRO FRE 5025

Sr
I must desire that you would be pleased to take away your Brother from me, he is so lewd & so unruly that twill be impossible for me to keep him in any due Decorum, I could mention very [word struck out] great motives (indeed not to be dispensed with) That forces me to give you this trouble I am

Sr
Your humble servant
Richard Goodenough

1° Oct 1681

For Mr Samuell Jeake Jun att Rye in Sussex

[129] *John Mackley to Samuel Jeake junior, 29 October 1681. Original letter.*
ESRO FRE 5027

Southwark October 29th 1681

Lo Cousin
These are to let you Knowe that I have bein [words lost] those 2 bills of Mr Bar one of £80 & one of £16=15s and the bill of £60 is accepted by Mr Haye it being all but my sarvis to my Uncle & love to youer good selfe & wife. I wrest in haste

Youer Lo Cousin
John Mackley

[You]er bro: Nat: is very well & Disiers to be Remembered to you all

[130] *Ann Wightman to Elizabeth Jeake, 29 October 1681. Original letter.*
ESRO FRE 5028

Loveing Cosen
Yours I received and Acoredg to yours desire I have borth your things all but the oranges the ships be not come in it but as sone as they come I will send sum yours stocings will not take noe couller but a bad grrene if I should advise you I would have them dide the same couller for that is as much woud as any if you plese to send me word wether your mind be soe to I will take care to get them done I have sent the other thing this weke wich I hope you will have sone the box of sweat meat cost 5s and three pound of wafer the one

pound is called chacolet wafer which lie upper most in the box and cost 2s-6d- and the to pound cost 3s the [words illegible] ar in the box with the wafer that cost 3s and the box 6d. You writ for clote line but I se noe string but I have sent one dosen yards wich is 1s 6d if it be big enouff if not, when you have ocaison to send to London send it Againe and Aprise that is fit and I will send it I write soe with mine and my husband service to you my unkle & your mother and love to you and husband I remaine your loveing coson to sarve

Anne Wightman

October the 29 1681

Cost of the things sent 15s 6d[54]

These for Mrs Elizabeth Jeake in Rye Sussex

[131] *Michel Savary to Samuel Jeake junior, 8 ? 1681. Original letter.*
ESRO FRE 5030

London the 8th [?]ber 1681

Mr Jeake
Sir yours of the 28th Xber last past have receved for the which I give you thanks although not conserned yet if can serve you in the like please to freely command.

The present is to Crave your friendship againe in favour of sume poore French protestant which are Latly arrived from about Rochel by the persecution which is to teadious to Rehearse the which his Majestie hath been pleased graciously to Receive into this kingdome, & since there arrivall granted them letters of Denisization, soe that now wee are considering where to Recommend them for setlements & Indeed have diverse times thought upon your towne for the Publicke good, Being a thing which I have this day moved & will bee farther considered one in the meane time you will be pleased to communicate it to sume persons which you thinke fitte, & to consider if bee not for the good of the towne, & to send me your answer & oppinion, & will abboundantly oblige

Sir Your humble Servant
Mich Savary

My service to your good father. They are all fisher men.

For Mr Samuel Jeake Junior Marchant in Rye Sussex

[54] Note of the costs added in Samuel junior's hand.

[132] *James Wightman to Samuel Jeake junior, 11 March 1681/2. Original letter.*
ESRO FRE 5044

London March 11th 1681/2

Loving Cosin
Yours I receved and have according to your desire sent the shoose and the quire of bonds allsoe; and the bill you wrote for which you will find in one of the shoose and theer is in the other my uncls watch which I would desire you to give him with mine and my wifes sarvis. I had sent the bill if I had thought of it when I had opportunety to send it, but was loath to put you to the charg of 4d in sending it by letter; my wife was brought to bead with a Girle this day three weeks, a little after two in the afternoon and is very well blessed by the lord considering her condition but the child hath been very weake thought att present we have some hopse of its Recovery through infinet mercy, this with mine and my wifes respects to your selfe and wife is all att present

From your loving Cosin
James Wightman

For Mr Samuel Jeake Junior in Rye Sussex

[133] *Richard Goodenough to Samuel Jeake junior, 21 March 1681/2. Original letter.*
ESRO FRE 5045

Sr
I received your letter, I beg you to present my service to Mrs Hartshorne, as to her son I know nothing of his going into the Country, but about a Weeke before for severall notorious faults I had discharged him my service, & desired him to acquaint his relations there with And as to what money should be returned I told him it should be referred to two indifferent persons, I perceive he is not ashamed to say or write anything to palliate his owne offences I am

Sr
Your humble servant
Richard Goodenough

21 March 1682

For Mr Samuel Jeake Junior att Rye in Sussex

[134] *Samuel Jeake junior to Richard Goodenough, 23 March 1681/2. Copy letter.* ESRO FRE 5046

Rye Mar 23 1681/2

Sr
I have yours of the 21 Instant & ~~have accordingly~~ acquainted my Mother with what you write, and perceiving your unwillingness to keep her [words struck out] son (being as you intimate guilty of such notorious faults though none particularised) it is our desire that you write us word in answer hereto what summe you will returne, which if you propose with Justice & Equity we may adjust the business within our selves without the trouble of Reference. He hath not been long with you & now ~~you~~ is put ~~him~~ as much to seek of a place & imployment as when he [words struck out] went at first & I suppose you have made some profit of the money you had with him in the time, he hath had nothing but victualls. I must needs say you had done well to have acquainted his Mother with your putting him away; [words struck out] the articles being made with her not him ~~yet~~ This is certainly a very abrupt conclusion. I have ~~acquainted~~ informed my Br of what you say that you gave him no leave who still affirmes that he asked you leave to come down & see his mother which you granted him at your office door. & that you ordred him to receive 5s of your Brother which he did ~~in~~ I request the answer assoon as possible to

Sr Your humble Servant
S. J.

To Mr Rich: Goodenough

[135] *John Osmonton to Samuel Jeake junior, 22 June 1682. Original letter.* ESRO FRE 5055

Bury Street June 22 1682

Deare
Friends what ever Insurrections may in the Rectoral Justiss of God befall the world & the land of our nativity For the unrepented persisted in abominations of all most all sorts of mankind let us laber night & day by unfained faith Evangelicall & harty repentance sinceer obedence to all Gods will & plesure bee Resigning our selves & all that is in our power as a whol burnt sacrifice to the pleasure of our God that wee may Receive all in him to unspeakable advantage that it may bee with us as with Noah when the waters of the flood are abated, Gen 8 20:21 verses And Noah builded an alter unto the lord & took of every cleane Beast & of every cleane fowle & offered burnt offerings upon the Alter & the lord smelled a sweet savor & the lord said in his

heart I will not again curse the ~~world~~ ground any more for mans sake For the imaginations of mans heart is evill from his youth neither will I again smite any more every thinck living as I have done. O that by vertue of that well ordered Covenant made to David & his spirituall seed established in all things & sure wee may by the leading by the hand of soveraine grace bee made meet to receiv of these priviledges made to Noah & may bee found in the Caleb spirit following god full living down the ungodlyness & murmerings of this Generation that cannot bear our words beleeving that through all the disorders and confutions in the world & wofull contempt & blaspheming of the spirit of god that nevertheless his enimies shadow is departed from them & that god is for us against them & therfore bids us not fear them tiss veryly a good land & good for us & the enimies of the lord shall bee but food for our faith therfore fear them not. For the meek shall inherit the earth Math 5:5[55] & ther shall bee aboundance of peace for as long as the sun & moon endure the lord fill us with purity of spirit, prudence, sagasity & a mortified spirit to this present evill world being prepared to bear his Cross with inuincable patience & holy Courage that we may bee meet to weare his glorious & eternall thrown & inherit all things: prays your truly affectionate Brother & truly humble servant in our deare Lord Jesus John Osmonton

I pray deare sir by the First convenient oppertunity to let mee know how it is with your deare Father & the despised Interest of our Dear Lord Jesus in Rye.

For the Deare & much valued Mr Samuel Jeake Junior with unfained love & all true Respects

[136] *Nathaniel Hartshorne to Elizabeth Jeake, 8 July 1682. Original letter.*
ESRO FRE 5056

Deare Sister
I Received yours dated the 9th which is to morrow and will fullfill your request next returne of the Carrier I hope you are all in good health, since you indicated nothing to the Contrary I know not whether your letter was not brought me in its due tyme for I had it not till to day which is the 8th of this Instant so with my service to my Cosin Jay I saw her husband yesterday as well Mr Tournay is this day come for Rye who I presume will see you before these he

[55] Matthew 5: 5, 'Blessed are the meek: for they shall inherit the earth'.

hath a letter for my Mother from me. Pray my Duty to my Mother, uncle Bro: and so concluding with my hearty requests to your selfe I am in hast

Your truly Lo: Brother
Nath: Hartshorne

London July 8 – 82

These to Mrs Elizabeth Jeake att her house in Rye in Sussex

[137] *Elizabeth Mackley to Elizabeth Jeake, 18 August. Original letter.*
ESRO FRE 4873[56]

Loving Cousin
I must eckowledge my self much to blame to neglect writing to you it hath not been for of love but I have been presented I hope it will come in good time to you I am Glad to hare that you doe goe forward with your grett belly. My service to my honnored uncle with your mother & respects to your good self & cosin. At present I remain

Your Lo Cosin to serve
Elizabeth Mackley

August the 18

How to make tansed
Tak a qart of the thickest carem
& the yelkes of 30 egges
1 pound & halef of fine suger
3 quartese of nabell [word illegible]
1 nutt mang & rosewatter
& the juse of spinegs
& tanse erbers

[56] The date on this letter does not include the year but is placed here because it is addressed to Elizabeth Jeake, married in 1681, and refers to Elizabeth Mackley being presented, presumably for non-attendance at church, thus most likely to be during the early 1680s. The letter also refers to Elizabeth Jeake's great belly, a term that was not necessarily confined to the latter stages of pregnancy. Elizabeth would have been around 5 and half months pregnant with her first child in August 1682. For examples of the use of the term 'great belly' see Laura Gowing, *Common Bodies: Women, Touch and Power in Seventeenth-Century England* (New Haven, 2003), 148.

[138] *Nathaniel Hartshorne to Samuel Jeake junior, 26 August 1682. Original letter.* ESRO FRE 5065

Lo: Bro:
I have yours of the 24° and am sorry to heare my Uncle doth not mend any faster but hope ~~it~~ he may suddainly you would do me a particular favour if you could get me some dabbs but I feare the season is almost past but hope you may get some I will pay and also be thankfull for your trouble. My Master never asked any thing of security of me but if he continues next yeare I must. I must needs say the whole family are very sivill to me I have behaved my self so as to gaine theire good opinion. I now perceive by what my Mrs hath told me that my fellow Clerke was the occasion of my Masters parting with me now he hath gott our 2 maids with child as it is reported and another maid and Mrs Daughter saw it is turned out of doors and so I came into the office I will tell Tho: Clarke of your present we have another blazing starr[57] reported to be seen but I have not seene it yet it being bad weather: So with my respects to all I am in hast

Your Lo: Brother
Nath: Hartshorne

London August 26° – 82

These to Mr Samuel Jeake Junior att Rye in Sussex

Nathaniel in debt, 1682

[139] *John Mackley to Samuel Jeake junior, 7 November 1682. Original letter.* ESRO FRE 5071

Southwark November the 7th 1682
Lo Cousin
I had writen to you Last post but going to hoborn I Defered it Till now because I Coled att Nat Masters thinkin to have seen him but did not I understand he hath not beine att his masters this 10 Days so they could not Tell me whear he was he hath not beene Sicke as they Tell me. I have Received the bill of £120 of Mr Hays & I have payd to Mr Markewicke £140 which you Drewe. I have sent to you I Dozen of plates thay came to 3s More than the [word

[57] Possibly Halley's Comet.

illegible] you sente it being all but my Kind love to your good selfe & wife with my sarvis to my uncle & to your mother. I wres

Youer Lo Cousin
John Mackley

Nat hath not bein att my howes never sences you was att London but I coled on him Thinkin to have had the 25s he owes me.

To Mr Sa: Jeake Junior, Mearchant in Rye Sussex

[140] *James Wightman to Samuel Jeake junior, 8 November 1682. Original letter.* ESRO FRE 5072

London November 8th 1682
Loving Cosin
Yours I received with the bill and have alsoe received the mony I have this day enquired after my cosin Nathaniel but canot heare of him any where therfore canot deliver the letter you sent for him I feare he keeps very bad company he hath sent letters to Mr Grace for monyes but I suppose he hath sent him none, the last he sent was by a porter wherein he tell him that he was in prison and ready to starve but hath not lett him know where it is but one examination of the porter he tould him it was att a house on Saffron Hill but att the place where he tould him he is not, soe we canot tell whether ther be any truth in what he write, I have sent by Slowman the Carrier a basket for my brother Freebody, directed to be left with you which I would desire you to send to him by a messenger on purpose as soone as it comes to your hands and what the carrier will have for the carage be pleased to pay and if my Bro: Freebody doe not pay you again I will, this with mine and my wifes respects to you and my cosen with our sarvis to my uncle and your mother is all att present from

your loving cosin
James Wightman

My wife desires you would lett her know in your next how the things please you.

[141] *John Jaye*[58] *to Samuel Jeake junior, 14 November 1682. Original letter.* ESRO FRE 5073

London November 14th 1682
Cozen Jeak
Sir The occasion of these lines is to acquaint you that last Lords day in the evening, one Thomas Clerke a Pipemaker in Clerkenwell, came to my house, and told me that the Monday before Mr Nathaniel Hartshorne was under the constables hands in a place called Hockley in hole[59] for taking from one Mr Joseph Stead of Staples Inn two guineas for which he was going to be carried to prison, but procured so much favour as to send for some friend, upon which he sent for this Clerk, who he persuaded to be bound in a bond with him to pay forty three shillings upon demand to the said Stead and told him his uncle Jeake and Holman were in town and the next day it should be paid and did alsoe give him a note under his hand seal to bear him harmeless, which note he showed to me. But this poor man hath never seen him since, and the person hath been to demand the money of him, and the Bayleys lye in wait to take him, that he is faine to keep within doors and dares not stirr out for fear of being sent to prison. I would have had him write down to his Mother but he was very earnest with me to write because he said he feared that his [word struck out] writing would not be understood, which seeing the man in so much distress I promised him to write to you, that you might acquaint Coz Hartshorne with it and if it is thought convenient may order that the money [words struck out] may be paid for I believe if he were in prison he is not able to procure tenn shillings for his reliefe, and now is not in a capacity to follow his own concernes, I went this morning to inquire for this Stead att Staples inn but he went out of town yesterday that I could give you no better account than what I had from Clerk who made such a sad complaint to me that I much commiserated the man's condition and thought my self in confidence bound to signify to you what I have that the poor man may be in a capacity to follow his imploy and therefore hope you will resolve this trouble. My wife presents her service to my uncle, Coz Hartshorne, your selfe and Cozon your wife, the like I do myself and rest

your ingaged friend and kinsman
Jn° Jaye

Mr Hartshorne is gone from his master and hath binn so some time.

[58] John Jaye, an apothecary, was the husband of Samuel junior's cousin Mary, daughter of Anne Jeake and William Key.

[59] Hockley-in-the-Hole was a notorious area of London. It was the location of bull- and bear-baiting and frequented by thieves and highwaymen. Walter Thornbury, 'Hockley-in-the-Hole', in *Old and New London: Volume 2* (London, 1878), pp. 306–9. *British History Online* http://www.british-history.ac.uk/old-new-london/vol2/pp306-309

[142] *John Medley to Barbara Hartshorne, 18 November 1682. Original letter.*
ESRO FRE 5293

London att the Angell
Corner shop of fenchurch
street November 18° 82
Madam
Since your departure from Mr Jayes, (very unwilling I am to occasion this trouble of advice) your sonn Mr Nath: Hartshorne have gradually come into my Debt 15 or 20 pounds, for goods hee tooke up at our shop, which I thought necessary to acquaint you with by reason hee promised mee payment & have disappointed mee, your assistance in this business I implore, [words lost] I would not take any vigorous means to secure my debt although it lay in my power soe to doe, by reasons of t[he] small acquaintance I had of you, I shall ever acknowledge my selfe

Madam

Your Most obliged servant
Jn° Medley

pray give mee an answer next post

[143] *John Medley to Barbara Hartshorne, 23 November 1682. Original letter.*
ESRO FRE 5294

Mr Nath: Hartshorne
Bought of Thomas Jenney and John Medley 82

		£ s d
Nov 1	9 yds of Venetian Tabby at 9s 0d	£4 : 01 : 00
	10 yds of Chery Satting at 9s 0d	£4 : 10 : 00
	7 yds ½ of white Satting florance	£4 : 06 : 03
	8 yds of blew stripe at 7 : 0	£2 : 16 : 0
		15 : 13 : 3

Madam
Yours came safe to hand this day, the particulars mentioned above which is [word lost] to your order, your son I have not seen sin[ce] I sold him the last, I went to meet with him in the Temple, but could not finde him, I was informed hee was gone downe to you, into the Countrey, this is all that is need full from Madam

Your obliged servant
Jn° Medley

November 23 82

Samuel senior in exile, 1682–1683[60]

[144] *Samuel Jeake senior to Samuel Jeake junior, 1 December 1682. Original letter.* ESRO FRE 5076

Loving son
Yours of the 28th past received, and am glad to heare of your health with your wife & mother, which I pray God continue to you all, I am through mercy in health & our relations here, except old Mrs Mackley who is not well. Ere this comes to you I hope your brother N. H will be safe with you with the Mare I rode up hither upon & the Boots per Mr Miller, by whom I did not write sending him away on the sudden. I could not heare of him till Monday after my coming to Towne & then he sends a letter to Mr Grace to borrow £4 of him & acquainted him that he was in prison at Westminster Mr Grace brings the Letter with the porter that brought it to Cosin Wightman, who next morning tooke on him the trouble to go to Westminster & found out your brother in Custody where the Debt & charges was £3 13s and paid it & released him, the Letter ~~and~~ to Mr Grace & the discharge my Cosen Mr Wightman tooke for the Debt for which my Cosin was laid in I intend to send you by Mr Miller when he returns. I feare things will go bad here as well as in the countrey with those that feare the Lord the Lord fit you with double portions of his spirit and beare you up against all discouragement. I am more concerned in my thoughts for you than my self though I have left all in your hands. My love to all friends in great hast I remain

Your very loving father
Samuel Jeake

Dec 1 1682

[145] *Samuel Jeake senior to Samuel Jeake junior, undated. Original letter.* ESRO FRE 5081

Loving son
I sent by the carrier a few lines to you, as well to acquaint you of my health as to let you know that I had as soone as I could sent away my cosin N. H. your brother, and what occurred in procuring his liberty. The Receipt my Cosin Wightman took for the Debt he paid for him for which he was in Custody I herewith send you and the other charges that he paid made up in all £3 13s besides 4d or 3 ½d I well remember not which he paid for comming

[60] Samuel senior left Rye in November 1683 and remained in London until mid-1687. Hunter and Gregory, *Astrological Diary*, 161.

back by water I send you also the letter my Cosin in his custody sent to Mr Grace which may the better satisfie being his owne hand, since his going I have heard nothing but that he owes Mr Firman 20s and 23s for a hat he bought of John Allin I hope he got well to Rye and the mare I rode out upon came well also. I have taken up of Mr Miller Ten pounds & drawn a bill on you which pray honour with the payment. I have paid Mr John Greenwood the £4 7s I had in my hands of his mothers so as I owe nothing there. I desire you to keepe an Accompt of what you pay & disburse for me, I would have you call upon Mr Welsh for the money due from him to Cosin Jaye but when you have it return it to me. I have spoken to Cosin Freebody who is here to pay in the money he owes me to you & I suppose he will shortly because I understand he hath sold his land. Beware of negotiating any Bills of Mr Betteford of Calais Father or son because Mr Miller's Bill is forced to be protested. If any thing you desire satisfaction in or should occur amongst you extraordinary write to me you may direct your letter to Cosin Mackley. I desire you would by the Carrier send me up a couple of Shirts & my morning coat & order them to be left there. The Lord bless & keepe you in his feare & give you wisdome & innocency. Christ advises his owne disciples to. Remember me to our Relations in Speciall & the Christian friends in generall with you whose condition I shall not cease to spread before the Lord for though absent in body, I am present in spirit with you. For news I refer you to Mr Miller. I abide

Your affectionate Father
Sa: Jeake

At the end of [word illegible] in the superscription of your Letters to Cosin Mackely. Let it be [word illegible] & then he may know they be for me.

Send my Combe that I left in the broadest box under the cupboard in the studdy.

To his Lov son Mr Sa: Jeake in Rye, These

[146] *Samuel Jeake senior to Samuel Jeake junior, 6 January 1682/3. Original letter.* ESRO FRE 5083

January 6 1682/3

Lov: Son
Yours of the 1st instant gives me the good news [of] the health of your self & wife which I am glad of & pray for the continuance thereof. When Cosin Freebdy payes you returne me the money & when you receive that due from

Mr Welsh send me an Accompt of what you have received & paid for me since I left you. As to the business of Wid: Hood let the moveables be settled by deed of gift in which she may give grant & confirme them to him absolutly, for the considerations as well of natural love & affection as for & in consideration that he his executors admin[istrators] or assignes shall maintaine her with meet & sufficient meate, drinke & all things necessary during her natural life & range her to be decently buried after her decease. In this writing let there be a covenant on his part to find, allow & provide for her during her natural life meet competent & sufficient meat drink &c. And if she have any debts let there be a convenant or letter of Attorney in the writing to enable him to sue for the same in the name of her, her executors or admin[istrators] to his own use. This writing were best be made by indenture between her and him. It may be done in paper & the moveables may be mentioned by schedule or in the body of the writing. And let there be a bond for him to her in double the value of the goods to performe the covenant on his part as usually. As to the House Let it be by indenture in parchment wherein she may covenant to him to stand seized of the mesuag &c. to the use of her for her life, or to his use during both their lives & after her decease if he shall survive to the use of him, his heires & assignes for ever to the use of him, his heires & assignes for ever provided he shall pay his brother Jn° Hood £10 on such a day as his apprenticeship shall come out upon (which you may informe your selfe of) if he shall so long live & the said M. Hood shall be then dead, or within so many moneths after the decease of the said M Hood if she shall live after the end of his apprenticeship. And in default of payment put in a clause whereby she may grant her son Jn° Hood power to enter & distreine as in Leases. But if she shall survive her son Coskar then to the use of her for her life or her & her heires & assignes for ever as she shall think best. Let this Indenture be made between her of the one part & her sons Coskar & Hood of the other part because else she cannot give him power to distrein for the £10 & all signed & seale both parts of the Indenture though it matters not whether Jn° Hood seale if he be made party thereof. The consideration in this Indenture may be for natural love & affection & for settling the Inheritance of the mesuage &c. Here is little news, It yet remaines a cloudy & dark day The Lord be your light & salvation & the refuge & strength of you & other his people. Some take that Shaftsbury is gone from Holland to Dantzick as thinking himself not safe there,[61] others question the truth thereof & say the interest of Orange there is not so prevalent as formerly & that the Dutch Ambassador here hath lately

[61] The first earl of Shaftesbury (1621–83) was one of the leading figures in the Exclusion Crisis. Following the failure to coordinate uprisings against Charles II, Shaftesbury fled the country at the end of 1682. Tim Harris, 'Cooper, Anthony Ashley, first earl of Shaftesbury (1621–1683)', *ODNB*.

given in a memorial signifying that the states are resolved to stand by their treaty with the emperor & K. of Spaine with some other things not pleasing at Court. France it is said hath ordered his seaman to be aboard his ships the beginning of this moneth which hath quickened the Dutch in their naval preparations. The poling for Common Counsellmen is not yet over in some of the wards. Little Mary Mackley is sick of the measells she was took ill ♂[62] last ☿[63] was indifferent, but ♃[64] worse. ♀[65] they began to appeare. Old Mrs Mackley is not yet recovered. The rest of our kindred here are well & remember to you & your wife to whom with your mother, brother & Christian friends my hearty respects & affections. When you have leisure write me up the places of the planets in Long. & Lat. for the 10th & 11th daies of July 1647. Also their places for the 30th & 31th of January 1650/51. Likewise for the last of August & first of September 1664. And for the 24th & 25th daies of March 1665 & 1666. And for the 12th & 13th daies of December 1667. And for the 22th & 23th of August 1669. Also the years daies & Hours answering to 1. Degree & the daies & hours to .1. minute by Naibods Table in Lillies Introduction.[66] And the Long. & Lat of London & Ispwich by the Table in Lillie where I thinke Ipswich is that so I may get the difference of Meridians. I could not conveniently write you by the Carrier which made me send this [words lost] post. In hast I am

Your very lo father
Sa: Jeake

This For Mr Sam Jeake Junior in Rye Sussex

[147] *John Mackley to Samuel Jeake junior, 20 January 1682/3. Original letter.*
ESRO FRE 5086

Southwark Jan the 20th 1682/3

Respected Cousin
Youers of the 16th Instant I have Received and tharby understand you be willing to have youer Talow sould provided I could sell so as thar might be no Loss which I canot Due all theas marketes but to some Loss and when thay will be better I knowe not by Reason of Trobeles that Due a Risse which makes people have no mind att all to Trade but that Loss I will save you and

[62] Tuesday.
[63] Wednesday.
[64] Thursday.
[65] Friday.
[66] A reference to Valentin Naibod in William Lilly's *Christian Astrology*, which was to be found in the Jeake library. Hunter *et al.*, *Radical's Books*, 142–3.

Take it my selfe if you be willing I will make good all youer money. So if you please you may Drawe a bill For £40 one me as sune as you met with a opertunety but as for the Rest you must alowe me some Time for it will be a Grate while before I shall Despenses with it because Traide Holes of nowe sumer comes one but if I have any opertunity to sell any to save my selfe I shall be willing to sell some for I ame now Indited for 1 month for not going to Church so I have 29 sessions before thay can medell with mee. My wife aske my uncle howe he did and he said his could was as it was he was att ouer howse to Day it being all att present but my kind love to youer selfe and wife & mother. I wrest

Youer Lo Cousin
John Mackley

To Mr Sam Jeake Junior Merchant in Rye Sussex

[148] *Samuel Jeake senior to Elizabeth Jeake, 27 January 1682/3. Original letter.*
ESRO FRE 5141

Deare Daughter,
I am glad though you have lost your little one for which you endured so much paine; that you are through mercy pretty well recovered, and hope the remaining weakness upon you will in time be removed. The Lord sanctifie his dispensations to you & poure out his grace & blessings on you. My cold was inconsiderable through the goodness of God I am indifferent in health, some nights a remnant of my former paine continues with me. I am sorry to heare William Jeffrey is so ill I heartily wish his recovery. Yesterday cosins Mackley & Jaye eate your Goose & all send you their thanks with mine for it. It was exceeding good. It pleaseth me well to see you have mended your hand in writing, my earnest desires are for your happiness here & hereafter and ever shall remain, with my respects to your mother.

Your truly loving father
Samuel Jeake

January 27th 1682/3

[149] *Samuel Jeake senior to Samuel Jeake junior, 15 February 1682/3. Original letter.*
ESRO FRE 5090

Dear Son, This morning I received yours of the 12th currant by Cosin Wightman That the news of my not being well might not discompose you I took the opportunity of writing you an Answer to yours of the 10th instant the next post for I understand my Cosin Mackley had wrot you some thing thereof & therein. I answered your Queries and gave you an accompt of my paine that then continued from ♄[67] to ♂[68] since which through mercy my paines are abated though some Remnants remain, what the issue of these often visits from heaven may produce at last you may see & prepare to see me no more, Though your desires & filial affections (of which I never doubted) should be denied they shall have paternal reciprocations. Yet I know nothing but if God spare me life & the apsects from above be more propitious I may see Rye. If in my absence I shall find my life in jeopardy I shall be willing you have timely notice that I may set mine eyes upon you before I dye & you may put your hands upon mine when dying. God allmighty bless you, your wife & issue he shall give you and give me your society in heaven though I should have no more of it on earth, which would be as acceptable to me as you, And whether our Iniquities as well as the Iniquities of the times have not been conjunct to the accomplishment of this present dispensation may be considered by us distinctly or whether I only have eaten the soure grapes though your teeth are set on edge. But what ever the cause on earth hath been I am sure the cure is in heaven. I am willing to look thither & should I look any where else can see nothing from men, means, policy, power, care contrivance or such like that may render [word illegible] of help to the distresses, disruptions distractions, fears, snares trials &c of the sons & daughters of Zion. I am sometimes ready to fear in stead of my coming to Rye you will be forced from thence, And bless God you have yet been able to bear up against the storm & desire if it be his will you may dwell quietly under your own vine. I am not without hopes that in measure God will meet this storm now it is shot forth & debate with it & stay his rough wind. But if otherwise let all go rather than Christ and a good conscience. Feare not them that can kill the body but [word lost] in that can kill & cast both body & soule into hell. My true love to you my daughter your mother and all friends. I remain

Your truly lo father
Sa Jeake

Febr15th 1682/3
Deliver the inclosed.

To Mr Sa Jeake Junior in Rye

[67] Saturday.
[68] Tuesday.

[150] *Samuel Jeake senior to Samuel Jeake junior, 10 March 1682/3. Original letter.* ESRO FRE 5095

Deare Son
By yours of the 5th instant I understand you have received the money due from widow Hounsell as well to Cosin Jaye as my self. I have paid Cosin Jaye and cleared him off as to his wives portion & that mortgage also but have taken up no money of Cosin Mackley for by reason my sister Dighton hath paid me what she owes me I have money spare yet. I thank you for your invitation to Rye but were I weary of the City I cannot yet take the Journey being not wholly freed of my paines though by the good hand of God upon me much abated. I should be glad to see you but would not you should neglect your business & take such a journey & charge on you only to give me a short visit. I am glad to heare your mother is on recovery that your self & wife are well. I hear this week by a Gentleman as if they were intended to be a little milder with the dissenters & that the Lord Keeper had order to stop the Capias writs against Excommunication & the Judges in the Circuits to be favourable to dissenters & would they have petitioned they had been indulged but some think as if a design were if any had petitioned to compound with them for a yearly sume, for money is precious at court sometimes, yet they continue to stop the people from going in at their Meeting houses & some that get in before the Officers come turned out, though some of the Officers arre so friendly as to let them know when they will come that they may be gone before & few carried to prison. The Court is gone to Newmarket, some say the D of Mon[69] is coming in favour again & that Hyde[70] is going to Ireland & Y to Scotland agàin,[71] how true I know not. Yesterday I heard the Earle of Yarmouth is dead.[72] The French were buzzing into the Europeans the prize to be won at a Horsrace at which time they had a design to surprise the Charleroy & some other Towns whose Governors no had corrupted but was discovered

[69] The Duke of Monmouth. Following the failure of the Rye House plot, Charles II had a short-lived reconciliation with the Duke of Monmouth in the autumn of 1683. Tim Harris, 'Scott [Crofts], James, duke of Monmouth and first duke of Buccleuch (1649–1685)', *ODNB*.
[70] Possibly the second Earl of Clarendon, a supporter of Charles II during the Exclusion Crisis and known to have an interest in Irish affairs. He was appointed lord Lieutenant of Ireland in 1685. W. A. Speck, 'Hyde, Henry, second earl of Clarendon (1638–1709)', *ODNB*.
[71] James, Duke of York had been High Commissioner in Scotland from October 1679 to March 1682. W. A. Speck, 'James II and VII (1633–1701)', *ODNB*.
[72] Robert Paston, first Earl of Yarmouth, was Lord Lieutenant of Norfolk and an anti-Exclusionist. He died on 8 March 1683. John Miller, 'Paston, Robert, first earl of Yarmouth (1631–1683)', *ODNB*.

& prevented. Cosins remember to you And with my kind love to your mother self & wife & the rest of my friends I remain

Your truly lo father
Sa Jeake

Mar 10 1682/3

To Mr Sa Jeake Junior in Rye Sussex

[151] *Samuel Jeake senior to Samuel Jeake junior, 17 March 1682/3. Original letter.* ESRO FRE 5096

Lov: Son
Yours of the 12th instant received and thereby understand you & your Relations with you are in health which I am glad of and desire God to continue to you and others that feare him in your place. I suppose by this Mr Markwick is returned to Rye who was so kind as to see me here several times so I need not write you touching my condition that I am not so bad as you may imagine nor yet so well as to be free from paine. I desire to waite on God who hath often ransomed my life from destruction & crowned me with his his loving kindness and tender mercies. As to the house though I have sometime had thoughts never to sell it because if you should do otherwise then well and I should ever return to Rye I should like no other house for an habitation there but that yet taking the number of my daies to be short & not knowing whether God will dispose of my return or no I leave you to do therein as you please & if you cannot get above £50 to take that. My kind love to my friends in generall with the respects of my Cosins here I remain

Your lo: father
Sa: Jeake

March 17th 1682/3

To Mr Sa Jeake Junior in Rye Sussex

[152] *Samuel Jeake senior to Samuel Jeake junior, 12 April 1683. Original letter.* ESRO FRE 5097

My Deare son
This day I received yours of the 9th instant at which your mother send hers [word lost] both rejoyce to heare of your health with your wife. Though she is troubled because her son Nath: comes not at her. As to the outlaw which you mention Mr Knight informed Mr Shinner of would come out against me next

terme, I think it will be to no purpose to throw away 30s to keep it of for a .12. moneth seeing if that on the Oxford Act[73] be stopt, it will be no stop to the Capias upon the Excommunication but I may as well be taken upon that & sent to prison as upon the other, so I yet am resolved to rest on providence & let the Lord do with me as seemeth good in his sight. This no little refreshment to me and a great mercy to you to heare you are yet spared from prosecution, which if you should I doubt you must be forced to come away. As long as you are not prosecuted the Books may remain as they are But if there be any thing else that was mine which you can spare you may sell & put into money. The Great Table & Stools you may sell if you can get 40s though it be worth more. Or any thing else you have a mind to sell. The parcell of Books you mention that stood upon the shelf under the great map neere the window if you send me a catalogue I may see what I can get for them. I have informed Cosin Mackley what you write concerning him, Cosins & kindred here are well & remember to you. Remember my kind love to all my friends with you as if named. On the 5th instant I received a Letter from Mr Markwick date Apr .2. wherein he informs me that by the vigillancy of the Adversary he thinks you will not be able to gaine any opportunity to meet with more then 5. above the family. And would have my thoughts on that. Touching which the Lord direct you for I cannot. But if you cannot meet otherwise to enjoy any season of joyning your forces to send up your petitions to heaven without distraction you were better meet with that number then not att all. If the Lord deprive or suffer the Adversaries rather to deprive you of your solemne Assemblies, the sin will be the enemies, the suffering yours. I do not think the loss or deprivation of some ordinances will separate God & his people, seeing he was with the congregation in the wilderness when they wanted circumcision & the Passover & at first had no settled priesthood or ministry among them. If you did take some weeke day to set apart & seek God in the case and make it a Particualr request [words struck out] whether to meet with 5. or more as you have done & run the risque of it. [two lines struck out] The God of Jacob be your refuge, & put underneath you his everlasting Arms, make your enemies that promise to themselves great things Liars & make you to tread on their high places. If there by any worth or strength in my prayers you may all be sure you shall not want them, & perswade my self I have a share in yours & if I knew when you would set apart any time to seek God as above I would let my spirit be present with you & send up one sigh & groane for you. I can send you no news, sometime a talk of a Parliament, sometime none. Things are in the City much as when Mr Markwick was here, only is it expected a great many will be excommunicate for not receiving the sacraments at Easter or the next Lords day according to the order of the B. of

[73] The Five Mile Act of 1665 was also referred to as the Oxford Act.

London. E. of Salisbury[74] some say is dead, & E. of Musgrave. With kind love I rest

Your very lo father
Sa: Jeake

[April 1]2th 1683

To Mr Sa Jeake Junior Merchant in Rye Sussex

[153] *Samuel Jeake senior to Samuel Jeake junior, 15 May 1683. Original letter.* ESRO FRE 5099

Lov: Son
In answer to yours of the 7th and 12th instant. The information of Mr Miller touching Mr Wares his house at Winchelseas I suppose was misunderstood & referred to the house Mr Wares lived in, which an heire of one Purfield claimed & got from him, and not to this house which he bought of Mr Wats of Appledore, the writings for which I made and they were left in my custody & were in the upper drawer of the court cupboard when I came away from Rye you may nevertheless enquire concerning it of some Winchelsea man. As to Mrs Greenwoods land I think I wrot you before how Robert Brown might write to her son Mr Daniel Greenwood in Oxford in Brasenose Colledge if he had any desire to deale for the land. As to the case of Wm Eaton if he & his wife have levied a Fine of his lands to the use of such persons and their heires exended &c as he shall mortgage grant &c then is the Freehold in Abeyance and shall subsequently follow such uses as he shall appoint. And after the terme is done a mortgage may be made from him (in which his wife need be no party nor is it convenient she should) but the party to whom they levied the Fine may be a party (& if by the Indenture leading the uses of Fine there be any to serve for his consent to such disposal must be a party) otherwise the mortgage to run as usual, & so far as I see by the expression of the uses in your Letter need be no party but the mortgage may be made only from Wm Eaton who had the sole power to dispose, nor need there any mention of the Fine in the mortgage, but it will be meet the mortgage have the part of the Indenture that leads the uses of the Fine left in his custody. Mr Drinkers mortgage I was paid for but whether it lye in the upper drawer of the court cupboard or in the little Box under the little Table, or in one of the Boxes

[74] Probably the third Earl of Salisbury. Salisbury was a popular figure among opponents of Charles II, although probably not directly involved in any of the plots. He was gravely ill in April 1683 but did not die until 24 May. Victor Stater, 'Cecil, James, third earl of Salisbury (*d.* 1683)', *ODNB*.

between the little Table & the north wall I remember not. The Accompt of Mr Samson and Mr Holman touching Richard Youngs two children I were not paid for. You may take for them what you think reasonable I had not much trouble to write them. The Ryot charged on Sheriff Pilkington, Shute and severall others[75] was found against them last saterday at which tryal it is said the L. C. J. carried himself some passionately yet it is thought is not very easie in his place and either his dismission or resignation is expected. Yet since the trial a writ of Error is granted. Prince George the K of Denmarkes brother is expected shortly to came over & marry the Duke of Y daughter Anne, and tis said will be made Duke of Cumberland.[76] Some talk yet continues of a parliament about Michaelmas next. Sir Patience Ward is charged with perjury in his deposition at the tryal of the Scandalum Magnatum against Y & to come to his tryal they say next saterday.[77] The Argument for the Hartfordshire men upon the stat of the 23th of Eliz is to be argued too morrow it is thought the Judges will declare against the dissenters thereupon though yet that court hath shuffled off their judgment thereon openly in court so far as I hear what ever their particular opinions have been in private. The Lord increase and continue your Graces and blessings and helpe you to do his will & make you able to suffer for him. Take my kind love herewise to your self & wife being still

Your ever lov father
Sa: Jeake

May 15 1683
Respects to all friends.
I have wrot to Mr Greenwood that he may send the lowest price of the land to you.

To his loving son Mr Samuel Jeake in Rye

[75] Sir Thomas Pilkington and Samuel Shute were elected sheriffs of London and Middlesex in March 1681. They were both instrumental in attempts to turn the corporation of London into a political entity to rival Parliament. A series of disorderly meetings and polls led to both men being sent to the Tower and then charged with riot in 1683. Pilkington was pardoned by James II in 1686. Gary S. De Krey, 'Pilkington, Sir Thomas (1628–1691)', *ODNB*.

[76] The marriage took place on 28 July 1683. W. A. Speck, 'George, prince of Denmark and duke of Cumberland (1653–1708)', *ODNB*.

[77] Patience Ward was a prominent merchant and spokeman for London dissenters. He gave evidence in the trial of Thomas Pilkington who faced a charge of *scandalum magnatum* for alleging that the Duke of York had burnt London. Ward was charged with perjury after Pilkington's conviction. Gary S. De Krey, 'Ward, Sir Patience (1629–1696)', *ODNB*.

[154] *Barbara Hartshorne to Samuel Jeake junior, 19 May 1683[?]. Original letter.* ESRO FRE 5296

Lond May the 19th
Dear Sonne
I had a letter this day from my dear Betty am glad to heare of your good health. Capt Eve was at my Cusen Whitmans I thinke about Munday was aloan Mr Whitman would have come for me but he pretended hast saayd he would come agane a Thursday where I sat to expect him but he hath not been there since. I am never like to end my Business with Mr Goodenough I suppose he meanes to shew som trick Sir Thomas Player told Mr Firman he could have had forty pound but he did not except it & now cannot hear further. Mr Goodenough was not to be spoke with. Some did suppose the riot might be the cause some say he is not worth six pence but I rather fear he desigens to get more money of me though Mr Firmen told me they did not charge Nat with any wronge he had done his Master of money but that there was some small matter due to nat upon account. I have lost Nat againe cannot learne what is become of him. I am tired out of my life & my troubles doth discompose me. I was forced to my bed yesterday all day to be tired I would not undergoe soe much as I have done for a hundred pound twill certainly kill me I shall never se poore Betty again I feare tis not probable I can possible recover to goe through this trouble I am tumbled from post to pillar & nobody regards my busines wither was I willing to undertake it knowing my owne insufficience to performe it but hear I am afflicted tormented without any relief. I received this day of Mr Mun eight pound upon Mr Millers account pray paye him tell Betty a sute of riban will cost ten shilling, the girdles are mostly tied before your Good father is well & we all remember our kind loves & to all friends. I am Dear sonne yr loving Mother Barbara Hartshorne.

For Mr Sam. Jeake Jun. in Rye Sussex

[155] *Samuel Jeake senior to Samuel Jeake junior, 26 May 1683. Original letter.* ESRO FRE 5102

My Deare son
Yours of the 24th instant inclosing a note of the 19th with one for your mother this day received by the hands of Mr Stephen Porter who came well to London this day and besides his remembrance to you & my daughter desires you to remember him to both his Cosin Millers & Mr Sa: Gillart. Before your letter I heard this weeke by Mr Skeets that widow Girdler was dead but the bond

you mention she left not with me, when Mr Shamel and Mr Gibbons was with her at the house she had the bond there but carried it away with her againe. They desired her she would leave it with some body that in case she should dye might deliver the bond in which she promised she would but into whose hands she intended then to put it she mentioned not, nor when she was last with me at Rye did I see it. I had no more of hers to dispose of then the £6 which was lent Mr Padiham and the Bill for the same lay in her bag with the [words struck out] Paper wherein I had set down what I had paid her & received for her. When you write to Mr Curteis remember my love to him. I am sorry for your loss of Mr Tho: Crouch[78] who I doubt not but hath gained by his death, being gone where the wicked cease from troubling & the weary be at rest. I pitty his poore cosins of whom he took care, the Lord provide for them. I thinke no man can put downe any house to lay another open but he must make up the breach or else an Action of the case lies against him at the suite of the Owner of the house so dammified. As to the monies you have put out or remaining by you I shall as yet draw none from you till I see more. Things are bad enough yet. The Hartford dissenters the last ♀[79] in the terme cast who pleaded the 23th of Eliz: to be not intended against Protestants which they proved themselves to be & 5. before the end of the terme. Sir Patience Ward by the jury convict of perjury for words in his evidence at Pilkingtons trial though in his evidence delivered himself so warily as to the best of his remembrance, he heard no such words spoken by Mr Pilkington, not positive but reserving himself to his memory. Some say he is gone since. Other talke of designes against others. L C J. Sanders[80] is so ill it's thought he will not be able to officiate next terme. Some say the K of Spaine[81] is like to dye, & that 3. pretend to the Crown, the Emperor, the French King & the duke of Medina Coeli. Your Mother remembers to you & your wife & desired me to write you that Capt Eve hath failed to see her or give her other security here so she would have you write to him by some body that goes to Adlington Court next weeke, and to tell your wife that the things she wrote to her in the letter she this day received she cannot buy, it coming but now to her hands & she intending to come away Monday morning next by the Tunbridge coach.

[78] Not Thomas Crouch, jurat and mayor of Rye, who is recorded in the *Astrological Diary* as having died in August 1682. More likely to be same Thomas Crouch noted as a travelling companion to Samuel junior in several letters in chapter 2. FRE 4827, FRE 4833, FRE 4835–7; chapter 3, FRE 4862. Hunter and Gregory, *Astrological Diary*, p. 159.

[79] Friday.

[80] Lord Chief Justice Edmund Saunders presided at Pilkington's trial and that of Patience Ward but was taken ill in late May 1683 and forced to step down. He died on 19 June 1683. Stuart Handley, 'Saunders, Sir Edmund (*d.* 1683)', *ODNB.*

[81] Charles II of Spain (1661–1700).

Dr Stacey last time I saw him ordered me when I wrote to you to remember him to you [words struck out]. The Most High bless, keepe and be all in all to you for ever. Remember me to all true friends with you, for whom with your selfe & wife I often bow my knees to the Master of the whole family in heaven & earth. I am

Your very lo: father
Sa: Jeake

Take here with Cosins love
May .26. 1683

To Mr Sa Jeake Junior in Rye Sussex

[156] *Samuel Jeake senior to Samuel Jeake junior, 7 June 1683. Original letter.* ESRO FRE 5103

Dear Son
I hope these will find you, your wife & mother in health though I have not had a line from you this fortnight, but I understood by Mr Tournay & Mr Gillart that your mother got home well & that you were well when they left Rye so I am the better satisfied. I have little to write to you only the opportunity of conveyance by Mr Gillart hath put the pen in my hand. Stand fast in the Faith & having brought the truth sell it not. Be thankfull for what monies you have, put your trust only in the Lord and feare not. Let not the example of any that relapse stagger you. Nothing venture, nothing have is an old saying & may be verified in a Christians adventures for God. They that sow sparingly shall reape sparingly. I had rather see you a Martyr than an Apostate. None ever yet was a looser by Gods service, set your eye on the joy before you & endure the contradictions of sinners, [word illegible] the cross, contemne the world, Rejoyce under Temptation, Trials, Afflictions &c. Let the joy of the Lord be your strength. I have no greater joy in the Earth then to see you walke in the truth, as you have received a commandment from the father. The end will crown your work, fight the good fight of faith, lay hold of eternal life, press through discouragement to the price of the high calling of God in Christ, yet a little while & you shall not see him but againe a little while & you shall see him. Endeavour after more love to God & joy in him that none of his commandments may be grievous. Be instant in prayer, often in meditation. Trust not in uncertain riches, Avoid all distrustfull and distracting cares. Delight yourself in the Lord & he shall give you your hearts desires. The God of all grace stablish strengthen & perfect you, bless you & all yours make you a seed

of the blessed of the Lord & your offspring with you. True love to you & all friends with you from

Your truly lo: & tender father
Sa: Jeake

June 7 1683

Holwell[82] hath set out an Appendix to his former piece I have bought it for 6d.

To Mr Samuel Jeake Junior in Rye Sussex

[157] *Elizabeth Jeake to Samuel Jeake junior, 21 July 1683. Original letter.*
ESRO FRE 5107

Rye ~~Jy~~ July 21st 1683

My Dear
I received your ~~kink~~ kind letter and return you thanks for it. I am glad you got safe to your ~~joyrne~~ journeys end. I am sorry to hear my Father is so ill I hope this will find him better. Be sure make much of your self and be not to Melancolly. My Mother [words struck out] remembers her to your self and Father and all other friends with you. News we have none save only a Barge was ~~hear~~ here on Thursday. I am much concerned for your abscence. My Dear pray return as soon as possibly you can. Mr Waters hath not been here yet. My Mother hath disposed of part of her money to Mr Horne. I do intend if Knight and Videan come before you come home, I will get them to leave the money with Mr Smith and they to speake to Mr Finch to let the suit rest till he hear further from you. if you dislike it pray contradict it speedily lest they come before I receive your letter and send me word how to proceed in it. My respects for your Dear self. My Duty to my Father with service to Cousins. I am

Your ever Faithfull and Loving Wife
Elisabeth Jeake

I received your commission my Dear by Mr Edward and have executed it.

For Mr Sa: Jeake junior to be left for him at

[82] Not listed in the Jeake library catalogue.

[158] *Elizabeth Jeake to Samuel Jeake junior, undated. Original letter.*
ESRO FRE 5108

Deare Mr Jeake
I would pray you to buy me a pair of things to keep the sides from ringing they be for my Mother and one girdle with a pair of red shoe string let them shoestrings be sattin. I have nothing elsse to say but wishing this may finde you well I remain

your Loving wife
Elisabeth Jeake

My Mother continues very ill but the Chirurgeon flaters her still it pains her very much. [words struck out] My Mother greifs veary much for fear my Br will not be a good boy My Mother & self desire to be remembered to all our Cosins with you.

To Mr Samuel Jeake at Mr John Mackleys in Tooleys Street near the Bridgefoot in Southwarke

[159] *Samuel Jeake senior to Samuel Jeake junior, 4 August 1683. Original letter.*
ESRO FRE 5109

Lov: Son
The Letter your wife sent to Cosin Wightman came to my hands after you went. And by yours to Cosin Jaye I understand you got home well and found your Relations there in health which I am glad of. Through mercy I have gotten on my shooe again & begin to go with more ease but yet have not been abroad. Cosin Jaye went with her sister Mackley to Maidstone last Tuesday when they return I know not. Cosin Mackley remains as ill there as she was when she went home. I have heard nothing of your Brother since you went. Vienna is certainly besieged[83] but not taken that I heare yet. Excuse me from writing any news. If you have not put up the Books I spoke to you of put up with them Butlers & Farnabies Rhetorick[84] old that stood under the great

[83] Vienna was besieged by forces of the Ottoman Empire and eventually relieved by Habsburg forces. Geoffrey Holmes, *The Making of a Great Power: Late Stuart and early Georgian Britain 1600–1722* (Harlow, 1993) 12.
[84] Possibly Carolus Butler, *Rhetoricae Libri Duo* (London, 1649), Hunter et al., *Radical's Books*, 26–7.

map. My kind love to you, your wife Mother & other friends with you. Father, Son & Spirit bless you & keepe you. Farewell

Your ever lo: Father
Sa: Jeake

August 4th 1683

For Mr Samuel Jeake Junior in Rye Sussex

Nathaniel arrested, 1683

[160] *Nathaniel Hartshorne to Barbara Hartshorne, undated. Original letter.*
ESRO FRE 5291

Deare and ever Honoured Mother
I have not heard from you since I saw you which makes me feare you are gone out of Towne Pray Mother let me heare from you to night and whether you have done anything considerable for my preservation for I am very fearefull of the next sessions at the Old Bayly which as I am informed will be within this [words struck out] fortnight or 3 weekes at farthest for I am informed this Morning that there are severall Indictments ready drawne up to present against me at the next sessions. 2 of their names are My Ld Pagett and Mr Stratford which Indictments if I am burned in the hand upon will be very hard with me and then upon the other Indictments of Sir Roger Hill and others that I must afterwards be tryed upon both her & in the Country after that it will infallibly take away my life but if you get my pardon betweene this and the next sessions at the Old Bayly it will prevent the charge that will depend upon my Tryall there and that which is worse [word struck out] will prevent my being burned in the hand here for I had in a Manner as leave be hanged as be burned in the hand but to be first burned in the hand and then hanged is double shame as well as death after this manner. Consider Mother the Torment and perplexity that I have in my mind for feare of this ignominious death to dye in health, the prime of my yeares and all these things considered may be saved for £150 or £200 most. Mother if I had £10000 I would pay it all downe if I come to begg afterwards for my living I would do it ~~for~~ with as much cheerfullness and willingness as I would save my owne life to save yours if it should happen so which I Pray God Preserve and prevent. Pray Mother take me in to your consideration a little before it be too [late]. Deare Mother give some hopes of my life that I may be at Rest Mother this Cooke [words lost] have my 4d a day from does abuse me so that I am like to be starved he brings me alwa[ys] [words lost] stinking meate that it is enough

to poison me and so little that it does not satisfy [me]. Pray order me something more and better or else I cannot subsist I have been forced to sell my stockings for money to buy me meate Pray Mother send me a little money by this bearer to get me something to take when I take Phisicke which will be to morrow evening for have a very foul stomach and a severe griping in the Gutts Pray Mother do not faile to send me an Answer to all these requests but especially that I may have some assurance of my life so I am

Deare Mother
Your disconsolated But ever dutifull & obedient son.

[from the] Gatehouse Westminster.

For Mrs Barbara Hartshorne att Mr Jayes an Apothecary at the sign of the Golden Lion in Fenchurch Street in London

[161] *Nathaniel Hartshorne to Barbara Hartshorne, undated. Original letter.*
ESRO FRE 5299

Honoured Mother
I have this day seene Mrs [word struck out] Burt and she hath shewen me a letter from you that was as it seemes a letter to informe you that I were in some danger of my life which is really true for I were on Saterday last as my letter then sent from hence to you did express taken into Custody and Committed to the Gatehouse Prison and there is Sr Roger Hill my Lord Pagett and severall other Persons that have sworn positive Roberies against me for Robbing their houses and such like matters that I shalt be tried on Wednesday next being 2 dayes hence att the sessions house at the Old Bayly in London where I am informed that there all the Malicious Designes against my life as possibly can be justified in the whole world. I humbly begg of you for my life sake If you did not come to me at the sight of my last letter to come away directly upon the sight of these lines for I am prosecuted with all the Malice in the whole world for Jesus Christ's sake come to me directly or I am a dead man. If I have not somebody to come to me to look after I must bege of you as I did before to bring Captaine Hall with you to go to [word illegible] Jenkins and others and some others of my friends to do me all the kindness that may be done for I feare there is occasion you do not imagine what mercy can do. For God sake come come Deare mother for my innocence will excuse me. I hope for God knows I am innocent. I remaine in greate hopes of your coming or else I am a deade man. I am in hast

Your ever dutifull obedient and ever lasting loving son
Nath: Hartshorne.

From the Gatehouse at Westminster on Munday.
Deare, Deare Mother to me come away directly and save me deare Mot[her]. I will never trouble againe tis not my guilt brings this but Malice

For Mrs Barbara Hartshorne att her house in Rye in Sussex. These are sent with all speed.

[162] *John Vanderkers to Barbara Hartshorne, 30 August 1683. Original letter.* ESRO FRE 5300

Madam.
According to my promise I went to speake with them that were concerned with mee in procuring your Sons pardon but they are gone with the kings most Excellent Majestie to the Citty of Winchester, onely one is gone to Thissleworth at his country house, whither I now goe toe, and to-morrow morning I hope to bee heere againe to speake with you at the Horseshoe tavern or at the Apothecary's shop in Fenchurch Street about what is transacted in the business: Madam assure your selfe of your expectation & that what I promised shall bee performed, and every-thing done, and nothing [word illegible] but honestly on each side which I expect to-morrow by 10 a clock [words struck out] to be performed upon which pray Madam goe too bed & do not trouble your head more this night then I shall does in procuring what is desired. I am

Madam
Your assured friend &
servant
John Vanderkers

St James the
30th of August 1683
in haste

To Madam Hartshorne at Mr Ralph Birts at the Hors-shoe Taverne in Drury Lane.

[163] *Barbara Hartshorne to Samuel Jeake junior, 4 September 1683[?]. Original letter.* ESRO FRE 5297

Dear sonne
I hope these may finde you safe at home with Deare wife I can come to noe means to be further informed about the certainty of nats pardon but I doubt if there be not speedie course it will goe worse with him then I desir or you suspect. I am just now taken off his Irons which cost me 3 whole guines besides ~~thoo~~ two shillings to them that tooke them off I have had five pound of Mr Miller I would faine have the bed & Boulter weighed to give an account what it comes to before she bargain Your father I left ~~in as good~~ your father in as good health as you parted with him. I am in great hast & very weary

London from Mr Whitmans
seven a clock at
night your Loving Mother
Barbara Hartshorne

Sep the 4th

These for Mr Sam: Jeake att Rye in Sussex

[164] *Barbara Hartshorne to Samuel Jeake junior, 7 September 1683[?]. Original letter.* ESRO FRE 5298

Sept. the 7th
Dear sonne
To tell you of my troubles will be noe content nor newes only thus much, I have neither seen nor spoke with the Duch man since you saw him & hope he can take noe advantage by that, Nat a Thursday sent me word I must come to the horse shoe tavern presently for the Vanderkirsh was goeing to Winchester for his friend had wrot him word if he had not his resolution that post he would not meddle with it, by that I finde there is new plots a laying for a greatter sum. Oh that the lord would give me a spirit to bear these troubles or lay his healing hand on me to deliver me out of them all, iust now I have a lamentable letter from Nat which is like to breake my heart. Justice Newman is out of towne for two moneths as I am told. I have not seen son Holman neither if he were heer could doe me much good I looke upon friends but there is none to helpe. Your father is very well & gone abroad this afternoon but I a miserable creature my affectionate love

to you & your poore wife I hope she did not se Mrs Manooch child Cosins remember their loves to you both.

Your sorrowful Mother
Barbara Hartshorne.

These for Mr Sam: Jeake att Rye in Sussex

[165] *Rich. Brumfould [Nathaniel Hartshorne writing under an assumed name] to Barbara Hartshorne, undated. Original letter.* ESRO FRE 5292[85]

Honoured Mother,
I were last week to see you but you would not be seen so I went away againe and Saterday night I went downe to Gravesend to see what might be done there and there I found a Quaker that was going to Bardeaux and he would not carry me under £7 so that I were forced to come home againe to London for I considered that I know not what I should do then without either Money, friends, acquanitance nor Creditt for if I had some money to carry me to Parris and keepe me 2 or 3 Months till I could get acquainted to helpe me into some manner of employment if it would maintaine me in any manner of meane [word struck out] condition I could by degrees improve my selfe to live better. It is very strange to me to consider that you can in the least Imagine me safe here when I am dayly sought after and alwaies driven out from place to place in such ~~a~~ hazzardous wayes as perhaps you cannot believe. I were in Yorke buildings with Mr Bulger where we were surprised about 1 a clock at night with a search of 2 or 300 men so that we were both forced naked as we were out on the Topp of the house and if it had not beene for the pittifullness of some of the gentry that let us into their Garretts we had beene both taken. They shott their guns at us as we were on the houses but missed us. This is the Second escape from thence. Mother do but do as my Brother advised you to that is use your reason and you will do well enough but as you do now I am sure you do not. In the first place can you Imagine me safe in England and in the next place can believe that £10 will carry me to France. [word illegible] I have none Periwiggs I have none nor any sort of linen but just to my backe now nor shoes nor boots nor any thing that is fit or necessary for such a journey. Mother if you do but think on these things impartially you cannot but find ~~your~~ the errours of your judgement not to be small in this case. I have no horse neither. Pray send a letter by this Porter and tell me your mind as short as you can whether you had rather see me hanged than [word illegible] alive and in a good condition in another countrey. Consult what I have written

[85] The diary records Nathaniel's escape as having been in October 1683. Hunter and Gregory, *Astrological Diary*, 166.

here whether this is not very reasonable [word illegible] best be with my Brother whom I doubt not but you will believe when I were in Prison you grudged that charge but would not remedy it by getting me a Pardon or [word illegible] and now I have done it without your knowledge or helpe only by good natured strangers to whom I owe my life for their kindness to get me a Pardon you would not, as you said to backe me you would not because you dared not for feare should run away now I were told by your selfe as well as others that you would straighten your self and lay down so far as £200 would go all what I have saved as well as the other charge for before I could have beene cleared. If I had escaped hanging it would in all things have cost you between £50 or 60 thou you proposed to comply and compound that would have cost you £100 or more with charges and now for one quarter of the money that it would have cost you for my Pardon I can in all probability save my life by going beyond sea and for you to strike out and [word illegible] me that seems to not that you never designed my good or preservation because the sum is so much less than what you said you would give for my Pardon which I must needs [word illegible] if I should be taken but I hope to save that for I very much doubt and have a great deal of reason to believe that I should have no Pardon since my life is not worth £50 there hath beene a horse lost that there hath beene more proferred to find him than you are now willing to give for my life. Suppose that I were taken to night as God knows whether I shall or no I have little reason to beleive that if I should have a Pardon if £50 would buy it but I dare be positive that £500 would not, for you proferred to go as farr as £200 but I ~~do~~ am forced to believe you did but flatter me because in the first place you proffered it in the next place that when you saw it might be had you would not performe it all this treates jelousy in me to thinke you never designed to save my life and now in a manner convinces me that you had rather I should be hanged than not. People that were absolutely strangers to me that might have £100 rather than faile £200 and want bread besides where I lye will not betray my life but would rather go to Goale, severall that have [words struck out] beene brought upon their Oathes (who are strangers to me) to know where I were or whether they did not bring Tooles to bring me out though they really did it and had a reward put in their hands of 30 guineas to discover me refused both and also did their soules so much injury as to sweare falsely. I have no freind in the whole world now I see plainely what I never mistrusted nor would have believed if 10000 men had sworn that you had lay downe £50 for my life but this looks very suspitious. Perhapps you may ~~do~~ do as you do with the Imagination that I have other friends that will do any thing for me but believe me I speake it from my soul and desire never to escape this trouble I am in if I know any one in this world that will give me £20 to save my life sure [you] cannot thinke that if I had so much money as I do here desire which is but £40 in all that I would be so greate a sott and seeke my owne Ruine so apparently as to stay in England in so much visible danger of my life which is as sweete to me as yours is to loose you if you this kepe. Pray put the money into any bodies hands you can trust and let them not give me a penny till I am aboard and going off, if I should go to France as I am without money friend acquaintance or Creditt I must be forced to steale and there I should be starved in Gaole and hanged at last, Mr Bulger whose father spent more than £1000 to get him a pardon and ruined him selfe to do that is come to see his son and had but £12 in all the world hath given it him and his friends & acquaintances have raised him £100 as I am told though they never expect it againe and all this for to save his life they will do and more if neede required it & since in all probability this will be the last that I shall desire of you I pray to God to open your heart this case and never no more do I do find it to be so hard to me as to provide what I have of thus heartily begged of a Mother whom no body would believe but that the naturall tie of affection should stirr you up to this most charitable deed towards me who am

Deare Mother
Your poore distressed yet dutifull son
Rich. Brumfould

Remember my kind love to every body
I am sure all this is reason and you ought in Conscience to thinke that what I have done amiss to you before is not a good reason for you to deneigh what I aske for my life for I am sure if I am [words struck out] hanged I can lay the blame on none but you since I am escaped out of the greatest and worse danger and tis in your power to keepe me so though I am the Author of it I must Confess my selfe to be the Originall Cause of the trouble yet you may as well say that God is the author of sin as I the occasion of my death if I am taken but you are [words struck out]. My reasons are these first as I am your son there naturall affection ought to oblidge in one respect [word illegible] I have beene a great sinner and if I should be taken off by such a suddaine accident God have Mercy of my soul for I have deserved none. Pray thinke of this and send me an Answere by all means in the world for I am almost distracted and fuller of care than where I were in Prison for now I am sensible of my waies and unhappy Condition.

For Madam Barbara Hartshorne att Mr Jayes an Apothecaries at the sign of the golden Lion in Fenchurch Street in London

Trial at the Old Bailey, 1683

[166] Old Bailey Proceedings Online, Trial of Nathaniel Hartshorn, Samuel Starkey, Breaking Peace: assault, 12th December 1683, t16831212-28 and s16831212-1

Nathaniel Hartshorn, and Samuel Starkey, (formerly Servants to Goodenough and Aaron Smith) Indicted for coming to the House of William Lord Pagett, at West-Drayden, demanding Entrance at Three or Four a Clock in the Morning, with Pistols and drawn Swords in their hands, under pretence of Searching for Traytors, offering great Rudeness and Violence, forcing all the Servants (one excepted) into the Hall, set a Guard over them, then making the Steward shew them all the House; likewise confined him amongst the rest of the Servants, whilst for an hour or two they Ransack'd about the House, running their Swords through some of the Beds: And other like Misdemeanours. In their Defence they produced Warrants Impowering them to Search for certain Traitors; but no Instructions to Search the House of that Honourable Peer: Therefore they were found Guilty of a Trespass and Assault.

Nathaniel Hartshorn, and Samuel Starkey, for the Trespass and Assault; upon each of them was set a fine of a hundred pounds.

[167] *Calendar of State Papers, domestic, Charles II, February 1684*[86]

Samuel Starkey to Secretary Jenkins.

I presume you have had an account of the trial at the Old Bailey on Lord Paget's indictment of trespass against Mr. Hartshorn and myself whereon we were each fined 100*l*., Lord Sunderland's warrants (though they both expressly authorized us to search all suspected places) not being approved authentic to search his house, being a peer, but no law or precedent was suggested to or by the court to prove its illegality, and counsel are since of opinion that the verdict and judgment was misled by mistake or error and that our defence was not duly argued for want of counsel, that the same ought to be reversed by appeal to the King and Council, and that the statute that says a peer's house shall not be searched without the Lord Lieutenant or Deputy Lieutenant, etc., for arms does not affect our case nor exempt any house or place from

[86] 'Charles II: February 1684', in *Calendar of State Papers Domestic: Charles II, 1683–4*, ed. F H Blackburne Daniell and Francis Bickley (London, 1938), 253–302 http://www.british-history.ac.uk/cal-state-papers/domestic/chas2/1683-4/pp253-302 [accessed 23 August 2015].

being searched for traitors especially in so hot and close a pursuit as we then were in. But I refer this and all other matters to your more mature determination. After I had so eminently hazarded my life and fortune in accusing and actually apprehending Aaron Smith and Simon and Samuel Mayn, by virtue of your warrant and that of three Deputy Lieutenants to search for and seize arms, etc., and by the assistance of several parties of militia horse assigned by the Earl of Bridgwater, I made a strict search for above twenty days and nights together and seized a great quantity of concealed arms, etc., at Mr. Wharton's and Mr. Hampden's and narrowly missed Goodenough and Ayliffe at Enfield and also at Sir Roger Hill's. After Lord Paget and Justice Newman had trepanned me out of Whitehall and secured me without warrant or commitment a day and night close prisoner and without warrant seized and perused some of my private papers, and after I was released by you and committed four days to a messenger's custody and on an examination before a Cabinet council, then and not till then Lord Paget and Sir Roger, to stiffle my testimony, pretended I had robbed them in searching their houses, whereon I was recommitted to the Gatehouse to be prosecuted, but I was confined above five months and neither prosecuted, tried, bailed or discharged though I thrice tendered 10,000*l*. bail. At last Lord Paget shrank his pretensions to an indictment of trespass only and suffered that too to sleep for four sessions, so that at last I was forced to impanel a jury at my own charge and give notice of trial at Hicks' Hall, but then to deprive me of the defence I had there made ready of witnesses and counsel he removed the cause and without notice tried it by surprise at the Old Bailey.

Sir Roger resolves to prosecute me at the next Aylesbury assizes, 3 March. The guards assigned to assist us in our said search of Lord Paget's and Sir Roger's house are a party of Sir Francis Compton's troop and are our only witnesses. My life and reputation lie at stake and can be preserved only by their testimony at the trial. Being a young man and rendered defenceless through a long imprisonment, I am altogether incapable of taking such effectual measures as my case requires. Since I have fallen under these unhappy circumstances and through my said services have created many inveterate animosities amongst the factious party, and Lord Paget and Sir Roger and others through their instigation have made great stickling to stiffle my evidence and irritate his Majesty and Council and yourself against me, I hope you will not prejudge my cause but consider there is always a malignant party always ready to stigmatize those that are most loyal and indefatigable to serve his Majesty. Therefore I pray your favourable assistance that the said party of the Guards may be specially ordered to attend and give their testimony on my behalf at my trial at Aylesbury and that all my said warrants and papers may be forthwith redelivered me or secured in some safe hands ready to produce at my trial.

5

Friends and Family, 1684–1686

In January 1684 Samuel and Elizabeth's daughter Betty was born into what had become an affectionate marriage.[1] An exchange of letters in early 1685 saw Elizabeth express herself 'extreamly dissatisfied at [Samuel's] so long abscence'. She asked him to 'write me a letter to last a day ere it be read'. A postscript blamed her 'evil writing' on lack of sleep but her husband reassured her in his response that he had read her letter 'with great satisfaction, and as I doubt not of the sincerity of your affections' (FRE 5241; 5242).

Yet, the majority of letters in this chapter give an insight not into the intimacies of close familial relations but rather the importance of extended networks of kin and friends for early modern social and economic life. It has already been noted that the Jeakes were not a narrow nuclear family. Although it was more usual for an early modern couple to set up a separate household at their marriage, Samuel and Elizabeth's betrothal created a household in which they, Samuel senior and Elizabeth's mother resided.[2] Moreover, much scholarship attests to the importance of wide kinship ties.[3] For the Jeakes this meant important contacts with step-families, specifically Barbara's sons by her first marriage to John Holman, and close and distant cousins, the Keys, the Jayes, the Mackleys, the Wightmans, Richard Freebody and Mark Chiswell.

During this period of Samuel and Elizabeth's lives we see kinship ties called upon often for prosaic reasons: the provision of goods and the circulation of news, information and legal advice (FRE 5199). Kin provided connections in business and were appealed to for loans (FRE 5202). Indeed, we have already seen that family and close friends had proved important to Samuel in the establishment of his trading career. Kin also offered shelter and support against persecution. Samuel senior left Rye for London in November 1682 and in late 1683 Samuel junior also left Rye because he feared he would be prosecuted for nonconformity. He and Elizabeth remained in London living with his father and mother-in-law at the house of his cousins Mary and John Jaye until May 1684 when Samuel junior, Elizabeth and Barbara returned to Rye.[4] Family offered support, comfort and practical help in times of crisis.

Perhaps the most powerful example of the importance of networks of close kin and friends is presented in the mobilisation of help for Nathaniel Hartshorne. Nathaniel was condemned for his part in the robbery against Sir Roger Hill but, at the intercession of his family, he was not executed immediately but did languish in prison until August 1686 when he was finally granted an unconditional pardon.[5] While

[1] Hunter and Gregory, *Astrological Diary*, 168.

[2] Keith Wrightson, *Earthly Necessities: Economic Lives in Early Modern Britain, 1470–1750* (London, 2002).

[3] For a summary see Naomi Tadmor, 'Early modern English kinship in the long run: reflections on continuity and change', *Continuity and Change*, 25 (2010), 15–48.

[4] Hunter and Gregory, *Astrological Diary*, 165–9.

[5] 'James II – volume 2: August 1686', in *CSP Dom.*

Nathaniel was in prison, the letters show Samuel junior's London network of cousins, along with his friend Thomas Miller, executing Barbara Hartshorne's instructions, liaising with the influential individuals who might have been able to assist, passing on information and seeing to Nathaniel's needs. John Jaye, in particular, was 'very serviceable' to Barbara in this respect (FRE 5206). There are indications that acting on Nathaniel's behalf encompassed not a little inconvenience and some risk. He continued to accumulate debts, including to his washer woman who was 'poore & keept by the parishe' (FRE 5223). Another individual appealed to for support excused himself 'upon the account of Sr Roger Halls being a great man, and he a tradesman so was fearfull to appear upon any occasion for her sonn' (FRE 5180). Nathaniel did, however, justify his eventual release. He married and had two children, Barbara and Elizabeth, and returned to Rye in 1690 to take up the role of town clerk. He kept that position until his death in 1693.[6]

Kinship was not just useful, it was also meaningful. The death of Mary Jaye, Samuel junior's cousin, detailed in the letters below, revealed a network of concern and support among the Jeakes and the Jayes. Mary's final illness was presaged 'by the very sudden and amazing providence, by the Death of our Maid Anne who went to bed, well to all our apprehensions, last Thursday night, and my wife found dead in her bed in the morning' (FRE 5181). This death much affected Mary but clearly there was another underlying cause to her own illness. Subsequent letters detailed her slow decline (FRE 5185). Interestingly, in her illness Mary asked Samuel junior to 'send up her Nativity for one that you know too will look over it'. This was a reference to Mary's natal horoscope which Samuel junior was to draw up for his father to interpret. The elder man's verdict was that 'Cosin Jaye labours under that evill direction you mentioned & so much of it yet to come that I fear she will never recover it'. (FRE 5185, 5193). Samuel senior was obviously a regular visitor to the Jaye household and was there when Mary died in early February 1685, just a few days after Charles II. The reports of her death which came to Samuel junior from his father, Thomas Miller and John Jaye, Mary's husband, again demonstrate a network of concern.

Kin did not, however, always form the closest connections. Samuel junior's good friend and trading partner, Thomas Miller, also migrated to London during 1683 having been 'wearied out with the troubles & persecutions he met with at Rye'.[7] Once in London Miller became Samuel's principal business correspondent, displacing John Mackley. Trusted friendship clearly trumped kinship in this case. In return, Samuel junior acted as Miller's correspondent in Rye. The letters in this chapter offer an insight into Miller's attempts to manage his various investments and business dealings under these new circumstances and demonstrate the difficulties of dealing with business matters at a distance. He had problems in letting his properties in Rye, the larger of which he was reluctant to let 'to the french they do so much abuse a house' (FRE 5171; 5190). A consistent complaint in Miller's letters was his inability to get repayment of money lent to several individuals in Rye despite what he described as his 'great want' ((FRE 5178). The greatest outstanding debt was owed by his cousin Curteis. Frequent attempts to get him to repay over a period from mid-1684 to January 1686 proved fruitless. It is notable that although Miller consistently emphasised the 'very pregidishall' position in which he had been placed there was no attempt to prosecute Curteis for the debt (FRE 5217). This is consistent with Muldrew's findings

[6] Hunter and Gregory, *Astrological Diary*, 206.
[7] Ibid. 164.

which show that debt was often tolerated for a long period of time before recourse to law. This could be for a number of reasons, including the expense of a law suit and reluctance to escalate the situation because of the wider consequences for social relations.[8]

Samuel junior, too, was struggling financially during this period. The years between 1684 and mid-1686 were ones in which he did little business and indeed attempted to find paid employment to supplement his income. He approached a previous acquaintance, Thomas Morris, 'about getting me a place in the East India Company, or as an Accomptant to keep a Merchant's Liedger' but to no avail. Samuel suspected Morris of not working very hard in this endeavour.[9] When, on 1 January 1685, Samuel reviewed his own accounts for 1684 he found he 'had gone behind £54 13s 1d out of the stock or Principal of my Estate' and gave the reasons as his stay in London and 'not daring to put my self into any business by reason of the persecution'.[10]

As a way of repairing their problematic finances, Samuel suggested in early 1685 that he and Miller create a partnership for the negotiation of bills of exchange.[11] Miller sent 'many thankes for your proposition Concerning the Negotiating of Forraine Bills which I am very redy to Imbrace; but at presant my moneys is out of my hands as well as yours' (FRE 5195). Miller's struggles to call in debts owed at Rye clearly placed serious obstacles in the way of the development of his business. Other factors also stood in their way including the death of Charles II which led to a period of increased persecution of nonconformists during the Monmouth Rebellion. Meanwhile Miller was presented with additional reasons to distrust negotiating bills of exchange as a way of gaining profits. In June 1685 he was apparently cheated by the bankrupt Jonathan Everard. His bitter response was he 'would not advise you to meddle with any bills now for no man knows who are good & who are not' (FRE 5209). These two examples from Miller's business dealings demonstrate the primacy and problems of webs of credit in early modern society. Because there was relatively little circulating specie in the economy, credit was generally relied upon as the dominant means of exchange.[12] This embedded most individuals in complex relationships of debt and obligation which, as in Miller's case, made them dependent upon the dealings of others. The social and economic pressures which, in these circumstances, led to an emphasis on reputation and trust when borrowing and lending money have rightly been emphasised. Equally important to acknowledge, however, were the changing circumstances, competing obligations, poor economic management and unforeseen personal and wider crises that made paying debts on time problematic and placed many in a position where default was inevitable through no fault of their own.[13]

[8] Muldrew, *Economy of Obligation*, 200.
[9] Hunter and Gregory, *Astrological Diary*, 166.
[10] Ibid. 171.
[11] Ibid. 172–3.
[12] Muldrew, *Economy of Obligation*, 98–103.
[13] Ibid. 123.

The persecution of dissenters, 1684

[168] *Barbara Hartshorne to Samuel Jeake junior, 5 May 1684[?] Original letter.* ESRO FRE 5295

May the fifth
Loving sonne
Yours I have am glad to hear you are in health but as to my businesse I can efect nothing my lord told me that I must get bail[14] but it must be the Capt or master of a ship that would ingage to transport him to some of his [word illegible] Ilands For he must keepe to the warrant & when he was shipt off they should have their securitie againe being under the masters hand a sertificate it was soe done but I can finde nobodie will medle with it unless they might sell him I am not sure then but the taylor doeth much abuse me he must be turned to the comon side how I shall perswad the taylor soe I know not he takes noe notice of letters or if I could tie him up to five shillings a weeke he hath out done Mr Markwikes order but siaes by Mr Markwiks order he let him have thirteen shillings for his ocations besides severall fees he paid himselfe I mean the taylor paid. What to doe in it I know nat lets him downe for Ale & tobaco. I must intreat Mr Markwik to write to him & get an Answer from him I am unwilling to paie the money unless he could be set at libertie I believe they doe contrive all the means that can be to hinder transportation therefore I must leave him I mean nat or the taylor I dare not undertake it he must goe to the common side & then then he can set downe nothing. Tell my deare Bettie there is no such roles worne as her lace is but twisted roles with such small white lace as her former one was. What to doe with this taylor I remember he wrot to Benson for his bill at the Asies according to the contents of his former letter but there came none till now & exceeding one Your father & all friends are well hear & remember our kinds loves to you

from your unhappie mother
Barbara Hartshorne

Sir Thomas Ginner would not have patience to hear me speake to him bid me not trouble him yet I said somthing before him I fear may doe me a mischife I am not fit to you about any business doe nothing but hartly wishe I were wise.

Let Sara know I have bought her a basket I cannot tell how she will hav[e it] must not be by the carr[ier].

To Samuell Jeake in Rye in Sussex

[14] For Nathaniel Hartshorne.

[169] *Thomas Miller to Samuel Jeake junior, 13 June 1684. Original letter.* ESRO FRE 5170

London the 13th June 1684

Loving Friend

Sir Your acceptable one of this 7th Instant is well receved and have delivered yours to your Father and heare inclosed is one from him; he is not well. I went yesterday with yours to Mr Spiller but he was not at his lodging so I did not se him but I left your letter with his man who will give it him; the news you wrote me of the death of my Cozan Hawksworth proves true, which I am heartily sorry to heare; I do se you have receved for me 8s 3d for which I thanke you; I am sorry to heare what entertainement your Naighbours give you, but I do suppose it is no more than you did expect from them. I wishe they do not proseed hier, the good Lord keep you & direct you for the best for his glory & your owne Comfort. Your good Company I do much mise, my kind love to your selfe, wife & Mother presented and to all friends with you; my Brothers remember them to you; and Mr Smith & his wife present there loves to you all; I cannot yet advise you what will be done in our busines this Terme for I have not yet seen Mr Spiller, I do much feare an appearance this Terme; my kind love to my Uncle and Aunt Shinner if at Rye, I heare Mr Markwicke is removing his shope to Battle & hath hired a house & shope there; I wishe him well to whom present my respects when you se him. Capt. Fissend[en] is very ill in Towne; Sir Tho: Armestrong is brought from Holland prisoner & is in Newgate. I have not else needfull at present but am

Sir Your faithfull Friend
Tho: Miller

To Mr Samuel Jeake Merchant at Rye

[170] *Thomas Miller to Samuel Jeake junior, 19 June 1684. Original letter.* ESRO FRE 5171

London the 19th June 1684

Lov: Friend

Sir Both yours of the 7th and 16th Instant I have receved & returned you an answer by Mr Young. The latter I answer that the bill your Mother sent me I have receved and am promised the payment of it next munday; when receved I will advise her & I am free to paye my selfe the £30 she had of me & the remaine to Mr Jaye, I shall speake to Mr Spiller as you desire when I return but I suppose it is done alredy by Tho: Shooesmith, when you have occasion to write to me in hast you may direct it to Mr Jos: Smith & Inclose mine to me; I have acquainted your Father with what you wrote me at the bottom of your letter. I se you have the news of our Outlawry, which was obtained against us these may advise you we have reversed it altho it be with great charge; and all the benefit of it is the getting time till lent sises, at which time they will bring us to a tryall; for they are very violent upon us & I expect no favour from them; therefore I shall provide for the worst. I thanke you for minding the leting my houses, which I se you can not do; your Father is not well; Capt: Fissenden cam up to London & is dead heare, god hath taken him from the evil to com; all friends heare are well; my kind love with my Brothers presented to you & your wife & Mother & all friends with you; Mr Smith & wife are well and remember them to you; I have not else needfull but am

Sir your ever Lov: Friend
Tho: Miller

Sir I praye be pleased to receve of Capt: Eve for me £7 10s for one yeares Interest due the 10th May 84. I have ordred him to paye it you and you will oblidge me.

To Mr Samuel Jeake Merchant at Rye

[171] *Thomas Miller to Samuel Jeake junior, 26 June 1684. Original letter.*
ESRO FRE 5172

London the 26th June 1684

Mr Sa: Jeake Junior
Sir My respects to you presented, & to your good wife & Mother, I did returne you answers to both yours & these are to desire you to advise your Mother I did last Munday receve her bill of £41 17 s & I have paid my selfe the £30 she had of me & 3s for interest one munth & I have cansled her bond, more I paid to Mr Spiller 3s and the remaining £11 11s I will paye to Mr Jaye according to her order, when he returnes home for he is now out of Towne; I heare there is no pardon to be obtained for Mr Hartshorne he must either be hanged or transported; I suppose the women that were imployed by your Mother have given her a full account of that matter before this, I am sorry for him & his Mother & all of you his relations; I praye god it may be sanctified to all; your good Father is som what better than he has been for som time past I praye god continue it to him; it is a very hot and dry time with us; all friends heare are well & I hope they are the sam with you, Mr Jaye is this day gon with Mr Freebody to Lidd; I have not else needfull but my hearty love & respects to all friends in generall with you as if named, both my Brothers went last satterday

for France wheare I hope they are well arrived before now; I Commit to the Lord & rest

Sir your faithfull friend
Tho: Miller

To Mr Samuel Jeake At Rye these in Sussex

[172] *Thomas Miller to Samuel Jeake junior, 3 July 1684. Original letter.*
ESRO FRE 5173

London the 3^{d} July 1684

Mr Jeake
Sir Yours & your wifes I have receved & for answer these may advise you that I did write you all I knew of your Brother which I had from Mr Jaye who had it from Mrs Lennard & Mrs Booths maid at there returne from seeking a pardon; he advised them to acquaint your mother with a full account of it which I judged they had done all I know more is that Mr Jaye tells me the above two persons are gon downe to the Assises which was this weeke & at there returne I suppose they will advise you the full what is done about them; they are both under the same Condemnation, I have inquired for Mr John Binglos & I find he is gone out of Towne. I shall follow your wifes direction about the monys have not yet paid Mr Jaye; I thanke you that you will mind my Bussines with Capt: Eve when you se him; your Father & all friends heare are well; only Mrs Kennedy is taken ill this day of a feavour. I have heard from my Brothers who are well arrived and remember them to you & all at Rye; I have not else but my kind love with all your friends heare presented to you & your wife & Mother & to all our friends in generall in Towne I rest

Sir Yours to Command
Tho: Miller

[173] *Samuel Jeake senior to Samuel Jeake junior, 21 July 1684. Original letter.*
ESRO FRE 5175

Lo: Son
Yours of the 7th instant received and have since received of Mr Buckle the £12 on the Bill of Mr Smith which you sent inclosed. By Mr Kirby I received the 3. Books & have delivered Cosin Sa: Goph the coat you sent who returns you thanks for it. You may let the Rings lye a while longer. I have not yet seen Mr Kirby to pay him, if I should not see him you may satisffie him for bringing it

& his boy for leaving it at Cosin Jay's. I am glad to heare you are all well, my love to you all is herewith sent. I am through mercy in indifferent health. I heare the Parson threatens to informe against you in the Crown Office. Mr Scot hath lately shewed me some writing which he intended to have shewed you, had they been come before you went down for better satisfaction of you in his title to the lands mortgaged to you. I do not see but all is faire & cleer, but if you desire any further accompt I will give you a Breviat of their contents. She Cosin Jaye is yet in the countrey I purpose you will see her at Rye before she returns, He remembers to you is pretty well save only a cold, Mr James returns you thanks with his love to you for the paper you sent him. The God of all grace be with you, all in you & for you, bless you & yours that I may meet you another day in glory is the desire of

your lo: Father
Sa: Jeake

Lond: July .21.
1684

To Mr Sa: Jeake junior in Rye These

[174] *Thomas Miller to Samuel Jeake junior, 14 August 1684. Original letter.*
ESRO FRE 5178

Mr Sa: Jeake Junior

London the 14th Aug: 1684

Sir Yours of this 9th Instant is receved and in it your bill of £41 1s which yesterday I did get accepted & he doth promise to paye it next friday com seven night at which time I shall demand it & dout not but it will be paid at which time I shall follow your advise and deliver the noate to your father; I thanke you for receving my bond of Mr Gillart I praye keep it till further order; I do intend to write to Cousan Curteis to paye you the monys at least halfe of it, which he promised me when at London he would do at Michmus next & if he do I praye do me the favor to receve it & indorse it upon the bond & remit me the monys to London, if you meet with returnes; your good Father is well & so thro mercy all our friends heare are; my hearty love to you and all friends with you, wishing you all hapines & peace & quiet. I Commit you to the Lord & rest

Sir Your Faithfull Friend
Tho: Miller

Sir since the writing heare of I receved [yo]ur Mothers letter & I have ingaged Mr Monck to do what she desires & will write to his friend next post; which is all with my respects to your Mother I rest T Miller

To Mr Samuel Jeake Junior at Rye these in Sussex

[175] *John Jaye to Samuel Jeake junior, 29 August 1684. Original letter.*
ESRO FRE 5180

London August 29th 1684

Lo: Cosin
Yours I received and have accordingly sent you down the oranges and Limons which with the baskett cost 2s I bless God wee gott safe to London in good time a wedensday but my wife is not well otherwise shee had write to my Cosin, Pray acquaint Mrs Hartshorne I was with Mr Moncke and he can give me no account concerning her son he write to his Chapman at Aylesbury, but he would not concerne himself in the business excusing it upon the account of Sr Roger Hills being a great man, and he a tradesman so was fearfull to appear upon any occasion for her sonn, I Returne you many thanks for all your kindness which with mine and wives service to Mrs Hartshorne, your self and Cosin, I rest your Lov: Cosin to serve you
You Jno Jaye

To Mr Sam Jeake, Junior

The death of Mary Jaye, 1684–1685

[176] *John Jaye to Samuel Jeake junior, 6 September 1684. Original letter.*
ESRO FRE 5181

London September 6th 1684

Lo: Cosin
Wee having binn visited by a very sudden and amazing providence by the Death of our Maid Anne who went to bed, well to all our apprehensions, last Thursday night, and my wife found dead in her bed in the morning, hath prevented [words struck out] her writing to Coz Jeake as shee designed, for indeed it hath so much afflicted her that shee fears that with her former Indisposition shee shall not quickly recover her selfe againe, my sister Mackley is also very sick, which adds much more to indispose her, wee Desire a Remembrance of us in your Prayers for a sanctifying of this astonishing

dispensation, that Instruction may goe a long with it and wee may hear His voice in it that wee may be alsoe [word struck out] Ready that wee may be upon our watch in this evill day. Present our service to Coz: Hartshorne which with the Like to you, and Cosin I rest your Lo: Cosin to

Serve you Jn° Jaye

My Uncle desires to be Remembered to you all. Wee shall be glad to hear how my Cosin is whether shee hath recovered the Indisposition wee left her under.

To Mr Sam Jeake Junior att Mrs Barbara Hartshornes In Rye Sussex

[177] *Samuel Jeake senior to Samuel Jeake junior, 7 October 1684. Original letter.* ESRO FRE 5182

Lov: Son
Yours of the 4th instant inclosed in Cosin Jay's by Mr Young received, & am glad thereby to heare of the health of you & yours, in whose welfare part of mine consists, and am at present indifferent through mercy, but she Cosin Jaye continues ill still & though somewhat better then she hath been, is very slow in recovery and sometimes puts me to question whether the issue may not be mortall. Mr Miller long since gave me the note you mention, which I have here sent you enclosed, & thought it not worth while to send it by post to put you to charge, when I see him I intend to tell him what you wrot of Mr Curteis. I hope because you write nothing to the contrary you are yet peaceable [words struck out] The Lord will be yet a Sun & a Shield & give grace & glory to them what walke uprightly. Seeke him & he will be found of you. Be not ashamed of, nor a Shame to the Gospel of Christ, Walk humbly & holily with God, Redeeme your time from Earthly things to heavenly. Keepe up a Sence of the mercies you have to be thankfull, Trust in God alone for all. Love the world less & Christ more. Let not any thing below him take up too much roome in your heart. God almighty bless you & yours with all spiritual temporal & eternal blessings & preserve you all spotless to his heavenly kingdome with exceeding joy. Cosin Wightman hath been ill with this Fever that is abroad & is not yet thoroughly recovered but except he & Cosin Jaye, your other Relations here are well. With my kind love to yourself, wife, Mother, Little one, & other friends I remain

your ever lo: Father
Sa: Jeake

October 7th 1684

To Mr Samuel Jeake in Rye These

[178] *Thomas Miller to Samuel Jeake junior, 10 October 1684. Original letter.* ESRO FRE 5183

London the 10th Oct: 1684

Lov: Friend
Sir At presant having so fit an oppertunity to write to you I could do no less then present my most hearty love & due respects to you & your wife & Mother being glad to heare by Mr Young of your good health as thro mercy all our friends [are] heare only Mr Whiteman who hath been v[ery] ill but now upon mendment; & Mrs Jaye who [has] been & still is very ill of a feavor & som do ques[tion] her recovery but I hope she may do well; but she is very weake & lowe. Your good Father is in good health blessed be God for it; Sir according to your former order I did receve the monys one the bill sent me & have made a receipt upon the noate you gave me & delivered it to your Father as sone as I had receved the mony & dout not but he hath or will send it you; I am glad to heare you are at peace & quiet at Rye. I praye God continue it. Sir my Cousan Curteis whose bond you have did promise me when in London to paye me in £50 in part of said bond; about this time but I heare nothing from him, which doth cause me to desire the favor of you to speake to him to paye it you & do you indorse it upon the bond, tell him I have need of it as indeed I have, and that at presant it will do me great pleasure; if you could let my house I should be oblidged to you; which is all needful but my love with my Brothers to all friends with you & at Hasting. I Commit you to the protection of the Almighty & rest

Sir Your Faithfull friend
Tho: Miller

To Mr Samuel Jeake Junior these in Rye

[179] *John Jaye to Samuel Jeake junior, 14 October 1684. Original letter.* ESRO FRE 5185

London October 14th 1684

Lo: Cousin
Yours by Mr Younge I received, and had the bill paid me by Mr Loyd last Saturday. I have according to your desire sent your note with my receipt on the back side. My Wife continues very weak wee have had the advice of two Physicians, her belly is extreamly swelled, and last Saturday, and the Lords day was so very full of pain and sick, together with vomiting that I very much feared her, but I bless God yesterday and to day shee hath binn better, but ~~very~~ wonderfull weak, that the Dr would have no company come to her shee

riseth every day towards noon, and hath comfortable nights for rest beyond expectation, I bless the Lord for her spirit is much composed, and very comfortable to her relations that are about her and I hope hath resigned her self to the Lord to do with her what pleaseth him. Shee desired me to signifie to you that if you thought good, and it was not to much trouble to you, shee would pray to you to send her up her Nativity for one that you know too will look over it,[15] and Indeed I own it as a great Mercy, and very good providence of the same person hath had opportunity now and then to visit her, for it hath binn much to satisfaction. I did believe this account would not be unwelcome to you, and therefore have the more Inlarged, but now shall conclude with mine and Dear weak wives love and service to your Mother self and wife Desiring an Intrest in your Prayers

I Rest your Lo: Cosin
To Command Jn° Jaye

Although my wife riseth every day shee is so weak that she is fain to lye upon the bed almost continually not being able to get Across the roome without help.

To Mr Samuel Jeake Junior att Mrs Barbara Hartshornes in Rye Sussex

[180] *Samuel Jeake senior to Samuel Jeake junior, 25 October 1684. Original letter.* ESRO FRE 5187

Lov: Son
Yours of the 20th instant, and am glad to heare you & yours are in health. I perceive you received mine by Mr Y. but mention nothing of the letter I sent you by Mr Kirby wherein I acquainted you that Mr Scot had paid me one & twenty pounds for you, and I desired to know how you would dispose of it. This day I saw him & gave him your Letter, & excused your writing to him for that which he had done before, because I thought you had not my Letter when you wrot, but if you send an [word struck out] Acquittance for him I will take in mine againe for I only mentioned so much were received for your use. I delivered Mr Miller and Cosin Mackley your Letters as you desired, & when I wrot all desired to have their loves remembred to you. They are all in health save she Cosin Jaye who remains still very weak & bad. Cosin Wightman is got abroad again but is yet weak. Your presentation at Rye is no other than that I thought would have overtook you sooner. The Lord fit you for it. And if you do stay there you must expect it or worse. So far as I can see, I know no friend you have there that will shelter you from the storme, unless God do

[15] Samuel senior.

more for you than he hath done for many others of his own, & what ground you have to expect it you may consider. John White may sell the part of the house Mr L: dwells in because it come to him as heire and is Gavelkind[16] provided he have a valuable consideration & deliver the possession actually, but otherwise the Sale is not good. I think £25 is not a valuable consideration. The buyer must looke to it. His part in the land cannot be sold till he is full 21. because the land is not Gavelkind. The security taken in the names of Infants I think is good being for their advantage. God Almighty bless you & yours with his chiefest blessings my love to all remaining

Your lo: father
Sa: Jeake

October 25th 1684

For Mr Sam Jeake Junior in Rye Sussex

[181] *Samuel Jeake senior to Samuel Jeake junior, 2 December 1684. Original letter.* ESRO FRE 5189

Lov: son
Yours received by Mr Markwick and am glad to heare of your health & the like of your Relations with you. I am through mercy in health at present but Cosin Jaye is still ill and hath been but twice out of her chamber in the Dining Roome these 10 weeks, her belly much swelled, sometimes full of cutting paines, and some nights restless, yet some daies pretty cheery, speakes yet pretty hearty, & though wasted of her flesh, yet breaths free, let her have a share of your prayers. Your Aunt was not very well last time I saw her. Others of our Relations are well here. Several remember to you particularly Mr Scot & his son. The Letter inclosed from Mr Scot I have read and thinke you may safely write so to Mr Kingsford as he desires but you were best send your letter up hither that Mr Scot may send it to Canterbury. I shall send you the Almanack you desire when to be had. I hope you have scraped cleere this last session. I can do nothing but wish you and yours well both here and hereafter For which I shall still pray, and remain with the affections of a

Lo: though aged Father
Sa: Jeake

Dec 2 1684

Your bill I paid Mr Pope.

To Mr Samuel Jeake junior in Rye These

[16] A system of land tenure used particularly in Kent.

[182] *Thomas Miller to Samuel Jeake junior, 2 December 1684. Original letter.* ESRO FRE 5190

London the 2d Dec: 1684

Lov: Friend,
My most kind love with my Brothers to you & your wife & Mother presented & to all friends with you I am glad to heare of your good healths and also that you continue in peace I praye God continue it to you; I thanke you for your speaking to my Cousan Curteis about my busines, but se you can not prevail; I am sorry for it, but I praye when you have convenient oppertunity be pleased to mind him of it againe & let him know that I have great want of it; by reason my Brothers do call for there monys of me; I praye if you cannot get the ~~intrest~~ principle get the Intrest due & make it receved upon the bond; I thank you for your indevors to let my house, you desire to know what rent I demand that I will leave holly to you & what you do I will stand to; but as for the great house I do not care for letting of it to the french they do so much abuse a house; but the little house; you may let them, for what you can get; if my Cousan Curteis will paye you but £25 at a time in part of the bond I am willing to take it & so be pleased to tell him; I have not else needful but to let you know your good father is well, all other things I refere you to the bearer. I Commit you to the Lord & rest

Sir Yours to Command
Tho: Miller

To Mr Samuel Jeake at Rye in Sussex

[183] *Samuel Jeake senior to Samuel Jeake junior, 1 January 1684/5. Original letter.* ESRO FRE 5193

Lo: Son
The last I received from you had in it the note for Mr Scot which I sent him and acquainted him with what you wrot me, but have not seen him since, so as whether he will make use of it or not I yet know not. Inclosed is the Almanack you desired wherein I observe ♀[17] & ☿[18] will be conjunction about the beginning of March & both far enough from ☉[19] to be seen in the mornings if cleere. Cosin Jaye labours under that evill direction you mentioned & so much of it yet to come that I fear she will never recover it all meanes used

[17] Venus.
[18] Mercury.
[19] Sun.

have hitherto been ineffectual, she is extremly swelled and now cannot rise, & sits up in her bed but little, some little hope is left, yet is she when the extremity of her paines are over pretty hearty, though worn to skin & bone. Our other relations here are well & hope you are all so, my love to you all, and prayers for your temporal & eternal happines I am

your very lo: father
Sa: Jeake

Jan 1 1684/5

Several remember to you which I omit to mention.

For Mr Sam: Jeake Junior at Rye in Sussex

[184] *Samuel Jeake senior to Samuel Jeake junior, 13 January 1684/5. Original letter.* ESRO FRE 5194

Lov: Son
Your present in the box came safe to hand and thanks from Cosin Jaye & my selfe are hereby returned to you & your wife for the same, but would not have you charge your self with the like for the future. Our Remembrance also to your mother and he desired me to write you that he had sent her the Accompt which he hoped she had received. I suppose you received the Almanack I sent you that week your box came up. She Cosin Jaye was so ill she could take none of the good things you sent. She still continues alive but cannot so much as sit up in her bed, nor lye but on one side and that with paine because excoriated and forced to be plaistered. Other Relations here are well, Cosin Freebody is in Towne he came up last Friday. The Lord bless and prosper you and yours is the daily desire of

your truly lo: father
Sa: Jeake

January 13 1684/5

To Mr Samuel Jeake in Rye Sussex. These post paid

[185] *Thomas Miller to Samuel Jeake junior, 22 January 1684/5. Original letter.* ESRO FRE 5195

London the 22th Jan 1684/5

Mr Sa: Jeake

Sir After my kind love & respects to you presented & to your good wife & Mother these may advise you that I have receved your Mothers letter & I have been this day at Mr Lukes his Chamber and find he is not yet com to Towne, so that I will goe to him againe next weeke & will do all your Mother desires me; I am glad the Coate sent doth like her; Sir I have just now receved your of this 19th Instant & am very glad to heare of your welfare; and do give you many thankes for your proposition Concerning the Negotiating of Forraine Bills which I am very redy to Imbrace; but at presant my moneys is out of my hands as well as yours; but I will indevor to call it in; & as I can get it in I shall very redily complye with your desire; I have you know £250 owing at Rye which I have Called in but cannot get it I do intend to write to write to them againe & order them to paye it to you; that is my Cousan Curteis his £100 & Mr Wilmshurst his £150 which will make a stocke of £500 which will be enufe to begine with I have also £50 in Tho: Longlys hands which I will call in; if we do goe one in this busines we must if we can get 10s per £100 for returnes of moneys downe & that will helpe for the lose of time & port of letters; & all bills you do dra heare one me to be draen at 4. or 6. dayes sight; we may consider more heare after; Sir your Father is well to whom I delivered your letter, & he remembers him to you & your wife & Mother, & little one; & saith he hath receved £6 of Mr Scot & desires to know your order conserning it; Mr Jeake I am desired by a friend heare to get him 2 or 3. hands full of Misseltoe[20] that growes upon an Oake; & I could thinke of none fitter to get it then Tho: Shoesmith, I praye therefore desire him to do me that favour & to send it me up per Carrier; I would have stackes and leaves together & he must be sure he hath it for an Oake for other will not do, for it is for a medisine. All friends heare are well but Mrs Jaye & he [*sic*] is very bade. Heare inclosed is a letter to Cos: Curteis to paye you that £10[0] which if he do you may begine; I have not else needful but am Sr you[r] [section damaged] Tho: Miller

To Mr Samuel Jeake Jun Merchant in Rye in Sussex

[20] Mistletoe had a variety of medicinal uses. G. Hatfield, *Encyclopedia of Folk Medicine: Old World and New World Traditions* (Santa Barbara, 2003), pp. 239–40.

[186] *Thomas Miller to Samuel Jeake junior, 29 January 1684/5. Original letter.*
ESRO FRE 5196

London the 29th Jan 1684

Mr Sa: Jeake
Sr Yours of this 26th Instant is receved; and take notes you are minded to proseed in the bussines of Bills with which I do agree, but feare it may be sum time before I shall get my monys In, but in order there unto I written to divers & heare inclosed I do make bould to send to you for conveyance to the partes; one is to Tho: Longly who oweth me £50 & 1 yeers Interest due the 9th of January the other is to Wm Backer for £40 & 1 yeers Interest due the 1st Nov: last, the other is to Capt Eve for £150 & 1 yeers interest due the 10th of May next; I have desired the two first named to paye it in to you with all speed; praye therefore if they be in Towne a satterday deliver the letters to them your selfe & aske them whether they will paye it to you at Rye or me heare & when they will pay it for if they will pay it to you I must send you downe the bonds; I have receved a letter from Cos: Curteis in which he doth promise to paye you sum money very suddenly & doth mention £50 let it be more or less take it, I have written also to Mr Wilmshurst about his mony but know not wheather he will paye it heare or at Rye when I know I shall advise you; but we must begine as you say with a little as monys coms in. I do approve of 2 Bills if you can bring them to it; I thanke you for speaking to Tho: Shosmith but se it cannot be had I have acquainted your Father of what you say about your monys; he is well & remembers him to you & wife & Mother & little one; praye desire my Cos: Curteis to secure the £10 Jacob Scarvil oweth him upon bond; by getting sum goods into his hands if he can; I have nothing more at present but my hearty love to you & your wife presented Committing you to the Lord, I rest

Sir Yours to Command
Tho: Miller

Sr Praye seale these letters. Tell Cos: Curteis I receved his letter & thanke thim & expect he should be as good as his word.

To Mr Sam Jeake in Rye

[187] *Samuel Jeake senior to Samuel Jeake junior, 10 February 1684/5. Original letter.* ESRO FRE 5197

Lov: Son
The seizing of the late King with an Apoplexy on ☽[21] Febr 2 and his death on ♀[22] 6 instant, & the proclaiming of the D of Y[23] in the afternoon here, I suppose is no news to you, but the following I suppose may be news your Cosin Mary Jaye yesternight about 12° a clock finished her course and fell asleep, had her senses to the last though falltred in her speech. I hope you need not be sorry for her as one without hope, for in the morning yesterday being asked how it stood with her soule & if she held fast her hope to the end she answered yes. And about 10 the last night when her speech was not articulate being asked by another whether she had any sense of the love of God upon her heart & desired if she had she would hold up her hand as a signe though she could not speake & she forthwith held up her hand. Her paines were great in her sickness, but her death was easy. The Lord fits us all for our change, other Relations here are well and hope the same of you and yours which shall be glad to heare when occasion serves. With kind you [*sic*] to you all I remain

your ever lo: Father
Sa: Jeake

♂[24] February 10th 1684/5

When you happen with oppertunity of sending without charge send up my Cosin Jayes bond that he gave on the marriage, it did lye in the box next the little Table towards the window together with Br Keys will & Inventory &c Cosin Jaye remembers to you all.

To Mr Samuel Jeake Junior in Rye Sussex

[21] Monday.
[22] Friday.
[23] James, Duke of York who was proclaimed James II on 6 February 1685.
[24] Tuesday.

[188] *Thomas Miller to Samuel Jeake junior, 12 February 1684/5. Original letter.*
ESRO FRE 5198

London the 12th Feb 1684/5

Mr Sa: Jeake
Sir Yours of this 9th Instant is before me & I thanke you for your Care in delivering my letters, I have receved a letter from Tho: Longley who talkes of sending up his hopps to paye me heare; & the contents of the Inclosed you sent me from Mr Backer is that about a munth hence he will paye me £20 & the full of the intrest due; & desires longer time for the rest; so that I find moneys will com in very slowly; I have not heard from Capt: Eve; I have receved & paid the bill of £11 5s you charged upon me; & placed to your Account; I do not send you the book you write for this week but may do it heare after, for I thinke best to rest a little while; therefore I desire you not to drae upon me any more bills till I give you order, but I praye contine your indevers to get all my moneys of Cos: Curteis & Imploye it that waye; if your moneys coms in before mine, if you do any thing upon your owne account I am ready to serve you heare to my power but for my part I can not, till I can get my moneys & when that will be I see is very unsertaine; I delivered your letter to your Father who is well but Mrs Jaye is buried this daye; pray tell your Mother I receved her letter & according to my promise I went the next daye to Mr Lukes Chamber but he was not within & since I have not been with him for he is very unsertaine to be found & besides the Kings death I believe hath put a stope to the Generall pardon; but there is expected an Acte of Grace from this K & it is like he[25] may have benefite by that but if the generall pardon did goe one & was signed by the late King I beleve her son is inserted for Mr Luke promised me it should be done & I beleve he durst not omit it; so that what money had been given him had been lost for I am of your mind there is noe fees due to him; I have not else need full but my hearty love

Sir Yours to Command
Tho: Miller

I write this post to Cos: Curteis to paye you.

To Mr Samuel Jeake Junior in Rye in Sussex

[25] Nathaniel Hartshorne.

[189] *John Jaye to Samuel Jeake junior, 18 February 1684/5. Original letter.* ESRO FRE 5199

London February 18th 1684

Loving Cousin

Sir I understand by my uncle you have heard of the Lords takeing my Dear & Loving wife to himself after her long & painfull sickness, the Lord help me to hear his voyce in it and learnd me Instruction by this as well as former Corrections. I have sent you, and Cosins your wife and Mother, each a pair of Gloves which I desire your acceptance of, I have alsoe sent a pair for Brother & Sister Holt, and for Brother and Sister Chiswell, which I would desire you to send to them.[26] Cosin I have one thing to acquaint you with which is that last Michaelmas Terme, I and my wife Raised a fine in Westminster Hall upon the house att Rye [word struck out] whereby it was settled upon the longer liver of us and Heires, so against my Dear wives decease it is fallen to me. Sir my request to you and Cosin Hartshorne upon this is to Intreat you to look after it a little for me and what you see to be needfull to be done to it, to gett done if Goodman Gowin cannot disburse the money if you please to do it for me I shall thankfully so pay you againe and if you can have a Chapman to buy it I would sell it, being I am att so great a distance from it and the concerne that great I hope you will decrease this trouble and if I can any wayes serve you or yours in my station you may assure your self none shall be more ready. I Returne you and Cosin your wife and mother, my hearty thankes for all your expressions and Manifestations of Love to my poor Dear wife and my self, and shall be glad to see you all in London, which when any of you come I hope you will make my house your quarters where you or any of my wives relations shall be really Wellcome which with my service to Cosin Hartshorne your self and wife

I rest your oblidged Loving
Cosin Jn° Jaye Junior

To Mr Samuel Jeake Junior In Rye Sussex with a brown paper parcel, caridge paid

[26] It was typical to distribute mourning tokens, such as scarves, rings or gloves, to be worn in remembrance: K. Thomas, *The Ends of Life: Roads to Fulfilment in Early Modern England* (Oxford, 2009), 244.

[190] *Mark Chiswell to Samuel Jeake junior, 21 March 1684/5. Original letter.* ESRO FRE 5200

Sir
My kind respects to you this is to searteyffey you that my vessell is in the carpenters hands and I hope by the Later end of the next weeke shee will be prittey well fineshed and then I think I shall goe For newcastell I shall want ahole stock which will be about twenty fower pounds Sir if you please to lett me have it heare according as I just to have it I shall give you maney thanks. I Remain wishing you well but desiering to hear from you the first oportunetey. If you derect youer letter to my Brother Mackley house I shall call there for it. I Rest your Loving friend

Mark Chiswell

London March 1684/5 the 21 day

This For Mr Samuel Jeake Living in Rye in Sussex

[191] *Samuel Jeake senior to Samuel Jeake junior, 25 March 1685. Original letter.* ESRO FRE 5201

March 25th 1685
Lo: son
My last to you Febr: 10th acquainted you of the death of Cosin Mary touching which I have nothing more to write but that after my Letter was wrot Cosin Jaye had her opened & found besides about 2. Gallons of water in her belly, a Mola or lumpe of unshaped flesh in her wombe of great bigness.[27] Since mine to you I have received two from you the first inclosing your Encomium on Morinus,[28] And to be returning your kindness I have herewith sent you a sheet of Scripture instances of Rhetorical Tropes & Figures the most pertinent I could call to mind in so short a time as I have been about it, the unevenness of the lines you must beare with for I have neither Ruler nor Compasses. Your other Letter inclosed the Bond I sent for which I had by Mark Chiswell by which I was glad to heare you are all in health, and hope you are still so. Your

[27] Autopsies were an unusual occurrence in seventeenth-century England and John Jaye's willingness to allow his wife to be 'opened' might be read as a deferral to the 'apparent objectivity and expertise of the medical profession in determining the cause of death'. Wear, *Knowledge and Practice*, 148.

[28] Writing on Jean Baptiste Morin, a French astrologer. A manuscript preserved in the Rye Museum Archives appears to be work by Samuel junior following Morinus's principles. This manuscript was begun in May 1695 and worked on until 1698. RMA, Selmes, RYEYT: N39.56.1.

Bill for the six pounds I received for you of Mr Scot I have paid March 2d instant. On the 21th February last I removed my quarters and am at Cosin Mackleys. Since the writing above, I received your Letter by Mr Markwick & therein your Receipt for the six pounds of Mr Scot but yet have not seen him since. I hope this Burgessing time[29] Mr Wares will pay off the money on the mortgage if you mind him of it. I can write you no good news & ill is not worth sending. The Good Lord bless & preserve you & yours and keepe you unto his heavenly kingdom, my love & respects to you all as if named, that still am

Your truly lo: Father
Sa: Jeake

I am glad to heare by Mr Markwick your little one thrives so well, & that you are all in health.

To Mr Sa: Jeake in Rye these

Managing legal matters, 1685–1686

[192] *John Mackley to Samuel Jeake junior, 28 March 1685. Original letter.*
ESRO FRE 5202

London March the 28th 1685

Lo Cousin
After my kind love with my wives to youer good selfe and wife hoping youer health as blessed be the Lord we are att present. Lo Cousin [word struck out] the Cause of writing to you now is to Disier you if you cane to spare me £25 while Christmas nex which then you shall have it a gaine it will Due me a kindness if you will spare it me so Disiering to hear frome you I rest

Your ever Lo Cousin to Command
John Mackley

Youer father hath not bein well some tim of a could but we hope it is agoing away againe.

To Mr Sam: Jeake: Marchant in Rye Sussex

[29] Probably a reference to elections to the appointed time for elections to local political office.

[193] *Thomas Miller to Samuel Jeake junior, 30 March 1685. Original letter.*
ESRO FRE 5204

London the 30th March 1685

Mr Sa: Jeake Junior

Sr Heare inclosed I do send you Mr Markwicks receipt for £47 which he hath receved of me heare which I praye imploye upon bills & all you can get of my Cousan Curteis & Mr Backer. I thanke you for what you have gotton; Heare inclosed I do send you Thomas Longly his bond of £50 upon which is due for Intrest to the 17th March 84 is 1 yeere 9 weeke at 5 per % is 59s 6d then I paid for waying & wharfage of his hopps 6s 7d and spent in selling & post of letters 17d makes 8s & paid since I write to Mr Longley 18s to Rob Barthelmew fraight so that all Charges upon his hopps is 26s besides what he pleaseth to allow me for selling of them which I leave to him; so that my prissiple & Intrest upon the bond is £52 19s & 26d paid in Charges upon his hopps is £54: 5s: 6d and his hopps com to £52: 1s: 0d & have receved so there rest due to me £2: 4s: 6d besides what he will allow me for my paines; I praye deliver him this letter & bond he paying you this 44s 6d due to me & what more he pleases for I leave it to him and so I do write him word; when receved advise me what he hath paid you; underneath I do send you a receipt for the 48s you receved of Mr Backer for me; if you can get the £40 of Mr Backer doe but the £20 he promises do not refuse; praye be earnest with Cos: Curteis for more monys I intend to write to him; praye desire him to secure the £10 due by Jacob Scarvil in mony or goods I desired him so to do long agoe & I hope he hath for he write me word as if he had praye aske him what he hath done in it & advise me in your next. Your good father & all friends heare are well blessed be God & remember them to you & all friends with you. I have no more but am

Sir Yours Tho Miller

Receved the 24th March 1684 of Mr Sa: Jeake Junior forty eight shillings which he receved for me of William Backer I say receved per me 48s

Tho Miller

To Mr Samuel Jeake Junior In Rye in Sussex

[194] *Samuel Jeake junior to Elizabeth Jeake, 21 May 1685. Original letter.*
ESRO FRE 5206

London May .21th. 1685

My dear wife

This is only to give you an account of our Travells & that now through mercy we are come safe to London, on Monday last about 1. a clock we got to Tenterden, & by that time we came thither Mr Naldread was quite tired, & could go no farther a foot, he had a little fit of an ague and feaver that afternoon, next day because he would go no farther on foot we hired horses to Maidstone & there coming very opportunely for the Tide it being very fair weather within an houre after we came to Maidstone we went down the River to Rochester, & then it being 6 a Clock afternoon & a fine evening we walked on foot to Gravesend where we lodged on Tuesday night & next morning the tide fitting at 7 a Clock & very calme we came thence in the Tiltboat & landed at London a little after noon, but Mr Naldread had another fit of an ague in the boat & was ill all day yesterday. But this day he is fine & well & walks out again. I found my father and mother & all friends here well. My Mother has not yet got your Brother out of prison. She is now gone about it I hear with Cosin Jaye, who is very serviceable to her I perceive therein. Pray let me hear from you & how little Betty does, her Grandfather & Grandmother enquire much after her & are pleased to hear she thrives so well have a care of her. The Parliament met on Tuesday last but tis said the King has not made his speech to them as yet, so I cannot send it you. Yesterday Oates was whipped at the Carts taile from Aldgate to Newgate.[30] This being all at present but my affections to you & respects to friends I remaine

Your Ever Lo: husband
Sa Jeake Junior

To Mrs Elizabeth Jeake at Rye in Sussex

[30] Titus Oates, fabricator of the Popish Plot which alleged a Jesuit plan to assassinate Charles II. He was eventually convicted of perjury and sentenced to be imprisoned for life. Prior to the commencement of that sentence he was pilloried in Palace Yard Westminster on 19 May 1685, whipped at the cart's tail from Aldgate to Newgate on 20 May and then from Newgate to Tyburn on 22 May. Alan Marshall, 'Oates, Titus (1649–1705)', *ODNB*.

[195] *Elizabeth Jeake to Samuel Jeake junior, 26 May 1685. Original letter.*
ESRO FRE 5207

Rye May the 26th 1685

Dearest
I received both the letter & the speech I am glad to hear that you are safe arrived at your Journeys end I hope Mr Naldreds illness by this time is worn off My Dear I much bemoan the loss of thy good company but my comfort is the greatest part of your abscence is expired. Little betty continues very well her coat is to little I designe to send it up a saturday to be made bigger I would desire you to buy me a needle book I am in hopes my mother will have finished her business by that time you be ready that she may come home with you pray remember to buy besse a coach or waggon my Dear remember my Duty to mother & Father with my Dear love to thy self and service to others as you see occasion. Dearest thy
affectionate wife
Elisabeth Jeake

To Mr Samuel Jeake at the Golden Lion in Fenchurch Street in London

[196] *John Jaye to Samuel Jeake junior, 11 June 1685. Original letter.*
ESRO FRE 5208

London June 11th 1685

Loving Cosin
Yours of the 2d Instant I received, and was glad to hear of your safe getting home, as for the Capps you Mention I have inquired about them, but as yet I cannot find them but if they should come to my hand, will convey them to you. Be please to acquaint my Cosin your Mother that I was with younger Benson this Morning, and I believe in a few weeks her sonn will be transported, for he told me, the Merchant hath binne once or twice with the L. C. J.[31] who was so full of business he could not be spoken withall but he intends in a few days to Give in bail, as any thing further doth offer in that I shall acquaint her with it. I did see my uncle yesterday who was very well. My Aunt was with me this Morning and is likewise and desires to be remembered to your self wife & Mother, which with my service to you my Cos: your Mother, self and wife
I Close your
Real Lo: Cosin to Command
Jn° Jaye Junior

To Samuel Jeake Junior in Rye Sussex

[31] Lord Chief Justice.

[197] *Thomas Miller to Samuel Jeake junior, 27 June 1685. Original letter.*
ESRO FRE 5209

London the 27th June 1685

Lov: Friend Mr Jeake

Sir These may advise you that I have receved the letter & box sent per Carrier & shall follow your directions as sone as I se Mr Scot; I have receved of him for you £6 & placed it to your account. I thanke you for what you have done for me. The [£]7 you receved of Mr Waylet is placed to your Debt; Your Father & [all] friends heare are well; If Mr Frebody pay me any money [for] you I will advise you; Sir These may advise you that Jonathan Everard is brock & hath given me a Cheat for 1200 ϖ̃ in bills Paris & Rouen, which is a very great lose to me. The Lord sanctifie it to me; pray beware of his bills & advise Mr Freebody of it. I would not advise you to meddle with any bills now for no man knows who are good & who are not; get what moneys in you can for me for this will put me to a great none pluse for mony for they will drae upon me from Morlaix for this mony I have paid already praye mind Cos: Curteis & se if you can get that mony & Mr Backer praye desire Mr Smith to mind Mr Tutt & get that £8 for me. I have not else but my respects to you wife & your Mother & all friends with you I rest

Sir Yours
Tho: Miller

To Mr Samuel Jeake Junior these at Rye in Sussex

[198] *Thomas Miller to Samuel Jeake junior, 4 August 1685. Original letter.*
ESRO FRE 5210

Mr Sa: Jeake Junior

London the 4th Aug 1685

Sir Yours of this 1st Instant I have receved & the bill of £46 5s upon Mr Sneath Junior I have presented & it is accepted and when due shall receve it for you; I did receve yours of the 29th of June last & followed your order there in & did send you the 10th of July per Carrier your two bonds canseled; which I do wonder you have not receved the Carrier Moon his sone did promise me to deliver it to you at Mr Foules they were sent you unsealed & being in hast I did write to you a letter one the Cleane side of one of the bonds in which I did advise you I had delivered the writings you sent to Mr Scot in the presence of your Father who was very well yesterday; I receved also of Mr Scot for you 6s for intrest & 10s for your charges & have placed it to your account. I have receved the £20 upon the noate you sent me from Mr Backer & have made it receved upon his bond of which please to advise him; I se you have receved £5 of Cos: Naldred who is at present heare. Mr Freebody hath not yet paid me any money for you but writes me he will suddenly; I praye if you have not yet receved the two bonds I sent you inquire of Moon for them & if you have them advise me & looke on the cleane side of one of them & you will find my letter to you to the purpose above mentioned; I desired you there in to be earnest with Cos: Curteis for more monys which is my request to you at this time; having more then ordinary occasion of monys at present being drane upon for the moneys I formerly paid to Everard; which I hope Cos: Curteis will consider & paye me all he oweth me or a great part thereof it will com very reasonably; I heare no less the 4. of the Callis Merchants are brocke which was the occasion of Everards failing; all friends heare thro mercy are well. My respects to you & your good wife presented & to all friends with you I rest

Sir Your Lov: Friend
Tho: Miller

To Mr Samuel Jeake Junior at Rye in Sussex

[199] *Thomas Miller to Barbara Hartshorne and Samuel Jeake junior, 22 August 1685. One original letter.* ESRO FRE 5213

London the 22th Aug 1685

Madam Hartshorne
Yours of this 20th Instant is receved & for answer what advise I can give your son Holman shall not be wanting & what moneys he desires upon your account he shall have when he calls upon me but as yet I have not seen nor heard of him till I receved your letter, which with my love to you presented I rest

Madam Yours to Command
Tho: Miller

Mr Sa: Jeake junior London the 22th Aug 1685
Sir Yours of this 20th Instant I have receved & am glad to heare of your good health & of your wifes; I se you have receved 44s: 6d of Tho: Longly & £13 of my Brother Edward, for which I thanke you; I have not receved any money of Mr Freebody yet but I would not have you to put your selfe to the truble of getting a bill for as yet I do not want the moneys. I hope my Cousan Curteis will pay you sum suddenly & then you may remit it together pray mind him as you have occasion & you will oblidge me, your Father is very well & all friends

heare thro mercy; I hope you did receve the two bonds I sent you per Carrier. I have not else but commit you to the Lord & rest

Sir Your ever Lov: Friend
Tho: Miller

To Mrs Barbara Hartshorne in Rye in Sussex

[200] *Thomas Miller to Samuel Jeake junior, 9 September 1685. Original letter.* ESRO FRE 5214

London the 9th Sept 1685

Sir My respects to you presented; these are to advise you that yesterday I receved of Mr Ric: Freebody for your account £30 ster: which I have placed to your Credit; I shall be mindfull of your bill when due upon Mr Snel; pray advise your Mother I did furnish her son Holman with £9 ster: for which I have his receipt; your Father and all friends heare are well thro mercy. Mr Grace presents his respects to you & desires you at your lashur to walke over to Mr Longleys & se how things are there & give him an account in your next to me: I suppose he meanes what Crope of Corne & hopps he hath this yeare; he presents his love to Mr Longley & his wife; which is all needful at present. I rest

Sir Your Lov: Friend
Tho: Miller

To Mr Samuel Jeake Junior at Rye Sussex

[201] *Samuel Jeake senior to Samuel Jeake junior, 19 September 1685. Original letter.* ESRO FRE 5215

Lov: son

Yours of the 22th of June, & your other by Cosin Freebody received and thereby was well satisfied to heare both you & yours well as then enjoying your health but now Mr Miller acquaints me your self & little one are both ill at which I am not a little concerned but comfort myself with hopes that yours will not exceed 2. or .3. fits of an Ague, and little Bettys fits may be over if then return not again which will be your care to prevent if it may be. I desire I may hear how it fares with you both by the next you may divert your Letter to Cosin Mackley, that accordingly addresses my be made to the Great Physician or praises returned as the case requires. Through mercy I am in health & Relations here are the same except Cosin Freebody who hath been ill of a fever this week yet I hope may do well, but you need not mention it for I think he hath not sent his wife word yet. The God of mercy bless you all with spiritual blessings in heavenly things in Christ, and heal your sicknesses & take away your sins, be neer you in what you want & call unto him for. With my love to you, your wife, mother, and child. I remaine

Your lo: father
Sa: Jeake

Sept 19th 1685

To Mr Sam Jeake junior in Rye Sussex

[202] *Thomas Miller to Samuel Jeake junior, 29 September 1685. Original letter.* ESRO FRE 5217

Mr Sam Jeake Junior
London the 29th Sept 1685
Sir All yours to the 24th Instant is receved & I do give you many thanks for your paines in going to Mr Longley's house & for the account you give I will acquaint Mr Grace with it when he com's to Towne he is yet at Eltum;[32] I am glad to heare you have lost your ague & that your Child is better then it was; your good Father thro mercy is well & all friends heare only Sa: Freebody is ill; These may advise you that I have paid to Mr Jaye £30 as you ordred me. I have receved for you of Mr Scot £21 ster: & this daye I have receved your bill of £46 5s upon Mr Sim: Snell; both of which sumes I have placed to your Credit; heare inclosed is a letter to Mr Horne of Bread[33] which I praye send him by a safe hand; it is to call in £100 my Brother John hath in his hands upon bond & I have ordred him if he please he may paye it to you the 9th Oct next which ends the halfe yeare if he do be pleased to receve it & I will send you the bond, there is 50s due for Intrest; I do write this post very earnestly to Cos: Curteis for to paye you the full bond & Intrest; and advised him I owe you above £50 which must be paid speedily & have desired him to do it; & if he have not mony to take up money for I can not stay any longer; I pray be pleased to mind him of it & let him know how that it is very pregidishall to me; I pray do me this favor to get this money of Cos: Curteis & you will very much oblidge me; for he doth not deale well with me. I have ordred Mr Edw: Wilmshurst to paye you £5 that is due for intrest of £100 there is now due 1 ½ yeare the 1st of Sept 85 at which time I desired him to paye in principle & Intrest to you but I heare nothing from him doth cause me to

[32] Possibly Eltham in Kent.
[33] Possibly Brede, which is around 4 miles west of Rye.

desire you to speake to him & know what he doth intend to doe; & advise me; your money in my hands is at your disspose when you will; in your next send Mr Scot a receipt for this £21 & then I will take in mine. I am glad to heare my uncle Shinner is upon Recovery the Lord continue it; I not else needful but am

Sir Yours to Command
Tho: Miller

To Mr Samuel Jeake Junior at Rye in Sussex

[203] *Thomas Miller to Samuel Jeake junior, 15 October 1685. Original letter.*
ESRO FRE 5218

London the 15th October 1685

Mr Sa: Jeake
Sr Both yours of this 6th & 13th Instant I have receved & thanke you for sending my letter to Mr Home who hath sent me word he will paye you the hundred pounds with Interest the 9th of Nov: next if not before, & therefore I do send you the bond & desire you to receive it for me there will be due for Interest the 9th Nov: just 7 munths; I have not seen Mr Grace since I receved yours I will acquaint him with what you write Tomorrow & will send you his answer; I se you have receved £5 of Mr Wilmshurst and that he will paye in the principle next March praye desire him not to faile of it then; I thank you for speaking to Cos: Curteis I pray follow him & get if possible these two payments he hath promised you & I shall be obliged to you for it will do me great pleasure at this time; I will speake to Mr Wildeman to send you your watch per Carrier; I do send to Abr: Wildes a letter this post & in it on for you from your Father; I do mind all you write about Nat: and am willing to do him & your Mother all the servis I can but as to what she desires I can not get it done for Mr Monck his friends there have formerly refused to do it, & I cannot desire Mr Monck to desire it a second time & I know none else that deales there. Mr Jaye tells me the best waye will be to do it by the Carrier that lives next door to the prison, & he & I have agreed next Tuesdaye to goe to the Carrier & talke with him about it, I will send him shose & stockens as you desire next week & 10d for his washer woman per Carrier; Mr Jaye tells me Mr Benson is coming up to Towne in order to get him transported; what is done in it Mr Jaye will advise you when he heares; your good Father with all friends heare are thro mercy in good health. I am sory for your Childs Illnes but I hope it will pas over; I have not else but my kind love with my Brothers presented to you & all friends with you; I do not heare Mr Longly hath been yet in Towne if you se him be pleased to tell him his Land Lord is well &

expects to se him heare very spedily or to heare from him at least for it is time; I Commit you to the Lord & rest

Sir Yours to Command
Tho: Miller

Pray advise me of the receipt of this letter per next post.

To Mr Samuel Jeake Junior at Rye in Sussex

[204] *Samuel Jeake senior to Samuel Jeake junior, 15 October 1685. Original letter.* ESRO FRE 5219

Lov: son
Abraham Wilde when he was here in Town acquainted me that the money he had of that given him by his Father while he had purchased a house in the Lower Street in Rye & settled it on his son, and that you made the writings & knew it to be true. And that he had now purchased a part of a vessel and was to pay for it £25 and desired me to give order that so much might be paid him, but had not the copy of the will so as I could not tell whether by the will he may have it or no. If the former money he had be laid out for the childs use upon the house then as I remember his wife might take £20 or what sume I certainly know not for her necessity but if it be not so, then I know not how he can have it. For if the money be given absolutely to the son, the Father cannot take it without he give Security to pay it againe, and whether he can get security I know not. I desire you would consult the will, And if it may be done to let him have it. I sent you by Mr Kirby a pot of Venice Treacle[34] which your Aunt gave me to send you. She & your cosin Sa: Goph remember their kind love to you, Last ♂[35] in the afternoon his wife was safely delivered of a son. Cosin Mackley is not yet brought a bed. Cosin Freebody this week hath taken his son down into the countrey again. We are all here through mercy in health. I hope by this little Betty hath lost her Ague, which I should be glad to heare with my kind love to you all in hast I rest

your lo: father
Sa: Jeake

Oct 15 1685

To Mr Sa: Jeake Jun in Rye

[34] Venice treacle was composed principally of honey and made with numerous other ingredients. It was used as a cheap remedy for a variety of ills. *DTGC*, 'Valencia almond – Vermilion'
[35] Tuesday.

[205] *Samuel Jeake senior to Samuel Jeake junior, 22 October 1685. Original letter.* ESRO FRE 5220

Lov Son

Yours of the 17th instant received and touching Abr: Wilde, if his brother will let him have £25 let the receipt be made to him as Executor in part of the legacy but do not you take the receipt to your self nor give any order under your hand to the Executor or any other to let him have it. If the Executor thinke not his receipt sufficient to discharge him. Abra: W: may give him his bond to save him harmless for the payment thereof to him. But if it be as you writ, the will is cleer enough for £20 that she may have, & if no further clause direct the disposall thereof to any other Legatees in case of the death of Mary or her son I see not but they may have £25. I am sorry little Betty keeps her Ague. The Lord bless preserve & keep you all here & herafter in his fear & favour. My kind love to your self & all with you, in hast I rest

Your lo: father
Sa: Jeake

Oct 22th 1685

To Mr Sa Jeake Junior in Rye in Sussex

[206] *Thomas Miller to Samuel Jeake junior, 14 November 1685. Original letter.* ESRO FRE 5223

Mr Sa: Jeake Ju:

London the 14th Nov 1685

Sir Yours of this 12th Instant I have receved advising the receiving £52: 18s: 6d of Mr Horne & that he will paye the rest next munth, for which I thanke you; I am sorry to heare Cousan Curteis hath not paid you what he promised, These may advise you I do write to him this post to hasten the payment for I hoped he had paid you according to his promise, so that if he com not to you in a little time be pleased to call upon him & you will much oblidge me; as for Mr Grace he saith he will not buy it; & for your Mothers busines, the letter sent to Mr Jaye was receved & both of us have done all we can with The Tailor & he hath promised to do all he can to get him transported & then did not dout of Effecting it; but since Mr Jaye hath been with his sonne & he tells him he meets with so much truble in that he feares he shall not be able to do it, but saith he will do all he can to do it & when done he will advise Mr Jaye & he you, but nothing being yet done was the reason he nor I did write to her; which is all I can say in it yet; the things you ordred me to send him I did send

& do com to 21s: 7d which is put to your Debit. The Taylor did tell me that Nat: was in a good Condition & wanted for nothing no more than he did before for he did meate with him as formerly & that he wanted nothing but those things I sent him; heare hath been with me the poore woman that washed his Linnen & tells me he oweth her 30s for washing and that she hath not had one penny of him ever since he hath been there I did paye he [*sic*] but 10s as you ordred me but I do thinke it most just to paye her the full for she is poore & keept by the parishe & hath no reason to washe his linnen for nothing; I am informed a great part of her arrant to London was to get this money; your good Father thro mercy is well & I will tell him what you write; all friends here are well & remember them to you; I am sorry to heare my uncle Shinner is still so il I praye remember my love to him; Cos: Naldred desires you to send him up his cane that is at your house by the first vessell that coms up; which with my hearty love to you presented I rest

Sir Yours
Tho: Miller

To Mr Samuel Jeake Junior at Rye in Sussex

[207] *Thomas Miller to Samuel Jeake junior, 5 December 1685. Original letter.* ESRO FRE 5225

Mr Sa: Jeake Junior

London the 5th Dec: 1685

Sir My last to you was the 14th last past in answer to yours of the 12th past; to which I refere you since which I have none from you; which doth make me feare Cos: Curteis hath not yet paid you; I would desire the favor of you to be very earnest with him to paye you next weeke for I have great occasion for it & he doth very much disappoint me; I will mind him againe next post & pres him all I can; Sir I shall owen it as a very singular favour if you could get me in that debt for I am very much abused that I cannot have my moneys paid me when I have so earnest occasion for it as I have at present; I praye mind Mr Horne that he paye you the other £50 the 9th Instant according to his promise for I expect it; I praye also advise Mr Wm Backer that I expected he should have paid you the 1st of Nov: last the other £20 due with Interest for 1 yeare; and that I now desire it may be paid to you with all speed; or to me heare, if he will paye it you I will send you the bond; your Good Father is well & all friends heare only Mr Mackly's sonne John is dead of the small pox; Mr Jaye tells me now that the Taylor hath been againe in Towne & hath done all he can to get Natt: Transp[orted] but saith he cannot get it done by no means he can use; I have paid Mr Jaye for you 48s 6d which is put to your Dr. Sir when you se Mr Wilmshurst tell him I do expect to have my moneys paid in the first of March heare at London at which time the yeare is up, I hope you will excuse this truble if I may be servisable to you heare command me which with my kind love to your selfe wife & Mother presented and to my Uncle & Aunt Shinner & tell him the £20 in my hands is at his dispose when he will I rest

Sir Yours to Command
Tho: Miller

I have receved the Cane you sent by Herly.

To Mr Samuel Jeake Junior at Rye in Sussex

[208] *Thomas Miller to Samuel Jeake junior, 22 December 1685. Original letter.* ESRO FRE 5226

Mr Sa: Jeake Junior

London the 22th Dec 1685

Sir Yours of the 17th Instant is receved advising the receipt of £50: 5s of Mr Horne for which I thanke you; These are to advise you I have written againe to Cos: Curteis & have been very presing upon him to paye you & I hope he will paye you I praye be earnest with him & get what you can tho but £10 at a time; there is a bill of £100 drane upon him from Deep[36] payable in London the 24 or 25th of January next; soe that I would desire the favor of you to get all you can of him before that growes due; praye keep it to your selfe; praye what moneys you have or can receve for me of any body be pleased to remit it me up as sone as you can for I want it much. I thanke you that you will mind Wilmshurst & Backer to paye me in there moneys when due as I did writ you; your good Father & all friends heare are well thro mercy; my kind love with my Brothers to you & all friends presented. I rest

Sir Your much oblidged Friend
Tho: Miller

To Mr Samuel Jeake Junior in Rye Sussex

[36] Dieppe.

[209] *Thomas Miller and Michael Godfrey to Samuel Jeake junior, 22 December 1685. One original letter.* ESRO FRE 5227

Mr Sa: Jeake Junior

London the 22th Dec 1685

Sir These are only to desire you to follow Mr Michel Godfreys order in paying sum moneys for him at Rye & who as he shall direct you; & drae upon him payable to me; which is all needful. I rest

Sir Yours to Command
Tho: Miller

[In Michael Godfrey's hand]
Sir The Inclosed is for Mr Wm Antony Master of a Smack Vessel called the Dove of Foy:[37] who was bound for St Mallo, Laden with Herrings, & by Extremity of Weather was forced up into the Port. The Master has wrote hee shall want some Repayres to his Rudder & forsayles, & som other Repayrs, pray doe mee the kindness, to see what hee may want & let him have, as far as Ten pound, or a small Matter more if you find hee wants it, & wich pay the bill for what [word illegible] I pay him pray hasten him out the first opportunity of Weather that presents & if hee requests a Bote to help him out of the Harbour; Let him have the mony to pay it [word lost] the trust & Command mee who am

Your affectionate friend toward you
Michael Godfrey

To Mr Samu: Jeake Mercht in Rye

[210] *Thomas Miller to Samuel Jeake junior, 29 December 1685. Original letter.* ESRO FRE 5230

Mr Sa: Jeake junior

London the 29th Dec 1685

Sr Both yours of this 24th & 26th Instant are receved & In the former a letter to your good Father which I carefully delivered him who thro mercy is in good health; as for the 5s you mention your Cousan now tells me he did receve it of Tho: Knight but I knew not of it till now & I yet have it not, but when I have I will pay it you; as for bills I does not se but if you be wary & take good bills but you may doe well; what servis I can doe you heare in it I am at your servis & will doe the best I can for you in it at all times; I give you

[37] Fowey in Cornwall.

my hearty thankes for your care in my consernes at Rye. I have receved a letter latly from Cousan Curteis promising to paye me all in a little time & that I shall lose nothing by him, but I looke upon it only as a put of to gaine time; but I cannot staye any longer & so I will write him; & I pray continue your minding of him & get it as you can, by little & little for I feare I shall never get it all at a time. In your last letter I receved a bill of £60 upon Mr Hays which I left at his house this day for acceptance & will call for it in a daye or two & if accepted I will keep till due as you desire if not I will returne it you per post; but I suppose noe feare but it will be accepted; as for my moneys in your hands I desire it may be remitted per bill at sight or a few days & not in a forraine bill. Your Cos: Freebody tells me his wife will give you a bond of mine of £10 from Godfrey Cros payable to my Cos. Hacksworth. I praye Sir receve it of her & doe me the favor when you have occasion or conveniency of sending to Lidd to write to Mr Cros in my nam & tell him you hav the bond & that I desire him to paye in the principle & Intrest due to you with all convenient speed & then give him in his bond; I have som moneys you know in Capt: Eves hands I have often write to him to paye it me in; but I can have noe answer from him; if I might not be to trublsom to you I would only desire the favour of you that when he comes to Towne that you would speake to him for me to paye it in ether to me in London or you at Rye & know his answer & advise me; of if he comes not in a short time be pleased to write to him & you will much oblidge me which is the needfull with my & my Brothers hearty love to you & your good Lady & Mother & all friends in generall I rest

Sir Yours to Command Tho: Miller

To Mr Samuel Jeake Junior in Rye Sussex

[211] *Samuel Jeake senior to Samuel Jeake junior, 31 December 1685. Original letter.* ESRO FRE 5231

Loving Son

Yours of the 24th instant I received, and am glad thereby to hear of your health & the health of your wife & little one, which I pray God to continue but truly sorry to hear of the unhappy condition of Cosin Freebody which I feared before but heard thereof but a little before your Letter. His brother I know was bound for Mrs Grebels money, but not for the other £50 you mention, as to the case you mention, I will not be so positive but think if 2. be bound in a bond & one of them dye yet the Executors or Administrators of the deceased shall stand obliged as well as the Survivor and intend to satisfie my self fully therein as soon as I can conveniently, & let you know for Mrs Grebels better satisfaction to whom pray commend me. As to James

Knight I refer the whole matter to you, what you do therein or any other concern of mine I shall & do accept. Cosin Mackley is well up againe, & Mary is well recovered of the smalpox but John died thereof the 4th instant being taken ill thereof ☉[38] was a sennight before. Since his death the rest hold well, but the pox and spotted fever are pretty much amongst the city & sub-urbs & what it may prove in the Spring I know not. If you could spare Secrets revealed,[39] I think there was 2 of them send me the worst, & Cottons Concordance.[40] Direct them to Cosin Jays I will call there for them. Spero te Magistrum Secreti Magni Philosophorum Facere ante Morior.[41] God almighty bless you and yours with all Spiritual, temporall & Eternal mercies. My love to you all and prayers for you that you may stand perfect & compleat in all the will of God, and be kept faithfull to his cause & interest. Remember me to all Relations & Friends with you. I am

Your lo: father
Sa: Jeake

Dec 31th 1685

Dr Stacey last time I saw him which was not long ago charged me to remember him to you. Your Aunt about a week agoe with a fall hurt her leg & is lame & be sides hath a great cold, yet I hope will do well. The rest are well there.

To Mr Samuel Jeake the younger in Rye Sussex

[212] *Thomas Miller to Samuel Jeake junior, 5 January 1685/6. Original letter.* ESRO FRE 5232

Mr Sa: Jeake Junior

London the 5th Jan 1685

Sr Yours of this 2d Instant with the Inclosed I have receved & delivered the Inclosed but have not yet conferred with him about the Contents but I doe judge it is Mrs Grebells £50 & the Scole £50 if it be so I can tell you he hath taken care about it & I would not have any words about it, for he will be honest, the two bills you sent I have receved & am paid one & Mr Godfreys I shall be paid when I call for it; Your bill of £60 is accepted & I have it bye me;

[38] Sunday.

[39] Possibly *Secrets reveal'd, or an open entrance to the shut-place of the king*, authorship unclear but noted in Hunter *et al.*, *Radical's Books*, 280–1, also referred to in chapter 2, ESRO FRE 4827.

[40] Clement Cotton, *Compleat Concordance* (London, 1648), Hunter *et al. Radical's Books*, 46–7.

[41] I hope you will have achieved mastery of the great secret of the philosophers before I die.

I thanke you for speaking to Mr Wilmshurst I have not yet heard from him, but I intend to write to him as you advise me & get part if he cannot paye all; I am sorry my Cos: Curteis gives you & me so much truble I se noe way but patience; I hope Mr Backer will be as good as his word; you may defere writting to Godfrey Cross till further order I have heard from him & he desires further time. I will speak to Mr Mackley as you desire but I feare he cannot yet pay it, trade being so very dead & of late he hath had a great Expence by his wifes Lying in & visitation of his children with the shall [*sic*] Pox. Your good Father is well & when I se him shall acquaint him what you say; Sir A friend of mine in Towne hath occasion of sum mose that growes upon dead mens scules & bones;[42] & your Father saith he has formerly seen a great deale at Winchelsea in or neare the Church; These are to desire the favor of you to speake to Cos: Tho: Shosesmith to goe over & get me all he can & send it me up per Carrier in a box directed to me & what he will have for his paines paye him & put to my account let him goe as sone as he can. I have not else but my kind love with my Brothers to you & your wife Mother & Mrs Freebody presented tell the latter her husband is well & I have delivered her message to him who will be carefull I am

Sir Your ever Lov: Friend
Tho: Miller

To Mr Samuel Jeake Junior in Rye Sussex

[213] *Richard Freebody to Samuel Jeake junior, 7 January 1685/6. Original letter.* ESRO FRE 5233

January 7th 1685

Loving Cousin

Within these few hours I Receved yours which if I had Receved it but one houre before my uncle should have seen it but he was newly gon from me, But you may be sure that I doe nothing here without his Advice, who hath seen both debts & deeds And doth take care for the scooll. And as for Mrs Grebells, it is sure, my sister being bound, But I think it best to desire her (as yett) not to Acquaint my sister with it untill I have exchanged A letter with her, As for Mr Weekes mony I know nothing but you may safely Receive it, And I would pray you to doe it, And keep it till further order, for I doe not judg it best to pay it as yett unto Any body, because it will be some disadvantage in my compostion, I shall write at the beginning of the weeke to Mr Mascale, And

[42] Moss from a dead man's skull was used for curing bleeding and headaches. Hatfield, *Encyclopedia of Folk Medicine*, pp. 244–5.

to other creditors, And hope noe blame will fall upon my Cosin Norman, I have Inclosed a Receipt to my cousin John Freebody And think it best for his bill to be sent hither that Mr Miller may have it, the money not only being properly his, but it will be just enuff to make up his debt who is left out of the Cattiloge of debtors & Creditors for that Reason, my Cordiall Respects unto your self & Cosin my true love to my wife & Ann, being what at present I know to be needful. In hast I am

Sir Your affectionate Kinsman
Rich: Freebody

I Receve my wifes dateless letter I presume the same day shee had mine And leave it to her to discourse with Mr Manooch or any other person about what household or other consernes as shee thinks fitt. Our friends here are well to day, but my uncle was not very well yesterday. Mr Naldred goes homeward to morrow where god will he desires to be next Monday.

To Mr Samuel Jeake in Rye Sussex

[214] *Samuel Jeake senior to Samuel Jeake junior, 9 January 1685/6. Original letter.* ESRO FRE 5234

Lov: Son
Yours of the 4th instant with the 2 Books, I have received & am glad to hear you are all well. For Mrs Grebels satisfaction I went yesterday to Mr Hurst and propounded the case to him, who tells me (as I did believe and wrot you before) that if the parties bound in a bond be bound joyntly and severally then the creditor if any of the debtors die before payment yet hath the liberty to Arrest which they will, the Survivor or the Executor or Administrators of the deceased, but if the bond bind the debtors joyntly (that is if the words joyntly and severally be not in the bond) then if one dye the survivors must be sued & the Executors or Administrators of him that dies first is not chargable. So as I hope Mrs Grebel may be satisfied, and wherein I can be serviceable to her shall not be backward. Remember me to her & all friends with you. I wish in your letters you had let me heare how Mr Shinner doth your Aunt is pretty well again I hear but have not seen her this fortnight. My love to your selfe Wife & Mother with little Betty. In hast I rest

your very lo: father
Sa: Jeake

Jan 9th 1685/6

To Mr Samuel Jeake the younger in Rye Sussex

[215] *James Wightman to Samuel Jeake junior, 12 January 1685/6. Original letter.* ESRO FRE 5235

London Jan 12 1685/6

Loving Cousin

Yours I received and intend to send you the quire of bonds by the Carrier on fryday, as for your Testemony Consarning our Tryall with Lernara I think it will be necessary and will be the next terme but when the time is fixed I will endeavour to give you timely notice and a supenia, I am sory I have such dull partners that they should lett Martell goe before we had his Testimony when I did write soe earnestly about it, I are afraid we must send for him from franc[43] or or some other from [Ghent], which will be Great Charge to us, I shall now write to Mr White about it, and pray Cosin if you see him be pleased to sturr him up to be diligent, that the bisnes may not miscarye through ther neglect, this with mine and my wifes Respects to you and our Cosins with my kind love to sister Freebody and tell her my brother is well and desirs to be remembred to you all, I Remaine

Your Loving Cosin
James Wightman

To Mr Samuel Jeake in Rye Sussex

[216] *Thomas Miller to Samuel Jeake junior, 16 January 1685/6. Original letter.* ESRO FRE 5236

Mr Sa: Jeake junior

London the 16th Jan 1685/6

Sir Yours of this 12th instant I have receved & thanke you for writting to Capt: Eve when you have an answer praye advise me; I se you have receved noe more moneys for me; the bill of £70 ster: you sent me I have gotten accepted & will keep till due; as for my moneys in your hands I desire if you can to remit it to me by bill because I have present want of it, which is the only reason I doe not accept of your kind offer you make me in your last; I am sorry my Cousan Curteis doth serve me as he doth for it is greatly to my prejiduce having great want of my moneys, this being the best time for giving order for goods at Morlaix & a good time to remit; but I know not how to helpe my selfe. Mr Wilmshurst money also would be very usefull to me if I could have it but I se I am like to be disappointed there also. I will write to him, & I would desire once more the favour of you to speake to him & let him know I have great

[43] France.

need of it & if possible that he would pay me in the full of the bond the 1st of March but if that cannot be done he must not faile me to paye in halfe with the intrest of the hole; I have told Mr Jaye I will pay him 41s for your Mother when he calles for it; underneath is account of the severall payments I have paid for your Mother which comes to £5: 11s: 01d ster: with the 41s I have promised to paye Mr Jaye; your Father & all friends heare thro mercy are well in health. I have receved the 40s 6d of Mr Godfrey. I have not else at present only the Ld de Lainer is found not guilty by his peares. My kind love to you and all friends with you presented together with my Brothers I rest

Sir Yours to Command
Tho: Miller

1685

			£	s	d
Oct	22th	To things sent Nat	0 -	11 -	3
	24	To 10 paid Mr Bats	0 -	10 -	0
	24	To 4d to a porter to Carry Natts things	0 -	00 -	4
N[ovember]	28th	To Mr Jaye	2 -	08 -	6
		To Mr Jaye	2 -	01 -	0
			5 -	11 -	1

To Mr Samuel Jeake junior in Rye Sussex

Married Life, 1686

[217] *Samuel Jeake junior to Elizabeth Jeake, 26 January 1685/6. Original letter.* ESRO FRE 5239

London Jan: 26th 1685/6

My Dearest Wife
I am through mercy safely arrived here, where found my father & all friends very well; I hope you, my mother, little Betty & my Cosin are the same since I parted from you; I am sorry my stay here must be so long from you for the Tryall I understand is put off till Thursday come sennight next, so that I think I shall not be at home till the Saturday following, & if there by any other demurr then it will be longer. Pray have a care of my little Girle her Grandfather enquires much after her & so do other relations. Give my duty to my Mother & tell her I have conferred with Cosin Jaye about my Br Nats enlargment & he thinks it will never be done by any application to Mr Luke, nor any way else but by the Taylor & his effecting it next assizes by peticion to the Judge

that comes the Circuit, & then it must be by Transportation, but he hath not promised the Taylor any thing but means to put him in hopes of a reasonable gratuity in case he do effect it, for he saith there is no other way to do it, he thinks the Taylor will be in Town this term; if he be possibly I may talk with him about it: & about some reasonable allowance for his diet for the future, for my Cosin fears he doth spend the 5s per week & run on with the Taylor as before; but I know not how it is. I will do what I can to rectify it if I see him before I come away. Mr John Miller is lately married to a Doctor of Physicks daughter one Dr Fielding who lives in Covent garden. I hear he hath £800 with her & her father a man of great estate, keeps his [section damaged]. John lives with him now; & so doth another [son] in law that married another of them; for the old man wont part with his daughters; I think tis a very good hit for John if he make good use of it they say also 'tis a very sober family. If you write me not a Letter this post let me hear from you by next & direct your Letter to Cosin Jays. My cordial love to your selfe & respects to Cosin tell her her husband is well, remember me to Little Betty, & to friends that ask after me. I have no more at present but that I am

Your ever loving husband
Sa: Jeake Junior

To Mrs Elizabeth Jeake at Rye in Sussex

[218] *Elizabeth Jeake to Samuel Jeake junior, 26 January 1685/6. Original letter.*
ESRO FRE 5240

Rye January the 26th 1685

My Dear
this is to acquaint you that a saturday I received a letter from my cousin wightman wherein he desired you to bring up the bills of sale I went to John white to enquire concerning them he told me you had them with you as my cousin desired, my cousin Freebody holds up still she remembers her service to you betty hath a little of her ague today I hope it will not continue pray my Dear take care of your self this cold weather I must desire you to buy me a piece of laced quoif with a pair of ear Knotts if worn the Knot they be to be worn with are red green and white. I hope you will not be forgetfull of my hangings and carpet pray dont buy ~~the~~ it to little. My Duty to my Father and love to your Dear self with Service to those you please to give it I am my Dear

Your real affectionate
wife
Elisabeth Jeake

My mother remembers her to you and my Father. I expect to hear from you this post excuse my writing for my Fingers are very cold.

To Mr Samuel Jeake at Mr James Wightman a watch maker over against the salutation Tavern in Lombard Street in London

[219] *Elizabeth Jeake to Samuel Jeake junior, 2 February 1685/6. Original letter.*
ESRO FRE 5241

Rye Feb 2 1685/6

My Dear
These will serve to let you know that my Cousin Freebody is safly I hope delivered of a ~~Dage~~ Daughter this day it being about a quarter of an hour past one of the clocke as neer as could be ghessed little Betty free from harm still thanks be to God My Dear I received your letter it was very acceptable to me in regard I heard of your welfare and that of my Father with other relations but I am extreamly dissatisfied at your so long abscence but am in hopes your return will be ere long else it would be more insupportable to me then now as for Robert Bartholomew of Hasting I have heard nothing from him since your departure I did hear that he was gone out of town but know not whether it be certain or not and have not time to enquire at present pray my Dear let me have a letter from you befor your return if possible for I long both to hear from you and see you as soon as your affairs will permit you; in the interim be pleased to accept of my real and unfeigned love to your dear self with duty to my father and service to those you shall think fit. I am my Dear your real & truly affectionate wife
Elisabeth Jeake.

On thing I forgot to instance in my last to you when I mentioned my hangings I must desire you to buy some of the same of the carpet enough to cover three of the little stools I have since sent to know if Robert Bartholomew were gone as I heard but I find he is still in town but waits only for a fair wind which he expects every day little Betty remembers her duty to her grandfather and you and sends you a kiss my Mother presents her service to my Father with love to your self and others. It grieves me my Dear to leave of writing when I consider it is to you [word lost] paper will not permit me to write so much as I would. I must [th]erefore be forced to leave though much against my will but I fear you [will] tax me with impertinence for what I have already wrote but I hope [you] will excuse this.

I could wish you would write me a letter to last a day ere it be read. Methinks you are to brief that you cannot fit half as [damaged section]

Excuse my evil writing but I slept but half an hour last night [damaged section].

To Mr Samuel Jeak at Mr John Jays at the Golden Lion in Fenchurch Street in London

[220] *Samuel Jeake junior to Elizabeth Jeake, 6 February 1685/6. Original letter.* ESRO FRE 5242

London Febr: 6. 1685/6

My dear & entirely
beloved wife
I had thought to have seen you this day which was the Reason I wrote not by last post but I could not be discharged as it fell out till neer noon & then it was too late to reach home to night & better for me to spend the Lords day here then upon the Road. So I intend God willing to set out next Munday morning & hope to see you before Tuesday night, I thank you for your last letter of the 2d Instant which I read with great satisfaction, and as I doubt not of the sincerity of your affections. So assure your selfe my dearest that nothing can alienate mine from you. I think my time as long ere I revisit you, as you can possibly before you see me. I received not your Letter till yesterday morning. The things I have sent which you will receive by Hawkherst Carrier were put on on Thursday in a box & sent down Friday morning because the Tryall being on Thursday I thought I should have come down yesterday morning, but Cosin Wightman being desirous to Conferr with his Counsell afterwards whether any thing more could be done this terme would have me stay to know the result lest I should be subpenaed again the same terme, & we could not find him to have his opinion till a few hours ago. There is in the Box the hangings which are green & white a very large leaf & pretty figure, which I liked so well that I bought 24 yds and judged that it would do better to cover the Stooles & for a Carpet & every thing else of the same, which will be better then to have the stools covered with another stuff. But I suppose you will do nothing about it till I come home. The box is very full of things therefore if you have it open'd take care you do not tear the stuff, for I don't know but the nails may take hold of it at some places. I am glad to hear little Betty is well & your selfe with my Mother & Cosin Frebody, & that she is safely delivered. I have a letter for her in my Pocket but shall now keep it & bring it my selfe it is from her husband who is well but I happened to miss of him yesterday. My

father is well & all Relations & friends. Severall remember to your Cosin Mackley. I must particularize because I am there. Give my remembrances to Mother & else where due. The spoon for little Betty I shall bring with me. My dear & true affections to your selfe & little Bess. I am

My Dearest wife
Your ever lo: husband
Sa: Jeake Junior

To Mrs Elizabeth Jeake at Rye in Sussex

Postscript: Nathaniel settled down

[221] *Nathaniel Hartshorne to Elizabeth Jeake, undated. Original letter.*
ESRO FRE 5336

Deare Sister
Just as I had sent my Wife over the Water with your Fruits I Received yours. I had sent them long since but being very ill neglected itt I have had them in the house these 3 weekes I sent for Mr Mannoch and paid him this afternoon he never asked me but one and then I were in the streete and gave him that Guinea which was all I had about me then, and as for Mr Miller I shall pay him speedily with use and thankes which had beene done if I had not beene sicke and now my disease showeth itt selfe to be the spotted Feavor but my Doctor tells me (as I find) that the Danger is over, I cannot by any meanes have my health here and have thoughts of coming to Rye. Pray send me word who is in your Towne Clerkes Place and by whom elected and I will go and gett a Warrant for itt, so soon as I dare go abroade and with my stocke I will trade in Wine or some other gainefull Comodities and take little house if there be any Vacant: Madam Fochee liveth in Row Alley in Bishops Gate Streete Madam Boteet was here this day and telleth me her Mother is dead: Mr Richard Goodenough is in London att Liberty Pray aske my Mother what I shall say to him as to the Remainder of the Money My wife is a good Nurse hath milke enough for 2 or 3 and the Girle thrive bravely. I cannot tell how much Money certainly I shall have to cleare but I am sure a greater sume then I had to begin with besides some bad debts and one greate one of £120 which I feare I must compound or loose all. My Mother needs not feare any thing of me for I have farr more owing me than I owe and I am sure I have been no extravagant husband of my Money by what I have left but my sickness hath cost me considerably I am sure I have not had one peny but what I have gott to keepe me my wife in lying in buying clothes for her my selfe and other necessaries besides my owne pocket expenses in my business and our

lodgings which costs us 4s per weeke meate drinke and washing for our selves and young child which the must needs imagine only costs money considerably buying all att the worst hand not having a house and conveniences I hear Mr Cadman is or is to be Mayor with ~~my~~ our humble Duties to good Mother and respects to your selfe and the rest of the family from your loving Bro Nathaniel Hartshorne

Pray my Mother to send me the cloth for the Coate and I will gett itt made upp before I goe abroade lett it be good and strong I wish you all a merry Christmas and wish I had some of your Fatt Geese and Turkys and some more of those puddings I have not eate 2 peny worth of anything till yesterday since I were sicke yesterday I eate some of a Chick or else nothing but watergrass[44] & cordials when my Mother sends any thing I desire her to direct itt home to me is the cheaper way

These to Mrs Elizabeth Jeake at Rye Sussex

[44] *OED*, n. 2. Watercress.

6

The End of the War, 1696–1697

With the persecution of the early- and mid-1680s behind them, Samuel and Elizabeth's fortunes appeared secure. During 1686 Samuel junior began to trade again and made a profit of £165 15s. In 1687 and 1688 his profits were £160 4s and £143 12s respectively.[1] While much of his profits came from interest on loans and discounting bills of exchange, he was seeing good returns on a trade in wool and hops. By the end of 1688 he computed his capital at £2,195 8s 8½d, nearly £400 of which was held in wool, lockrams and other textiles.[2] That Samuel was optimistic about his prospects at this time is confirmed by the building of a storehouse which, with some other building work carried out in 1689 and 1690, required an outlay of around £300.[3] As we have seen in the previous chapter, from the mid-1680s he had also begun to put some investment into negotiating bills of exchange. This yielded a profit of around £20 per annum in the years prior to the start of the Nine Years' War.[4] In 1687 Samuel senior returned to Rye after his long sojourn in London. The persecution of dissenters had lessened during the reign of James II and the Act of Toleration which followed the Glorious Revolution of 1688 confirmed relative freedom of worship. In 1688 Samuel junior also celebrated the birth of a son. He named the child Manasseh, meaning 'to forget', after a promise made in 1673 when he had experienced a 'support of faith' and had, briefly, made him forget his 'toil and cares'.[5] But if the later 1680s were comfortable years for the Jeakes, the 1690s were to bring a change of fortune.

The family experienced significant personal loss. In July 1690 Manasseh died after suffering a fever. Around one quarter to a third of early modern children died before their fifteenth birthday and ten to fifteen per cent died before the age of one. Thus, Samuel and Elizabeth's loss is not surprising.[6] Their reactions to the death of their child were not recorded aside from a rather emotionless account in the *Astrological Diary*. Samuel simply recorded 'About 10h a.m. My dear & only son Manasseh Jeake died of the Feaver abovementioned'.[7] Nonetheless, it was not uncommon for both parents to be involved in the care of a sick and dying child and for that child's suffering to provoke intense emotions.[8] Perhaps Samuel's silence points to a depth, rather than a lack, of feeling. In October that year Samuel senior died. In this case the younger man showed no reticence of emotion. In one of the most poignant passages in the *Astrological Diary*, Samuel junior described his father's death and their final goodbye, 'When I said farewell Dear Father, & kist his dying lips; he answered;

[1] Hunter and Gregory, *Astrological Diary*, 68.
[2] ESRO, RYE145/11, fo. 132.
[3] Hunter and Gregory, *Astrological Diary*, 68–9; 196–7.
[4] Ibid. 68.
[5] Ibid. 125; 194.
[6] Hannah Newton, *The Sick Child in Early Modern England 1580–1720* (Oxford, 2012), 2.
[7] Hunter and Gregory, *Astrological Diary*, 206.
[8] Ibid. 4.

Farewell my Dear Lamb, The Lord bless thee, & prosper all that thou undertakest'.[9] Another loss came in 1693 when Nathaniel Hartshorne died. Samuel recorded that he was 'much troubled' by his brother-in-law's death but did not specify whether the trouble was of an emotional or practical kind.[10] What we know of Nathaniel points to the latter, as does the fact that after his demise his daughter Bab lived with Samuel and Elizabeth.

No surviving letters describe these bereavements. Indeed, there are no surviving letters for the period between late 1686 and 1696; neither do Samuel junior's account books survive after 1688. The letters in this chapter cover 1696 and 1697 and chiefly detail the political and economic consequences of the final years of the Nine Years' War. They are unique in this collection because they represent a series of letters from Samuel junior to his wife, thus revealing not only details of the family's financial and economic activity at this time but also Elizabeth's contribution to that activity.

With no surviving account books for the period after 1688, we are reliant on the *Astrological Diary* to detail the economic consequences of the early years of the war. In it Samuel recorded a continuance of a purely domestic trade in wool and hops. He also began a trade in flaxseed some time during the 1690s and this emerges as a key concern in the letters below. Keeping in mind that the diary was written with hindsight and that consequences might not have been so clear cut at the time as they appeared later, Samuel noted that the war started to impact upon his business early in 1689. In January and February he found that his business in negotiating bills of exchange was buoyant. He had negotiated nearly £1,300 in bills during that period. 'But afterwards it decreased & the war coming on I gave it over'. Likewise profits on bottomry ceased in February 1689.[11] Indeed, foreign trade proved close to impossible for the small merchant during the war. The French fleet were unquestionably dominant and posed an ever-present danger. As residents of a south coast town, Samuel and Elizabeth experienced this threat at first hand. The *Astrological Diary* recorded sightings of enemy ships and fears about the risks to Rye which prompted Samuel on at least two occasions during July 1690 to send his family away and out of danger.[12] The primary risk, however, was to English merchant shipping. By 1693 ships worth £3 million had already been lost. In June of that year there came the decisive loss of the Smyrna convoy. This convoy of around 400 ships bound for Turkey was attacked and around a quarter captured or sunk. This had a powerfully negative impact on London's merchant community and resulted in a significant decline in trade.[13]

The *Astrological Diary* offers no indication that the war subjected the Jeakes to serious hardship. Once again Elizabeth's dowry offered a cushion against loss of income through trade and other activities, and Samuel's financial position was further stabilised by legacies from his father and Thomas Markwick.[14] There were other indications that Samuel was comfortably off since he was able to offer to assist in paying

[9] Ibid. 205–8.
[10] Ibid. 221.
[11] Ibid. 195.
[12] Ibid. 203; 204
[13] Julian Hoppit, *A Land of Liberty? England 1689–1727* (Oxford, 2000), 100.
[14] Hunter and Gregory, *Astrological Diary*, 208; 222. Samuel junior received around £540 from his father, although this sum was transferred prior to Samuel senior's death, and around £100 from Thomas Markwick.

off the town's debt in return for being absolved from civic duties.[15] Nonetheless, he clearly worried that his income was stagnating and, when a visit to London in April 1694 offered him new opportunities, he took full advantage.

London, at this time, was in the grip of much excitement about financial innovation. The nascent stock market had been buoyant since the start of the war and investors, many new to the market, were profiting from speculations in a wide range of companies that had emerged to supply goods that could no longer be imported from France or were essential to the war effort.[16] By 1693 and struggling to pay for what had become an extremely expensive war, the state also turned to financial innovation. Prior to 1693 William III's government had relied upon short-term borrowing to cover the rising costs of war against France but by the end of 1692 the state's credit was very low and discounts on existing debt high enough to deter further lending. Without innovative solutions, the English state must have been forced into effective bankruptcy and surrender to the French.[17] What was needed, therefore, was a means of restructuring the debt to be repaid over a longer term, as well as the development of instruments that would appeal to a much broader section of the English population. The solutions offered have rightly been called a financial revolution.[18] They included the sale of life annuities, expensive instruments for the state but appealing to the English investor, the setting up of the first state lottery, the Million Adventure, and the establishment of the Bank of England and later the New East India Company as vehicles for funding the state. Together these projects raised a limited amount, just £6,900,000, but it was sufficient to keep the English war machine going until an uneasy peace could be agreed.[19]

Samuel's interest was first piqued by the Million Adventure. This lottery offered tickets at £10 and all tickets secured a return. The buyer could not lose and, if he or she were in possession of a prize-winning ticket, they stood to make a considerable amount of money paid out annually over a sixteen-year period.[20] Samuel regarded it as a happy chance that he had come to London when the lottery was being floated, otherwise he would not have considered investing. Nonetheless, the scheme did give him some pause since if God's will, rather than chance, determined the outcome of events then to engage in a lottery and rely on chance to yield a profit was immoral. Samuel consulted several books on the matter and eventually concluded that the lottery had 'become necessary for the support of the Government in the War' and thus he could justify involvement. He purchased 20 lottery tickets on his own account and more as part of a part of a syndicate with others in Rye. He also persuaded Barbara Hartshorne to invest in tickets.[21] Samuel later invested £300 in annuities and £500 in

[15] Hunter and Gregory, *Astrological Diary*, 69–70. Samuel junior had served as overseer of the poor during 1686.

[16] Murphy, *Origins of English Financial Markets*, 16–19.

[17] P. G. M. Dickson, *The Financial Revolution in England: A Study in the Development of Public Credit 1688–1756* (London, 1967).

[18] A term first used by Dickson, *Financial Revolution*.

[19] Dickson, *Financial Revolution*, 48–9.

[20] A. L. Murphy, 'Lotteries in the 1690s: investment or gamble?' *Financial History Review*, 12 (2005), 227–46.

[21] Hunter and Gregory, *Astrological Diary*, 234–5; 238–9.

the Bank of England, thereby effecting a significant transfer of his capital from local to national investment opportunities.[22]

The *Astrological Diary* account of the decision-making process that led to Samuel's investments is of immense importance to historians. It is the only account of the financial revolution from the perspective of the small investor that has come to light thus far. But equally important are the series of letters in this chapter because they offer an insight into investors' reactions as the promise offered by those innovations began to disappoint. This is one aspect of the financial revolution that is often overlooked. The financial credibility of William III's new regime, seemingly reinforced, as Douglass North and Barry Weingast have argued, by the political changes which followed the Glorious Revolution, was illusory.[23] Poor tax planning, the high costs of the new financial instruments and the length and expense of the Nine Years' War had brought the system under significant strain. By 1696 the tax funds that were supposed to support the state's borrowing had fallen short: investors could not be paid and the new system of public debt seemed on the verge of collapse.[24] Parliament's woes were compounded by the parlous state of the England's coinage. Undermined for years by wear and clipping, the coinage by the early 1690s was little more than a token currency, reliant on users' willingness to exchange coins at their nominal value regardless of their actual weight. The war, however, acted as a serious drain on the currency as bullion was shipped to the Low Countries to pay troops and fund provisions and supplies.[25] A recoinage enacted to address the problem merely created a further drain on the currency and caused a severe shortage of coin in circulation. In total silver coin totalling around £5.7 million in nominal value was called back to the Mint. When recoined and reissued it amounted to just £3.3 million.[26] It is little wonder that vigilance regarding the value of coin was a regular theme in Samuel's letters during this period (FRE 5301, 5313, 5315, 5316, 5322).

Samuel recognised that the end of the war would bring a significant turning-point in the country's economic situation. Peace had the potential to buoy the failing market and the recall of Parliament and return of the king would also allow the public creditors to petition for a restoration of interest payments. Moreover, the end of war would bring changes in trading patterns and the prices of commodities. As Samuel noted as the end of the war was announced, 'now there is a peace there will be a noise made of the importing of forrain hops' (FRE 5306). His visit to London in September 1697 was, therefore, a visit with purpose. With more than £1,000 invested in the new public funds and significant stocks of hops and flaxseed, as he told Elizabeth '…the greatest of our concerns are now here. If they were not I should not stay from you' (FRE 5318).

The letters in this chapter allow us to observe the methods used by Samuel as he sought to protect his interests. They point to a world in which face-to-face contact mattered. Margaret Hunt has described Samuel as a 'man fully assimilated into the

[22] Ibid. 239–41. A. L. Murphy, 'Dealing with uncertainty: managing personal investment in the early English national debt', *History,* 91 (2006), 200–17.
[23] D. North and B. R. Weingast, 'Constitutions and commitment: the evolution of institutions governing public choice in seventeenth-century England', *Journal of Economic History*, 49 (1989), 803–32.
[24] A. L. Murphy, 'Demanding credible commitment: public reactions to the failures of the early financial revolution', *Economic History Review*, 66 (2013), 178–97.
[25] D. W. Jones, *War and Economy in the Age of William III and Marlborough* (Oxford, 1998).
[26] Dickson, *Financial Revolution*, 349.

world of print' and cites this time in London as a point at which the post and news dispatches took on a new significance for him.[27] That was quite true of Samuel's world and yet what this series of letters show most prominently is not a world of print but a world in which face-to-face conversation and action mattered. Newspapers were still not published daily and breaking news was slow to make the printed page.[28] Samuel would have heard important news, not read it. Indeed, when the news of the end of the Nine Years' War arrived in London, he *heard* it 'assoon as I went out' (FRE 5306). Information gathering took Samuel away from Thomas Miller's house where he was staying and to the Royal Exchange or one or several of the coffee houses or taverns around the Exchange. He also went regularly to Southwark, across the river, to enquire about the value of commodities. Thus, he wrote to Elizabeth: 'I pray tell Mr Tucker I was in Southwark to day, but could hear no news from Sturbridge Fair.[29] Mr Travell told me hops had some stur on them' (FRE 5306). That this process of information gathering was a daily chore is indicated by one letter noting times when he would be available at the Millers' house (FRE 5309). The letters reveal that Samuel regarded as important the acquisition of formulaic information, of the type that could be found in some newspapers or printed price lists, as well as in conversations. Nearly every letter recorded prices, for example, especially the price of Bank of England shares. But he also sought to interpret that information in conversations with brokers and discussions with other investors and men of business (FRE 5303, 5305). Moreover, he was embedded in influential networks. In May 1699 he dined with the Bank director Robert Bristow and was invited to 'Sir R. Ashton's but went not because I went out of town'.[30]

Influence, however, was chiefly to be found in numbers and Samuel's letters demonstrate that when it came to defending their investments, the public creditors joined forces. That Samuel was aware of the importance of using such opportunities for gaining a say in the management of his capital is indicated by his investment of £500 in the initial subscription of Bank of England shares. A minimum holding of £500 was required to secure the right to vote on the institution's decisions.[31] And Samuel regularly attended shareholders' meetings, known as the General Court or the Court of Proprietors (FRE 5306, 5307, 5315, 5322, 5323). While he was in London in 1696 and 1697 the shareholders were most concerned with the political dangers to the Bank. In this respect, he clearly assumed his voice would be heard for, with regard to proposed actions that might have affected the Bank he thought 'it necessary to stay till [Parliament] sit & use that little interest I have against it' (FRE 5319). Equally, he emphasised to Elizabeth the need to be watchful and observe how 'Parliament, will act about the Bank of which we have a good prospect that they will favour us rather than our adversaries' (FRE 5321). The adversary in question was the Land Bank and the risk was that the Bank of England would lose its place and privileges to a rival who might provide the state with a greater level of financial support.[32] Samuel also followed,

[27] Hunt, *Middling Sort*, 181; 180.

[28] James Sutherland, *The Restoration Newspaper and its Development* (Cambridge, 2004).

[29] Stourbridge Fair was held each September on Stourbridge Common on the outskirts of Cambridge.

[30] Hunter and Gregory, *Astrological Diary*, 256.

[31] Ibid. 241.

[32] D. Rubini, 'Politics and the battle for the Banks, 1688–1697', *English Historical Review*, 85 (1970), 693–714.

and got involved in, the lottery ticket holders' fights to get their prizes paid. Thus he noted on 21 October 1697: ticket holders 'are to meet next Wednesday to concert the best methods to obtain the Arrears where I intend to be with them' (FRE 5315). In a later letter he informed Elizabeth of the resolution to that meeting: 'Our Lottery Ticket men were consulting to petition the Lords of the Treasury for their arrears & if they do nothing in it I believe the Parliament will be peticioned assoon as they sit' (FRE 5317). Although it is impossible to measure the impact of the public creditors' actions on Parliament, after the war interest and annuity payments were resumed eventually. It was only after having seen the Bank of England placed on a sounder footing and having received some of the outstanding payments on his annuities that Samuel decided to return home in December 1697 (FRE 5323).

This series of letters is significant not just for what it can tell us about England's financial revolution. With her husband away for an extended period of time, it was left to Elizabeth Jeake to manage affairs at home and, in addition to caring for the household, her children and her niece, Samuel relied on her to transact his business in Rye. The letters show that this included instructing carriers and messengers, negotiations with Samuel's business partners and acquaintances, managing property and tenants, negotiating bills of exchange, borrowing and lending money, tending to the preservation of grain, hops and flax stored against future sales, the employment of men to help with these various tasks and the negotiation of the complex monetary environment of the late 1690s.

Accepted gender roles did not allow for female autonomy. The family was supposed to be 'a miniature commonwealth in which the father was king'.[33] Although early modern women did not necessarily contest this patriarchal model, the reality often differed from the theory. In a godly household, like the Jeakes', marriage might have been regarded as a partnership and Elizabeth as a 'helpmeet' to her husband.[34] Moreover, the practicalities of life, not just in godly households, required cooperation and a degree of female authority both within and outside of the household.[35] Equally, it is now clearly established that the assumption that early modern women's labour during marriage was purely domestic and unpaid is incorrect.[36] Many wives would have worked, either in their own right or in cooperation with their spouse. Erickson argues that even into the eighteenth century the evidence supports Ivy Pinchbeck's assertion that women were indeed expected to engage in employment.[37] There is no evidence that Elizabeth worked in her own right. Nonetheless, although, at first glance, the Jeake marriage seems to have conformed to a male-breadwinner model, in fact, Elizabeth and Samuel worked cooperatively to support what can be reasonably described as a family economy.

It is possible, however, to read between the lines of these letters to see that Elizabeth was not always happy with the responsibility that had been placed on her.

[33] B. Capp, 'Separate Domains? Women and Authority in Early Modern England' in P. Griffiths, A. Fox and S. Hindle eds, *The Experience of Authority in Early Modern England* (Basingstoke, 1996), 118.

[34] Ibid.

[35] Richard Grassby, *Kinship and Capitalism: Marriage, family and business in the English-speaking world, 1580–1740* (Cambridge, 2001), 92.

[36] A. L. Erickson, 'Married women's occupations in eighteenth-century London', *Continuity and Change*, 23 (2008), 267–307.

[37] Erickson, 'Married women's occupations', 295; I. Pinchbeck, *Women Workers and the Industrial Revolution, 1750–1850* (London, 1930).

Even with maids and the assistance of her mother, running a home and caring for her children was a full-time job, especially as the family grew larger during the later 1690s.[38] Elizabeth gave birth to a daughter, Barbara, in May 1695 and a son, Samuel, in June 1697. Samuel's absence added to her burdens, as he was ready to acknowledge. Thus, in September 1697, with regard to flaxseed he wrote to Elizabeth to say that he was 'troubled that I cannot ease you of that trouble by my presence' (FRE 5308, see also FRE 5311). He also acknowledged his own desire to return to Rye (FRE 5317).

Although Elizabeth may have undertaken the tasks required of her with some reluctance, she did demonstrate skill and the ability to engage in complex negotiations and decision-making. With regard to the purchase of flaxseed, for example, Elizabeth had to make judgments about quality based on samples provided (FRE 5307). Understanding the monetary environment meant keeping up with a constantly changing situation and being able to tell good money from bad (FRE 5301). Samuel's instructions also placed Elizabeth in difficult and confrontational situations as when she was asked 'to send to Mr John Curteis junior or his wife & give them warning either to continue in my house at £4 per annum or else to leave it at Ladyday' (FRE 5308).

As a schoolmaster's daughter, Elizabeth probably received a basic education from her father but there is a hint in a previous letter that her education was continuing at the start of her marriage, perhaps under the guidance of her father-in-law. Samuel senior, in a letter written in late 1682, commented that he was pleased she had 'mended [her] hand in writing'.[39] Moreover, the work Elizabeth undertook required more than just basic literacy. Numeracy would have been essential for managing household accounts, which was usually a woman's domain, and, as we have seen, for interaction with Samuel's business world. Since girls would not have generally received a great deal of instruction in numerate skills we can suppose that these too were skills acquired within the marriage.[40] Although we cannot judge directly Elizabeth's skills, her husband did praise her actions, particularly with regard to her purchases of flaxseed, where he noted 'you manage it so well that I can give you no directions' (FRE 5320, see also FRE 5309, 5312). Moreover, that her husband regarded Elizabeth as intelligent and interested in the world outside of Rye is indicated by his sending her news and reports from London, including the 'The Resolutions of Parliament' and the Kings speech 'which is worth you reading' (FRE 5302, 5322).

Elizabeth was also required to demonstrate authority while her husband was away. Again, while seeming to transgress accepted gender roles, it was essential for wives to be able to wield power in some arenas. The management of the household was women's work and that encompassed authority over the children and servants.[41] While we may only speculate on this point, since Elizabeth was just thirteen when she married and remained living under her mother's roof, achieving authority within her marriage and household cannot have been an easy task. Nonetheless, the letters show her not just in charge of the household but also employing and giving instructions to men who were to be hired to manage the Jeakes' stores (FRE 5308 and 5315). Equally, one of the most notable things about Samuel's instructions to Elizabeth are how often they

[38] Mendelson and Crawford, *Women*, 308.

[39] ESRO FRE 5141, chapter 4.

[40] B. Lemire, *The Business of Everyday Life. Gender, practice and social politics in England, c.1600–1900* (Manchester, 2012), 204.

[41] Capp, 'Separate Domains?', 127.

forced her to step outside of her domestic space. Whether negotiating loans or passing on instructions and news, Elizabeth was clearly interacting in public spaces (FRE 5306, 5311). Business could also encroach into the domestic space as Samuel's contacts came to the house to collect or deliver commodities or receive or deliver information (FRE 5312 and see also FRE 5310). For the Jeakes, as for many early modern families, the boundaries between public and private and home and work were blurred.[42]

Samuel in London, March–April 1696

[222] *Samuel Jeake junior to Elizabeth Jeake, 26 March 1696. Original letter.*
ESRO FRE 5301

London Mar. 26 1696

My Dear
This day the Parlia[ment] [word lost] voted that Guineas shall not pass for above [words lost]. Therefore I send you this that you take [none] [a]bove that rate. And you may tell Mr [Tucker] for though the vote is that they shall not pass [words lost] after Apr. 10. Yet no-body will take them for more assoon as they hear of the Vote. If Goody Pavis have not paid her money before you receive this don't take it at all Because now Guineas are settled, clipt money will not be current I believe for above a week or fortnight except tolerable good shillings & six pences. Therefore take no half Crowns. But if Pilbeam bring his rent you may take it because I promised him if brought in fortnight after Ladyday, only take no Guineas for above 22s. Here is a doctor an Acquaintance of Mr Thompsons, a sober man that would come to live at Rye, when Dr Wright goes away. Therefore you may signify so much in the Town to prevent another from stepping in before him & let me know by Tuesdays post, whether any body else have made any offer to come. But I suppose there has not yet so when you send me word I will acquaint him with it. My duty to mother, love to Betty & Bab.[43] Mr Miller & his Lady's service with [Mr] Edwards to you &c In great hast I am

Your ever lo: husband
Sa: Jeake

Mind the payment of the Kings tax as I ordered you.

To Mrs Eliz: Jeake in Rye in Sussex

[42] Flather, *Gender and Space*, 6–7.
[43] Barbara Hartshorne, daughter of Nathaniel Hartshorne.

[223] *Samuel Jeake junior to Elizabeth Jeake, 4 April 1696. Original letter.*
ESRO FRE 5302

London Apr: 4th 1696

My Dear

I received yours of the 31th past [and am] glad to hear you are all well; I will mind the [words lost] for both for my Mother & you assoon as [words lost] Madam Miller is now under some [distress] [words lost] of the loss of her Boy, who died last [words lost] Tell Betty that my Cousin Jay's Letter & [words lost] needle book with silver Clasps and Bosses is sent this [word lost] per Carrier, so you will receive it on Munday. When you write again, let her return him thanks in a letter in yours to me. You need not seal it only write the supscription to save postage. Tell Betty also Cos: Jaye remembers to her. I was at the Nags Head in Jewen Street about the books you call Bibles. But they askt so excessive dear for those that were handsomly bound that I have not yet bought any. The reading is very little not so much as you have printed for 2d. And the book not above 2 Inches square & they ask 12d a book. I suppose one may have them for 11d or 10d. But then I question whether any body will buy them. There are some they ask 8d for & perhaps will take 6 but they have no lines of gold on the Covers. You may write me what they that have any of them give for them, & then I shall know if they ask too much. But I believe a dozen will be as many as she will be able to dispose of. It's thought now that Sir G: Rook[44] will return with our fleet, before the French. And I hope we are in no danger from France neither by sea nor land. But if the French should attempt to come into the Channell, we are satisfied that we have fleet enough in the Downs to fight them. And the French forces I believe are certainly withdrawn from Calais back into Flanders. So that I hope if there should be any idle reports you will not be afraid nor in any danger. For all things go well here & we are not under any apprehensions of any thing the Jacobites or French can do. Yesterday Sir W. Parkyne and Sir J: Friend were executed.[45] The Resolutions of Parliament in Thursdays votes are worth your seeing, you have them [word lost] Rye. Dr Wright need not be disturbed about what I [word lost] to you, for I thought of the same that he does. And so [word lost] person does intend to come before Midsummer to see the Town & hire an house; & will I suppose take it kindly if Dr Wright will inform him any thing about the methods of practise there used. If he can fit his business I suppose

[44] Sir George Rooke was, in 1696, admiral of the fleet and in command in the English Channel. John B. Hattendorf, 'Rooke, Sir George (*c.*1650–1709)', *ODNB*.

[45] Sir William Parkyns and Sir John Friend were Jacobites involved in a conspiracy against William III. They were executed on Tower Hill on 3 April 1696. Paul Hopkins, 'Parkyns, Sir William (*bap.* 1649, *d.* 1696)', *ODNB*; Paul Hopkins, 'Friend , Sir John (*bap.* 1640, *d.* 1696)', *ODNB*.

he will come with me rather than ride alone being a stranger. I know not when I shall return but it will be fortnight at least if not more. Doubt not but I have you always in my thoughts with requests to the blessed God through Jesus Christ for your welfare in this life but especially for your eternal happiness. And so much the more earnestly as you express your [desires] for it. My duty to my Mother which with true love to you, respects to friends, love to Betty & Bab is all at present from your ever lo husband Sa: Jeake.

Tell Wm Mercer I have bought him a Bible. And I hope he will [word illegible] to be at Rye on the [word lost] day the 16th Inst though I can't be at home [for him].

To Mrs Eliz: Jeake in Rye in Sussex

Samuel in London, September–December 1697

[224] *Samuel Jeake junior to Elizabeth Jeake, 4 September 1697. Original letter.* ESRO FRE 5303 [Upper portion of the letter is damaged, transcription commences at line 14 of the letter]

[Damaged section] So that you will have time to write to your sister Holman [and] her husband about it, & let him send me a letter & [word lost] speak to Sir Jn° on his behalf, & let my sister also write to [word lost] how great a kindness it will do her to prevent her removing [word lost] & then I will shew the letters to Sir Jn° & move him to it again [word lost] Mr Pulteney and Mr Austin to use their interest for him & if I can before; I will leave it with Mr Miller, for Sir Jn° ordered me to [word lost] memorandum with him to mind him of it at his return. So [word lost] have no precipitation about it for nothing can be done this mo[nth]. Give my service to Mr Maior, & tell him I have spoke for the [word lost] to be sent him every Post, & it was ordered to be done accordingly. [word lost] is very well pleased to hear he is Maior, & said he would write to him before long, I find our management is very well liked of, as I [intend] to signify further by letter to him assoon as I have leisure & op[portunity]. In the mean time I know he lacks no courage to do that which is for [the good] of the Corporation. I was busied also yesterday in buying 100 in the Bank which was then at 86 or 87. but the broker tells me to not buy yesterday & he did not doubt but he should get it to day viz for 85 ½. He has appointed to meet me at the Bank Munday [word lost] when he saith I shall have it transferred. It was at 91 or 92 but [down?] since upon some demur about the peace, and if there be a further d[elay] I suppose it may sink to 80 for such is the humor here up & down everyday almost. So that this is the venture: next Monday comes [news] from Holland mail & it depends on that rise or fall but I must venture [some]thing or else do nothing, so that I mean to buy one 100 more & [word lost] the demur of the peace, for I hope that may not be a long demur, & if [news] of the conclusion of the peace should come then I believe it will be at 100 in a days time, so that then it will be to late, for I am resolved not to follow it so high. E: India stock is sunk to 54. & I find no encoura[gement] to do any thing there at present. I resolve to be very cautious of that. I shall have money enough here with my bank note of £27 16s 9d to pu[rchase] this 100 in the Bank, so I shall not need to take up any of Mr Fer[ris] except what I shall pay him again here whilst I stay in London. [If] John Dickson ask you about the bond I have to receive for him the man says he will pay it about a week hence perhaps it may be fortnight since but I am apt to think it be paid in some little time. Flaxseed I have not thought yet about: so proceed according to the Instructions I left with you. I [word lost] Mr Tucker may have wrote his son the prizes of Hops. I have [no] leisure yet to go into Southwark nor seen him since we parted [word lost] Mr Miller's folks are all in the country. My duty to my mother, love [to] children & all friends. Which with my affection to you is all at present.

Your ever lo: husband
Sa: Jeake.

Tell Betty I intend to write to her before long. I hope you will not complain now of a short lett[er].

To Mrs Elizabeth Jeake at Rye in Sussex

[225] *Samuel Jeake junior to Elizabeth Jeake, 7 September 1697. Original letter.* ESRO FRE 5304[46]

London Sept 7th 1697

My Dear

The enclosed I desire you to deliver. I send them this way because I would not send that to Mr Maior by post. I suppose old Mr Tucker will give directions to his son sufficiently cautious about hops. I am not forward to give 10 in the Country, because the risque is great in coming up. For if one bag come to damage it sweeps away the profit of a load. As to flaxseed, proceed according to the directions I left you; Only if you find any one that is positive that he will not take under 4s 6d per bushel for brown flaxseed & if it be very good. Then

[46] The final third of this letter is extensively damaged.

if you can possible get so much time to write to me about it and let them know [its like] I may buy it but I left no order for [words lost] high price. Neither would I do it unt[il] [words lost] very good & a parcell something considerable. I bought £100 stock in the bank yesterday at [words lost] & before night it fell to 83. Such is the hum[our] because the Holland post brott no [news of the] advance of the Peace. But if [words lost] My duty to my [mother] [words lost] [children] & Bab, as also to [my friends]. [In great] hast I am

Your affectionate
Sa: Jeake

To Mrs Eliz. Jeake at Rye in Sussex

[226] *Samuel Jeake junior to Elizabeth Jeake, 11 September 1697. Original letter.* ESRO FRE 5305

London Sept. 11th 1697

My Dear
I received yours by the Carrier with the Box safe. I am glad to hear of your health. I suppose you will expect to hear from me once a week & therefore write now though have not much business. I am told that the Lottery tickets due at Michaelmas 1696 are sold for 17s per Ticket that is 3s in the pound loss, & I do think to sell mine that remained after I purchased the Annuity at that rate if I can. For there will be no money to be had on them till next summer at soonest. Mine that I have remaining of that year come to £12 for which I shall have £10 4s at that rate which if I can get I am inclined to take: Now I write you that you may let my Mother know of it, she has £40 in Tickets of that year which at 3s per £ discount will make but £34. If she be willing to sell hers at the same rate I will do my endeavor for it. I think it will be the best way, for then she will be nothing behind till next Michaelmas: But if I can[not] meet with an opportunity to sell them, then she must either keep them till next summer when it's thought the Parliament will provide for [word lost] payment or else if she care to buy 16 Bla[nk] Tickets more which she may have at 17s [word lost] she may purchase a Reversion of some [word lost] life with them & those she has for which she may have £14 per ann when the party dyes, if the security continue. You must let me know her mind per next post. As to flaxseed follow my directions already given & buy what offers at those rates. As for Hops, I must leave that to Mr Tucker, he [knows] my mind how far I am willing to be concerned [word lost] not above £50 as I remember he said also he did not intend to go above. I know not what price they are at for I have no time to go into Southwark till next week. If he can buy for .9. I

believe there is no danger. His father thought he could do something in the country so I left it to him, for I take his judgment to be better than mine. I have put off my bank note at par. And got off [word lost] of my bank bill. Bank stock is now again at .86. Great expectations there are that next mail from Holland will bring news of the peace: but I fear it will not be so soon. Mr Miller's child has been very ill he is now gone into the country. Cosin Jay (& his wife) give service to you & Mother & Betty. Particularize mine, Paper fails. I am your etc. Sa: Jeake.

To Mrs Elizabeth Jeake at Rye in Sussex

[227] *Samuel Jeake junior to Elizabeth Jeake, 14 September 1697. Original letter.* ESRO FRE 5306

London Sept 14th 1697

My Dear

I had not written you to night, but that the good news of the peace coming this morning. I thought would be more welcome to you from my hand than another, though I doubt not but other Letters will come assoon to the same purpose. Tis I believe now certain, this coming by express from Holland, with this account that the peace was signed last Friday night by the Plenipotentiarys of England, Holland, Spain & France with liberty for the Emperor to sign in such a time and Strasburgh to be restored to the Empire or the Equivalent which of the Two the Emperor chuses. The King is now expected over in a very short time. And things will look with a good face again. Bank stock was yesterday at 86 & I thought to have ventured another 100 today or tomorrow. But to day morning assoon as I went out he[ard] the welcome news of peace which [thanks] be God is much better. For now to day at Exchange time Bank stock was at 98 a good rise in a days time. So that now I have given over all thought of buying hoping 'twill rise so that so that I [may] think of selling before long. Tomo[rrow] we have a Court at the Bank where I hope we shall be ordered our Bonds in & to receive our dividend. Pray don't trouble me with any errands. I pray tell Mr Tucker I was in Southwark to day, but could hear no news from Sturbridge Fair. Mr Travell told me hops had some stur on them, at least would not go currant at above £10 or £10 5s there I think it not prudence to run much above 9 in the Country, for now there is a peace there will be a noise made of the importing of forrain hops. I wrote you last I did not care to go above £150 deep in that commodity. As to flax seed buy what you can, but do not exceed what I ordered for now forrain flaxseed will be imported. Tell Mr Tucker I would willingly have a letter from him [and] know what he has done about hops, or what he is like to do. In hast I am your [words lost] husband Sa: Jeake.

To Mrs Elizabeth Jeake at Rye in Sussex

[228] *Samuel Jeake junior to Elizabeth Jeake, 16 September 1697. Original letter.* ESRO FRE 5307

London Sept. 16th 1697

My Dear

I have yours of the 14th I do approve of your buying Chetons flaxseed. But as for Apps's, if it be so bad as you write it is no matter whether he come again or no. However what you have bid him I would have you stand to. You had best keep their samples for sometimes they are apt to bring samples better than their goods are. I doubt not but you will buy all you can & get them to bring it in assoon as they can. & keep the white by it self & the brown by it self. I could not hear how hops were at Sturbridge fair last post & I have not time to go into Southwark now. I wrote you last post what I heard that hops were then at a stur, but how it is now I know not. But I depend that Mr Tucker will have advice from Southwark by the man he said he write to for that purpose. I refer you to my last letter about hops. I still think it's not worthwhile to give above 9 in the country. I do not hear anything since of my Chapman about the Tickets. But now there is peace I doubt not but we shall be paid in time. I went to Mr Offley this week & he promised me to speak for Br Holman to some of the Commissioners that he knows, of which have given her account by post. For me to go to Mr Strong &c. whom I know not will signify not a farthing. I am glad to hear so many new freeman made &c. There's no need of certificates yet about the Annuities. Yesterday I was at the Bank Court, where the Governour told us we should have our Bonds del[ivered] up when we would, & should have warrants [word lost] our overplus viz. 3 ½ p Cent. at Michaelmas. You may tell Mr Manooch I will take care to receive his when I receive mine. I suppose it will be paid by Michaelmas. Bank is now at 95. That's usual for it to waver here every day. I mind what you write about other things, but now cannot enlarge. My duty to mother, love to you & the childr[en] & all friends. I am

Your ever Lo husband
Sa: Jeake.

To Mrs Elizabeth Jeake at Rye in Sussex

[229] *Samuel Jeake junior to Elizabeth Jeake, 21 September 1697. Original letter.* ESRO FRE 5308

London Sept. 21st 1697

My Dear

I have yours of the 18th & like well what you do about flaxseed, only am troubled that I cannot ease you of that trouble by my presence but there is no help for it at present for I think it necessary for me to stay some time longer here. I would have you imploy Goddin when you want any help about the flaxseed, and of all you buy get it in assoon as you can, for when there is a quantity of 30 or 40 quarters I intend to have it to London. As for money if my mother be willing to let you have £30 I will pay interest for that which with what you have will do for the present & £10 I suppose Mr Curtis will bring soon after Michaelmas. But if you find you shall want more let me know a week before you think you shall need it & I can have it here, for Mr Miller being to have ½ will pay his part here, & I shall take care to remitt it you. I would have you send to Colman the Tailor & tell him before my Mother (who may be a witness) that if he intend to stay in my house I shall not let it under 50s per year. Only because he may be unprovided I will condescend that he may tarry till Ladyday at the rate of 40s per annum. And know his mind one way or other before Michaelmas day. Then after you have done this send to Mr John Curteis junior or his wife & give them warning either to continue in my house at £4 per annum or else to leave it at Ladyday, be sure give warning before Michaelmas. I shall never get any rent of them & therefore I must take this occasion & now there is peace I do not fear a Ten[an]t. If Colman refuse to continue as above then you may tell Mrs Curtis if she will remove thither at 50 s per year, she may which I will admit of because she was your midwife, for I shall be always troubled to get the Rent. But that keep to your self. If Col[man] leave his house its like he will go back into his own & [word lost] perhaps Smith may hire or buy mine, which my Mother m[ay] mention to them if it should so fall out. Bank stock continues at 95 1/2. I wrote you before I had received my Bank Note of £27 16s 9d. And I have received £41 7s 5d on my Bank seal'd bill & tomorrow I am like to receive £30 more & this week or next I shall have my dividend of 3 ½ per % which is £31 10s and my Bonds in. If John Dickson enquire about his Bond tell him I have received £25 of it & am prom[ised] the rest on Saturday & hope it will be then paid. When it is I will write word. I thank God for preserving our house from fire & for all his special Providence.

The Peace I hope will prove very advantagious to us. I would fain stay a little longer in hope the Bank will rise higher & though it costs me something more here in expenses & diet it must do if I continue here then it would do at home, yet I hope your saving there will make some compensation for it. I do think it may be worth my while to stay a month longer & to see how things will be when the king comes over, which I believe will give the stock another rise. I cannot sell our tickets at 17 therefore I mean to keep them, for I think they will be paid next year. If you can spare so much time hear Betty to construe some Latine & to say over the declensions & conjugations, else I shall have all to begin again at my Return. Give my duty to my mother, my love to you & the Children & Bab. I have sent the letter to her Mother[47] & seen her, & she will send a Cap before long. Give my service to Mr Maior, Mr Tucker, Mr Mannooch & other friends. If I have no business I shall write but once a week, therefore be not troubled when you have no letter, for if I should be ill you may depend on it I will not fail to write. But I have my health very well I bless God for it. Tell Mr Tucker that I have been in Southwark this afternoon to enquire about Hops. & now they tell me that Hops were run down at Sturbridge fair before it was done to £8 10s per hundred though I understand it was because the weather was very wet & dirty & they sold so rather than carry them back to London, some say there is a good crop in Flanders & many are expected from thence. There lyes our greatest danger in bringing over Flemish hops. The market in Southwark is dull from £9 10s to £9 15s or £10. But tomorrow is the great market day for hops there & Mr Travel has promised me to send me by penny post how they go there & I will not fail to give him further advice by next post. But I believe it will be a dull market. For the weather being so very wet they will come up in a dirty condition & being dull already are not like to quicken this week. In the mean time I think it best to forbear buying any more till he hears further. And as for those already bought I am clear of opinion to send them up assoon as possible, for after this dulness it's very like they may quicken again in October & then we shall be ready for the market before forrain hops can possibly come in. Besides the price being considerable it will be best to make our returns assoon as we can. Mr Miller & wife &c remembers to you, to my mother & Betty, as also to Mr Tuckers. I remaine

My Dear Your Ever Lo: husband
Sa: Jeake

To Mrs Elizabeth Jeake at Rye in Sussex

[47] Anne Hartshorne, wife of Nathaniel.

[230] *Samuel Jeake junior to Elizabeth Jeake, 25 September 1697. Original letter.* ESRO FRE 5309

London Sept. 25 1697

My Dear

I received yours of the 23rd with Betty's which are very welcome, but have not time to write to her yet. Tell Mr Tucker that I hear by Edw: Newton who lived at Canterbury that there is a great crop of hops there & the price now but £8 5s per hundred & the very best under £9 there. I am told that the Million Lottery Tickets which will be now due this 29th of Sept. 1697, will be paid first soon after Michaelmas, which makes me sorry that I did not cut them off & bring up with me.[48] Therefore I would have you some day next week when you are at leisure, to look in my Chest & you will find uppermost a large bag with papers in it amongst which you will find one parcell superscribed [Benefit Tickets in the Million Adventure][49] open it & cut off neatly one payment which you will find dated 29 – Sept. 1697 both of my Mother's benefit & mine. Then under the said Bag you will find 2 parcells of blank Tickets which are my Mothers & mine, 20 in each. Take them & cut off the payments which you find dated 29. Sept. 1697. You may observe how to cut them off by observing how the former have been cut, tis best done with a penknife. When you have them all off the Total will come to £55 viz: my Mothers benefit £10 & her 20 blanks & my benefit £5 & my 20 blanks. Then double them once & fold them up in a brown paper or two & so put them in a letter directed to me at Mr Millers in Dunstan Court Mincing Lane & keep them till Mr Harris or Mr Tucker come to London & desire either of them to bring it to me & if I not be within to leave it with Mr Miller or his wife (you need not tell Mr Harris what it is, only desire him to have a great care of it there being papers of concern in it). I am within always at 3. a clock afternoon to be sure. I am glad you do so well about flaxseed. Take note I paid Geo: Hills 2s 6d which outset when you pay him if his be so bad as you write perhaps he may be willing to abate something or to stay till I may return however I would not have you differ with him for the matter will not be great. I have received £30 more on my bank bill & shall have my dividend next week. Stock is at 97. Tell Mrs Bridon, Mr Ferris & I have some hopes of getting her husbands liberty & she may hear more [fr]om me about it in a short time. No news from beyond [seas] the winds being contrary.

Give my service to Mr Harris I wish him joy of his son & should be very glad to see him here. My duty to my mother, love to you & my children & Bab.

[48] Samuel refers here to the coupon which had to be presented to the Exchequer to collect payment.

[49] Samuel's own square brackets.

Service to Mr [word lost] Mr Tucker & other friends. My prayers are to God for all your welfare in soule & body I remain [your ever] lo: husband S J

To Mrs Elizabeth Jeake at Rye in Sussex

[231] *Samuel Jeake junior to Elizabeth Jeake, 30 September 1697. Original letter.* ESRO FRE 5310

London Sept 30th 1697

My Dear

I received yours of the 28th as to the Tickets they will come time enough by Mr Harris so send them by him, unless Mr Tucker or his father should come sooner. You do very well about the flaxseed. I do not find any rise of the prizes here so keep at 35s per quarter the highest unless you think fit to 36s for any prime parcell but be sure don't exceed that for any. Don't go after Reubens if he don't come to you let it go for we had better sit still then buy too dear. If Tho: Morrow don't come till November, I hope you may have it all in in October & if he will carry it reasonable I had rather have it by him because I have imploy'd him before. I suppose he will not expect above 2s per quarter now there's peace. You may also ask him if he will carry it & at what price & let me know. You will have time enough for you cannot have all in this month. As to wheat you must buy as the market price is what you want. I don't trouble my self about your buying the Horse but seeing you may either take or leave him till maytide you need not resolve yet till I come home which hope may be in November for I am desirous to see another dividend at the Bank which will be at the end of October hoping that may advance it something more. However I have received my Bonds this morning & cancell'd them & have also received £31 10s besides in money for my dividend of 3 ½ p Cent. The Stock is sunk a little viz to 96 but there's nothing in it but the humour of the people. I am sorry to hear my Mother is ill, & you also I will take care about the Prunes if I can get those that are good. I wish you would accustom yourself to drink more, & then I believe it would be better. I am glad to hear Mr Tucker & his wife are on recovery. I have wrote to him severall times to send the Hops up his father bought by way of Maidston but hear nothing from him. I would fain have them sent up assoon as possible. Now they are dull indeed between 9 & £10 per hundr[ed] but the charge of standing is inconsiderable now they are at so great a price & here we shall have them ready for a market. For now we expect peace will be proclaimed next week at furthest & then there will be fitting of ships to sea apace for Irela[nd] & the West Country & much brewing here, so that it's very likely they may be quick in a fortnight, but perhaps not hold so long. For when they hear of it in the country then they will send them up from Canterb[ury] & Maidston whereas this week it being dull there were but few brought up that I heard of. My Remembrances where due. I am

Your ever Lo: husband
Sa: Jeake.

Keep the eyebright from growing mouldy.[50] If Mr Manooch ask about his dividend tell him Mr Miller has received it & assoon as I come home shall have it.

Tell John Dickson I have now received all his money of Mr Eyre & when I come home shall either pay him or continue it at Inte[rest as] best suites his & my occasion.

To Mrs Elizabeth Jeake at Rye in Sussex

[232] *Samuel Jeake junior to Elizabeth Jeake, 2 October 1697. Original letter.*
ESRO FRE 5311

London Oct .2. 1697

My Dear
In answer to yours of the 30th past. You may enquire among the shopkeepers & assoon as you will draw Thirty pounds on me & write your bill thus

Rye Oct: th .1697.
per £30

At three days sight hereof pay to Mr A.B. or order the summe of Thirty Pounds Sterling value of himself as per advice of

Your Lo: Wife
E: J.

To S J at Mr T Ms mercht[51]
in Dunster Court Mincing Lane London

[50] *Euphrasia officinalis*, more commonly known as 'eyebright', was a popular remedy for weak eyes, something which Samuel had suffered from since contracting smallpox during his teens. *DTGC*, 'Etruscan – Eyebright water'.
[51] Thomas Miller, merchant.

But if my mother be willing to lend you £30 till I come home I had rather so. For I can use the money I have here to pay for my part of the hops Mr Tucker bought & perhaps I may meet with something else that may be probable to do well. However if you think not fit to do so, draw it on me for you shall not want as long as I have it. I hope I may return by the middle of November. But I would fain tarry till then. I wrote you word last post to mind Mr Tucker to send up the hops which I think of greater importance to me than the flaxseed because they come to more money, & are a hazardous commodity. I wonder I hear nothing from him nor his father as if they minded it not though to me it seems of concern. The Bank is at 96 & I hope now in a very good condition our bills being at par. For now I hear any one may have his money upon the old sealed Bills, & after the 10th of Oct it's said the Bank will allow no interest for any sum under £100 & for all greater sums put in they allow now but 3 per Cent which I doubt not but will raise the stock. I wrote you before, I have my dividend & bonds in. And the latter end of this month we do expect another of 2 2/3 per Cent which will be to me £26 13s 4d so I would stay this month to see what effect this will have upon the stock. I was about buying another 100 if I could have got it for 95 but I think not to exceed that. For if it rise above 100 I intend to sell some. I think never more to give above 100 as I did before. I am heartily sorry I am forc't to give you so much trouble about flaxseed but I know not how to help it my concerns being so great here. There are [no] good Prunes to be got at London however I sent you 14lb of the best that were to be had which yet are none of the best though very dear 4d per lb. You will have them on Munday per Carrier. I am sorry to hear my Mother is ill. My Respects to you all with Children [and friends] I am your lo: husb[an]d S: J.

To Mrs Elizabeth Jeake at Rye in Sussex

[233] *Samuel Jeake junior to Elizabeth Jeake, 7 October 1697. Original letter.*
ESRO FRE 5312

London Oct 7th 1697

My Dear
I received yours of the 2nd instant for answer I cannot affoord to give any more than 36s per quarter for the best flaxseed that is, therefore so write to James Snoad. You have done as well as if I had made him the answer for unless it be extraordinary good it will be too dear at that price. And as for little parcells don't give above 34 at most. You do manage it so well that I cannot do better. As for white flaxseed by no means give above 26s per quarter

& not so unless it be of the very best, for some of it is dear enough at 20. And if it be very full of dirt you had better not buy it at all for it will spoil the rest. It still troubles me that I can not free you from this fatigue. But I believe shall return about mid: Nov: if not before. Mr Miller's remembrances to you & Cos: Jay's. If Mr Bernard should come to our house, I desire you to receive him with respect. I am sorry I could not be present for I should have been glad to have some discourse with him. Mr Tucker it's like will spend a little time with him. I have not heard how hops go today, but I fear dull still yet I would not care if all ours were here, though have no great hopes of getting by them, we shall come off well if we don't lose. Bank 95 ½ if it come to 98 I am minded to sell the 100 I bought since I came up I shall see this month. No good to be done upon buying any thing this winter as I can see yet. E: India is not for me to meddle with. My Duty to mother love to you & child[ren] respects to friends I am

Your Ever Lo: husband
Sa: Jeake

To Mrs Elizabeth Jeake at Rye in Sussex

[234] *Samuel Jeake junior to Elizabeth Jeake, 16 October 1697. Original letter.* ESRO FRE 5313

London, Oct .16th.1697

My Dear
I received yours of the 12th & that by Mr Harris with the Tickets safe. I thank you for your care about the flaxseed which is the most sensible trouble that I am forc't to put you to. I am apt to think I shall return about mid November. Guinea's are falling to 21s 6d so I would not have you take any more. They go indeed yet for goods at 22s but we have no such occasion to take them. Bank Stock is fallen to 92. But no cause except great demands for money at the E: India house & [to] the Government, so that I am not much concerned at it. [I] hope we shall have another dividend shortly. [Deliver] the enclosed to Mr Tucker. My duty to my mother & love to you & children. Committing you to God's protection I remain

Your Ever Lo: husband
Sa: Jeake.

To Mrs Eliz. Jeake at Rye in Sussex

[235] *Samuel Jeake junior to Elizabeth Jeake, 19 October 1697. Original letter.* ESRO FRE 5314

London Oct 19th 1697

My Dear

These are to let you know that Flaxseed is somewhat fallen therefore I would not have you give above 32 s per quarter at most for brown & not that neither unless it be very good & well clean'd. And for white give not above 20 s per quarter at most. And for that which is very dirty you had best not meddle with it at all. But what you have bought before the receit of this letter, perform what you have agreed for. I hope you mind that what you have be good measure for it used to exceed our Towns but fell somewhat. But at least if it do not hold by our bushell you must have them make it up to that. If it have not been turned, I believe it is time for you to imploy Goddin to do it lest it heat. I desire to know whether you have spoke to Morrow about carrying it & let me know what he saith. I would not have the brown mixed with the white as yet. But keep them apart & send me up about a Quart of each in Two bags for a sample by the Carrier next week. The Peace was proclaimed this day. Bank Stock is at 93. My duty to my mother I have a hood for her which sister Hartshorn brought, but I suppose she will not want it till I come home which makes me not send it. My love to you & my children & Bab with respects to all friends I am

Your Ever Lo: husband
Sa: Jeake

To Mrs Eliz. Jeake at Rye in Sussex

[236] *Samuel Jeake junior to Elizabeth Jeake, 21 October 1697. Original letter.* ESRO FRE 5315

London Oct 21st 1697

My Dear

I am much troubled to hear by yours of the 19th that you are so ill & indisposed & also that my little Girl is ill. I will not give you so much trouble as to send the flaxseed but tell Morrow I shall not send it till after Christmas which as it will free you from that fatigue which I would not by any means should fall upon you; so we think also it will come to a better market toward spring than now. Truly I am much concerned for your trouble but I hope this will be some ease to your mind that I shall be home before it will need to be sent. I wrote you last post not to give above 32s for any brown, nor above 20s for white per quarter. & to let Goddin turn it. I thought I had wrote you every week if not I forgot my self. But if Mr Tucker did not tell you about Guineas it was his fault for I desired him particularly to acquaint you & I thought he might have done so much. To day in the Gazett is an advertisement that they [guineas] shall be taken for Custom & Excise &c at 22s. so that I am apt to think they may pass a while & many do take them so here for goods I believe no body refuses them. I will take care about your Petticoat & Combs. I do think as I wrote before to return in mid: Novemb[er]. I would fain see whether we shall have a dividend first. To morrow we have a General Court at the Bank & I find most of the Members are for it, so that I hope there will be an order for one & when I have seen what Influence it has on the stock that if it rise I may sell some, and withall have waited a little to see whether hops will mend I shall think of returning. There's no money on the Million Lottery. Several of the Proprietors are to meet next Wednesday to concert the best methods to obtain the Arrears where I intend to be with them. I suppose it will be to petition the Parliament about it assoon as they sit, before they fall on other business. Trouble not your self about the Poor Tax, thats all the mischief they can do. My duty to mother. With love to you & children is all at present from

My Dear Your Ever Lo: husband
Sa: Jeake.

To Mrs Eliz. Jeake at Rye in Sussex

[237] *Samuel Jeake junior to Elizabeth Jeake, 23 October 1697. Original letter.*
ESRO FRE 5316

London Oct 23rd 1697

My Dear
Yours of the 21st received. You have done very well about Snoads flaxseed. Nevertheless if he should bring it in & insist upon your agreement I would have no difference with him but would give him 34s p quarter if he be so satisfied. For I would have every body easy that I deal with: Or if you find him much dissatisfied (as you know at the return of your messenger) I had rather give 36s then have any brawling about it. And so you may send him word if you find it convenient. For it's a pretty great quantity & if it be very good I am willing to have it, for I find there will not be much more to be had. If he have brought it in before you receive this then it must be adjusted when I return. But as for any other parcells I say as before give not above 32s per q[uarter]. Nor above 20s for white. I wrote to Mr Tucker to furnish you with £30 & that I would pay so much the more here towards the hops. But if he cannot or be not free then you must put away some Guineas for my mother at 22s as they

go currant for Goods. Or you may draw £30 on me. Only if you draw on me let me know when you write again which way you intend to make use of that my money may be ready. I hope you are better in health & am glad to hear my little girl is mending. Madam Thompson says bole Armoniack[52] & white sugar candy powdered & blown through a quill into her mouth is good if it be of the nature of the Thrush. I wrote you last post that I will not send the flaxseed till after Xmass. So you will not be troubled with shipping it. The Commiss[ioners] of Excise would [word lost] nothing this winter but next spring I think some[thing] may be done for Br H[olman]s remove. I hear nothing yet about Mr Bridon. Ask Mr Tucker if there be any vessel going to Exceter, because he wrote he was inclined to send our hops thither. The Dividend was put of at the Bank till December. Stock is at 92. The King is expected the beginning of Nov My remembrances to Mother & your self with the children also to Mr Maior Mr Tucker &c. I am

My Dear Your Ever Lo: husband
Sa: Jeake.

To Mrs Eliz. Jeake at Rye in Sussex

[238] *Samuel Jeake junior to Elizabeth Jeake, 28 October 1697. Original letter.* ESRO FRE 5317

London Oct 28th 1697

My Dear
I was very glad to receive your letter by the Carrier, & with all to ~~you~~ hear you & the children are well for which I bless God. I intend to send your Coat & things Madam Miller has bought to morrow per Carrier. She will send you a letter to tell you your Coat must be lined so need say no more about that. I shall also send my mother's hood & almonds that [sister] Hartshorn bought for her & a Tippet she sends to B[ab] & a few almonds my Aunt sends to Betty. I thank you for sending the samples. As for Snoad I approve of your resolution. But if he sends it in at 32s p quarter I should like it well enough because its a quantity. Or if you should hear from him anymore if you give above 34 s per quarter for it, if you find he will not let it go under you may venture so far. I will take care about the spectacles. I doubt not but you will send up the butter. You may send it by Morrow for I believe he will take most care of it. I would not have you draw any money on me at present because I have bought £100 more of Bank Stock at 91½ so that I cannot well spare any

[52] Defined in the Dictionary of Traded Goods as an 'astringent bole or earth brought from Armenia' and used as an antidote or styptic. *DTGC*, 'Board nail – Bone comb'.

at present. And I hope you will not have occasion to draw because you have paid for most of the flaxseed already bought. & if you should buy Snoads you may agree with him to stay till I come home, which I believe he will not stick at seeing he may expect it in a month, which is as ready money for goods. You may send a letter to Mr Wm Curteis if you please for £10 interest due to me at Michaelmas, which I believe he will pay assoon as he receives notice from you. The King is expected next week. I am as desirous to be at home as you & think I may return by mid: November unless any thing more than ordinary prevent me. Our Lottery Ticket men were consulting to petition the Lords of the Treasury for their arrears & if they do nothing in it I believe the Parliament will be peticioned assoon as they sit. My remembrances with Mr Millers to mother & your self as also to the children. I can add no more but that I am

My Dear Your Ever Lo husband
Sa: Jeake

To Mrs Elizabeth Jeake at Rye in Sussex

[239] *Samuel Jeake junior to Elizabeth Jeake, 4 November 1697. Original letter.* ESRO FRE 5318

London Nov: 4th 1697

My Dear
I have received yours of the 2nd & am very glad to hear you are all well. I carried my Mothers spectacles this morning to Mr Pope's to be sent down to Mr Tucker so she will have them next Monday. I did mind the Chocolat though you had not mencioned it & intend to buy some before I come away. If you look in the 2d fir box from the window behind the chair where I used to sit you will find the Contract between Mr Bishop & Thorp lying one of the uppermost papers & loose, only perhaps it may be shook down towards the bottom of the box with your removing it. Bank stock was yesterday run down to 86. & before night 'twas up at 88. For to day 'tis 88 ½ or 89, it is grown mighty uncertain & so I am apt to think it will continue all this winter which makes me desirous to tend its motion a little longer in hopes I may have an opportunity to sell some of it for you know how much it concerns us. Besides I find it necessary to stay about disposing of some of the hops, which though there will be some loss upon, I think it best to get out of the briers at the best I can. You know the greatest of our concerns are now here. If they were not I should not stay from you. If you don't hear from Snoad this week (or by Saterday) you may send him a letter to this effect, that when you wrote to me of his coming over about the seed, I was willing to divide the difference so that if he

thinks fit to send it in at 34 s per quarter if it be of the best brown seed he shall have so for it. My duty to my mother & love to you with Betty & 2 Babs Sam is to little to take notice. I commit you to God's protection and remaine

Your Ever Lo: husband
Sa: Jeake

Tell Mr Tucker I have sold the 2: bags of fine hops for £9 [number struck out] 2s 6d of the best of the 18 for £8 2s 6d [words struck out] which was the best I could do & if he not like of it I am content to take them towards my third part of the parcel; & to divide them I fear there will be more loss by them & therefore think the first loss will be least.

To Mrs Eliz. Jeake at Rye in Sussex

[240] *Samuel Jeake junior to Elizabeth Jeake, 9 November 1697. Original letter.* ESRO FRE 5319

London Nov. 9th 1697

My Dear
I received yours & am very sorry to hear my Mother is so ill & should very gladly hear of her Recovery. The letter to Robt Myre you may put in at the Post house of Rye, it will go well enough to London. The king is daily expected if not hourly some thinking he put to sea yesterday. The Bank is at 88 ½. Some are afraid of another engraftment[53] which is the thing makes it sink. But though I do not apprehend the Parliament will do any such thing, yet I think it necessary to stay till they sit & use that little interest I have against it. I have been fain to sell some of our hops to loss, but I would not have you discouraged about that it being no more than what I hope we may well bear & recover again without much feeling it. I look on my concerns about which I came hither much more considerable & if these do well (as there is a good prospect now we have peace) I hope to rub through the other well enough. I am apt to think November will expire before I can conveniently return, but I am not without hopes that I may compass to come in December. Give my

[53] In 1697, having failed to raise money through a proposed scheme to set up a Land Bank, Parliament sought to relieve some of its debts by asking the Bank of England to engraft some of Parliament's short-term debts into the Bank's capital. This was accepted by the Bank but here Samuel is clearly reflecting the view that a repeat of that measure was not welcome. Murphy, *Origins of English Financial Markets*, 63–4.

duty to my mother, remember me to Betty & Babs, which with my hearty love to you & prayers for you is all at present from

Your Ever Lo: husband
Sa: Jeake

~~If you think convenient to mention to my Mother what I spake to you about the goods, at least if she should be dangerous ill in my absence but [if not] there will be no such occasion for her death would add much trouble to blot this out.~~[54]

To Mrs Eliz. Jeake at Rye in Sussex

[241] *Samuel Jeake junior to Elizabeth Jeake, 16 November 1697. Original letter.* ESRO FRE 5320

London Nov 16th 1697

My Dear

I have yours of the 13th Instant & am exceeding glad to hear my Mother is recovered & that you are all in health blessed be God for it. I am well satisfied about Snoad's flaxseed, there will be nothing to be got by it at that rate I would not have you give above 4s per bushel for any nor that neither unless extraord[inary] good. But you manage it so well that I can give you no directions. If Mr Stone should come again you may ask him whether it be about his money, if it be tell him you will write to me & I will take care he shall have it or what part he desires in a month. This day the King came through the City to the great joy of the people who desired he might come in the day that they might see him, he came in a coach, but the Glasses afforded a good sight of him on either side the way. Tell Mr Tucker that I can advise him nothing new about Hops. The King's coming has made every body keep holiday. But if he can sell those hops between us that cost 8 for £9 or upwards in the country I am of opinion to take it. For they are certainly dearer there than here. It's true it's possible they may hold up. But if the Parliament should take off the duty on forrain hops for this year which is 50s per Cent, or if they should make another tax on goods as they did last, either of these will sink the price what ever other accidents happen. I tarry a little to see what effect the sitting of the Parliament will have on the Bank (which is now at 89) for if they be favourable to us as there is no great fear but they will, then I shall return the better satisfied. I believe Miller is come away [before] this. I have not had time to mind a cheese at present. The Jack I did not send because I

[54] Probably struck out by Elizabeth Jeake.

was afraid you would run it into your fingers at opening the parcell so keep it till I come. I received yours by Mr Warner. My duty to Mother, my love to you & Betty & 2 Babs & Sam. I am glad to hear he thrives well. I commit you to God's protection & remain.

Your Ever Lo: husband
Sa: Jeake

To Mrs Elizabeth Jeake at Rye in Sussex

[242] *Samuel Jeake junior to Elizabeth Jeake, 27 November 1697. Original letter.* ESRO FRE 5321

London Nov 27th 1697

My Dear
Because I have some good news to tell you I could not forbear making you partake of it by this post. And that is that I have gotten £30 for my Mother & £25 for my self on our Lottery Tickets. And that I have sold the Land at Wadhurst for a Market price, and as for my Mother's money on it will be continued upon the same security I gave her which is without dispute. Tell Mr Tucker I have accepted his bill of £100 & shall pay it next week. Hops continue as they were. I am not for selling any more as the markets go but waiting till spring when I hope they may be somewhat quicker. I hope you have not neglected to send the Butter. I have bought you a cheese which shall be sent by the vessell that brings the Butter. The Bank is up at 87 ½ standing at a stay. I wrote to know if my mother would buy £100 if it fell to 80 which if she be inclin'd to I shall be ready to serve her if there be an opportunity. I tarry now to finish the receiving the money for the hops I sold here & some money I am to receive on the sale of the Land & also to see a little how the Parliament will act about the Bank of which we have a good prospect that they will favour us rather than our adversaries, & when these things are over I think of returning which I hope may be in a fortnight. But you shall hear from me about the day senight or the day following & then I hope to tell you more certainly of my return. My duty to my mother, which with love to you & Children Committing you to the protection of God I remaine

My Dear Your ever lo: husband
Sa: Jeake

To Mrs Elizabeth Jeake at Rye in Sussex

[243] *Samuel Jeake junior to Elizabeth Jeake, 4 December 1697. Original letter.*
ESRO FRE 5322

London Dec 4th 1697

My Dear
I expected a letter from you this post but none is yet bought & I cannot defer writing any longer being now evening: so if I receive any after I have sent my letter you will see the reason I cannot answer the contents of it. I have spoke to Moon the Carrier to bring me up a horse next week which he will do, & so you may hope to see me this day sennight if God assist. But if any extraordinary business should make my stay necessary till the week after I may then continue the horse here till that time. I mean chiefly in reference to the Bank which is now at 90 or 91 & some think we shall have a dividend ordered the 15 of December at which time will be a General Court. And this would make it rise higher were it not for fear some Tally men will petition the Parliament for a new engraftment, yet I think there is no real fear [of] it. I am told they begin to pay some [of] the Annuities. So I intend to see about that next Tuesday. I send you the Kings speech which is worth you reading & hope things will go well with us at last. I hope to be at home before the Gooders come I intend them 6d a piece. I would not have you take the Guineas unless you could put them away immediately as you took them, nor meddle with any Pistols for they are worth but 17s 4d. My duty to mother & love to you with my children. In hast I am

My Dear Your Ever lo: husband
Sa: Jeake

To Mrs Elizabeth Jeake at Rye in Sussex

[244] *Samuel Jeake junior to Elizabeth Jeake, 14 December 1697. Original letter.*
ESRO FRE 5323

London Dec 14th 1697

My Dear

I received yours of the 11th & am glad to hear you are all in health. These are to let you know that I intend God willing to be at home this week but I believe it will not be before Saterday for I shall hardly get out hence till Friday. I would have you send to Hounsell (if Morrow will not come so soon) & if he be not loded I intend to send the flaxseed by him if we can agree for the freight of it when I come home. But I won't give you any trouble to ship it, for there is no such hast, I have sold it & am at liberty to send it when I please. I have received ¼ s Annuitys at the Exchequer which is £9 10s so there's less behind. I have paid Mr Thompson his £100 & taken in my bond. I have bought £100 stock for my mother in the bank, & £100 more for myself at 89 per Cent which is to be transferred to morrow on which day there is a General Court & we expect a dividend will be ordered of 4 per Cent which will reduce the stock I bought for my mother & self this day to 85. It was uncertain whether it would come lower, & therefore I thought it best for her to be concerned a little in it as it is which I hope will do well. I shall take care to pay for it here & reckon with her when I come home. Tell Mr Tucker I would not have him draw any money for the hops till I return for if they [will] take the £100 due at xmas for hops at Rye I can pay it better there. I write this post because I would not have you expect any letter by next hoping to see you this week. I commit you to God's protection & with remembrances to you & mother & children I remain

Your Ever lo: husband
Sa: Jeake.

To Mrs Elizabeth Jeake at Rye in Sussex

7

Elizabeth and her Children, 1699–1736

Samuel returned to London in the spring of 1699. The letters sent during that time echo those in the previous chapter. While in London Samuel focused on managing his investments while Elizabeth dealt with business at home in Rye. The task for Samuel was a less anxious one in 1699 as annuity payments were being honoured and the price of Bank of England shares was rising. Yet, decision-making was no more straight-forward. He told Elizabeth: 'As for telling when tis a good time to purchase [shares] that's past my skill or any body's else' (FRE 5329). With a stable political and economic situation, there was, however, more time for consideration of domestic matters. For the first time in Samuel's letters it is possible to find fairly frequent mentions of his children. During his previous trip to London Samuel had dismissed the need for love to be passed to his son Sam arguing that he was 'too little to take notice'.[1] In this series of letters, while he was no more specific when sending his regards, he did relay concerns for his children's health (FRE 5324, 5325, 5326). His instructions to Elizabeth with regard to the care of the children indicate a shared responsibility for at least some aspects of parenting at a time when fathers were not expected to take much notice of their young children. Given that parenting was, and remains, partly based on experience and observation, perhaps Samuel senior's significant involvement in his son's early life offered a model.[2]

Samuel also spent time while in London purchasing things needed by his family. His lengthy shopping list detailed various items of clothing, shoes and household goods including a brass pot-lid, a whisk and an iron kettle that Samuel feared would be too small for the purposes for which it was required (FRE 5330). The letters imply discussion of the suitability of various items and point to what Grassby has described as a 'bustle of shared activity' with regard to the household rather than a strictly gendered delineation of tasks.[3] This was undoubtedly typical of early modern households.[4] Yet vignettes of domesticity elsewhere in the letters in this chapter also reveal Elizabeth's household responsibilities. When Barbara Hartshorne wrote to her grand-daughter later in 1699 she noted 'Mother is busi a baking' and on another occasion 'Mother says she is busie, she cannot write, folding clothes take up her time at present' (FRE 5360, 5361). That laundry should take up so much time should not surprise. Even with maids to assist, washing day was labour-intensive. Samuel Pepys noted one occasion in his diary when he retired after 1.00am leaving his wife and the maid 'washing still'.[5] A letter from Elizabeth to Barbara written in 1701 also indicates

[1] ESRO, FRE 5318, chapter 6.

[2] Mendelson and Crawford, *Women*, 159; J. Bailey, 'Reassessing parenting in eighteenth-century England' in H. Berry and E. Foyster eds, *The Family in Early Modern England* (Cambridge, 2007), 229.

[3] Grassby, *Kinship*, 94.

[4] Flather, *Gender and Space*, 40.

[5] Cited in Tim Reinke-Williams, *Women, Work and Sociability in Early Modern London* (Basingstoke, 2014), 64.

the younger woman's domestic authority. In response to Barbara's complaints about a new maid, Sarah, Elizabeth replied: 'I hope when return to quicken her or get another' (FRE 5353). This suggests that Barbara deferred to her daughter's decision-making and that Elizabeth was comfortable asserting authority within their shared household.

Although Elizabeth relied on Samuel's judgement in the purchase of household items, when it came to her own clothing she turned to the advice of Thomas Miller's wife. Letters in previous chapters have demonstrated Elizabeth's consistent interest in fashion and, in particular, her desire closely to follow and keep up with fashions in the capital. Hence Mrs Miller offered advice on the way clothes were worn and ways of dressing hair (FRE 5329). As Tankard suggests, after following Mrs Miller's advice Elizabeth would have been able to 'receive guests and make social visits in and around Rye confident that she was wearing the latest London fashions'.[6] When in London Elizabeth informed herself about the prevailing fashions and passed information on to both her mother and her teenaged daughter. For the former she was 'at a loss knowing you will not conform to high heads which young & old wear here'. She clearly expected her daughter to be more fashion-conscious, informing her that 'No glove tops worn…hair trussed up as mine used to be is the way low dresses & two double ruffles' (FRE 5340).

Samuel and Elizabeth's elder daughter, Betty, by now aged fifteen, was also away from Rye during 1699. She had been sent, probably to school, 'at Mrs Brewer's' at Hawkhurst in Kent at a cost of £20 per year.[7] Two of the three letters sent to her at this time were from her grandmother and were concerned chiefly with local and family news but indicated a very affectionate relationship. The third letter must have been one of Samuel's final communications with his eldest daughter. The letter enquired after Betty's health. Although not mentioned in the letter, the *Astrological Diary* records Betty as suffering from greensickness at this time.[8] The letter also imparted spiritual advice. In this respect it was an echo of Samuel senior's letters to his adolescent son in 1668.[9] This was one of the few times Samuel included overt expressions of his spirituality in his letters. Equally, the *Astrological Diary* has what Hunter and Gregory describe as an 'overwhelmingly worldly air'.[10] The family were, however, clearly actively pious. Both Samuel and Elizabeth were active members of the nonconformist community in Rye. During the 1690s Samuel also raised money and commenced the building of a nonconformist meeting house. This was a common undertaking by prominent dissenters under the more tolerant conditions that pertained after the Glorious Revolution. The meeting house was begun by Samuel and completed by Elizabeth after his death.[11] Samuel found it 'a comfort' that Betty shared his religious convictions and that he could observe 'in you some good thing towards the Lord God of Israel & I trust he will perfect that good work he has begun in your conversion to him to serve the living God' (FRE 5359).

[6] Tankard, 'They tell me they were in fashion'.
[7] Hunter and Gregory, *Astrological Diary*, 258.
[8] Hunter and Gregory, *Astrological Diary*, 259. It was believed that young women were prone to greensickness as a result either of the suppression of menstruation or an overabundance of seed, a distillation of the blood which would drive women to sexual activity. P. Crawford and L. Gowing, *Women's Worlds in Seventeenth-Century England: a sourcebook* (London, 2000), 29.
[9] ESRO FRE 4823, chapter 2.
[10] Hunter and Gregory, *Astrological Diary*, 9.
[11] Ibid. 35.

The letter was written in September 1699 and on 22 November Samuel died aged forty-seven. He was buried in Rye the following day.[12] A published obituary, reproduced below, is all that remains of the reactions of his family and friends. It speaks of a 'loss to great to baer; Too great for Words'. After eighteen years of seemingly contented marriage, thc loss to Elizabeth was perhaps so devastating. It was compounded by the fact that, at the time of Samuel's death, Elizabeth was pregnant with their third son. Francis was born on 11 April 1700. Two of her three other children were still infants. Barbara was aged four, and Samuel was two. Betty was fifteen.

Following Samuel's death, Elizabeth was left to manage his affairs and business interests. Although his will does not survive it is possible that Elizabeth was his executrix since in 1701 she was forced to spend an extended period of time in London dealing with various business matters. What most occupied her time was resolution of a dispute with Mr Benge. Although details recorded in the *Astrological Diary* are scant, it appears that Samuel had either lent money to Benge or sold him some land and a farm and was awaiting payment. By May 1699, however, Benge was in severe financial difficulties and there were rumours that a 'statute of bankrupt' would be issued against him.[13] The issue had not been resolved at the time of Samuel's death. While the previous chapter showed Elizabeth to have been experienced in matters of business, she clearly did not relish the legal battle with Benge. Her letters to her mother during this time tended to focus on relatively trivial matters and she described her business as 'tedious' (FRE 5357) and to have achieved little except ensuring that she could be 'stiled a Philosopher for my learned talk…' (FRE 5356).

A notable topic in one of the letters written during her stay in London during 1701 was Elizabeth's denial of a relationship with Joseph Tucker (FRE 5348). A possible relationship between the pair had clearly become the subject of some gossip amongst the community in Rye, something that had been communicated to Elizabeth by her mother. She responded saying, 'for what people at Rye say I look on ill their chimeras… I care not what they say only wish for their sakes they would not endeavour to make lyes pass for truth…Its probable after all Mr Tucker is in no want of a wife, especially of other people's chusing'(FRE 5348).

Reader, she married him. They had been long acquainted. Tucker was engaged in business with Samuel and the latter had from time to time recommended Elizabeth to seek Tucker's advice during his own absences in London. Elizabeth and Joseph married in London in November 1703. No correspondence between them survives but the contents of letters between Elizabeth and her children indicate a loving marriage. They had two children together: Joseph, baptised in February 1705, and Philadelphia, who was probably born in 1707. Philadelphia appears to have been the only one of Elizabeth's children to have children of her own and it is through that line of the family that most of the Jeake family papers survive.

Although there are few surviving direct insights into Elizabeth's second marriage, the letters reproduced in this chapter do reveal much about her relationships with her children and indeed her own role as the adult child of Barbara Hartshorne. In this respect the letters give a rare insight into parenting over the life course, rather than just the parenting of children. Six of Elizabeth's eight children survived into adulthood but Betty and Francis do not appear to have been long-lived. The last mention of Betty Jeake was in the will of her grandmother, Barbara Hartshorne, written in 1703.

[12] ESRO, Rye Parish Register, PAR 467/1/1/4

[13] Hunter and Gregory, *Astrological Diary*, 258. See also 253; 255–256.

By that time Betty was married to a Mr Brownsmith, of whom there is no obvious trace. Betty obviously died young and perhaps with no issue. Likewise, mentions of Francis Jeake did not persist. He corresponded regularly with his mother while he was at school and serving his apprenticeship but was not mentioned in Joseph Tucker's will, which was written in 1721. It is likely, therefore, that he died in his late teens. Joseph Tucker junior lived at least into his early thirties, Samuel Jeake III and Barbara Jeake both lived into their sixties and Philadelphia Tucker lived into her late eighties, dying in 1795.

Motherhood would have been one of the defining roles of Elizabeth's life and arguably one of her greatest satisfactions. She wrote lovingly of her children when they were young, calling them variously her 'little tribe' (FRE 5343), her 'cubbs' (FRE 5350), and her 'two pair of illmatched clogs' (FRE 5348). When they were older that affection persisted with Elizabeth often writing of her 'dear children' and expressing her desire to see them when they were apart. Yet, most early modern mothers would have subscribed to the adage 'spare the rod and spoil the child'.[14] And Elizabeth did show herself to be aware of her children's faults, mentioning Betty as a poor correspondent and impatient (FRE 5338 and 5347). Her greatest disapprobation was reserved for her son Samuel who, in adulthood at least, was neglectful of his parents. In a letter penned in 1725 his mother admonished him: 'I am sorry Dear Sam the Town has so many charms that Business & Relations may all be sacrificed to its allurments'. The letter went on to accuse Samuel of selfishness and extravagance. Elizabeth 'despair[ed] any remonstrances of mine will ever have any effect on you' (FRE 5389).

Elizabeth's other children were more dutiful as indeed was Elizabeth herself in her relationship with her own mother. This was a close relationship but one also in which the formal expressions of obligation continued to be expected and expressed, as she responded to one of Barbara Hartshorne's apparently querulous complaints: 'it is my Duty to inviolably observe your commands having not missed one post since I came here' (FRE 5357). What is obvious here is a relationship which follows Ben-Amos's model of reciprocity in parent–child relationships throughout the life cycle.[15] Barbara continued to reside with her daughter and provide care and household management when required. Elizabeth provided a home and care for her mother. There were obviously tensions in the relationship but it appears to have been generally cooperative and at least outwardly affectionate.

Based on the letters that have survived, Francis was by far the most diligent correspondent among Elizabeth's children. His letters from school in Tenterden were short, sometimes making little requests but always remembering his sisters, mother and Joseph Tucker, whom he referred to as father. Both Francis and Samuel III were apprenticed to lawyers in London and later letters from the city were full of more news and things that Francis had witnessed. He appears to have taken an interest in politics. This interest is confirmed by a manuscript book of political verse in Francis's hand compiled during his time at school in Tenterden and including verses on the dangers of Popery, the War of the Spanish Succession and especially Marlborough's victories and subsequent fall from grace, the financial crisis of 1710–11 and the impending

[14] Mendelson and Crawford, *Women*, 161.

[15] I. Krausman Ben-Amos, 'Reciprocal bonding: parents and their offspring in early modern England', *Journal of Family History*, 25 (2000), 291–312.

succession of George I.[16] His letters record his gratitude for the support of Joseph Tucker in securing his apprenticeship (FRE 5380 and 5381; RYEYT N39.59.3; .4) and his thoughts about that apprenticeship, which reveal an admirable evenness of temper. He informed his mother 'I believe indeed there are better places and I believe there are worse then since I have not met with one of the latter the best way is to rest contented' (FRE 5383). Samuel Jeake III was in London at the same time as Francis but was mentioned little in the letters and does not appear to have written home regularly. He did apparently send greetings through his brother, although, of course, those greetings might reflect Francis's diplomacy rather more than his brother's intentions.

The chapter is brought to an end with Elizabeth's death in 1736 at the age of 68. She was buried on 3 June 1736.[17] The wills left by Joseph and Elizabeth are reproduced below. Both left legacies to a very narrow group of kin, Joseph to his wife and the children of his marriage to Elizabeth. To his other children, sister and surviving step-children, he left only a small legacy for the purchase of mourning. Elizabeth's will left her estate to her four surviving children: Samuel and Barbara Jeake and Philadelphia and Joseph Tucker. It also shows her to have been an affluent woman with around £2500 in money to distribute along with significant furniture, silver and jewellery. She reserved the bulk of her property for her daughter Barbara who remained single until very late in her life, marrying Christopher Booth Howard in Lewes in 1741. Barbara was thus unmarried at Elizabeth's death and perhaps perceived to be in greater need of financial support. Both Joseph and Philadelphia had received legacies from their father but were also recognised in Elizabeth's will.

The contents of both Joseph and Elizabeth's wills were consistent with findings from other studies. Testators typically left legacies to a small circle of close kin and the determining factor in deciding legacies was perceived obligation towards family.[18] Thus single daughters might be well-provided-for and married daughters left a smaller legacy. Nonetheless, the position of Samuel III in Elizabeth's will is most interesting. He received only £200, although with substantial amount of furniture and some silver and gold table pieces and his father's library of books. With few details of Samuel III's life having been preserved it is impossible to judge the significance of this legacy. Nonetheless while disinheritance was not common, 'preferential giving' was used to punish wayward offspring.[19] Perhaps Elizabeth's will was intended as an encouragement to Samuel to mend his profligate ways. If so it did not have the desired effect. Samuel III was bankrupt by the mid-1740s.

[16] Rye Castle Museum, RYEYT: N39.60, Quarto verse commonplace book.

[17] ESRO, PAR 467/1/1/5

[18] D. Cressy, 'Kinship and Kin Interaction in Early Modern England', *Past and Present*, 113 (1986), 43–59.

[19] Ben-Amos, 'Reciprocal Bonding', 301.

A final trip to London, 1699

[245] *Samuel Jeake junior to Elizabeth Jeake, 30 March 1699. Original letter.*
ESRO FRE 5324

London Mar 30th 1699

My Dear
Through the blessing of God I came safe hither yesterday about 2. a clock afternoon & found all Mr Miller's family in good health. & hope this will find you & all ours the like of which I should be glad to hear. I have seen Mr Lock & he saith he did receive Wid: Seals bill safe. Pray do not forget Madam Miller's butter because it's wanted by the first vessell. You need not make any hast to dispose of the wheat unless it come to 7. Neither will it lack any turning as yet. Bank was yesterday at 103 ½ & in a rising strain so I know not how I shall proceed as yet. I hope Sam's Eyes continue well as I left them. Yet if they do I would have you give him an ounce of manna, & then you need not purge him any more. I expect to hear from you once a week & you may expect the like from me & if any thing extraordinary happen then oftner. My duty to my mother & love to you and the children with Bab and remembrances to friends concluding this from

Your Ever Lo: husband
Sa: Jeake

To Mrs Eliz: Jeake at Rye in Sussex

[246] *Samuel Jeake junior to Elizabeth Jeake, 8 April 1699. Original letter.*
ESRO FRE 5325

London Apr 8th 1699

My Dear
I received yours of the 4th and am very glad to hear you are all well, If Mr Maior be willing I shall return the £80 that was paid by Sir Robert Austen to Mr Miller by his order then I desire Mr Maior to write an order to Mr Miller to pay it me & do you pay the £80 to Mr Maior, borrow money of my mother to make it up with the £24 I left & I will answer it to my Mother. I do write to Mr Young this post to know Mr Maior's mind about it. But if he have otherwise disposed of it & cannot do it then assoon as you have an opportunity see if Nic: Stone can return it for he told me he should have some money in London about this Time. I have bought some stock & done some other business since I came so desire to hear from you about this per next post. I shall be very busy next week so may not write but once a week. I have not

been at leisure to buy [word illegible] cloths yet. But pray send word what things you would have bought that I may have the more time. Madam Miller is very ill with a cold, but the child's cap Ruffles fan gloves & lace for her coat was sent you this week per Carrier, as also the Rhenish wine for Ed: Coskar which being to be had neer me I had time to do. I shall see sister Hartshorn[20] next week I sent the letter to her. I am glad you have put the butter on board I hope you ordered him to send it by a Porter with the box, if not let [me] know whether he be come from Rye. You m[ay] give Sam the manna assoon as you think fit. [The] weather is warm enough for that if you keep him neer the fire. Mind to send my things a Munday if you can. My duty to my mother & love to my children & friends. Mr Miller & his wife remember to you all. I commit you to God's protection & with my affectionate love to you remain

my dear Your Ever lo: husband
Sa: Jeake

Let me know whether you paid 14s 6d for the butter for the present till the Crock is weight & what it weighs in all I think it was 36 ¼ lb.

If you cannot have this return of Mr Maior enquire if you hear of any other & send me word. Let Mr Young speak to Mr Maior first about it for I wrote the letter to him.

To Mrs Eliz: Jeake at Rye in Sussex

[247] *Samuel Jeake junior to Elizabeth Jeake, 11 April 1699. Original letter.* ESRO FRE 5326

London Apr 11th 1699

My Dear

I have received yours of the 8th Instant with the enclosed which I do send this post to sister Holman that she & the others may be in readiness about that time mentioned to come to Rye, So if you hear ~~again~~ from Sister Holman what day she & they appoint to come to Rye you must I think send in purpose to Mr Taylor to let him know so much that he may not fail to meet them. I have ordered Sister Holman to send me word also what day she appoints that I may give notice to Mr Tournay which I can do by post. I am sorry little Bab has an ague, you write Sam's eyes are not worse whereby I hope they are somewhat better which should be glad to hear. I wrote you last post to see if Mr Maior would let me have the money that Mr Miller received for him &

[20] Probably Nathaniel Hartshorne's widow.

you to pay him the money there which this confirms. If you can have that money I shall want more besides & therefore I did speak to Mr Ferris this day & he saith that Robt Brown[21] can return 80 or £100 if he have not disposed of it already which he thinks he hath not & therefore doth write to him this post to let me have it before any one else. So pray go to Robert Browne & get a bill of him for £100 or for as much as you can if he cannot let you have the whole, & send it me up next post for then Mr Ferris will pay it me upon sight. Borrow money of my mother to pay for it. I will allow her Interest for the time I keep it. The Land Tax is not yet past so that you need not speak any thing about my Tax till I [mention] it, but I hope to be at home & do what [is] need full my self before the day of appeals comes, for that cannot be before the end of May. Mr Miller &c give remembrances to you. Things go pretty well at present but for particularities you must expect at my Return, my letters may be opened you know where which makes me forbear. My duty to mother, love to you & the children concluding this from

My dear Your Ever lo: husband
Sa: Jeake

To Mrs Eliz: Jeake at Rye in Sussex

[248] *Samuel Jeake junior to Elizabeth Jeake, 15 April 1699. Original letter.*
ESRO FRE 5327

London Apr: 15th 1699

My Dear
I received both yours of the 11th & 13th Instant with Mr Maior's bill of £80 & the box you sent per Carrier. Mr Dupper is a man I don't know & therefore he may be content that I should receive the money here before you pay him at Rye. But if you be satisfied about him by Mr Tucker or Wm Mercer then if he desire it you may let him have the money when you take his bill, if you have not his bill before this comes to hand then let it be drawn at 3 days sight which I had rather than at sight for fear of miscarriage. If you cannot have the whole £100 of him then see to get it of Nic: Stone, Mr Wilmshurst, John French or Robt Brown or some other that you know is sure, and assoon as you can. I hope to be back sometime in May, but cannot yet fix the time. I saw Cosin Betty Wightman in London & suppose she will come to Rye if I come by Maidstone which I think to do. I am glad to hear Sam's eyes are well but very sorry that Bab's ague continues. I see you have given Betty physick with

[21] Robert Brown was a mariner and wealthy inhabitant of Rye. He and Samuel had dealings on various occasions during the 1680s and 1690s. Hunter and Gregory, *Astrological Diary*, p. 266.

good success hope she may be better after it. I have had no time yet to consider your letters about what you desire to be bought, but I shall mind it next week. I wrote you I had bought some Bank stock which will excuse my Tax, but I hope to be at home time enough to plead that, for it is not yet past & cannot be in the country before the end of May. Bank was yesterday at 105. I have received my mother's dividend £9 which will account with her when I come home. I have also received ½ yr Annuities at the Exchequer £19 Mr Manooches also is paid which I received of Mr Miller by his order & will reckon with him at my return. But you need not mention it to him unless he ask you. It's no matter for the shirt seeing I shall return in May. Give my duty to my mother, tell her sister Hartshorn remembers to her & Bab. I paid her 24s for the things she sent by my mothers order. My love to you & the children & Bab H. Remember me to friends. I am my dear

Your Ever Lo: husband
Sa: Jeake

If you meet with returns to your mind you may send me bill for 20 or £30 more besides the £100 & take up money of my mother.

To Mrs Eliz: Jeake at Rye in Sussex

[249] *Samuel Jeake junior to Elizabeth Jeake, 18 April 1699. Original letter.*
ESRO FRE 5328

London Apr: 18th 1699

My Dear
I received yours of the 15th with the enclosed bill of £40 such I doubt not but will be well paid. You may remit £80 more assoon as you have opportunity from safe hands, but I would not have you hurry your self about it, for I can shift well enough till you meet with it conveniently which I suppose you may in a week or fortnight time. I had a Letter from Sister Holman wherein she writes me word that she and her Brothers & Sisters will all be at Rye on Wednesday the 26th of Aprill. I do write to Mr Tournay this post to give him notice of it & that he may pay his money here if he please. But however if he do not pay his money at Rye do not let him have the Bond till you have advice from me first that the money is paid here. I do also write to Mr Taylor this post to let him know that they appoint to be at Rye on the 26th of April. But lest my letter should not come to his hand, I think it would be meet for my mother to send one over to him to Tenterden on Friday next to acquaint him with it. I suppose you may get one to go over afoot for 2s. As for Mr Tournay you need not trouble your self for if he do not come the fine may be levied

without his being there. Tell Betty I have not time to answer her letter now. She may take the Spirit of Savery Grass she mentions, it may do her good. I shall Endeavour to do all the errands you have mentioned in all your letters. & am glad you have sent them all already for I would not have any new things mentioned when my time draws neer to come away, because I shall dispose of what money I have more than the things come to for other purposes & then that will put me to a non-plus to have other things to buy besides I shall want time. But if you have forgot anything that you would have for your self I will endeavour to oblige you, but not any body else. Bank was yesterday 105 1/2. I would have you keep on Sam's bongrace[22] & let him be led till his eye is thorough well for a fall will make it return again. Better lead him about a month too long than a day too short. I am glad Bab has lost her ague & bless God for all his mercys, my duty to my mother & love to you & the Children. Mr Miller remembers to you, I am my dear Your Ever Lo: husband

Sa: Jeake.

To Mrs Eliz: Jeake at Rye in Sussex

[250] *Samuel Jeake junior to Elizabeth Jeake, 25 April 1699. Original letter.* ESRO FRE 5329

London Apr 25th 1699

My Dear

I received yours of 22nd Instant I shall take care about the errands you wrote, as time & opportunity serve me. I am sorry to hear Betty is not well, nor Sam's eye. I hope he has had no more falls. I had a letter from Mr Tournay that he will be at Rye to morrow and pay the money there; The Butter is come by Tho: Morrow. Madam Miller says that Trains are worn still with womens upper petticoats but not so long as formerly; And as for fringes she saith they wear them strait but she would not advise you to alter any for they are worn both ways. Twas a good time to have bought in the Bank yesterday for it fell from 105 to 104 upon a blind story of the Frenches coming. But that being blown over it rose again today to 104½. As for telling when 'tis a good time to purchase that's past my skill or any body's else. I have taken up sixty five pounds of Mr Newman of Winchelsea for which I gave him a note payable the 26th of May before which time I hope to be at home. Madam Miller desires to know whether the silk you would have drawn with Indian sprigs be for a Mantua or for a Lining, for she saith if it be for a Mantua it will be so very tedious for you to work it that she would rather advise you to have it painted

[22] *OED*, n. 2. A broad-brimmed hat worn to shade the face.

with lively flowers which shews exceeding well & may be done for about 15s & will wear very well provided it don't come to wet which you will have no occasion to use it in. So she would have you send word next post. I cannot yet meet with any iron kettles that hold above 8 gallons or 10 at most. So have not bought yet. I have received one & Twenty pounds & nineteen shillings of Tho: Morrow for which I being absent Mr Miller hath drawn a bill upon you this day by my order paiable at sight to one Mr John Atkins or order, which I desire you to pay when bought to you. I think he is a Lydd,[23] man but that is not material. Take a Receit on the bill when you pay it, If he come not himself then see if his name be endorsed on the bill or else do not pay it. I have spoke to Mr Ferris & he saith he will write to Robt Brown to let you have a Return the first he can. So I would have you get £100 ~~more~~ of him unless you can meet with it or part of it before he can let you have it, you may take up money of my mother till I come home. My remembrances & Mr Miller's [to you] all in hast I am my dear Your [ever] Lo: husband

Sa: Jeake.

To Mrs Eliz: Jeake at Rye in Sussex

[251] *Samuel Jeake junior to Elizabeth Jeake, 2 May 1699. Original letter.*
ESRO FRE 5330

London May 2nd 1699

My Dear
I received yours of the 27th & sister Holmans of the same date. I know not how to inform her any thing more about Allington Court than what Mr Tournay told her & so you may write her for its not worth while to put her to 2d charge to send her a letter from hence. Your silk is put out to paint & will be done next week & with your mantua. I intend to send your best petticoat, being of most value. Other things I have put aboard Tho: Morrow to day viz: 1. fir box full of things viz: A large Bible which when it comes to hand pray lay it up carefully till I come home. There is also my watch in a little box which mind to take care of. Then there is all the shooes you sent for except 1 of your shoes which was not brott till the box was sent away so I must send it to you hereafter. Then there is my Gown, the ovens door, 1 p Holland of 19 ½ ells, Nans bible. 3 lb Hair powder. 6 washbals. 1 pr shoes for me. the point pattern. Wafers. 1 pr stockings. 2 shirts. 2 caps. 2 cravats. 2 pair wristbands. 3 pair gloves, & that you sent. 4 pillowcoats. 1 flannel petticoat. 1 pair pattens. 1 pair clogs. 2 pewters for washbals. 1 Frock or Gown for Bab cut out. 1 Green

[23] A village in the Romney Marshes, about ten miles from Rye.

Girdle & other green Ribbon. ¾ yd black stuff anterine.[24] All this is in the box together with other small things. Then there is a parcell tyed up together where you will find 6 psalm books for Wm Mercer & the stuff that Mrs Betty bott for Nan 16. Yds. & a brass potlid & a whisk. Besides I sent by Morrow an armed chair black with rush bottomed & also an Iron Kettle, which will be too little I fear but I could meet with no bigger though were at a many shops. Morrow talks of going down to morrow so I hope you will receive the things safe in a weeks time. I cannot buy the lining of the bed at present & I will tell you the Reason when I come home. As for Mr Tournays bond I don't think it worth while to send it up if he pay any money here I can give him a Receit till he comes to Rye. As for the Report you have of the sickness being at London, there's nothing in it. The City is very healthy at present. I have the promise of Mr Ferris & Mr Cox for £100 from Ro: Brown assoon as Mackrells come in viz. the first money he can draw for fish & therefore I would have you mind R B[rown] of it for I perceive you cannot get any elsewhere if you can of a sure hand then you may return what you can otherwise & so take the less of R Brown. I hope you are all well because I hear not to the Contrary, my duty to my mother love to you & the children & friends concludes this from

my dear Your Ever Lo: husband
Sa: Jeake

They begin to leave off trains from all their petticoats.

To Mrs Eliz: Jeake at Rye in Sussex

[252] *Samuel Jeake junior to Elizabeth Jeake, 4 May 1699. Original letter.*
ESRO FRE 5331

London May 4th 1699

My Dear
I received your stays by the Carrier & Mr Tournays bond enclosed in them, which I shall take care of. I have spoken to Mr Ferris again & he has promised me I shall have a return of £100 of Robt Browne, which he has appointed that you shall pay the £100 for Robt Browne & take his bill & send up to me & then he will pay me the money here next week. So I desire you not to fail of paying the money to Rob Browne & sending me his bill on Mr Ferris by next post. Mr Ferris promised me to write also himself & order Ro: Brown to give you a bill for the said summe which he may draw at sight or 3 days sight as he

[24] Antherine, n. a light fabric made from a mixture of wool and silk, or of cotton and mohair: *OED*. Stuffs were usually textiles made from mixed fibres.

pleases. If Mr Ferris should forget to write him, yet he need not question the thing for it's true & Mr Ferris directed me to write to you to pay the £100 to Browne & saith I may depend on it that he will furnish me with it next week here. You had best get the wheat turned once, though it do not lye very thick. Here was a report of the K: of Spain's death last night, but tis not much credited as coming from the French Ambassador; what more may be said about it before night I know not, for, I write now at 4. afternoon. I tarry now for Mr Benge coming to London, & if I could finish the business with him I should return but it may be about 3 weeks yet before I shall dispatch to [word lost]. My duty to mother & love to you & the children hoping you are in health. I commit you to God's protection & remain

my dear Your Ever Lo: husband
Sa: Jeake

I know not whether I have any letter from you to day, because I have not time to go to Mr Miller's before night.

To Mrs Eliz: Jeake at Rye in Sussex

[253] *Samuel Jeake junior to Elizabeth Jeake, 11 May 1699. Original letter.*
ESRO FRE 5332

London May 11th 1699

My Dear
I received yours of the 8th Inst. You have done well to depend upon the return from Robt Browne, so I would have you tarry till he can do it, & not go to any body else. I am glad to hear Morrow is safe arrived & that the things are all dry & well. Pray mind my Bible & the watch. I know not what price wheat is, but if so as I told you viz 7 s you might if you had opportunity sell 12 bushells, but if not it's no great matter till I come home which I hope will be about the 29th of May so that if the Cistern be not begun you may have it omitted till I come home, or how you please for it will please me either way it being a good time of year to do it in & dry weather. I hope you give the wheat air now & then; But have a care of your or any one's falling out of the doors. Madam Miller will direct you about your head washing which is now done without the brush. The Tax is hardly printed yet so I suppose shall be at home before the day of appeals can possibly come, I am not taxable now for personall estate. But you need not mention any thing unless only you may write me when you hear the Tax is made for when that is made there is 10 days after for appeals. Bank is at 104, has stood at a stay for about a week. As for Winter's Rent it's no great sume so you need not send to him. I conclude you are all

pretty well in health because you mention nothing to the contrary. My duty to my mother Love to you, & Betty, Babs & to Sam: & all friends. I commit you to God's protection praying for your prosperity & remain

My dear you Ever Lo: husband
Sa: Jeake

To Mrs Eliz: Jeake at Rye in Sussex

[254] *Samuel Jeake junior to Elizabeth Jeake, 18 May 1699. Original letter.*
ESRO FRE 5333

London May 18th 1699

My Dear
I received yours of the 16th with the Enclosed bill of £100. But having last Tuesday drawn on you £60 payable to Mr Ferris's order & it being all I have occasion for he has ordered me to send down the bill again to you. So that if you have not paid any bill of £60 then let Ro: Brown make you a Receit on that & pay you back £40 & then give him this bill in again. But if you should have paid the bill of £60 besides before you receive this letter, then let Rob: Brown give you in my bond of £100 (you delivering him in this bill & paying him the years interest.) I am now thinking if the Carrier have a horse that will fit me to come from London this week by way of Maidstone & so home the beginning of next week. But I have not yet seen the Carrier so cannot tell whether I can have a horse if not I intend to speak to him for one next week, so cannot say yet whether I can do any of the things you write. My duty to my mother & love to you & my children in hast I am

My Dear Your Ever Lo: husband
Sa: Jeake.

To Mrs Eliz: Jeake at Rye in Sussex

Letters to Betty, 1699

[255] *Barbara Hartshorne to Elizabeth Jeake junior, 1699, undated. Original letter.*
ESRO FRE 5360

Rye Satt morning

My dear
I doubt I shall tire thee with my scribbling I have nothing to write but to let thee know we are all in good health at present as I hope thou art. I must tell

thee some newes I know ore else I should have nothing to write which is to tell thee that thy mother cusin Betty Bab went a wensday affter dinner to udimor[25] to cusins Odiarns lay there that night thursday morning designd to goe a Foot to my brother John Clarks with my cusine Odiearn, Cusin nanci Holman and two or three of my cusin Odiernes children but as they were setting forth tooke the convenience of a waggon goeing for wood very near the house where they were bound and took the opportunity of the coach with six oxen and a postilion an a single horse by; were very kindly entertained and they thought very welcome dined there with very pleasing cheere after dinner returned to udimor lay there that night and last night came home just before fell a violent great raine. I write in great hast for fear my messenger will be gone or else I could tell you some rye news. Just as I was writing Cussin Betty came to my chamber to desir me to give you her servis which I pray to accept with all the rest of our kind loves, with mine in particular Mother is busi a baking Bab a bed my dear I hartily kiss thee in my thoughts

Thy loving Grandmother
Barbara Hartshorne

Remember the beans

To Mrs Elisa: Jeake at Madam Brewers at Fowlers in Hawkhurst Kent, these

[256] *Barbara Hartshorne to Elizabeth Jeake junior, 7 August 1699. Original letter.*

ESRO FRE 5361

My dear Betty
Yours I have to day by carrier am glad to hear your well I have sent you an old lace for a tucker which your mother had ocation for som of it last week. She persuaded me twas good for nothing for bab not to make her a tucker and now she would have it to make you one, but I am ashamed to send a thing good for nothing to beg thy acceptance I have sent thee another I have bought at Mrs Warners, tis not fine but better then the other because it is stronge thy mother would not have thee thinke her displeased because thou writs for things she is very ready to co[mp]ly with thee for that because she knows thou wilt write for no[thing] but what thou wants thy father sent thee a letter last munday he doubts thou hast not had it. Rye news hear is to fast Bucks to be eaten a wensday at the mearmaid forty pounds to be spent upon a dinner by

[25] Probably Udimore, a village about 8 miles to the west of Rye.

Burgess this is all I have to say saving our kind love to thee cosin betties servis farewell my dear from thy loving grandmother

Barbara Hartshorne

Mother says she is busie she cannot write folding clothes taks up her time at present

Rye 7th Aug

[257] *Samuel Jeake to Elizabeth Jeake junior, 9 September 1699. Original letter.* ESRO FRE 5359

Rye Sept. 9th 1699

Dear Child

I am glad to hear by your letters yesterday that you have been something better since your mother was to see you. I pray God continue it & restore your health & to him return thanks and in all your ways acknowledge him & he shall direct your pathes. I suppose the pain of your head may return again, but if it do be not out of heart: as it returns so it may remove. Man is born to trouble. Endeavor to make a sanctified use of all afflictions, & let all the dispensations of providence draw you nearer to God & more off from the world in which you are but a stranger as the Apostle speaks of the believer in the 11th of the Hebrews who did not take up their rest in this world but looked for a City that hath foundations whose builder & maker is God. Look upon sin as the greatest Evil of all & pray to God not to lead you into Temptation. Avoid all occasions of sin, lest you be left to your own strength & fall, Keep in the way of God's providence & in doing your duty & then you may expect his protection. Chuse affliction always rather than iniquity. These directions that I give you will be of use to you in after times as well as now even thro the whole course of your Life. It is a comfort to me that I have observed in you some good thing towards the Lord God of Israel & I trust he will perfect that good work he has begun in your conversion to him to serve the living God. If you acquaint your self with Christ it is not so much matter for acquaintance in the world. I commit you to God & remain

Your affectionate father
Sa: Jeake

To Elizabeth Jeake at Madam Brewers at Fowlers in Hawkhurst in Kent

The Death of Samuel Jeake, 22 November 1699

[258] *Obituary Poem for Samuel Jeake printed for W. Marshall at the Bible in Newgate-Street, 1700*. RMA, Selmes Manuscripts, RYEYT: n39.58

IN OBITUM VERE
Deploratum Samuelis Jeake, Gent. (*qui Obijt* 22 Novembris, 1699) *Carmen Lugubre*.

Go mournful Muse! In sable Dress appear,
Th'Occasions sad, the Loss too great to baer;
Too great for Words: Let then our tender Eyes
Express the rest in Liquid Elegies.

Could'st thou alone in gen'ral Terms relate
Of transitory Things the common Fate;
Tell us how Scepters break and Crowns do fall,
How time first shakes and after throws down all;
How that fair lump of animated Clay
Which seems to thrive in Health and Strength to Day,
To Morrow's broke, enclosed in its Urn,
And to its native Dust will soone return;
How the gay Tapour which appears so bright,
Burning with Vigour is extinguish'd quite
By sudden Blasts, and never holds till Night;
How Death, the cunning Marksman, strikes the best
Of Vertues Favourites and spares the rest:
Could'st thou but cease, and give no nearer touch,
We should not be affected half so much,

But Ah! The tydings of so dear a Friend
Dear by Desert, who did so far transcend
The vulgar Sort, crop't off in blooming Years
By fatal Stroke, claims our unmeasur'd Tears;
So small, so just a Tribute let us pay:
Where Love Commands the Passions must obey.
Had we the Gums or Spice our famous Isle
Yearly receives from Rich *Arabia*'s Soil
In stately Ships, where Silver *Thames* doth fall,
To his Embalming wee'd devote them all.
Great Blessings whilst enjoy'd too common seem,
But when remov'd they raise our just Esteem:

Thus Heav'n thinks fit our Folly to Chastise,
And teach us by their want their worth to Prize.
Yet since our Loss to him proves greatest Gain,
Methinks he bids us now from Tears refrain,
Who knows no Tears, no Sorrows, Grief nor Pain,
And would not for Earths glitt'ring Crowns renew
His former Conflicts, having bid Adieu
To this vain World, whole Pleasure most pursue.
There no Eclipses can his Joys impair,
Now he hath reach'd that sweet Celestial Air,
Free from the Fogs of Earth, Divinely clear,
To which his Soul was not a Stranger here.
But often would it like the Lark or Dove,
Mount up by Contemplations Wings above
This shaken Globe, to seek its Central Rest
Forestalling that whereof 'tis now Possess't
With things unseen, by Prelibation blest?
And if to such Refreshments 'twas inur'd,
Or to those Tents of *Kedar* close confin'd,
Which ne'er for pleasnt Mansions were design'd,
How rich, how Glorious, how immensely great
Must his Enjoyments be when they'r compleat?
Cou'd we but soar beyond each earthly Thing,
Or hear those Joyful Anthems he doth Sing,
Since joyn'd in Confort with the Quire above,
And ravish'd with those Extasies of Love,
Our Minds might then some due Ideas frame
Of his refulgent Bliss; which now to Name
In this imperfect State, or comprehend,
Our Tongues and Intellect doth far Transcend.
But since that Glory's veild, wee'll think upon
His well spent Life, and strive to follow on
In those sweet Paths which yield such great encrease,
The choicest Pleasures, and whose End is Peace.
Though often Foil'd, wee'l fresh Attempts renew,
At humble distance still his Steps pursue,
And learn that great, that noble, useful Art
Of dying Daily; then our better Part,
Drawn by th'Almighty Pow'r which gave it Birth,
Will soar like his above the Cloggs of Earth.

Thrice happy they whose Thoughts are thus sublime,
Who pass like Thee, the cooked Paths of Time!
Whose Life's a constant Warfare, rais'd by th'Wings
Of Faith above all transitory Things!
Whose Aims are always good, whose Actions try'd.
Free from the Stains of Avarice and Pride!
Whose gen'rous Mind no longer craves to stay,
In these unsettled Orbs than whilst they may.
Their fellow Mortals serve, and spend their Days
In setting forth the great Jehovah's Praise!
Who having 'scap'd the Labyrinths of Sin,
The Snares the Dangers which they once were in,
And pass'd the Surges of a restless Sea
Into the Haven of Felicity,
Are entred on those everlasting Joys,
Which Pain, nor Grief, nor fear of Change annoys,
Where Sweetness never gluts, nor Fulness cloys.

Could'st thou dear Pious humble Soul, impart
They present State and Thoughts to Us, whose Heart
Was wont to be unbosom'd, open, kind,
To good Discourse as well as Acts inclin'd,
Sure we might hear Thee from th'Ætherial Spheres
Sweetly drop down such Words into our Ears,

S ince this more noble Part hath taken flight,
A nd reach'd its Center in the Orbs of Light,
M y former Mists are fled, and now I find
U nmixed Transports seize my boundless Mind,
E ncreasing always raising new Desires,
L ike Love's Seraphick holy endless Fires.

J nto these blessed Mansions hast to come;
E xert your Utmost Vigour, here's your Home,
A ll my surviving Friends; Let Faith and Love
K indle such Flames as Death can ne'er remove,
E ternal, constant, like the Joys above.

EPITAPHIUM

Beneath this Sable Tomb are hid
The last Remains of Him who did

As we and others, lately dwell
In such a fading Mortal Cell:
His better half, by Pass-port gain'd,
The upper Regions hath attain'd.
See here the best of Natures Glory,
The end of all things transitory.
A welcome Bait this Structure falls
To Subterraneous Animals:
Yet in this one Thing we may boast,
Altho' dissolv'd it is not lost:
The scatter'd Atoms must rejoin
When summon'd by that Pow'r Divine,
Which did at first from nothing raise
A Word, to shew its Makers Praise,
Then rest in Hope, thou precious Dust,
The Resurrection of the Just,
Both Soul and Body shall ag'en
Unite in perfect Bliss. *Amen*.

Elizabeth in London, 1701

[259] *Elizabeth Jeake to Barbara Hartshorne, 13 May 1701. Original letter.*
ESRO FRE 5337

London May the 13 1701

To tell you Dear Mother how I got to London is a difficult task but thro the goodness of our gracious protector I am safe arrived two persons besides my self sate on my end the Gentleman not at all less than capt Martin so [word illegible] in his full bigness the Lady not inferiour in Bulk. [word struck out] So Mrs Hall thus sate up I rode 3 [word illegible] other side a gentleman of which held a young Lady on his knee, warm riding for us all. I called at Dr Curteis where I was civily receiv'd and importun'd to stay 'till the next coach day which will be Thursday next if I could not have got a corner in the coach intended to have accepted so ~~civil~~ kind an offer. I find Mr Miller his family are all very well I had the happiness to see Mr Miller who came pat to meet at the Inn. he presente his service to you, my Duty to my Dear Mother with Love to my Children & service to the Dr: & his Lady not omitting the rest of my Friends I am

Dear Mother
[final section damaged]

To Mrs Barbara Hartshorne at Rye in Sussex

[260] *Elizabeth Jeake to Barbara Hartshorne, 20 May 1701. Original letter.*
ESRO FRE 5338

London the 20th of May 1701

To keep my word Dear Mother & to let you know I am by the goodness of God in health I write this for have nothing to communicate as touching my business if there should an opportunity offer during my stay would have Betty send me a piece of red Indian sattin the same of my gown tis in the chest rolled up with other silk I hope I shall hear next post that you are all well Betty is very thrifty of her scrawl she might be more liberal unless twere Better. I just now saw cousin jay have not been at the other end of the Town yet my most Humble Duty to my Dear Mother with sincere Love to my children & niece Bab. Service to my Friends if you do but know the true from false I am

Dear Mother
Your most obedient
Daughter
E Jeake

If my Mother has any service for me I beg she would not defferre her commands.

[261] *Elizabeth Jeake to Barbara Hartshorne, 1701, undated. Original letter.*
ESRO FRE 5339

I have this day Dear Mother seen Mr Benge who is full of talk says his money is ready & that a conclusion will be made which I heartily wish the carrier came to town a day sooner than ordinary which has much disappointed me in some little remembran[ce] as I intend for home & Marys gown & petticoat. Betty tells me not whether she has sent a Box for sugar for us per Hoy I would by no means have Bacon forgot it is pretty late so cannot extend this to a greater length only desire to know if Mrs Young would have muslin for ruffles as well as head & hood which is alredy bought. I bless God I am well & heartily wish you & my dear may be so Duty to my Dear Mother & love to my children. Service to all my friends I am

Dear Mother
Your ever dutiful
Daughter
Elisa Jeake

Thursday night past ten.

[262] *Elizabeth Jeake to Barbara Hartshorne, 24 May 1701. Original letter.*
ESRO FRE 5340

London May the 24th 1701
This serves Dear Mother to inform you anew of my health which thanks be to God is still continued I hope the same blessing attends you and my children I received yours not till yesterday if you had directed to me at Mr Millers Merch and in London it had come on Thursday but adding Dunster Court and not Mincing Lane 'twas carried into Fleet Street I have bought you petticoats but for head linen am at a loss knowing you will not conform to high heads which young & old wear here no glove tops worn tell Bettie her hair trussed up as mine uses to be is the way low dresses & two double ruffles. Tell Sarah I will mind her trunk & hope she will mind her business to dispatch it nimbly out of the way that I may have a clean garden and see the effect of her diligence in spinning these long days. Mr Miller and his Lady send their service to you & Madam Miller wishes she had you and the children to make much of that I might never go to Rye again, be pleased to give my service to Mr Tucker & his sister & let 'em know I have a gratefull sence of all their civilities to my Dear Mother and shall not be wanting in my acknowledgements whenever oppertunity offers. My most Humble Duty to your Dear Self & Love to my Dear creatures with service to the Dr: and where else you please I am

Dear Mother
Your obedient
Daughter
Elisa Jeake

Love to the Maids
Past ten a clock says the watch man good night

No news of Bacon yet 3 pints of shelled pease sold for £3 for some Aldermans Daughters weding.

[263] *Elizabeth Jeake to Barbara Hartshorne, 27 May 1701. Original letter.*
ESRO FRE 5341

London May the 27th 1701
I shall take care Dear Mother to execute your commands in all the particulars & hope if Madam Shonkburgh have the horse for her journey he will not be received into her family & if not I ~~hope I may~~ shall be glad to have him after her which I confess is manners & as much as I desire at present Mr Short has not yet been at Dunster Court nor was yesterday morning come to Town I

have not waited on the foremenconed lately but intend to pay my devoir so soon as I know how my business stands shall communicate it to my Mother. Let Betty send me the piece of red Indian Sattin by Mr Chiswel to leave at Mrs Tomkins if it be not sent per carrier I wou'd know what Mrs Seal wou'd have instead of her carnation Tape I have forgot I am glad you have so much good company Madam Miller advises Betty to weave bone lace rather than Point which is quite out of voge if she incline to the Ladys sentiments will buy a pieke of Lace. The Box for sugar wou'd have sent as Betty says to Mr Wilmoore & when Mr Chiswel's Hoy is come up would have word. Madam Grace & Ashurst have given a visit to Madam Miller were pleased to invite me but have not yet been nor made any visit but a perpetual hurry of buying things I have bought my Aunt's Lace but did not think worth while to make a pacquet of that alone the first oppertunity of convenience she may expect it. My Humble Duty to my Dear Mother with Mr & Madam Millers service to you and Betty. My Love to my Children service to my friends. Your cordial was proper for your [word illegible] I am Ð

Dear Mother
Your most Dutifull
Daughter
Elisa Jeake

Love to the Maids.

To Mrs Barbara Hartshorne at Rye in Sussex

[264] *Elizabeth Jeake to Barbara Hartshorne, 29 May 1701. Original letter.*
ESRO FRE 5342

Thursday 29th of May

Excuse Dear Mother the brevity of my Letter which is only to inform you I am well & received the Bacon so too with the other things I heartily thank you had the Dr's Letter the day & shall return him answer in the mean time beg his acceptance of service & thanks which with humble Duty to my Dear Mother & Love to my Children conclude

I am Dear Mother
Your most Obedient
Daughter
Elisa Jeake

Mr Millers & Madams Service to you all Include niece for I esteem her one of my Dear children. Love to the maids.

[265] *Elizabeth Jeake to Barbara Hartshorne, 31 May 1701. Original letter.*
ESRO FRE 5343

London May 31st 1701

I rejoyce Dear Mother to hear of your & my little tribes good health which I pray God continue I canot conveniently pay good wife Davids bill for good wife Seals will if I can but do not promise the last ten pounds if Betty send her gown wou'd have her send the lining & petticoat belonging to it as well as the other. I was too late for the carrier this week or I had sent Marys gown petticoat & aprons a maker she may better fit her Lace with at Rye I shall send the things needful by Tenterden carrier good wife Seals commissions will take care of. I can say little of Mr Benge's & my business only Mr Short is come to town & the other gone out but comes next week again. I have made no visits ~~yet~~ the weather has been so bad & of buying part not yet quite over Mackrel are here 7 d per piece & cherry 2 p penny. My most Humble Duty to your Dear self, real Love to my children and service to the Dr with the rest of my friends I am

Dear Mother
Your most Obedient
Daughter
Elisa Jeake

Love to the maids

[266] *Elizabeth Jeake to Barbara Hartshorne, 3 June 1701. Original letter.*
ESRO FRE 5344

London June the 3rd 1701

I am sorry Dear Mother I incurre so much displeasure for my good will I know of no advantage I shall reap by what I buy for people my readiness to serve 'em should not encourage em to be to severe on me for 'tis most certain if greater motives than those commissions received had not induc'd me to go for London I shou'd not have been there on purpose for their occasions my Aunts Lace I bought long agoe as likewise cousin's stuffe but for making it up I never understood twas to be done here nor canit be unlesse her stays were with me I shall send it the week with Mary Jones's. I wish I could as easily dispatch my affairs which are of more importance but I know not what to do 'tis necessary for it to be done whilst I am here but the advances are small & since my Dear Mother & Children are at Rye I can do no other than with my self which em that I might shew my self

Dear Mother your most obed[ient]
Daughter
E. Jeake

I have my nieces her mother promise to see & thank her for her pretty Letter I think I have a stronger tye to be serviceable to her than to any other. Your Dear Self & my children excepted. Let her not be dis[quiet]ed I hope always to acquit my self her friend. My Duty Love & Service where due. Cherrys four [words lost]

[267] *Elizabeth Jeake to Barbara Hartshorne, 7 June? 1701. Original letter.*
ESRO FRE 5345

I saw Mr Benge Dear Mother yesterday but from what he says never take direction and have not heard from Mr Short but am in daily expectation I shall acquaint you with what he says and what hopes there is of a conclusion which I earnestly desire to be rid of so troublesum an affair & because I might then speed home which I would gladly do to my Dear Mother and children which are the only tyes to engage me to Rye. I shall be glad to hear you have received the things safe per Tenterden Carrier Mrs Seal doth not say what she would have instead of her carnation Tape excuse brevity for I am in great hast and can add no more than my humble Duty to my Dear Mother with Love to my little creatures & service to my friends as if particularised [words struck out] Mr Miller & his Lady present their service to my Mother I am

Dear Mother
Your most Obedient
Daughter
Elisa Jeake

Saturday the 7th 1701
Love to the maids

[268] *Elizabeth (Betty) Jeake junior to Elizabeth Jeake, 1701, undated. Original letter.*
ESRO FRE 5346

We received the things Dear Mother for which we remark our hearty thanks. I have sent my things viz gown & petticoats & linen by Chiswell ~~be~~ will be at London shortly the things will be left at Mrs Tompkins I would pray you to remember a pair of shoes for Sam Mrs Young desires you to buy her knots. Mary Jones: gives her service & thanks for buying her things which she likes extraordinaryly & desires you to send her word concerning her hood & Sarah's trunk my Grandmothers love & she prays you buy her a pair of shoes I have almost worn out mine I desire you to send me word who all them sad couller gloves are for & whether you had not a pair of my cousins sent us with your gown lineing. My cousin Mary desires her petticoat to be made her everyday petticoat is a yard & 2 half long. I should be glad if you'd please to send my dust gown & [word illegible] or fan with it I received my night raile[26] wich I like very well & return my humble thanks for them. If you have the 2 pair of parl nippers with you desire canst send me one pair for I can find none & Sam in great want. All our serv to the family I am & in your most Dutiful Dau E J.

I have not had opportunity to enquire of your health since his return.

To Mrs Jeake at Mr Tho: Miller's merchant in London

[269] *Elizabeth Jeake to Barbara Hartshorne, 17 June 1701. Original letter.* ESRO FRE 5347

London June the 17th 1701

I desire Dear Mother that good wife Seal would let me know how much is due to Mr Lock he charges more than she gave me he charges a parcel may the 23th which makes 9s 3d more than the bill she gave me there is nothing due for changing Laces I shall not clear off the account 'till I hear from her I have ordered her sope there is some more than what she appointed of which will give account for at my return. I have paid the old debt which was with the confectioners goods is ordered to Mr Wilmots likewise I shall go thither presently if he be at home order what things she desires from him. I have a letter from Mrs Cross & shall I hope have the Satisfaction of terminating that long business if Mary Jones can buy her alamode hood at Rye twill be best so to do I send per Mr Chiswell's Hoy Sarah's Trunk & Broom besides what shall order from Mr Wilmots but let not Sarah desire to have her Trunk open before I come & I charge Mrs Bettys impatience to let it alone for I have the Keys with me on purpose to secure it till I come. I hope according to the old saying these few lines will find you all in good health as I am at this present writing thanks be to God. My humble Duty with Love & service as you judge necessary concludes this Dear Mother from

Your most obedient Daughter
Elisa Jeake

Twill not I hope surprise my mother to tell her my Christian name is changed since my surname is still Jeake and I am wrote Elisha

[26] *OED*, n. a loose wrap or dressing gown, worn after undressing or before dressing, usually by a woman.

[270] *Elizabeth Jeake to Barbara Hartshorne, 1701, undated. Original letter.*
ESRO FRE 5348

You cannot be more desirous to see me Dear Mother than I am to return I am under a great perplexity Mr Benge's business moves so slowly tis no fault of mine for they both know me to be in Town that I wait on purpose for em which is all I can do. For what people at Rye say I look on ill their chimeras as with that indifference I ought have been so accustomed to be [word illegible] I can take it without any concern for whilst they have no reason to discant upon my actions I care not what they say only wish for their sakes they would not endeavour to make lyes pass for truth & I am sure this is most abominable falsitie its probable after all Mr Tucker is in no want of a wife especially of other peoples chusing but be it how it will as I came out Betty Jeake so there is no danger but I shall if providence blesse me with life & health return with the same name it is most certain if any body was so mad to take me with my two pair of illmatched clogs I shall not be so eager to dispose of my Person without the approbation or knowledge of so good a mother as is mine please to buy Sam a pair of shoes will you & I will do so too I believe I did pay Hunsder & Miller the window Tax[27] but whether there may be another half year I know not due since however it be tis not I think usual to pay more than half a year at a time & that's but five shillings. Remember me to Betty & tell her I hope she will supply my place in Love & Duty to you in my absence & not desire to go much out & especially on the Sabbath Day no more than to church & home again above all I would not have her go to Mrs Shephards shop if she be good to you & keep my Dear mother company she shall lose nothing by it at my return let Mary Jones remember to get me the receipt for the Itch my Duty to Love & Service Dear Mother as it properly belongs I beg you to accompt & dispose of from Dear Mother what ever the mistaken world suggest not only your most obedient Daughter but

Elisha Jeake

[Wed]nesday past 10 at night.

[27] The Window Tax was the successor to the Hearth Tax and was introduced in 1696. M. J. Braddick, *The Nerves of State: Taxation and the financing of the English state, 1558–1714* (Manchester, 1996), 103.

[271] *Elizabeth Jeake to Barbara Hartshorne, 1701, undated. Original letter.*
ESRO FRE 5349

Mother
I perceive my dame designes to try that hard countrey again I wish her the success she proposes I will mind her quillt & blanket the other things are on board the Hoy The windows I promise shou'd be mended so far as was needed but in regard they have but ½ the house hope they won't expect all the glass repaired what is necessary am willing should be done & no more for will be all lost when I repair the house. There is neither silver gold nor precious stones in the Trunk but yet I wou'd have it safe as if the treasure of the Indies were contained in it by this I raise expectation but indeed there is nothing of any considerable value but such little things & papers they are as would be troublesom to me to repair if lost I shall heartily rejoyce in my return because tis the habitation of my Dear Mother & children. Mr Short is now in town but goes out to morrow but says this Term will undoubtedly conclude this long tedious affair. I shall send cousins gown & petticoat to morrow morning & for Betty's Dust gown tell her I designe my silk one for her I cou'd not please my self in a new one for her nor shou'd I have bought her so good I do not promise her the Ribbands nor need she take em of before I come home. I cannot help the woman's not coming so soon I saw my Cousin last week she is in daily expectation of her heaven send her a good hour and mary a good place pray mother don't let your Oranges rot for want of eating nor the cakes stale. Mr Millers & his Ladys service with my Duty, Love & Service to you all is what offers from Dear Mother

Your ever Dutifu[l]
Daughter
Elisha Jeake

Thursday past 6
I will be sure to remember your purse I write no treason nor think no harm if pryers find any in what I write the old motto be their portion: evil to em that evil think.

[272] *Elizabeth Jeake to Barbara Hartshorne, 21 June 1701. Original letter.*
ESRO FRE 5350

London June the 21st 1701
Yesterday Dear Mother I sent Cousin Marys gown and petticoat which I hope will prove to her satisfaction. I put up a pair of shoes for niece Bab for sumer & a pair of winter shoes for Bab Jeake but the main cargo is in the

trunk since my last I cannot give you a further account of business having heard nothing of the matter but I am in great hopes twill be ended this Term I beg Dear Mother you wou'd not expect a longer account from me now than that I am well and your most obedient Daughter

Elisha Jeake

My most humble Duty to my Dear Mother, love to the little cubbs service to my friends & Love to the maids.

[273] *Elizabeth (Betty) Jeake junior and Barbara Hartshorne to Elizabeth Jeake, 1701, undated. Original letter.* ESRO FRE 5351

Dear Mother this is to inform you of our welfare my aunt gives you many thanks for her lace which she likes extraordinary well. I did not desire you to & make a particular paquet of those things I pray'd you to send with cousin Mary but to put them up with hers & I believe they are so light they won't make her pay any thing the more for carriage for her things I am to take care to send them to Hawkhearst whither she went last week. My Grandmother who gives her love to you would have you buy cousin Bab (who gives her service to you) a pair of collered gloves. I desire to know whether I must make my night rails without hallowing away before or if as usual. my scarfe is all to peices. Mary Jones gives her service to you & desires you to send her word concerning a hood. Mr & Mrs Tucker give their service & think your stay long. Humble duty to my [word illegible] from your ever Lo dau E J.

I be just going to fishing

[*On reverse of FRE 5351*]

My Dear goodi Seal desires thee to buy her a good large white Blanket and a quilt for her bed she gives her service to thee tels thee if thou doest not make hast home she will be gone before thou comest to Stone & suppose if thou stay this twelve moneth one or other will finde business…but the french doe much desire thee to let the glassier to mend their windows they say thou didest promise them it should be done. Mary Jones is much out of patience the woman doth not send to her yet remember me a purse. Old and young Mrs Tucker Doctr Young and his wife Mrs Waters, Betty & Bab are gone to fishing this afternoon. Betty bids me finish her letter. I hope thou hast noe great tresure in the trunck but the last letter was opened. Send noe wafer. Thy longe stay is very troublesom to me my kind and harty servis to Mr and Madam Miller not forgetting the good old gentleman my dear love to thy selfe

from her who is thy
loveing Mother Barbara
Hartshorne

To Mrs Elisha: Jeake at Mr Thomas Millers Merchant in Mincing Lane in Dunster Court, London, these

[274] *Elizabeth Jeake to Barbara Hartshorne, 26 June? 1701. Original letter.*
ESRO FRE 5352

London the 26th 1701

I have at last Dear Mother gotten a fair account from Mrs Crosse & Mr Miller has an order from her to pay what remaine in her hand if it please God to give me as fair a deliverance from Mr Benge I shall heartily rejoyce I live in hopes this Term will conclude this business as luckily as that Exon is ended I saw Old Grayburn here but did not pay his Daughter's forty shillings he having no order from her to receive it She is almost of age of which I am glad. I wish my Dame soft dealings in the hard Countrey and you Dear Mother health and long life my Humble Duty Dear Mother to your Dear Self love to my Dear little children & service to my Friends tell the Dr he was not so good as his word to his servant

Your ever dutiful
Daughter
Elisa Jeake

And love to the Maids.

[275] *Elizabeth Jeake to Barbara Hartshorne, 28 June 1701. Original letter.*
ESRO FRE 5353

Yours Dear Mother I received am sorry to hear you are so much alone. I hope in a short time I shall have the satisfaction of seeing you and my Dear Children Mr Benge has given Mr Miller a Bill for £200 which he has received this day so there is now some hopes there will be an end of that tedious business. For your money when I come home will give you an account what I have done the business will be free for you still if you approve it tis not in the govenment. I wish the Bride joy now she has left me she is out of fear of my leaving of her Bettys journey is an unimpeded frolick. I am sorry to hear Sarah makes out so badly I hope when return to quicken her or get another. Marys Mrs is not brought to bed as I hear she thinks the time long as Mary can do I add no more but humble Duty to your Dear Self with Love to my children and service to my friends I am

Dear Mother
Your most obedient
Daughter
Elisa Jeake

Saturday June the 28th
1701 Love to the maids.

[276] *Elizabeth Jeake to Barbara Hartshorne, 1701 undated. Original letter.*
ESRO FRE 5354

My last I think acquainted you Dear Mother with what preparation Mr Benge had made for the conclusion of that affair I am really impatient of my long stay & earnestly desire a dispatch that I might return to my Dear Mother & children whom I ardently wish to see the term draws towards an end so that I shall in a few days know whether twill be done now or no my Humble Duty to your Dear Selfe, my little Dear children with Love & Service where you think convenient I am

Dear Mother
Your obedient
Daughter
Elisa Jeake

Thursday night

[277] *Elizabeth Jeake to Barbara Hartshorne, 3 July 1701. Original letter.*
ESRO FRE 5355

London the 3rd of July 1701

Your express your self Dear Mother to be tired with providing answers and I am as weary of writing since I cannot fix the day of my departure I gave you what account I could of the matter that stays me I have wrote to Mr Short but no return yet I have this day seen Madam Fouchè & Mrs Paine Madam Fouchè presents her service to you her Husband is gone into Holland to see his sons. Madam Miller is indisposed & has been thus these 5 or 6 days a faintness [all] over her no appetite a disorder in her head pardon Dear Mother my brevity Mr Miller is newly gone out and Madam is alone which I am unwilling she shou'd whilst I am here. Duty, Love & Service Dear Mother accept & dispose of as you please from

Your most dutiful Daughter
Elisa Jeake

[278] *Elizabeth Jeake to Barbara Hartshorne, 4 July 1701. Original letter.*
ESRO FRE 5356

London July the 4th

Think not Dear Mother I will prolong my stay farther than necessary I think the time long till I see you all again which I hope it will please God to grant me in a little time I earnestly desired to know how Sams hat fitted & Bettys thoughts are so filled with her admirer it justles other things quite out for the Coats I can have remedied by the maker here who had rather do it her self than any body else should for sending any thing down before I come would not have it desired it is sufficient have bought all the things they send for & hope to see 'em safe att Rye. I have been at the exchequer once & next week must go again some other business have to disput & shall return I fear I shall make no merchandize of my shells nor other advantage than being stiled a Philosopher for my learned talk be shewed the rarities at Gresham College & have the honour to be acquainted with a fellow of the Royal Society The King is gone this day in order to go for Holland. Cherrys are three farthings a pound my unfeigned Duty to my Dear Mother & tender Love to my sweet children & niece I hope the Oranges were not rot & that my Dear little Frank can make a shift by this to eat a sugar cake I have bought him three caps I have bought all the maids desired service to the Dr Mrs Geer has not been sick nor did the Child receive any damage in their journey more than that of being thorough wet which they were all of in I am

Dear Mother
Your most obedient
Daughter
Elisa Jeake

To Mrs Barbara Hartshorne at Rye in Sussex

[279] *Elizabeth Jeake to Barbara Hartshorne, 1701, undated. Original letter.*
ESRO FRE 5357

You see Dear Mother as it is my Duty to inviolably observe your commands having not missed one post since I came heare I wish I had more considerable opportunities of shewing my Love & obedience to so indulgent a Mother as mine I am under a real perplexity about my return I can give no further account of my business than what I have already done I think to have lawyers put into the litany is very necessary their proceedings are so tedious & I believe I am none of the greatest sufferers by them neither. Madam Miller continues ill, she presents her service to you & Betty. I would have her send me the gallon [words illegible] if it be sweet per carrier next week. I wish I could say I expect to see you at the end of it my utmost diligence shall not be wanting to lay hold on the first opportunity of shewing you Dear Mother

Your most obedient Daughter
Elisa Jeake

My Duty Love & Service where due

[280] *Elizabeth Jeake to Barbara Hartshorne, 8 July 1701. Original letter.*
ESRO FRE 5358

Tuesday the 8th of July 1701

At last Dear Mother I have done with Mr Benge for the present in order to conclude the affair & my presence is no longer necessary on that score I therefore entreat you will please to send horses for me to Tunbridge on Friday. I have taken a Place in the coach for that day that I may if God permit be at home on Saturday I wou'd have the Horses early in at Tunbridge Friday [word struck out] afternoon that they may rest against I come for if I come thither in any tolerable time designe to pursue my journey that I may have some thing the less for Saturday 'tis long since I heard from my Dear Mother but hope now to see her and my Dear children in a short time I am with due remembrances

Dear Mother
Your dutiful Daughter
Elisa Jeake

Death of Barbara Hartshorne, February 1707

[281] *Will of Barbara Hartshorne* TNA, PROB 11/502/107[28]

In the Name of God Amen. The Thirteenth Day of March in the Third year of the Reigne of Our Soveraigne Lady Anne by the Grace of God of England, Scotland, France and Ireland Queene Defender of the Faith etc. and in the yeare of our Lord One Thousand Seaven hundred and three I Barbara Hartshorne of the Antient Towne of Rye in the County of Sussex widow being aged sick and weake in body but of perfect and disposing memory Thanks be to God Doe make and ordaine this my last will and Testament in writing in manner and forme following. That is to say Imprimis I commend my soule into the hands of God hoping in his mercy through the meritts of

[28] The Rye Parish Registers record Barbara's burial on 13 February 1707.

Jesus Christ to receive Remission of my sins and eternall salvation and my body I yield to the Earth to be buried in decent manner. And as touching that temporall Estate which God hath given me I will and dispose the same as herein after followeth. That is to say I will give and bequeath unto my Grandchildren Thomas Holman and Honor Holman the summe of Two hundred pounds that is to say to Each of them One hundred pounds of lawfull money of England to be respectively paid by my Executrix herein after named to the said Thomas when he shall accomplish the age of one and twenty years. And to the said Honour when she shall accomplish the age of one and twenty years or on the day of her marriage which shall first happen. And if the said Thomas shall happen to dye within the said age of One and twenty years or if the said Honour shall dye within the said age unmarried Then it is my will and mind that the survivor of them my said grandchildren shall have the whole Two hundred pounds. And if both my said grandchildren Thomas and Honour shall dye before their said ages and the said Honour be unmarryed then and in such case I give and bequeath the said Two hundred pounds unto my Executrix herein after named. Item I give and bequeath unto my Grandaughter Barbara Hartshorne the summe of foure hundred pounds to be paid unto her within One month next after the day of her Marriage provided allways and my Intent and meaning expresly is That my said Grand Daughter Barbara shall and doe marry by and with the joint Consent and approbation of my said Executrix herein after named and of my good and trusty friend Francis Young of Rye aforesaid Gent or the survivor of them but if the said Barbara shall happen to marry without such Consent and Approbation as aforesaid Then and in such Case I doe absolutely give and bequeath the said four hundred pounds legacy of the said Barbara unto my four Grandchildren Elizabeth Brownsmith, Barbara Jeake, Samuel Jeake and Francis Jeake to be equally divided between them. Item I will and devise give and beaqueath unto my said Grandaughter Barbara Hartshorne All that my Annuity issuing and coming out of Fordths farme situate lying and being in Brede in the County of Sussex lately purchased by me of Francis Young, Stephen Odiame, Samuel Durrant, Thomas Horne and Joseph Horne some or one of them to be and remaine to my said Grandaughter and the heire or heires of her body lawfully to be begotten forever. But for want of such heires my will and meaning is That the Annuity shall be to the said Barbara for and during the Terme of her naturall life And immediately after her decease I will and devise it to my Grandaughter Elizabeth Brownsmith and her heires forever. And my will and meaning further is That my Executrix herein after named shall receive all the Rents and profits issuing and arising from the said Annuity untill the said Barbara come to the age of one and twenty years or till the said Barbara be married which shall first happen and the money soe received to lay out for the said Barbara at her owne Discretion without being liable to be called to accompt for the same when the said Barbara shall attain her age of one and twenty years or be married. My will and meaning further is that my Executrix for the better maintaining the said Barbara soe long as she remains unmarried shall expend out of my personal estate ten pounds a yeare upon her and lay out for her without being accomptable to any person at any time for the same. Item I give and bequeath unto my Grand Daughter Elizabeth Brownsmith the summe of five pounds a yeare during the Coverture between her and her now husband to be paid half yearly out of my personall estate (vizt.) Att the feast of the Annunciation of the blessed Virgin Mary and at St Michael the Archangel by equall portions unto her owne hands separate and apart from her husband And a receipt under her hand only to be sufficient Discharge to my Executrix for the same The first payment to be made at the next of the said feasts after my decease. And in case my said Grand Daughter Elizabeth Brownsmith shall happen to survive her said now husband then (but not otherwise) I give and bequeath unto her the summe of one hundred pounds to be paid unto her within one month next after the decease of her said now husband. And from thenceforth my intent and meaning is that the payment of the said five pounds a year shall cease and determine. Item I give and bequeath unto my said Grandaughter Elizabeth one double Rose noble piece of Gold. Item I give and bequeath unto my three Grandchildren Barbara Jeake, Samuel Jeake and Francis Jeake the severall summes of one hundred pounds a piece of lawfull money of England to be paid unto them by my said Executrix when they shall attaine their respective ages of One and twenty yeares or be married which shall first happen. And if any or either them the said Barbara Jeake Samuel and Francis shall happen to dye before such age or Marriage Then the said Legacy or Legacies of her him or them soe dying shall goe equally to the survivours or survivor of them. Item I give and bequeath unto my Daughter in Law Anne Hartshorne[29] one twenty shilling piece and one Two and Twenty Shilling piece of Gold. Item I give and bequeath unto my five Grandchildren Elizabeth Brownsmith,[30] Barbara Hartshorne,[31] Barbara Jeake, Samuel Jeake and Francis Jeake one purse of Gold that was my GrandFathers to be equally divided betwixt them. Item all the Rest and Residue of my Gold plate, wearing Apparell, Goods, Chattels and personall Estate whatsoever or wheresoever (after my just Debts and Legacies and my funeral Expenses with the probate of this my last Will are paid and discharged I give and bequeath unto my Daughter Elizabeth

[29] Nathaniel Hartshorne's widow. There are no further mentions of Anne in the Jeake or Tucker papers.

[30] Betty Jeake, now married.

[31] Nathaniel Hartshorne's daughter. Likewise there are no further records of Barbara in the Jeake or Tucker papers.

Tucker the Wife of Joseph Tucker of Rye. Item I make ordaine nominate and appoint my said Daughter Elizabeth Tucker to be sole Executrix of this my last Will and Testament. And Lastly I doe hereby revoke and make void all former wills whatsoever by me heretofore made and declared In Witness whereof I the said Barbara Hartshorne the Testatrix have to the first sheete of this my last Will and Testament sett my hand and to this last sheete sett my hand and seale Dated the day and yeare first above written. Barbara Hartshorne signed sealed published and declared by the said Testatrix in the presence of us Ann Costler, Mary Jeffery, Francis Young.

Francis Jeake at School and at Work, 1710–1716

[282] *Francis Jeake to Elizabeth Tucker (Jeake), 10 March 1709/10. Original letter.* ESRO FRE 5378

Hon: M[oth]er Tenterden Mar: the 10: 1709/10
I make [word lost] to trouble you with these few lines, hoping they will find you in good health, as I am at this present. I desire you to send me a Greek Grammar for I have great need of it. We received no letter last week, pray send me a line by the Carrier. I desire to know how you & the rest of the family do. Pray give my duty to my Father, & love to my Brother & Sisters, I am
Your dutiful son
Francis Jeake

To Madam Tucker a Rye in Sussex

[283] *Francis Jeake to Elizabeth Tucker, 18 July 1712. Original letter.* RMA, Selmes Manuscripts, RYEYT N39.59.1

Hon: Mother
I desire you to send me one word how you got home last Saturday & about what time. Pray send me some paper for I have not one quarter of a sheet. Pray give my duty to my Father, & my love to my Brother & Sisters. I am
Your dutifull Son
Francis Jeake

Tenterden July 18 1712

To Madam Tucker at Rye Sussex

[284] *Francis Jeake to Joseph Tucker, 3 December 1714. Original letter.*
RMA, Selmes Manuscripts, RYEYT N39.59.3

Sr
The manifold Kindnesses and Obligations which I have received at your hands put on me no small concern that I am not able to repay them at present however as a mean requital I dedicate my first fruits to you, begging that you would please accept of them, 'till I am in a better Capacity to make a more suitable return to you, and in the mean time assure yourself That my endeavours to make you amends shall not be wanting. This Sr emboldens me to present these Lines to you, desiring you would accept the same from
Your Obedient Son and Servant
Francis Jeake

Tenterden December 3 1714

To Mr Joseph Tucker at Rye Sussex

[285] *Francis Jeake to Joseph Tucker, 18 July 1716. Original letter.*
ESRO FRE 5379

London July the 18th 1716

Hon: Sir
I hope this Letter which brings you the news of my safe Arrival here (that Day that I parted from you) about 3 a Clock, may be answered with the agreable news of your and my Mothers Safe Arrival at Rye and finding the family well. Whether this be news to you or no I cannot tell, as such I write it, viz That as Parson Paul[32] was riding to Tyburn a man in a certain house in Holborn threw some dirt at him and hit him whereupon the Parson pulled off his Hat & said Sir I Thank you, upon which the Mob rose & had seized the Fellow had he not been carried off with a Guard, and finding they could not come at him they brake all the Windows in the House, & they were forc'd to set a Guard upon the House all that night for fear of its being demolished as the Mob threatened to do; likewise when they were at Tyburn the Mob began to be insolent, upon which an Officer who was there drew his Sword & cut one fellow (who was more insolent than the Rest) severely, upon which Wholsome Severity the Mob presently vanished. July the 13th last being Sunday a certain man in Moorfields who had a Place in the Pay Office hanged

[32] William Paul, a Jacobite, hung, drawn and quartered at Tyburn on 13 July 1716. Robert D. Cornwall, 'Paul, William (*bap.* 1679, *d.* 1716)', *ODNB.*

himself in his Garret. He had been melancholy for some time before. But least I should trespass upon your Patience I shall conclude (with Presenting my Duty to you & my Mother, my Love to my Sisters & my Remembrances to all my friends) subscribing my self

Your Dutiful Son & Servant
Francis Jeake

I Like my Place very well as yet

Mr Slade gives his service to you & my Mother, & my Brother remembers to you all.

To Mr Joseph Tucker at Rye, with care, in Sussex

[286] *Francis Jeake to Elizabeth Tucker and Barbara Jeake, 8 August 1716. Original letter.* RMA, Selmes Manuscripts, RYEYT N39.59.2

Hon: Mother
I have now sent Mrs Bishop's shoes which I had sent by Mr Slade had I known of his being in Town soon enough, for I knew of it but on ~~Wednes~~ Tuesday in the afternoon & he went away a Wednesday morning; The Shoemaker said that perhaps the shoes might be lost out of the parcel as it went down & that then there was no reason he shou'd lose a pair of shoes, But if on the contrary he had ~~omitt~~ omitted 'em he was sorry for it, & would willingly make 'em up whereupon he gave me the shoes which I here send. I have been likewise with the Gold thread man & bought ¼ ounce for which I gave 2s whether I have done well or ill therein I know not I can only say I got it as cheap as I cou'd & I hope I have pleased you therein. Mr Hudson hath sent the whole piece of Linsey per Hoy which he chargeth at 30s & he saith that if you have not occasion for it all you may use so much as you want & send him back the rest. My Brother having seen the letter which you wrote to me last says that he wrote a letter to you about coming into the country; but however I am of opinion that if you wrote a Letter to the Dr he would willingly enough come. The Town is very barren of news nor have I much time to enquire after any. I must ask your pardon for troubling you with such long impertinence & bad writing but I hope your goodness will excuse it both & that you will believe ('till I forfeit that Opinion) that I am

Your dutifull son
Francis Jeake

London August the 8th 1716

My Brother remembers to you all.
[*On reverse of RMA, Selmes Manuscripts, RYEYT N39.59.2*]

Dear Sister
I have according to your desire bought you Waller's Poems[33] for which I gave 2s. I would fain have got it cheaper but could not, however I think it is as good as mine which cost 2s 6d. If at any time you have any business wherein I can be serviceable to you; Please to let me know it and it shall be willingly performed by

Your Loving Brother
Francis Jeake

London August the 8th 1716

I like my place very well.

Pray give my Duty to my Father & remember me to all my Friends at Rye.

Please to give my Love to Sister Phill & tell her I expect her to perform her promise.

I have now sent per Carrier
1pair of Shoes
¼ oz of Gold thread
Wallers Poems

To Madam Tucker at Rye in Sussex

[287] *Francis Jeake to Joseph Tucker, 15 August 1716. Original letter.*
ESRO FRE 5380

London August the 15th 1716

Honoured Sir
After a Tryall of 5 Weeks, I liking my place I have engrossed my Indentures which I have now sent to you. If you please to sign them & send them up, they shall be deposited either in Mr Vandyke's Hands or mine (as you shall judge

[33] Probably Edmund Waller whose work was published in at least 4 editions during the 1660s and 1680s and was widely read during the late seventeenth and early eighteenth centuries. Warren Chernaik, 'Waller, Edmund (1606–1687)', *ODNB*.

convenient) till the other are sent to you. Pray date the Indentures the same Day you sign 'em otherwise there is a £500 penalty. Pray give my respects to all my Friends but especially to my Mother & Sisters; I am

Your dutiful Son & Servant
Francis Jeake

The City is very quiet not a Dog moving his Tongue against the Government. My Brother remembers to you all.

To Mr Joseph Tucker at Rye, with a parcell, with Care, in Sussex

[288] *Francis Jeake to Joseph Tucker, 1 September 1716. Original letter.*
ESRO FRE 5381

Honoured Sir,
I once more give you the trouble of a Letter (per Post) to let you know that this day the Indentures were signed & the £125 paid. I received the residue of the £133: 19 being £8: 9 whereof £6:5 is to be paid to the King, the other £2:14 shall be disposed of by me as you shall please to order. So Sir presenting my humble duty to my Mother, my Love to my 2 Sisters, & to you (for your great kindness to me) my hearty & sincere Thanks (which I confess is but small amends) I subscribe my self
Your dutiful Son & Servant

Francis Jeake

London: Saturday Sept. 1st 1716

[*On reverse of FRE 5381*]

Honoured Mother
I have (I must confess) too long neglected writing to you but I hope you will not account it out of any disrespect to you. God forbid that I should be guilty of such a Crime. I have not as yet received any Accompt from Rye whether you received the things which I sent by the Carrier about a month agoe viz. ¼ oz. of Gold thread, Mrs Bishop's Child's Shoes & Wallers Poems. I have nothing more to say at present but that I am
London Sept. 1st 1716

Your dutifull Son
Francis Jeake

My Brother is very well who joyns with me in Remembrances to the whole Family.

To Mr Joseph Tucker at Rye, Sussex

[289] *Francis Jeake to Joseph Tucker, 12 September 1716. Original letter.*
RMA, Selmes Manuscripts, RYEYT N39.59.4

Honoured Sir
Yesterday being Tuesday I went to pay the Duty where they made me pay 6s 7d more than we reckon'd For they said that your paying the duty was equivalent to giving my Master so much mony, & necessity having no law I were forced to pay it; they taxed the £6 5s at 1s per £ which came to six shillings & three pence, then they taxed the 6s 3d so the produce of that till they could bring it no lower, so that I paid in all £6 11s 7d & have by me still £2 7s 5d. This Sir I thought fit to let you know, which my hearty respects to my Mother & my Sisters concludes this epistle from

Your dutifull Son & Servant
Francis Jeake

London Wednesday Sept. 12th

My Brother gives his respects to you all.

Tho' I am very sorry to hear that Mr Waters is failed yet it would be some satisfaction to me to hear something of the particulars & what will become of his Wife & children.

To Mr Joseph Tucker at Rye with a parcel in Sussex

[290] *Francis Jeake to Joseph Tucker, 22 September 1716. Original letter.*
ESRO FRE 5382

London Saturday Sept. 22nd 1716

Honoured Sir,
I went yesterday to Mr Gybbon, who happened to be gone out, so to day morning I went again, & went very luckily, for the man who had the Bill from Mr Sharp came within two minutes after me, so I received the money which I paid to my Brother, & the Bill which I now send you. Mr Gybbon gives his Service to you, my Mother & Sister, & says that he would have writ this Post

but that I writ, & he having no business will defer it till another time. His Lady too gives her remembrances to the Family. She looks very big upon one, but is very brisk and well. Yesterday the 5 Rioters were hanged against Salisbury Court in Fleet-Street,[34] where was a vast Croud of Spectators; The poor deluded Populace (after they were hanged) cut off Chips from the Gallows which they sold for half pence or pence apiece to keep as Relicts of such pious martyrs of their Cause. That same Day also the Sign of the Roebuck was erected in Cheapside as likewise the Sign of the Mug under which is writ the Loyal Society of the Mug house which some poor wretches have peppered with dirt. I am very sorry to hear of the Chimmney's fall. The wind did no damage at London (Thanks be to God). My Brother is very well who joyns, in remembering to you all, with

Your dutifull Son & Servant
Francis Jeake

I received Broth: Joseph's Epistle. I have now sent the Ordinary's Accts of the Rioters.[35]

[291] *Francis Jeake to Elizabeth Tucker, 31 October 1716. Original letter.*
ESRO FRE 5383

To Madam Tucker at Rye, Sussex, with a parcel.

London October 31st 1716

Honoured Madam,
I received yours this day; Thanks be to God I have my health very well; As to my liking of my Place, though some things occur not very pleasing yet they are trivial and scarce worth the mencioning so that I hope & entreat you

[34] The riot in question took place on 24 July 1716. It involved an attack on Mr Read's Mug House in Salisbury Court near Fleet Street. Witnesses recorded that the rioters, John Love, Thomas Bean, George Purchase, Richard Price and William Price broke windows, took down and destroyed the Mug House sign and destroyed household goods and papers. The Old Bailey Proceedings do not record the motivation for the attack but record the rioters as having cried 'High Church and Ormond. No Hanoverian, No King George, Down with the Mug-house' suggesting that they were Jacobite sympathisers or, at least, that the riot had been instigated by Jacobite sympathisers. Love was a dock worker, William Price an apprentice sword cutler, Richard Price a Welsh tailor who had come to London seeking work, Purchase a journeyman shoe-maker and Bean a servant to a gentleman who had been involved in the 1715 Jacobite rebellion. OBP, September 1716, Trial of John Love, Thomas Bean, George Purchase, Richard Price, William Price (t17160906-2); OBP, *Ordinary of Newgate's Account*, 21 September 1716 (OA17160921).

[35] OBP; OA17160921.

(since I do not) not to make your self uneasy at it; For when I first went there I did not expect to find it as I did at home; I believe indeed there are better places and I believe there are worse then since I have not met with one of the latter the best way is to rest contented as doth
Your dutifull Son & Servant

Francis Jeake

I sent a Letter last week which had nothing in it materiall but my hearty thanks to my Father for his Care & trouble about the things last mencioned which I now reitorate.

My Brother joyns with me in presenting our Devoirs to the whole family.

Elizabeth and her adult children, 1716–1733

[292] *Elizabeth Tucker to Barbara Jeake, 23 June 1716. Original letter.*
ESRO FRE 5387

Rye June the 23rd 1719
I told my Dear Bab Father was returned ill from his journey, he was indeed extreamly out of Order Saturday & Sabath day but yesterday I bless God he was something better & is rather better today he was full of pain in all his Limbs & yesterday began to be out of order in his stomach brought up what he took which was but little & a considerable quantity of Phlegm his stomach is mighty qualmy still but he is not so much enfeebled to day as before. Father would have Brother call at Mr Falkner's the upper end of abbchurch lane & get such a silver watch chain as that he had of him when in Town about seven or eight shillings to pay for it to tell Mr Falkner Father hopes he will not make him give dearer than when in Town 'Tis for Capt Pigrams new watch. I shall be glad to hear when you will come home begin to long to see you & my Dear Sam Our joy[f]ul Salutes to all the Cousins & Love to you both I am

My Dear
Your truly loving
Mother
E Tucker

[293] *Elizabeth Tucker to Barbara Jeake, 27 June 1716. Original letter.*
ESRO FRE 5388

Rye June the 27th 1719
I am sorry my Dear Bab I cannot send word Father is better I yesterday had hopes he was but this day he is again very ill the pain in his bones a soreness in his breast & sick in his stomach no appetite since he came home & no good tast in any thing he takes I am inexpressibly uneasie know not what to do his spirits are excessivly dull & down for the three last nights he has I bless the Lord enjoyed pretty good rest & since his coming home has brought away abundance of Phlegm by spit chiefly Though at the beginning of the week he cast twice & [words lost] of that kind away. I long for thy coming home & thy Brothers [words lost] in a sorrowful state as you well can guess the Lord in mercy [words lost] as I wish I had a sample of that sope to try it & then if we [words lost] could send afterwards knowing where & to whom call for my great scizers at Mr Davis's going over the Bridge Father left [words lost] I have nothing to say of Hats for this summer If it please the Almighty to restore the Health of my Dear Husband & bring my Dear Children safe & grant us all our health I shall think my self [words lost] happy Father was [word illegible] that did not send the Trunk Miss Pigram is much disappointed mary Sisly desires you to know her silver buttons for her sleeves forget not to send Fathers shoes in the old Box with what other things you think fit by sea And Fail not to send the Trunk into the Carrier by Wednesday evening fail not to send Mrs Pigrams linings & Mrs Dixon's things either in or out of the Trunk as you can fit it but be sure carefully put up I am my Dear, your Dear Brothers & your tenderly Loving Mother

Elisa Jeake

Dear Father sends his with my service to the Family where you are & to Mr Vandykes as well & your Dear Brother & self, take our Love with Jo & Phils. Mrs Cook tells me Bab has the measles full but knows not how the news came to Mr Bird who says Dr Woodward has been with her.

[294] *Elizabeth Tucker to Samuel Jeake III, 10 March 1725. Original letter.*
ESRO FRE 5389

Rye March the 10th 1725
I am sorry Dear Sam the Town has so many charms that Business & Relations may all be sacrificed to its allurments I persuade my self real advantage has not employ'd one half of the time you have now spent in that bewitching place it entirely bereaves you of your sence of every thing for neither can you

afford to write to your absent Friends but very sparingly & then take no notice of answering what they write concerning when you promised your Father so positively you would be back to be present at the Commission I really depended on your word but there is no such thing to be looked for when London is in the case if you wou'd but consider the extravagancy of your expenses & consider the rest of mankind that are worth taking Notice of it would put you in a better method. I despair any remonstrances of mine will ever have any effect on you. Your Father is very ill had a most terrible night the last he puff and is much out of order. I am very much troubled to see how far short my son falls of that assiduous care your Friend here expresses for his Relations I wrote to you concerning my watch & your sister Your Father desired you to leave £75 in Mr Slade's hands but you take no notice of any thing, no more than of what your sister wrote in Mr Proctor's Letter if tears wou'd appear on paper I have stock enough to write this & much more you are not expressive enough to let us know what you mean by Mr MacEven's account there is 2 Guineas for the Lace & two mounts of Fans & one entire Fan the price of these I never know. Yesterday Mr Lamb called & swore Mr Carleton the Freeman but Davis & Horsfield are not come on the Bench Mr Lamb tells Proctor he has no Authority to Administer an Oath nor should he have opened his Cask. You send word of 15 Tickets you have provided without saying who are to be proprietors your Towns Duties & all goes to wrack. Mr Button is quite tired for no Body now you are absent takes any care if either you Mr Slade or Capt Pigram will please to pay £7 10s to Mr Ferguson & take a Receipt in full for your Father & Mr Button. The Money shall be paid at your return they have [words illegible] to drink his Health. Your Father bid me tell you the Commission is adjourned to Thursday next & if you do not appear a lot there are none of your Friends will ever trouble themselves any further nor have any dependence on you. Pray Buy some Sp[iri]t of Sal Armoniac.[36] Farewel my Sam, think for 'tis true we all Love you but none more Ardently than

Your truly Loving
Mother
E Tucker

[295] *Elizabeth Tucker to Barbara Jeake, 3 September 1728. Original letter.*
ESRO FRE 5390

Every Epistle I receive from Rye is acceptable to me nor can I ever be tired with the length of any that comes from my Dear Barbara I bless God the

[36] Sal Armoniac was used in dyeing and medicine: *DTGC*, 'Saddle band – Sal volatile'.

weather has been very favourable since we have been here I yesterday attempted to see Mrs Mead but she was gone to Sun Court Miss Mead is yet at Bristol where the Capt's station is continued. Mr & Mrs Shortis I have seen once they Lodge on Ludgate Hill near the Bell Savage. The side saddle is bespoke but requires so much time to make the Hoy must return without it this time the young Ladies send their service to you all I am sorry your Brother did not go to Bro: Blackmore. I believe I shall not be less glad to see my Dear Children if it please God to Bless me then they will be to see their Mother. On Thursday we purpose to go to Battersy wou'd have Dick set out from Rye munday next which will be the ninth instant; If the weather & other things concure we intend for Lewes Wednesday after Dick's arrival. Send by him two of the Double Diapre affairs you put in your portmanteau & [word illegible] Bottle. I can send you no account of Spinnet yet Chocolate is five shillings per lb & like to be dearer I shall wean my self from that nor do I think it so good as what I had in 1726. I hope my Dear Children will take care of themselves & keep good hours & may the Almighty Bless & keep you all from every danger is the constant prayer of my Dear Barbara

Your Truly Loving Mother
E. Tucker
Sept the 3rd 1728

Fathers & my love to all our Dear Children with service to Mrs Beeching, Capt Pigram & the rest of our friends. Capt Pigrams Harness is bought, his other commands shall be obeyed.

[296] *Elizabeth Tucker to Barbara Jeake, 24 July 1733. Original letter.*
ESRO FRE 5391

By Father I am deputed to answer my Dear Barbara's Epistle that coming first in course we all rejoyce in the account we have of our Girles good Health and satisfaction by which hint hope your self & sister are free from those inconveniencies you have been incident to when in Town. The Hoy is not yet arrived so can give no account of the receipt of what you sent your Father & I are glad our Children have not in the midst of various diversions forgot their parents. Capt Pigram (says for no body else says any thing about 'em tho' miss Jeny promised long agoe). They [word struck out] ought to be dyed Black since there is no other colour they will take I have not seen Mrs nor Miss Beeching since last week suppose by your sisters the silk did not come but do not know. Mr Harrison appointed yesterday to be here but sent his Man suppose he is come to day or not far behind. Mr Wicks of Romney would have two or three lb of three penny worsted of Mrs Green's mens colour and Blew he would be glad to settle a correspondence with her upon the foot of selling again if she can give him any encouragement. I believe he will be a very honest Chap. Brother Tucker purposes if the disappointment happen to meet Cousin Slade at the Race Shall take care to send per Hoy now I have the Keys the things sister mentions. I here Mrs Pigram the Mother was very Fine on the Lords day Miss Jeny and she having been at Tenterden to be Equipt I do not call to mind any News but that Mary Curd is to be married at Michaelmas Spouse Elect has given warning tis the mans son that sold you Damsins as he call'd them. Your Bro Jeake goes to Morrow to Tenterden to Mr Ed: Mullins for four or five days. Mrs Beeching is just come in & sends her service as do so many others every body you can think of. Mr & Mrs Lambs miss went to Tunbridge Wells Munday return Thursday. Am sorry the Spinet is out of your reach. Pray see Mrs Shortis I am which our joynt salutations to the Family & all Friends with Tender Love to our Dear Girles. I am my Dear Barbara

Your truly loving
Mother
E Tucker

July the 24th 1733

To Mrs Barbara Jeake at Mr Slade's the Corner of St Thomas, Southwark
Post paid 3d

[297] *Elizabeth Tucker to Barbara Jeake, 31 May 1733. Original letter.*
ESRO FRE 5392

I write this my Dear Barbara much unprepared being told Mr Manooch's just setting out I was willing to let you hear from us I suppose the Hoy sailed last night whether I forgot anything material in the paper seal amongst the things that was done pretty much on the sudden there is two Boxes one for Candles let there be three dozen of good working lights that will give good light you may remember the last winters lights were of little use for that the size we ought to have you must enquire of the person you have them of we have mould Candles sufficient for the table & company let there be of long fourteens & sixteen to make up the Box. Capt Pigram has been at New Haven but not at Litton hears they are very fond of one another 'tis to be hoped he will always avoid telling Lyes since in his Courtship he was so cautious the Husband will doubtless speake plain English truth the children are all dead they have had much company. The present I saw was a small low built Gold

Watch with a chased case but the story I could not tell twas a Lady siting in a Chair of State & two military men approaching her in Armour Generals to be sure the Top of the Hook Europas Flight on the Bull. Mrs Beeching said he said he had or would send for a Chair or Chaise she cou'd not tell which both were named att different times & I forgot to ask again. Your Father complains this morning of a pain in his Bones. I would be glad you would let me know ~~what~~ how many grains of Rhubarb I used to take for I must increase the dose. Mrs Norton miss & Miss Betty were here on Wednesday & Mrs Buttenville Mrs Weedon all send their service to you both as does your Father & Brother theirs with that my

Dear Barbara of your loving
Mother
E Tucker
May the 31st 1733

Service to all the Family
The clock just strikes eight don't forget a quarter of a pound of tenpeny thred we shall be out.

To Mrs Barbara Jeake at Mr Slades the Corner of St Thomas Southwarke, these
Post paid 3d

[298] *Elizabeth Tucker to Barbara Jeake, 8 September 1733. Original letter.*
ESRO FRE 5393

I have had the misfortune Dear Child to break your China Boat I desire you to buy another you know twas a burntin one buy also two Mops such as are us'd in the Family where you are Mr Knapton said would so suppose he has sent the Number of Rapin which was wanting you give me no account what Broken Flint Glass[37] will yield per lb. As you say Cousins & you think the Irish Cloth worth the money you may buy it Susan has been very ill but is I thank God got well again your Brother tells me Mr Norton of Rye goes to London next week with his two ~~Dau~~ Daughters who I suppose you will see. Rye affords but little news & my memory is so bad I can't remember whether I give you the occurrences of the Town or not. Father came not from Tenterden till yesterday the weather was so windy & rainy he could not dispatch his

[37] *OED*, flint-glass, n. 1. A pure lustrous glass, originally made with ground flint or pebble as the siliceous ingredient.

business. The carrying roads are very bad what a Black berry summer[38] may do towards mending them we cannot tell.

Mr Frewen told me of something your sister desir'd to be sent but he cou'd not make out if there is any thing unsent shc wou'd have she must explain it her self hope now the heat abates. Phil's[39] Enemies have made a Truce with her we have no Buggs at Rye. You Exceused your Blunders because twas almost dark I must mine since I write by Candle which is to me a very imperfect light. I am sorry the shortness of the days obliges us to so much of that kind. Fathers & Mothers Love to you and Phil with service to Cousins in General & particular with service to Friends as you think proper closes the scene without farther addition than that I am

My Dear Barbara
Your truly lo:
Mother
E Tucker
Sept. the 8th 1733

Mrs Page has a Quartan Ague

To Mrs Barbara Jeake at Mr Slades the Corner of St Thomas Southwarke, these
Post paid 3d

The death of Joseph Tucker, November 1733

[299] *Will of Joseph Tucker* TNA, PROB 11/662/135

In the name of God Amen. I Joseph Tucker of the Antient Town of Rye in the County of Sussex Gent being of sound and disposing mind thanks be to God for the same do make this my last Will and Testament in writing in manner following. Imprimis I commend my soul into the hands of my Lord and Saviour Jesus Christ and my Body to the Earth to be decently buried and as to my Temporall Estate I will and dispose of the same in the manner following. Imprimis I will give and bequeath unto my loveing sister Mary Tucker to my Daughter Hannah the wife of Mr Samuel Munn to my Daughter Mary the wife of Mr William [word illegible][40], to my Brother in Law Samuel Jeake

[38] *OED*, blackberry summer, n. *Eng. Regional,* a warm period in late September and early October.
[39] Philadelphia Tucker, only daughter of Elizabeth and Joseph Tucker.
[40] Possibly Blackwood or Blackmore.

and to my Daughter in Law Barbara Jeake five pounds a piece to buy them mourning. Item I give and bequeath unto my son Joseph Tucker all that my Garden called Birkwell Garden and those other Garden Spotts which lately I purchased of Thomas Ryder and which are in the Liberty of Rye and also all my house in the Lower Street in Rye wherein Andrew Burke now liveth which I lately bought of Thomas Nicholas to hold to the said Joseph Tucker and the heirs of his Body and for want of such issue to my Daughter Philadelphia Tucker and her heirs for ever. I give, devise and bequeath all that my messuage in the Middle Street which I lately purchased of Mathew Wilinshurst and his wife Elizabeth with the Barkside Garden and Stable thereto belonging or adjoyning to my above said daughter Philadelphia Tucker and the heirs of her body and for want of such issue to my above said son Joseph Tucker and his heirs for ever. Item I give devise and bequeath unto my said son Joseph Tucker Two hundred pounds of Good and lawfull money of great Britain to be paid to him when he arrives at his age of twenty one years. Item I give devise and bequeath unto my Daughter Philadelphia Tucker five hundred pounds of like lawfull money to be paid to her when she shall attain to the age of Twenty one years. Item I will devise and bequeath unto my loving wife Elizabeth Tucker and to her heirs all that my messuage called the Red Cross in Watchbell Street with the Gardens and appurtenances thereto belonging. Item I will give devise and bequeath all those my house and Lands at Hasting in the parishes of St Clements and all Saints with all their Appurtenances which I purchased of Richard Watts or his assigns unto my said loving wife Elizabeth for the term of her natural life and after her decease then to my abovesaid son Joseph Tucker and the heirs of his Body and for want of such heirs then to my abovesaid Daughter Philadelphia Tucker and her heirs for ever. Lastly I do hereby make constitute and appoint my said loving wife Elizabeth Tucker sole executrix of this my last Will and Testament to whom I give all the residue and remainder of my Goods and Chattels after my Debts and Legacies are paid and I do hereby revoke all former and other wills by me heretofore made or mentioned to be made. In witness whereof I the said Joseph Tucker have here unto set my hand and seal this twentieth day of February in the eight year of King George of Great Britain France etc. Anoqe Domini 1721. Jo: Tucker signed, sealed, published and declared to be the last will and Testament of the said Joseph Tucker in the presence of us who subscribe our name in the Testators presence, John Button, Wal: Waters, Mary Sisley her mark.

This Will was proved at London the fifteenth day of November in the year of our Lord One Thousand Seven Hundred and Thirty Three before the right worshipfull John Bettesworth Doctor of Laws Master Keeper or Commissary of the Prerogative Court of Canterbury lawfully constituted by the Oath of

Elizabeth Tucker Widow the Relict and Sole Executrix named in the said will to whom the Administration was committed of the Goods, Chattels and Credits of the said deceased being first sworn by Commission duly to Administer.

The death of Elizabeth Tucker, July 1736

[300] *Will of Elizabeth Tucker* TNA, PROB 11/678/209

In the name of God Amen. I Elizabeth Tucker of the Antient Town of Rye in the County of Sussex Widow being sick and weak in Body but of sound and disposing mind memory and understanding (God be praised for the same) do this twenty fifth day of February in the ninth year of the reign of Sovereign Lord George the second by the Grace of God King of Great Britain in France and Ireland defender of the faith etc. and in the year of our Lord 1735 make and ordain this my last Will and Testament in manner and form following (that is to say) in the first place I resign my soul to God my creator assuredly trusting through the meritts and mediation of my Lord and Saviour Jesus Christ to receive full pardon of all my sins and my Body I commit to the Earth to receive a devout private buriall at the discretion of my Executors hereafter named and as for my Wordly Estate I dispose thereof as follows. Item I give and bequeath unto my son Samuel Jeake the sume of one hundred and fifty pounds of lawfull money of Great Britain and if I shall happen to survive till after the five and twentieth day of March next (then and in such case and not otherwise) I give and bequeath unto my said son Samuel Jeake the further sume of fifty pounds of like lawful money making together two hundred pounds also I give and bequeath to the said Samuel Jeake one large silver Tankard with a Foot marked I ^{H} B, two silver porringers[41] one large the other small marked each S I, one double Rose Noble peice of Gold, the feather Bedd whereon he lyes with the Steadle covering and appurtenances thereunto belonging, the furniture of the best parlour (vizt) ten chairs the chimney glass and stoutes with the Furniture of the firehearth and all his late Father Jeakes Library of Books as contained in a Catalogue. Item I give and bequeath unto my daughter Barbara Jeake the summe of one thousand five hundred pounds of lawfull money of Great Britain (the summe of one hundred and eighty pounds upon a Mortgage made by John Tilden of Cranbrook in the County of Kent Timber broker to the said Barbara bearing date the two and twentieth day of June which was in the year of our Lord 1719 and all such moneys as were given or that she may claime a right to

[41] A shallow bowl.

under her late deceased Father Mr Jeake and her grandmother Mrs Barbara Hartshorne being included therein. Also I give to my said daughter Barbara my diamond ring with three stones and four sparks which was her Grandmothers, my diamond earrings, my silver coffee pot, one large wrought silver salver, the bed covering and Furniture of the room wherein she lyes, my wedding ring with which I was marryed to her Father Mr Jeake with a latin poesie[42] and one double Rose Noble peice of Gold to be paid and delivered to her the said Barbara by my executors within one month next after my decease. Item I give and bequeath unto my daughter Philadelphia Tucker the summe of seven hundred pounds of lawfull money of Great Britain (exclusive of the summe of five hundred pounds given and bequeathed to her by the last Will and Testament of her father my late husband Mr Tucker) which together make one thousand two hundred pounds payable to her. Also I give and bequeath to my said daughter Philadelphia Tucker my repeating Gold Watch with the chain and seal, my pearl necklace, my wedding ring with which I was marryed to her Father poesie No 9: 1703[43], my mothers wedding ring to my Father with a Latin poesie, one silver salver marked I ^{P} N and the Bed and furniture thereof two pillows and white quilt in the new Building to be paid and delivered to her by my Executors within one month next after my decease. Item I give and bequeath unto my said daughters Barbara and Philladelphia all and singular my wearing apparel, my silver Tea kettle and silver lamp my silver Tea pott and Lamp silver Milk pott with the Case Cannister Sugar Dish, twelve gilt Silver spoons, Tongs, Strainer and all and singular any China Ware of what nature or kind soever equally to be divided between them. Item I give and bequeath unto my said son Samuel Jeake To my son Joseph Tucker and my said daughters Barbara and Philadelphia all and singular my Linnen and pewter of what nature or kind soever to be equally divided between them. Item I give and forgive unto my said sons Samuel Jeake and Joseph Tucker and my said daughters Barbara Jeake and Philladelphia Tucker all such moneys as I may claime a right to for their or either their Board, Cloathing or Education since the decease of their respective Fathers and all such moneys as I can or lawfully may demand or take of them or any or either of them at the time of my decease. Item I give and devise unto my said son Joseph Tucker all that my Messuage or Tenement with the Backside and appurtenances thereunto belonging commonly called or known by the name of the Red Cross situate lying and being in the Watchbell Street in Rye aforesaid now or late in the Tenure or occupation of Richard [word illegible] or his assigns To have and to hold the said Messuage or Tenement and premises with the appurtenances unto my said son Joseph Tucker and to his heirs and assigns

[42] A verse, probably inscribed on the inside of the ring.
[43] The date of Elizabeth and Joseph's marriage.

for ever. Item from and after all my just debts, my aforesaid Legacies, funeral expenses and other incident charges in and about the probate of this my Will shall be paid off and discharged, I give and bequeath all the rest and residue of moneys, securities for money, goods, chattels and personal estate whatsoever and wheresoever be it of what nature or kind soever unto my said son Joseph Tucker and to his Executors administrators and assigns for ever. Item I nominate and appoint my said sons Samuel Jeake and Joseph Tucker joynt executors of this my will and Lastly I do hereby revoke all former and other wills by me at any time heretofore made and do declare this to be my last Will and Testament In Witness whereof I the said Elizabeth Tucker have to this my last Will and Testament written and contained in these two sheets of paper to the first sheet I have sett my name and to this last sheet my name and seal dated the day and year first before written Elisa Tucker. Signed, sealed, published and declared by the said Testatrix for and as her last Will and Testament in the presence of us who have in the said Testatrixes presence subscribed our names as Witnesses the words [thereof two pillows and white quilt] being first underlined. Ann Burton, William Wybourn, Edwin Wardroper.

This Will was proved at London the twenty third day of July in the year of our Lord one thousand seven hundred and thirty six before the Right Worshipfull John Bettesworth Doctor of Laws Master Keeper or Commissary of the Prerogative Court of Canterbury lawfully constituted by the Oaths of Samuel Jeake and Joseph Tucker Executors named in the said Will to whom administration of all and singular the Goods Chattels and Credits of the deceased was granted being first sworn by Commission duly to administer.

Afterword

Of Elizabeth and Samuel's children, the only one whose life left any significant trace was Samuel III. Samuel was born in 1697, and for that reason we met him only infrequently in his father's letters. Clearly a poorer correspondent than his brother Francis, he also did not feature much in his mother's surviving letters, aside, as we have seen, from a severe admonishment for a lack of attention to familial duty.[1] Samuel did, nonetheless, have a rather interesting life. He, like his brother Francis, was apprenticed to a London lawyer. He was described in a document written in 1745 as being of the Middle Temple but it is not clear whether he practised law for any period of time after his apprenticeship.[2] Equally it is not clear how long he spent in London but he, along with his brother Francis, signed a petition from Rye citizens to George III in 1715 expressing 'utmost Abhorrence' at the Jacobite uprising of that year.[3]

Samuel had probably returned to Rye by the early 1720s. He claimed his freedom of the Corporation of Rye in August 1719 at the age of 21.[4] He had been appointed jurat by 1721 and by 1724 had attained the post of Collector of his Majesty's Customs at Rye. His half-brother, Joseph Tucker, apparently worked as his clerk for a period of time, resigning that position in 1737.[5] These public offices required both men, as a result of the Test Act of 1672, to take the oath of allegiance and supremacy and also to worship at the Church of England or at least seem to be doing so. Samuel clearly did not share his father's and grandfather's religious views because numerous sacrament certificates in his name survive in the Rye parish records. These certificates confirm, via two witnesses, attendance at 'Divine Service and Sermon' and the receiving of the 'Sacrament of the Lord's Supper'. The certificates also allow us to trace Samuel up to 1738 and indicate that he did hold some form of local public office up until that time.[6]

Samuel was pursuing other means of advancement during the 1720s, 1730s and 1740s. In 1728 he published his grandfather Samuel Jeake senior's *Charters of the Cinque Ports, Two Ancient Towns and their Members*. The volume was dedicated to the Duke of Dorset and wished that 'You long continue the Delight of Your Friends, an Ornament of Your Country, and a *Conservator* of Liberty'. Samuel signed himself 'Your Grace's most obedient, most humble and most devoted Servant'.[7] In 1741 he

[1] Chapter 7, ESRO FRE 5389.

[2] 'House of Lords Journal Volume 26: November 1745, 21–30', in *Journal of the House of Lords* Volume 26, 1741–1746 (London, 1767–1830), 519–22 http://www.british-history.ac.uk/lords-jrnl/vol26/ 519–522 [accessed 26 September 2015].

[3] Monod, *Murder of Mr Grebell*, 175.

[4] Holloway, *History and Antiquities*, 577

[5] 'Warrants for Minor Appointments: 1737', in Calendar of Treasury Books and Papers, Volume 3, 1735–1738, ed. William A Shaw (London, 1900), 449–61 http://www.british-history.ac.uk/cal-treasury-books-papers/vol3/pp449-461 [accessed 26 September 2015], 205.

[6] ESRO, Sacrament Certificates, RYE19/299; 19/319; 19/325; 19/367; 19/371; 19/391; 19/395; 19/407; 19/420; 19/423.

[7] Samuel Jeake, *Charters of the Cinque Ports, Two Ancient Towns and their Members* (London, 1728), iv.

stood for Parliament but with no success.[8] Other schemes were more fantastical. At one point he apparently built a flying machine which he stored in the upper part of the schoolroom in Rye. It presumably was the same schoolroom in which Samuel III's maternal grandfather, Richard Hartshorne, had once taught but was now turned to less erudite purposes.[9] As well as the flying machine, it was discovered to be full of 'some Gross of empty Bottles and some Dozens of Full ones', hogsheads of wine and a great quantity of 'Fowl Tobacco pipes'.[10]

Samuel's schemes also led him into dispute. In 1743 he was indicted by the House of Lords for causing 'a Ditch to be made, to enclose Land belonging to the Earl of *Thanet*, in the Parish of *Lydd*, in the County of *Kent*, in Breach of the Privilege of the said Earl, and also of this House'.[11] In 1745 he appeared before the House and, having admitted his offence, was discharged.[12] It is possible that this attempt at enclosure of land was part of a scheme for inland navigation, which the *Gentleman's Magazine* reported was the cause of the dissipation of Samuel III's fortune.[13] Whatever the cause of his money worries, he was in serious financial trouble by 1750. In a document that gives no specific details, there is reference to the sale of land at Northiam forced by a commission of bankruptcy awarded against Samuel Jeake.[14]

Soon after this Samuel left Rye and sailed for Jamaica. The island offered plenty of opportunities for ambitious and well-educated men during the eighteenth century.[15] Precisely how Samuel secured a living is not known. He petitioned in 1761 for the post of collector of customs but it is not clear whether he was given the post. The *Gentleman's Magazine* claimed that he practised at the bar for some years and his will, presented below, does indicate a return to the law.[16] The will mentions his role as a Master of Chancery and many of his legacies were to men working in the legal profession.

Samuel III did not grow very rich in Jamaica, but he was certainly comfortable. His will, first written in 1768, left several hundreds of pounds in total to various friends and to his sisters Barbara and Philadelphia. There was no mention of a family, but he did leave a great deal of his estate to his black housekeeper, Juno Murphy. A later codicil left Juno and 'her Mulatto son Joseph Barlebo ten acres of my land in Saint Mary aforesaid to them to hold during their lives and during the life of the survivor of them'. While a relationship between Samuel and Juno cannot be positively

[8] Monod, *Murder of Mr Grebell*, 225.
[9] Holloway, *History and Antiquities*, 578
[10] Monod, *Murder of Mr Grebell*, 180.
[11] 'House of Lords Journal Volume 26: May 1744', in *Journal of the House of Lords* Volume 26, 1741–1746 (London, 1767–1830), 383–99 http://www.british-history.ac.uk/lords-jrnl/vol26/pp383-399 [accessed 26 September 2015].
[12] 'House of Lords Journal Volume 26: November 1745, 21–30', in *Journal of the House of Lords* Volume 26, 1741–1746 (London, 1767–1830), 519–22 http://www.british-history.ac.uk/lords-jrnl/vol26/ 519-522 [accessed 26 September 2015].
[13] *The Gentleman's Magazine*, vol. 65, 218.
[14] ESRO, Memorandum Book Concerning the Manor of Broomsmith [Brownsmith], DAP 267/8/1.
[15] Trevor Burnard, 'A Failed Settler Society: Marriage and Demographic Failure in Early Jamaica', *Journal of Social History*, 28 (1994), 64.
[16] *The Gentleman's Magazine*, vol. 65, 218.

stated, such bonds were common and tolerated in a settler society where 'fragile family formation' was the norm.[17]

There was no mention of religion in Samuel's will. With the exception of its standard opening, its concerns were all material. This collection commenced with a godly death, it ends with one that was wholeheartedly worldly.

[300] *Will of Samuel Jeake III* TNA, PROB 11/994/20

In the Name of God Amen. I Samuel Jeake of the Parish of St Mary in the Island of Jamaica make this my last Will and Testament as follows. In the first place I direct my executors herein after named to bury my body at an expense of fifty pounds current money of the Island of Jamaica. Item I give unto my friend James Lewis of Saint Mary Esquire One hundred Pounds of like Money. Item I give to each of my friends George Francis Hampson and John Brownrigg Counsellors at Law, Thomas Beach Esquire Chief Judge of the Grand Court of this Island and John Biuret of Kingston in Jamaica Gentleman twenty pounds of like money. Item I give my friend Simon Taylor of Kingston aforesaid esquire fifty pounds of like money and to my sister Barbara Howard of Rye in Sussex fifty pounds Sterling. Item I give John Rodon Attorney at Law in Jamaica fifty pounds current money of this Island Jamaica. Item I give to my housekeeper Juno Murphy a female slave named Climena and her Increase for her life and I give the said Juno farther the sum of fifty pounds current money of this Island Jamaica and a Bed with Bedstead, Bolster Pillows and a pair of sheets and the Residue of my Estate after payment of my Debts and Legacies I bequeath and devise to my sister Philadelphia Frewen and her heirs for ever in Trust that with the profits thereof she maintain my sister Barbara before mentioned in decent manner suitable to her condition during her life. Item I remit Francis Delap of St Thomas in the East Esquire all fees due to me as a Master of Chancery for any business by me for him done. Item I give my executors hereafter named power to sell as much of my estate as shall be wanted to discharge my debts and pay my legacies and I do hereby revoke all Wills and Testaments by me at any former time made and I publish and declare this to be my last Will and Testament and hereof I appoint James Lewis and Simon Taylor Esquires above mentioned my executors in witness whereof I have hereunto subscribed my name and put my seal this twenty second day of July in the year of our Lord One thousand seven hundred sixty eight, S Jeake, signed sealed published and declared by the within named testator as and for his last Will and Testament in the presence of us who have at his request subscribed our names as witness

[17] Ibid. 69.

thereto in the presence of him and of each other signed Ja Roper, Peter Clark, Willm Gordon.

I Samuel Jeake of the Parish of Saint Mary in the Island of Jamaica Esquire make this Codicil by way of addition to my last Will. I give and bequeath unto my good friend Abraham Chovet and his wife each the sum of ten pounds current money of this Island and to my housekeeper Juno Murfy I give and bequeath ten live Goats and one Ram Goat and four Turkeys and one Turkey Cock and six Dunghill hens and one Cock and my old shirts and stockings. In witness whereof I have hereto put my hand and seal this twenty second day of July in this year of our Lord 1768 S Jeake signed sealed published and declared by the above named Samuel Jeake as and for an addition to his last Will and Testament in the presence of us who have at his request subscribed our names as witness thereto in the presence of him and each other, (signed) Jas Roper, Peter Clark, Willm Gordon.

I Samuel Jeake of the Parish of Saint Mary in the County of Middlesex in the Island of Jamaica Esquire being of sound and disposing mind and memory make this Codicil to my last Will and Testament and declare this Codicil to be part thereof. Imprimis I add to the number of Executors in the said will appointed Robert Graham Esq. Brother by Affinity to Simon Taylor Esquire and I bequeath to him the said Robert Graham One hundred pounds Current Money of the said Island and I give and bequeath and devise to my Black housekeeper a free woman called Juno Murphy and her Mulatto son Joseph Barlebo ten acres of my land in Saint Mary aforesaid to them to hold during their lives and during the life of the survivor of them and I direct my Executors at their discretion to lay the same in such part of my land as shall be to my other land the least inconvenient. In witness whereof I have hereunto put my hand and seal this sixth day of May in the year of our Lord one thousand seven hundred and seventy, signed S Jeake, signed sealed published and declared by the said Samuel Jeake to be a part of his last Will and Testament in the presence of us who have at his request subscribed our names as a witness to the same in the presence of him and of each other, signed Robt Clarke, Joseph Levy Madoira, Wm Clarke.

On the fourth day of January in the year of our Lord One Thousand Seven Hundred and Seventy Four with the copy of the Will and two Codicils annexed of the Goods, Chattels and Credits of Samuel Jeake late of the Parish of St Mary in the Island of Jamaica Esquire deceased was granted to Philadelphia Frewen wife of Thomas Frewen Esquire the sister of the said deceased and Residuary Legatee named in the said Will limited untill the Original last Will and Testament and two Codicils of the said deceased or an

Authentic Copy thereof shall be brought into and left in the Registry of the Prerogative Court of Canterbury, she having been first sworn by Commission duly to Administer Robert Boutine formerly Graham Esquire an executor named in the second Codicil to the said Will having requested the Execution of the said Will and Two Codicils and James Lewis and Simon Taylor Esquires the Executors named in the said Will having been duly cited to accept or refuse the Execution of the said Copy of the said Will and two Codicils but in no wise appearing.

Appendix A. Jeake Family Tree

Henry Jeake m. Anne Peerson

- Anne (1618–1665)
  m. 1. William Dallet
  2. William Key
- **Samuel Jeake sen. (1623–1690)**
  m. Frances Hartridge (d. 1654)
  - **Samuel Jeake jun. (1652–1699)**
    m. Elizabeth Hartshorne
    - Elizabeth (b. and d. 1682)
    - Elizabeth (1688–?)
      m. ? Brownsmith
    - Manasseh (1688–1690)
    - Barbara (1695–*c.*1770s)
      m. Christopher Booth
      Howard (1741)
    - Samuel (1697–*c.*1773)
    - Francis (1700–?)
  - Thomas (1653–1656)
  - Frances (b. and d. 1654)
- Elizabeth (b. 1626)
  m. 1. Abraham Goph
  2. Nathaniel Bonnick
  3. Christopher Dighton
- John (d. 1630)

Appendix B. Hartridge Family Tree

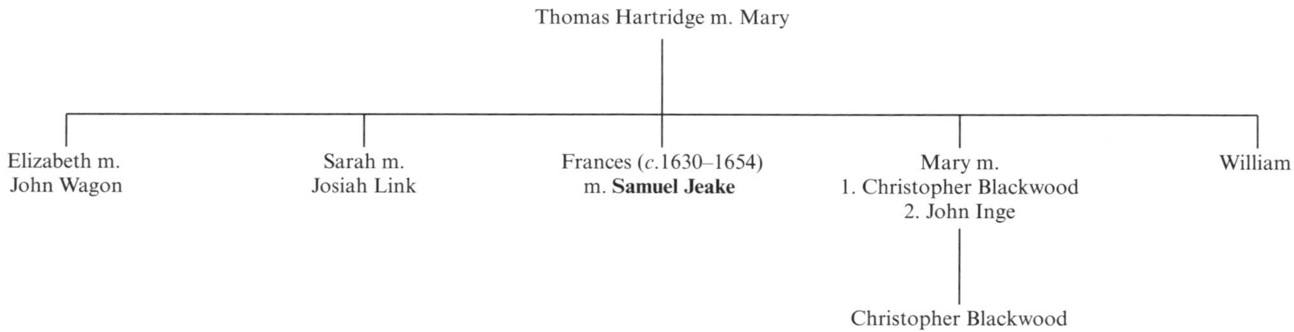

Appendix C. Hartshorne Family Tree

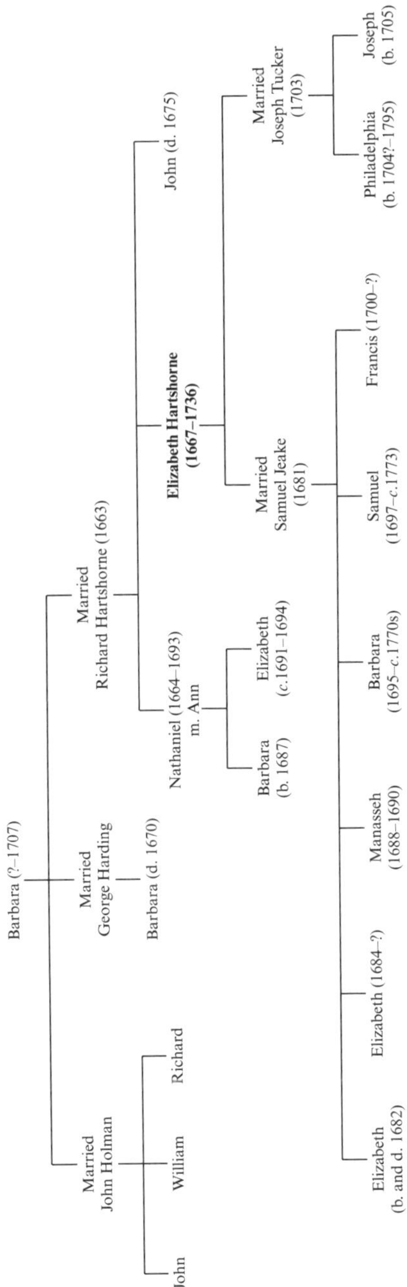

Appendix D. Key Family Tree

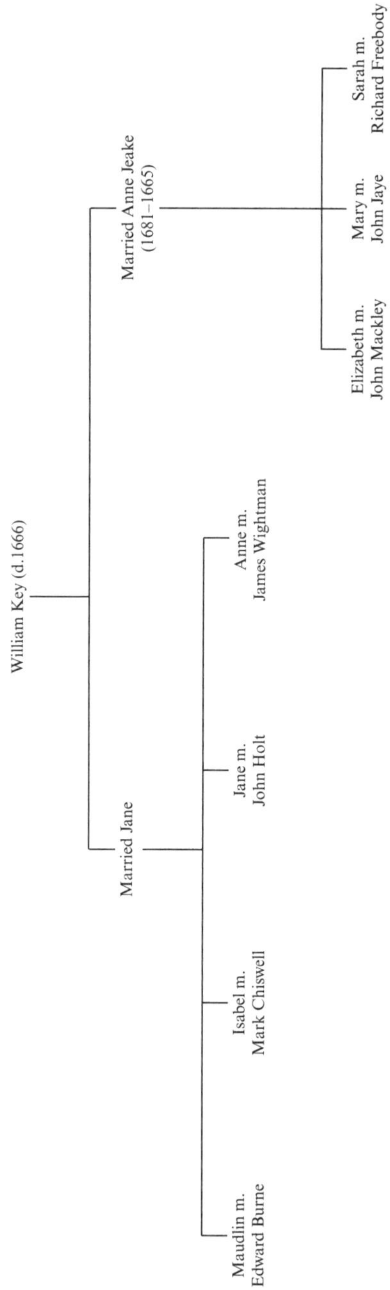

Bibliography

Manuscript Sources

EAST SUSSEX RECORD OFFICE

DAP 267/8/1, Memorandum Book Concerning the Manor of Broomsmith [Brownsmith].

FRE 4223 Volume of correspondence of John Peerson, Ann Jeake (née Peerson) and Samuel Jeake the elder; 1589–1675

FRE 4814–5249 Letters to Samuel Jeake the younger; 1664–1686

FRE 5263–5300 Letters to Samuel Jeake the younger's mother-in-law, Barbara Hartshorne; 1654–1689

FRE 5301–5333 Letters from Samuel Jeake the younger to his wife Elizabeth; 1696–1699

FRE 5334–5336 Letters to Elizabeth Jeake; 1693

FRE 5337–5358 Letters from Elizabeth Jeake, widow to her mother Barbara Hartshorne; 1701

FRE 5359–5420 Miscellaneous correspondence; 1661–1748

PAR 467/1/1/4, Rye Parish Register

RYE/13/82/82, Precept and rate made for the speedy provision of money for disbanding and paying off the forces in this kingdom, both by land and sea, September 1660.

RYE/19/299; 19/319; 19/325; 19/367; 19/371; 19/391; 19/395; 19/407; 19/420; 19/423, Sacrament Certificates.

RYE/47/162/11, General Files, Mayoralty of Thomas Greenfield; uncalendared, 1659–60

THE NATIONAL ARCHIVES, PUBLIC RECORD OFFICE

PCC, PROB 11/502/107

PCC, PROB 11/662/135

PCC, PROB 11/678/209

PCC, PROB 11/994/20

THE RYE MUSEUM ARCHIVE

RYEYT: N39.39.1–5 Samuel Jeake junior's stock accounts 1674–1680, except 1678

RYEYT: N39.40.1–6 Samuel Jeake junior's personal expense accounts 1674–1680

RYEYT: N39.41.1–6 Samuel Jeake junior's profit accounts 1674–1680

RYEYT: N39.42.1–4 Samuel Jeake junior's accounts for cash bag A 1675–1680

RYEYT: N39.43.1–5 Samuel Jeake junior's accounts for cash bag B 1675–1680

RYEYT: N39.57 Shorthand diary of Samuel Jeake junior from 28 March to 19 October 1699
RYEYT: N39.58 Obituary poem for Samuel Jeake junior, printed in 1700
RYEYT: N39.59.1–4 Letters from Francis Jeake, 1712–1716
RYEYT: N39.60 Commonplace book containing verses on several occasions

PUBLISHED PRIMARY SOURCES

Chester, J. L., compiler, and Armytage, G. J., ed., *Allegations for marriage licences issued by the Dean and Chapter of Westminster, 1558 to 1699 : also, for those issued by the Vicar-General of the Archbishop of Canterbury, 1660 to 1679* (London, 1886).
The Gentleman's Magazine, vol. 65
Holloway, W., *The History and Antiquities of the Ancient Town and Port of Rye in the County of Sussex* (London, 1847).
Jeake, S., *Charters of the Cinque Ports, Two Ancient Towns and their Members* (London, 1728).

ONLINE SOURCES

Calendar of State Papers, Domestic, Charles, II, http://www.british-history.ac.uk/search/series/cal-state-papers--domestic--chas2.
Calendar of State Papers, Domestic, James II, http://www.british-history.ac.uk/search/series/cal-state-papers--domestic--jas2.
Calendar of Treasury Books and Papers, Volume 3, 1735–1738, ed. William A Shaw (London, 1900), 449–61 http://www.british-history.ac.uk/cal-treasury-books-papers
Dictionary of Traded Goods and Commodities 1550–1820, http://www.british-history.ac.uk/no-series/traded-goods-dictionary/1550-1820.
Early English Books Online, http://eebo.chadwyck.com/home
Journal of the House of Lords Volume 26, 1741–1746 (London, 1767–1830), 519–22 http://www.british–history.ac.uk/lords-jrnl/vol26/
Old and New London: Volume 2 (London, 1878). *British History Online* http://www.british-history.ac.uk/old-new-london/vol2/
Old Bailey Proceedings Online, https://www.oldbaileyonline.org/
Oxford Dictionary of National Biography, http://www.oxforddnb.com/
Oxford English Dictionary, http://www.oed.com/

SECONDARY SOURCES

Adair, A., *Courtship, illegitimacy and marriage in early modern England* (Manchester, 1996).
Bailey, J., 'Reassessing parenting in eighteenth-century England' in H. Berry and E. Foyster eds, *The Family in Early Modern England* (Cambridge, 2007).

Bell, W. G., *The Great Plague in London* (London, 1994).
Ben-Amos, I. K., *Adolescence & Youth in Early Modern England* (New Haven and London, 1994).
Ben-Amos, I. K., 'Reciprocal bonding: parents and their offspring in early modern England', *Journal of Family History*, 25 (2000), 291–312.
Braddick, M. J., *The nerves of state: taxation and the financing of the English state, 1558–1714* (Manchester, 1996).
Burchall, M. J., 'Inhabitants of Rye in 1660', *Sussex Genealogist and Local Historian*, 4 (1982), 97–108.
Burnard, T., 'A Failed Settler Society: Marriage and Demographic Failure in Early Jamaica', *Journal of Social History*, 28 (1994), 63–82.
Capp, B., 'Separate Domains? Women and Authority in Early Modern England' in P. Griffiths, A. Fox and S. Hindle eds, *The Experience of Authority in Early Modern England* (Basingstoke, 1996), 117–45.
Coffey, J., *Persecution and Toleration in Protestant England, 1558–1689* (Harlow, 2000).
Crawford, P. and Gowing, L., *Women's Worlds in Seventeenth-Century England: a sourcebook* (London, 2000).
Cressy, D., 'Kinship and Kin Interaction in Early Modern England', *Past and Present*, 113 (1986), 43–59.
Davies, O., *The Haunted: a social history of ghosts* (Basingstoke, 2007).
Davis, R., 'English foreign trade, 1660–1700', *Economic History Review*, 7 (1954–5), 150–166.
Daybell, J., *The Material Letter in Early Modern England: manuscript letters and the culture and practice of letter-writing, 1512–1635* (Basingstoke, 2012).
De Krey, G. S., *London and the Restoration 1659–1683* (Cambridge, 2005).
Dickson, P. G. M., *The Financial Revolution in England: A Study in the Development of Public Credit 1688–1756* (London, 1967).
Dobson, M. J., *Contours of Death and Disease in Early Modern England* (Cambridge, 2003).
Edwards, Jeremy and Ogilvie, Sheilagh, 'What lessons for economic development can we draw from the Champagne fairs?', *Explorations in Economic History*, 49 (2012), 131–48.
Erickson, A. L., 'Married women's occupations in eighteenth–century London', *Continuity and Change*, 23 (2008), 267–307.
Evans, J., *Aphrodisiacs, Fertility and Medicine in Early Modern England* (Woodbridge, 2014).
Flather, A., *Gender and Space in Early Modern England* (Woodbridge, 2011).
Fletcher, A., *A County Community in Peace and War: Sussex 1600–1660* (London and New York, 1975).
Fletcher, A., 'Manhood, the Male Body, Courtship and the Household in Early Modern England', *History*, 84 (1999), 419–36.
Gauci, P., *The Politics of Trade: the overseas merchant in state and society, 1660–1720* (Oxford, 2001).
Gauci, P., *Emporium of the World: the merchants of London 1660–1800* (London, 2007).
Glaisyer, N., *The Culture of Commerce in England, 1660–1720* (Woodbridge, 2006).
Glennie P. and Thrift, N., *Shaping the Day: a history of timekeeping in England and Wales, 1300–1800* (Oxford, 2011).

Gowing, L., *Common Bodies: Women, Touch and Power in Seventeenth-Century England* (New Haven, 2003).
Grassby, R., *The Business Community of Seventeenth-Century England* (Cambridge, 1995).
Grassby, R., *Kinship and Capitalism: marriage, family and business in the English-speaking world, 1580–1740* (Cambridge, 2001).
Griffiths, P., *Youth and Authority: formative experiences in England 1560–1640* (Oxford, 1996).
Hargreaves, A. S., 'Lionel Lockyer (1600–72) & his Pillulae Radiis Solis Extractae', *Pharm Hist (London)*, 29 (1999), 55–63.
Harris, T., *Restoration: Charles II and his kingdoms, 1660–1685* (London, 2006)
Hatfield, G., *Encyclopedia of Folk Medicine: Old World and New World Traditions* (Santa Barbara, 2003)
Hipkin, S., 'The Maritime Economy of Rye, 1560–1640', *Southern History*, 20/21 (1999), 108–42.
Holmes, G., *The Making of a Great Power: late Stuart and early Georgian Britain 1600–1722* (Harlow, 1993).
Hoppit, J., *A Land of Liberty? England 1689–1727* (Oxford, 2000).
Hudson, P., 'Correspondence and Commitment: British traders' letters in the long eighteenth century', *Cultural and Social History*, 11 (2014), 527–53.
Hunt, M., *The Middling Sort: Commerce, Gender and the Family in England, 1680–1780* (Berkeley, 1996).
Hunter, M. and Gregory, A., *An Astrological Diary of the Seventeenth Century: Samuel Jeake of Rye, 1652–1699* (Oxford, 1988).
Hunter, M., Mandelbrote, G., Ovenden R. and Smith, N., eds, *A Radical's Books: the library catalogue of Samuel Jeake of Rye, 1623–90* (Woodbridge, 1999).
Jones, D. W., *War and Economy in the Age of William III and Marlborough* (Oxford, 1998).
Lemire, B., *The business of everyday life. Gender, practice and social politics in England, c.1600–1900* (Manchester, 2012),
Macfarlane, A., *Marriage and love in England: modes of reproduction 1300–1840* (Oxford, 1986).
Mendelson S. and Crawford, P., *Women in Early Modern England, 1550–1720* (Oxford, 1998).
Monod, P. K., *The Murder of Mr Grebell: Madness and Civility in an English Town* (New Haven and London, 2003).
Muldrew, C., *The Economy of Obligation: the Culture of Credit and Social Relations in Early Modern England* (Basingstoke, 1998).
Murphy, A. L., 'Lotteries in the 1690s: investment or gamble?' *Financial History Review*, 12 (2005), 227–46.
Murphy, A. L., 'Dealing with uncertainty: managing personal investment in the early English national debt', *History,* 91 (2006), 200–17.
Murphy, A. L., *The Origins of the English Financial Markets: speculation and investment before the South Sea Bubble* (Cambridge, 2009).
Murphy, A. L., 'Demanding credible commitment: public reactions to the failures of the early financial revolution', *Economic History Review*, 66 (2013), 178–97.
Newton, H., *The Sick Child in Early Modern England 1580–1720* (Oxford, 2012).
North, D. and Weingast, B. R., 'Constitutions and commitment': the evolution of institutions governing public choice in seventeenth-century England', *Journal of Economic History*, 49 (1989), 803–32.

O'Hara, D., *Courtship and constraint: rethinking the making of marriage in Tudor England* (Manchester, 2000).
Pinchbeck, I., *Women Workers and the Industrial Revolution, 1750–1850* (London, 1930).
Porter, M., *Windows of the Soul: Physiognomy in European Culture 1470–1780* (Oxford, 2005).
Raven, J., *The Business of Books: booksellers and the English book trade, 1450–1850* (New Haven and London, 2007).
Read, S., *Menstruation and the Female Body in Early Modern England* (Basingstoke, 2013).
Reay, B., *Popular Cultures in England 1550–1750* (London and New York, 1998).
Reinke-Williams, T., *Women, Work and Sociability in Early Modern London* (Basingstoke, 2014).
Rubini, D., 'Politics and the battle for the Banks, 1688–1697', *English Historical Review*, 85 (1970), 693–714
Shaw, J., *Miracles in Enlightenment England* (New Haven, 2006).
Shepard, A., *Meanings of Manhood in Early Modern England* (Oxford, 2003).
Smart, T. W. W., 'A Biographical Sketch of Samuel Jeake, senr. of Rye', *Sussex Archaeological Collections*, 13 (1861), 57–79.
Sowerby, S., *Making Toleration: The Repealers and the Glorious Revolution* (Harvard, 2013).
Spurr, J., *English Puritanism 1603–1689* (Basingstoke, 1998).
Sutherland, J., *The Restoration Newspaper and its Development* (Cambridge, 2004).
Tadmor, N., 'Early modern English kinship in the long run: reflections on continuity and change', *Continuity and Change*, 25 (2010), 15–48.
Tankard, D., 'They tell me they were in fashion last year': Samuel and Elizabeth Jeake and clothing fashions in late seventeenth-century London and Rye', *Costume*, 50 (2016), 20–41.
Tapsell, G., *The Personal Rule of Charles II, 1681–85* (Woodbridge, 2007).
Thomas, K., *The Ends of Life: Roads to Fulfilment in Early Modern England* (Oxford, 2009).
Wallis, P. and Webb, C., 'The education and training of gentry sons in early modern England', *Social History*, 36 (2011), 36–53.
Wallis, P., 'Labor, Law and Training in Early Modern London: Apprenticeship and the City's Institutions', *Journal of British Studies*, 51 (2012), 791–819.
Wear, A., *Knowledge and Practice in English Medicine, 1550–1680* (Cambridge, 2000).
Whyman, S. E., *The Pen and the People: English letter writers 1660–1800* (Oxford, 2009).
Willen, D., 'Godly Women in Early Modern England: Puritanism and Gender', *Journal of Ecclesiastical History*, 43 (1992), 561–80.
Wrightson, K., *Earthly Necessities: Economic Lives in Early Modern Britain, 1470–1750* (London, 2002).
Zahedieh, N., *The Capital and the Colonies: London and the Atlantic Economy 1660–1700* (Cambridge, 2010).

Index of Persons and Places

Index of Subjects